SIMPSON

IMPRINT IN HUMANITIES

The humanities endowment
by Sharon Hanley Simpson and
Barclay Simpson honors
MURIEL CARTER HANLEY
whose intellect and sensitivity
have enriched the many lives
that she has touched.

The publisher gratefully acknowledges the generous contribution to this book provided by the Simpson Humanities Endowment Fund of the University of California Press Foundation.

Canyon Cinema

Canyon Cinema

The Life and Times of an Independent Film Distributor

Scott MacDonald

UNIVERSITY OF CALIFORNIA PRESS

BERKELEY   LOS ANGELES   LONDON

The author is deeply grateful to the National Endowment for the Humanities for its support of this project in the form of an NEH Fellowship awarded at the end of 2003. Of course, it should be understood that any views, findings, conclusions, or recommendations expressed in this book do not necessarily reflect those of the National Endowment for the Humanities.

University of California Press, one of the most distinguished university presses in the United States, enriches lives around the world by advancing scholarship in the humanities, social sciences, and natural sciences. Its activities are supported by the UC Press Foundation and by philanthropic contributions from individuals and institutions. For more information, visit www.ucpress.edu.

University of California Press
Berkeley and Los Angeles, California

University of California Press, Ltd.
London, England

For acknowledgments of permissions, please see page 435.

Library of Congress Cataloging-in-Publication Data

MacDonald, Scott, 1942–
    Canyon Cinema : the life and times of an independent film distributor / Scott MacDonald.
        p. cm.
    Includes bibliographic references and index.
    ISBN 978-0-520-25086-4 (cloth : alk. paper)
    ISBN 978-0-520-25087-1 (pbk. : alk. paper)
    1. Canyon Cinema. 2. Independent films—United States.
I. Title.
PN1999.C335M33   2008
384'.80973—dc22   2007009532

Manufactured in the United States of America

17   16   15   14   13   12   11   10   09   08
10   9   8   7   6   5   4   3   2   1

The paper used in this publication meets the minimum requirements of ANSI/NISO Z39.48-1992 (R 1997) (*Permanence of Paper*).

Contents

3 : Revitalization   165

4 : Intellectualization   241

5 : Maintenance 399

Introduction

1

By the 1920s, once the commercial narrative feature had established its economic preeminence, the pervasive experimentation that had characterized the first two decades of film history tended to be redirected, roughly speaking, along two different avenues. Many of those who had explored the possibilities of cinematic form and style in the wake of the early experiments of the Edison Studio, the Lumière brothers, and Georges Méliès became lieutenants in the service of the generals of industry feature films. Others established an alternative history of cinema that explicitly and/or implicitly critiqued the growing hegemony of the commercial feature and the audience it was creating.[1] This alternative history developed in various places and at various moments. In Europe and in the United States during the 1920s, many visual artists explored the possibilities of using the movie camera as an instrument to extend their forays into expressionism, abstraction, dadaism, and surrealism. In Russia, new, experimental forms of film editing were attempts to celebrate and cinematically embody the "dialectic materialist" underpinnings of the Revolution of 1917 and of the new Communist government. During the 1930s in the United Kingdom and the United States, filmmakers frustrated with the problems of unbridled capitalism worked at creating new worker-oriented forms of cinema. In the United States the 1940s saw the emergence of the "psychodrama"—cinematic dramatizations of disturbed states of mind—and a wide variety of new forms of abstraction; by the 1950s and 1960s a full-fledged critical cinema movement (variously called "avant-garde film," "experimental film," "the New American Cinema," or "underground film"—depending on the orientations and interests of particular critics and chroniclers) had emerged.

In retrospect, we can read the development of alternative forms of cinema as something like a coherent aesthetic history, and as a history that reveals particular relationships with the social developments that surrounded it. Each form of alternative cinema that emerged at a particular moment seems to relate in a variety of ways to the alternative forms of cinema that preceded and succeeded it, and each form seems to have responded in a somewhat different way to the realties of modern society.[2] However, whatever social or aesthetic influences now seem formative, it is important to remember that the evolution of alternative cinema was determined not simply by the quantity and quality of the films that were produced within any given moment and set of circumstances, but also by the extent to which whatever films did get produced were seen by audiences, and by the nature of these audiences. Further, both the production of films that provided an ongoing critique of the film industry and modern society *and* the evolution of audiences for alternative forms of cinema were largely dependent upon the efforts of a very few farsighted and often courageous individuals who believed that alternative cinema was important enough—ideologically and/or aesthetically and/or economically—to deserve regular, dependable distribution, and saw various forms of alternative film distribution into being.

Canyon Cinema: The Life and Times of an Independent Film Distributor is an attempt to honor and historicize what became Canyon Cinema, a remarkable achievement in film distribution that evolved during the 1960s in response to the repressive and conformist tendencies of 1950s America and especially in response to the way in which the mainstream media of that moment, particularly film and television, tended to confirm these tendencies. Beginning as an informal exhibition alternative, Canyon Cinema developed into a three-pronged attack on the conventional film scene. Alternative exhibition—that is, the exhibition of forms of cinema not available in commercial theaters or on television—remained an important component of Canyon's work until the 1970s, when its exhibition function became the San Francisco Cinematheque.[3] Canyon's efforts to create a nationwide network of cineastes through its publication of a newsletter that supplied information about alternative film production and exhibition practices helped to establish the "underground" that for a time during the middle to late 1960s seemed poised to offer a challenge to the struggling Hollywood film industry.

But most important for our purposes here, Canyon's establishment of an artist-run film distribution organization in San Francisco that could serve Bay Area independent filmmakers and, later, filmmakers from across the country and across the globe created a lasting model for those who are committed to alternatives to commercial culture. During the past forty years, Canyon has evolved into the most dependable distributor of alternative cinema in the United States, and it has done so without betraying the fundamental principles on which it was founded. If the youthful exuberance and idealism that fueled Canyon's early years—note the nude pyramid of the Canyon board of directors on pages 158–159!—now can seem a vestige of a long-gone moment of utopian excess, Canyon Cinema distribution is one of those rare instances where the "counterculture" of the 1960s continues to prove its long-term value. Canyon has shown itself to be dependable both for filmmakers and for those who rent the films in its extensive collection.

Of the three processes that deliver finished films to the audiences that pay to see them—production, distribution, and exhibition—distribution is certainly the least discussed and the least appreciated. Of course, in the case of mass-market entertainment films, the process of distribution seems virtually automatic and becomes visible only if we live in places where some of the films we hope to see are unavailable. Indeed, the industrial production of cinema has always depended on an efficient nationwide and international distribution system.[4] But the moment we consider the full range of film experience—and, in particular, nonmainstream forms of film—distribution and exhibition can never be taken for granted.[5] Even the front rank of features made outside the Hollywood industry rarely get widely distributed in the United States—though they may find their way to specialized exhibition outlets in a few major cities and may be celebrated at film festivals. And when it comes to avant-garde film, opportunities for distribution beyond a local, coterie audience have been few and far between.

Of course, no one who is familiar with the full range of film history could fail to understand that the quality of a film has little to do with its being widely available; and if this is clear even in the world of commercial cinema, it is painfully obvious in that wide world of cinema that provides critiques of mass media and its audience—and nearly always has been. During the 1920s there was a good bit of interest in "amateur film." Once Eastman Kodak had introduced 16mm film in 1924, this interest resulted in thousands of amateur filmmakers, a network of amateur film clubs, the Amateur Cinema League, a small network of "Little Theaters," and what Jan-Christopher Horak calls "the first American film avant-garde."[6] For a time, there were efforts at distributing amateur cinema through the network of clubs and Little Theaters. By the 1930s, however, the Great Depression had limited theatrical distribution of anything but commercial films, though the amateur movie clubs continued to be active. According to Patricia R. Zimmermann, "The Amateur Cinema League . . . had two hundred fifty amateur-cinema clubs on its rolls by 1937," and its yearly "Ten-Best" contests provided some distribution for a few of the amateur films.[7] Also, for a time the various workers' movements of the 1930s created distribution opportunities for certain forms of leftist-oriented documentary and polemic.[8] In general, however, it seems clear in retrospect that the lack of distribution for anything other than features and shorts made for the nationwide commercial theater chains contributed to the general failure of even those films that did get made, by serious amateurs and by artists working with film, to achieve widespread recognition and influence in this country.

By the mid-1940s it had become clear to a few imaginative cineastes that there was probably an audience, and might be enough films, to support an alternative to the commercial theaters. First, Frank Stauffacher in San Francisco and then, soon after, Amos and Marcia Vogel in New York decided to see if the European film society (or "ciné-club") movement might find purchase in the United States, and in both cases this exhibition gamble met with considerable success.[9] By the end of the decade, thousands of filmgoers were regularly attending the presentations at Art in Cinema (Stauffacher's film society) and Cinema 16 (the Vogels'), and by the 1950s these efforts had helped to instigate a nationwide network of film societies.[10] Both Stauffacher and the Vogels struggled to assemble their programs, since few distribution outlets were available. Both were in large measure dependent on the Museum of Modern Art, which had begun to distribute a range of films in 1936,[11] and on word of mouth, which alerted them to new films being produced. Amos Vogel, who took charge of Cinema 16 once it was established, was committed to a wider range of documentary than Stauffacher: for example, Vogel regularly showed films produced by and for physicians and psychotherapists, and for use in educational institutions, and became familiar with the various film distribution organizations that serviced these fields. But as the film society idea swept across the country, it became increasingly clear that new distribution systems were needed to service the growing film society audience.

Beginning in the late 1940s, Vogel began to distribute selected avant-garde films and documentaries, and in 1951 he produced his first brochure announcing the availability of "20 Experimental/Rental Films, from Cinema 16." Vogel was not alone in trying to cater to this new audience for educational and artistic cinema. Tom Brandon had begun distributing political films in the 1930s; by the 1940s he was distributing a range of documentaries, as well as dance films and films about art, and by 1950 he was, somewhat grudgingly, including a few avant-garde films in the Brandon catalog: *Rhythm in Light* (1934; Mary Ellen Bute, Ted Nemeth, Melville F. Webber) and *Fiddle-De-Dee* (1947; Norman McLaren) were included in the 1950 catalogue; three films by Curtis Harrington— *Fragment of Seeking* (1946), *Picnic* (1948), *On the Edge* (1949)—and *Ai-Ye* (1951) by Ian Hugo were added by 1953.[12] Rosalind Kossoff distributed English versions of French documentaries through A. F. Films; Audio Film Classics in San Francisco included a number of experimental documentaries in its 1954 catalog (including *The Private Life of a Cat* [1945] by Alexander Hammid; Basil Wright's *Song of Ceylon* [1934]; *Notes on the Port of St. Francis* [1952] by Frank Stauffacher; and *The City* [1939] by Ralph Steiner and Willard Van Dyke); and Leo Dratfield's Contemporary Films distributed art films and social documentaries, including experimental documentaries (*The Private Life of a Cat, Song of Ceylon, The City,* and *The Quiet One* [1948] by Sidney Meyers and Janice Loeb), a number of what Dratfield called "Cinema 16 Films"—for example, *The Cage* (1947,

Sidney Peterson); *Psyche* (1947), *Lysis* (1948), and *Charmides* (1948) by Gregory Markopoulos—and several of Maya Deren's films.[13]

Particularly important for Canyon Cinema was Bob Pike's Creative Film Society, which was founded in 1957 in Los Angeles, for nearly the same set of purposes that were to instigate Canyon itself. As explained by Pike, this included "consolidating the efforts of the individual West Coast filmartists in terms of aiding closer communication of ideas, films, and equipment, as well as distributing the finished works of the members."[14] The Creative Film Society shared a number of clients with Canyon: Pike's first catalogue included Stan Brakhage and Larry Jordan (later, when Canyon Cinema incorporated, Jordan became its first president), and its rental collection grew until 1975, when it included some four hundred films. Not surprisingly, Pike was interested in Canyon's distribution efforts from early on, and for a time he regularly contributed reports to Canyon's newsletter, originally called the *News* (several of these reports are included in this volume). Pike's confident response to Robert Nelson's claim that he was a crass businessman who had treated Nelson and his films disrespectfully (see pages 87–92) was predicated on his long experience as an independent distributor committed to some of the same goals as Canyon.

All these distribution outlets had one thing in common: they were organized so that the distributors decided which particular films they would distribute. Further, all were committed to providing a profit-making service, and many asked filmmakers to sign exclusive contracts that provided them with a percentage (usually 50 percent or less) of rental revenues. Although filmmakers were grateful that someone was willing to take a chance on distributing at least some of their films, by the end of the 1950s there was also a move afoot to develop distribution possibilities that would be controlled by the filmmakers themselves. For Jonas Mekas and a number of others, the idea that Amos Vogel, or anyone else, should become the arbiter of which of a film artist's films should get to be seen by the public was increasingly untenable, and on September 28, 1960, the New American Cinema Group met to consider alternatives. By 1962 the New York Film-Makers' Cooperative was publishing its own catalogue and suggesting to potential exhibitors that they consider offering programs of films by individual film artists, rather than the "pot pourri programs" usually offered by film societies.[15]

The Film-Makers' Cooperative was, and remains, an artist-run organization. In the beginning, it provided member filmmakers with the opportunity for passive distribution of any or all the films they wanted to make available to exhibitors. This distribution was "passive" in the sense that while the Film-Makers' Cooperative was committed to producing a catalog of films for rent, all filmmakers were considered equal, and no film or filmmaker was to receive more attention from the distributor than any other. The "Coop" would not do any sort of advertising or promotion for particular films or filmmakers. Of course, if film-makers wanted to promote their own films, that was fine, but the Cooperative's job was to maintain prints, take orders from exhibitors, and provide a listing of available films, along with descriptions supplied by the film artists themselves, plus the Coop's rental terms. The lower overhead achieved by passive distribu-tion, it was assumed, would allow for a more generous percentage of the rental to go to the filmmakers: the Film-Makers' Cooperative began with a 75/25 per-cent split of rental monies, with 25 percent coming back to the Coop to cover its costs. The assumption was that those who worked at the Coop would receive a decent wage, but that the organization would not profit from the service it pro-vided beyond maintaining its viability as a distributor.[16]

The New York Film-Makers' Cooperative was the first cooperative distribution outlet to establish itself, but it was only a single instance of an idea whose time had come: groups of independent filmmakers in various parts of this country, and in Europe and Japan, faced with the same problem of how to make their films available to those interested in showing them, were coming to the conclu-sion that some sort of cooperative distribution might be useful. The formation of the New York Film-Makers' Cooperative proved that filmmaker-run distribution was possible, and other groups, here and abroad, followed its lead. Canyon was the most long-lived and influential of the American filmmaker-run distributors to emulate the New York Coop.[17] Canyon, which was formed in San Francisco in 1966, initially was called the Canyon Cinema Cooperative. Though it was estab-lished in the shadow of the New York Film-Makers' Cooperative, during its more than forty years of operation, Canyon Cinema has proved itself something close to a model organization of its kind, both for the filmmakers and for those who use Canyon's service. While the percentage of revenues returned to the film-makers has varied from the original 75/25 split (since 2001 the split has been 50/50), so far as I have been able to determine, filmmakers have *always* received the rentals their films have generated.[18] Further, Canyon has a particularly good record of providing good 16mm prints in a timely fashion.[19]

Canyon Cinema did not begin as a distribution cooperative, but rather as an unusually conceived exhibition outlet just north of Berkeley. Filmmaker Bruce Baillie was the instigator of Canyon Cinema, and he has described its origins:

> We started Canyon Cinema about 1960, in Canyon, California, over the hills from Oakland and Berkeley. Kikuko [Baillie's partner at the time] was paying the rent and giving me the chance to free up my time to make films. Immediately I real-ized that making films and showing films must go hand in hand, so I got a job at

Safeway, took out a loan and bought a projector. We got an army surplus screen and hung it up real nice in the back yard of this house we were renting. Then we'd find whatever films we could, including our own little things that were in progress—"we," there wasn't really any we, just myself for awhile—and show them.

So I made a *thing* of it. I had no occupation. I couldn't get a real job anywhere. So I thought, I'll invent my own occupation. I set up a little part of the house as an office. I had to call it something: I put up a little sign and it turned out to be "Canyon Cinema" with a light bulb next to it. Fairly soon, we had weekly showings. Kikuko made popcorn. The kids around the neighborhood gathered the community benches and chairs, and we'd sit under the trees in the summer with all the dogs and people and watch French or Canadian Embassy films and National Film Board of Canada stuff, along with our own. I let it be known immediately that I had a place to show films, if any filmmakers were coming through town. I let Jonas [Mekas] know right away. At first we were in touch with Larry Jordan, and later, Jordan Belson.[20]

As Canyon Cinema evolved, Baillie was joined by others—most notably, filmmaker Chick Strand and Ernest "Chick" Callenbach (longtime editor of *Film Quarterly* and author of *Ecotopia* [1975])—and the screenings moved from place to place, first into Berkeley, and then to San Francisco as well. Because there was so little precedent, at least in the United States, for the kinds of programming Baillie did, and so much suspicion of "underground film," the biggest problem was finding a space where Canyon could present films without fear of being shut down by the local authorities. In fact, Callenbach became involved in 1961 when Baillie "began telling me how . . . the fire marshalls were always after them. You know, you'd rent some hall and then it would turn out that, according to the authorities, it didn't have enough exits. And it wouldn't have toilets. And they'd get closed down. . . . They had tried schools, and they had done a lot of things, and none of them had really worked, so they were really desperate for a place to show."[21] While the original screenings in Canyon had been sporadic, by 1961–1962 Baillie, Strand, Callenbach, and others—Paul Tulley, Wes Patterson, Dave Cleveland, and a little later Emory Menefee—had made Canyon a regular, if still rather nomadic, showcase, sometimes presenting as many as three events a week. In Berkeley, Canyon screenings were held for a time at the home of Chick and Paul Strand. Baillie remembers:

Programming took place in Strand's backyard on sunny Saturdays. Husband, Paul Strand kept the VW bus going which we used to haul our growing *Circus* (as in von Richtoven circa 1915–18). Someone donated a large new screen which went overboard enroute on the freeway and was finally replaced. We showed at the

Oakland Arts Institute for awhile—always locked (later inspiring my screenplay, *The Shoe Salesman*), requiring some gymnastics to climb into a high window and descend onto the theater backdrop, suspended by ropes from the rafters, like in the dangerous Opera House of the *Phantom of the Opera*.

We also showed in North Beach, along with our weekly or bi-monthly Berkeley schedule, amongst the post-Beat folk, the books, bars, bands and poetry readings. The SF Mime Troupe and the SF Tape Music Center were emerging at this time, mid-60's. We cooperated with the Center in various ways—Morton Subotnik and Ramon Sender were giving concerts, while the Mime Troupe often performed in the park, as perhaps they still do.[22]

Another of the early venues was Bistro San Martin, an anarchist restaurant in Berkeley; still another was Chick Callenbach's backyard in Berkeley. Callenbach has described the scene:

> We would set up Bruce's old projector and a screen of some kind on the other end of the yard, and invite all the neighbors—because the soundtracks were often pretty raucous. And people would come in. It was really a neat scene because Chicky Strand, who had, and probably still has, a real sense of drama, would wear a kind of witchy cloak and her long black hair down, and she would sit with a couple of candles in the garage that went through from the street to my backyard, and that was the "box office." She would collect the money and chat with people, and then they'd go on in, bringing sleeping bags and jugs of wine and so on. They'd sort of crash all over the deck and after a while we'd show the films to maybe thirty or forty people. Not immense, but enough—and they were pretty regular; they would come . . . maybe once a month. Some of them helped out with Canyon's operation in some way, but most people just showed up hoping to see something unusual.[23]

According to Callenbach, Baillie would often begin the program with a Castle film he had found or brought, followed by local experimental films, including his own, and films from the East Coast and elsewhere. Evenings might end with the award of a door prize (a ticket to the presentation included a chance to win the prize), which might be a pie that Baillie had made, or tickets to a steam bath. Chick Strand remembers, "It was a real family kind of thing."[24]

Though the early, community-oriented screenings evolved into a formal organization, and in time became the San Francisco Cinematheque, the original Canyon has continued to have an impact; indeed, it was one of the primary influences on what has recently become known as the "microcinema" movement—a nationwide network of small, almost familial screening rooms. One of the major instigators of the microcinema movement was San Francisco's Total Mobile Home, a collaboration of Rebecca Barton and David Sherman, who

Chick Strand in the 1970s, a self-portrait.

hosted filmmakers and film shows in their home, once a week, from 1994 until 1997. For Barton and Sherman, Baillie's original Canyon Cinema was a crucial inspiration: "In fact, one of our early shows (in 1994) at Total Mobile Home was a series of morning salons with Bruce Baillie where the connection between what we were doing and Baillie's Canyon screenings was dialogued."[25] Barton also remembers that when she was first discovering and exploring avant-garde cinema, as a student at the University of Maryland, the Canyon Cinema catalogs were "great delicacies."[26] Sherman worked for Canyon from 1988 until 2000.[27]

Baillie's vision of Canyon as a kind of village nexus, an essentially spiritual gathering that could bring diverse people together, was obvious in the nature of the early Canyon screenings, but it also led to other activities and services as well, including both production facilities and the creation of local "news" outlets. When Chick Callenbach moved to a new home, Baillie and Callenbach transformed its large basement into editing facilities: "Bruce edited *To Parsifal* [1963] there and worked on a couple of other films briefly; we were trying to make it a sort of anarchists' cutting room, where anybody who needed to borrow equipment could come and work and schmooz and help each other."[28] Baillie's instinct seems always to have been collaborative and communal. In fact, Larry Jordan recalls that when Baillie received a Ford Foundation grant (sometime before 1968), "He sent me a thousand dollars out of it, which paid for the sound track of my long, dramatic *Hildur and the Magician* [1969]. Whenever I tried to express my gratitude, Bruce didn't want to hear anything about it; he just thought that's the way things should be. At that time, a thousand dollars bought a lot of film services!"[29]

Baillie's vision for Canyon also included regular access to news about the local community that surrounded Canyon's screenings. Baillie himself began filming "news items" early on and presented these at the screenings. *David Lynn's Sculpture* (1961) was one of Baillie's first films: "a newsreel of David Lynn's *big* log sculpture, made for the first Canyon Cinema up in Canyon."[30] Others include *Friend Fleeing* (1962; "I was leaving Canyon one day to go on a little trip, so I made a little film for everybody")[31]; *Mr. Hayashi* (1961), a portrait of a neighbor, "a real, living saint," as Baillie describes him in an early Canyon Cinema distribution catalog; and later on, *Termination* (1966; by the "Canyon Cinema Documentary Film Unit," according to catalog notes for the film), which was made for a small community of Native Americans near Laytonville, California. The desire to draw the Canyon community together by providing information also resulted in the establishment of the *News,* later called the *Canyon Cinema News* and the *Cinemanews*—over the years the title underwent several variations.[32] The *News* was Callenbach's idea. As editor of *Film Quarterly,* he frequently received information about film projects and events that was not suitable for an academic quarterly, but that he knew would be of interest to the independent film community.

The first issue of the *News,* edited by Alexandra Ossipoff, was published in December 1962. The publication quickly became a valuable source of information about film festivals, film projects, scheduled screenings of independent work, and contact information for filmmakers, distributors, and exhibitors—and, in time, it included interviews, articles, poems, drawings, photography, and debates. Baillie saw that the *News* even had its own logo: "We discovered a great logo, the front and back pen drawing of a beautiful guy from a nineteenth-century medicine catalog called: The Exothematic Method of Cure. It was a little kit with platinum tipped needles: you punctured yourself and used the 'Olium' that came with the needles. By this *advanced method* you were supposed to be able to rid yourself of 'morbid matter.' We really loved that; we had the image reproduced and it went on our news. Later, we had it made into stamps, stickers, and it went on the reels of film the Coop distributed."[33]

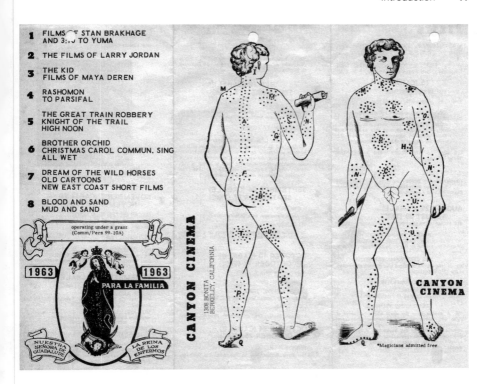

Program announcement for fall 1963 Canyon Cinema film series, with the "Exothematic Man" logo (the asterisked words under the right-hand figure's left foot are "Magicians admitted free"). Events in this series were presented at the Cabale, 2504 San Pablo, Berkeley, on Thursdays at 7.30, and at the Tape Music Center, 321 Divisadero, San Francisco, on Fridays at 8.30. The "East Coast short films" scheduled for November 7 and 8 were selections from the Film-Makers' Cooperative collection. Note the Christmas carol community sing scheduled in October and, in general, Baillie's diverse, and tactical, programming.

By the mid-1960s, Canyon had established itself as a three-part service to the community of independent filmmakers and cineastes. Emory Menefee, a research chemist working at a Department of Agriculture office in the Bay Area, was overseeing Canyon's exhibition program at various San Francisco venues, most notably at Intersection (then at 150 Ellis Street). The mixture of pop and avant-garde film that had characterized Baillie's early Canyon programming had been replaced by a more complete focus on avant-garde film and especially on one-person shows presented by film artists. Menefee oversaw Canyon's exhibition program from 1965 until the end of July 1967. In November 1967, Canyon screenings resumed with a new moniker, the "Canyon Cinematheque," under the directorship of Edith Kramer, Loren Sears, and Roy Ramsing. Screenings were still held at Intersection, which had moved to 756 Union Street. According to Steve Anker (who was director of the Cinematheque from 1980 until 2002), in the late 1960s screenings became extremely popular and seem to have recaptured something of the anarchic spirit of the early Canyon screenings organized by Baillie, Strand, and Callenbach: "Programming was egalitarian, with films frequently selected spontaneously while the events were in progress. Wacky door prizes, free drinks and popcorn, and lively masters of ceremonies (most notably filmmaker Anne Severson) added to the party atmosphere."[34]

The *News* was "edited"—during the early years there was little editing per se; news items would be collected or submitted, and arranged, typed up (for a time Bruce Baillie's mother was the typist), reproduced, and distributed—first by Ossipoff, then by Margaret Kerr (1963, issues 2–6), Chick Strand (1963, issues 7–9), Lillian Thibodeau (1963, issues 10–11; 1964, issues 1–4), and Strand again (1964, issue 5). From September 1964 until the March–April 1966 issue, no editor is listed in the *News* itself, but presumably Baillie oversaw these issues: the March 1966 issue announces, "In Bruce's absence, this month's News is being put out by Emory Menefee and next month Robert Nelson will take it." The Nelson issue (June 1966) was followed by an issue devoted entirely to a sequence of drawings by Neon Park; and then, again, from August 1966 until the March–April 1967 issue, no editor is listed. As of May 1967, Menefee took over and remained the *News* editor until his resignation in 1970.

In the November 1966 issue, the *News* announced that a distribution cooperative had been formed: "In its sixth year, Canyon Cinema felt the need to establish an independent film distribution office on the West Coast of North America to better serve the needs of film-makers in that part of the world. That facility came into existence on the 14th day of August, 1966, in the wake of the pioneer Film-Makers' Coop [in New York City] and in this year of new Co-ops in London and Boston and rumored Co-ops in Chicago, Philadelphia, Austin, Rome and Paris." Something of Bruce Baillie's sweet, spiritual anarchism is evident in the announcement's description of the new organization's members: "Canyon Cinema Co-op is a federation of willing devotees of the magic lantern muse, consisting of artists engaged in the creation of 16mm films, 8mm film and other related light and image projection media. The devotees have a policy of non-policy, and are subject to only the barest and most basic 'procedures' for co-operatively distributing their films or informing likely audiences of their light-projection capacities." All film artists were invited to join. The announcement outlines the process for renting and buying prints of films, then lists the filmmakers and their films available for rent—a total of thirty-one filmmakers and seventy-five films (plus one audiotape). Only six of the filmmakers—Baillie, Robert Feldman, Larry Jordan, Robert Nelson, Ben Van Meter, and Michael K. Wiese—listed more than one or two films, and only Jordan offered a substantial number of films (nineteen).

It is symptomatic of the committed, unmercenary temper of the Canyon group that they list *all* the distributors for each of the films offered for rental or sale in their catalog *and* include an equally detailed listing of independent films "*not* available, at this time, from Canyon Cinema Co-operative." Until Canyon formally incorporated on February 26, 1967, the distribution operation was handled by Earl Bodien (two of Bodien's films were listed in the catalog), who stored the prints in his living room. Lenny Lipton, an early Canyon board member (also a filmmaker whose films were distributed by Canyon and the author of two breakthrough books, *Independent Filmmaking* [New York: Simon and Schuster, 1973] and *The Super-8 Book* [New York: Fireside, 1975]), remembers Bodien's "funky little apartment in a little house near Howard Street [Bodien's address was 58 Verona Place], an area that's utterly gentrified now." The apartment doubled as Canyon's everyday office and its meeting place: "Sometimes at meetings we would enjoy Earl's manipulating a normal television broadcast using several magnets. *Earl* was the one who *did the work;* he was very steady and I'm sure that without Earl's participation there would have been no Canyon distribution."[35]

A catalog of films for rent was included in the November 1966 *News;* this catalog was reproduced in December 1966 as *Catalogue Number One* of the Canyon Cinema Cooperative. This simple listing (16 two-sided, 8½ × 11 inch pages stapled together) must have served a considerable need, at least judging from the fact that two years later *Catalogue Number Two* was a 128-page (6 × 9 inch) listing of nearly five-hundred films by 165 filmmakers (published with the help of "the [financial] contributions of Jonas Mekas and the American Film Institute"). *Catalogue Number Two* was followed quickly by *Catalogue Number Two, Supplement Number One* (1969), then by *Catalog 2, Supplement 2* (1970) and *Catalog 2, Supplement 3* (1970; all the supplements were 6 × 9 inches).[36] Spring 1972 saw the publication of *Catalog 3,* a 218-page (8½ × 11 inch) listing in which filmmakers—if they wished—could design their own catalog pages. Enough filmmakers did design their own listings to give the catalog a rather anarchic feel and to offer potential renters something of an adventure. The sanguine mood at Canyon at the time is suggested by the fact that seven thousand copies of the 1972 catalog were printed.[37] *Catalog 3* was updated in two supplements: Spring 1973 and Fall 1974. Also, from November 1966 on, the *News* regularly listed new films available from Canyon.

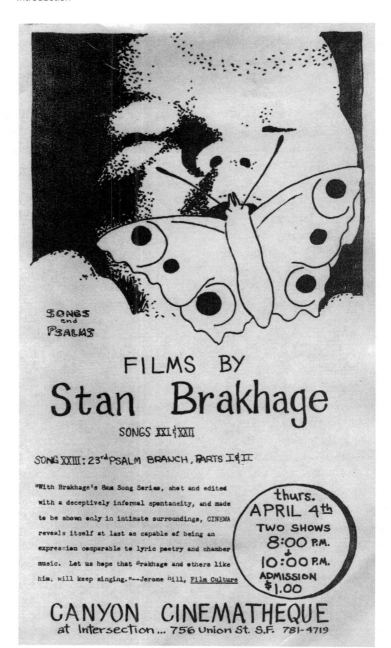

Posters advertising screenings at the Canyon Cinematheque at Intersection.

When Diane Kitchen became Canyon's manager in 1973, she was convinced that the look of *Catalog 3* was largely responsible for the falloff of rentals during the early 1970s, and she quickly put plans in motion for what became *Catalog 4,* which was published in 1976. *Catalog 4* did include photographic and graphic imagery supplied by the filmmakers, but only in special sections set off from the listing of filmmakers/films; it also included, at the end, a "subject index" in which the "filmmakers . . . selected the categories that they feel best describes [*sic*] their film(s)"—categories included "abstract," "animals," "animation," "assemblage/ collage," "autobiographical," "children," "cine poems," "comedy" . . . an attempt to assist potential renters find their way into the catalog and access the films best suited to their particular circumstances. *Catalog 4* was also the first listing since *Catalog 2, Supplement 2* not to list 8mm films separately from 16mm films. New catalogs continued to appear with some regularity.[38]

The fast-developing interest in alternative forms of film in the middle to late 1960s quickly rendered Earl Bodien's living room inadequate for maintaining the films available from Canyon, and by 1967 it was clear that the organization required a higher level of professional organization. In 1967 Bodien and Larry Jordan signed Canyon's incorporation papers. The papers named Jordan the president of "Canyon Cinema, Inc. (A Non-Profit Corporation)," and Bodien, sec- retary; they also established a board of directors to be elected by the members ("any film maker or any one interested in film making shall be eligible to apply for membership in the corporation"). The articles of incorporation list Jordan, Ben Van Meter, Robert Nelson, and Bruce Baillie as directors "until the selection of their successors." When the first election was held, five directors were chosen: Larry Jordan, Lenny Lipton, Emory Menefee, Loren Sears, and Ben Van Meter. The original address of Canyon Cinema, Inc., was 58 Verona Place, San Fran- cisco, but in 1967, when Earl and Mary Ann Bodien left San Francisco to move back to the Midwest, Canyon moved to the basement of the defunct church at 756 Union Street that had been taken over by Intersection. There, Jordan and Robert Nelson built storage space and an office for Edith Kramer, who had been working with Bodien for some months and was asked by the board to take over the day-to-day operation of Canyon distribution. "Edith," Jordan remembers, "was very hands-on and right there, and very capable; she got to make most of the decisions. The whole idea of forming the Coop was to get somebody else to take the burden of distribution off our [the filmmakers'] shoulders; we were very lucky Edith took the job."[39]

Beginning in the fall of 1968 (in undated issue no. 68.7), the minutes of board of directors' meetings were published in what was now being called the *Canyon Cinemanews.* The first item of business at the September 4, 1968, meeting was a bit of bad news: "In order to qualify for non-profit status, the Coop will have to reorganize. The Internal Revenue Service has refused our request for non-profit status." In the discussion that followed, it was clear that "non-profit status is important for attracting grant money . . . special mailing rates, etc. The Coop under IRS regulations will never be able to qualify it is clear. We will have to split into at least two organizations." According to Edith Kramer, the problem was that Canyon had incorporated as a membership organization. Legally, a nonprofit organization can make money, but this money cannot be shared with members. Since the whole point of forming Canyon was to help member filmmakers earn some money from rentals of their films without the hassle of being in distribution for themselves (even during this idealistic period, few filmmakers would have expected to make a *profit:* that is, more than it cost them to make their films), the State of California and then the IRS refused Canyon's request to be considered nonprofit.[40] It would be nearly a decade before Canyon would bifurcate into the distribution organization, which retained the "Canyon Cinema" name, and a nonprofit exhibitor, the San Francisco Cinematheque (the *Canyon Cinemanews* would become one of the nonprofit activities of the Cinematheque).

The Canyon Cinema rental catalog continued to grow, but by the early 1970s the number of rental requests was leveling off and operating revenues were down. When Intersection was forced to move out of its Union Street space, Canyon lost its facilities as well. Kramer moved Canyon to a warehouse in Sausalito, where the organization remained until Diane Kitchen moved it back to San Francisco. As Canyon distribution expanded and became increasingly professionalized, the community spirit that seems to have characterized the early organization did become more diffused, except at Canyon board meetings, which sometimes continued to suggest the organization's earlier anarchic spirit. A sense of community was maintained at Cinematheque screenings and expanded through the *News/Canyon Cinema News/Canyon Cinemanews/ Cinemanews,* which never entirely lost the small-town aura that Bruce Baillie had brought to the original Canyon Cinema screenings and that was pervasive during his editorship (1965–1967). As the years went by, the periodical developed a national, even an international, readership; by the time Emory Menefee took over as editor in 1967, the *News* was beginning to publish longer essays: polemics of one kind or another, discussions of technical issues, reviews, letters from traveling filmmakers and from people organizing film events—especially avant-garde film events—around this country and in Europe, Australia, and Japan. By the end of Menefee's editorship, the *Canyon Cinemanews* had become an important voice—one of the most important voices for the developing community of alternative filmmakers.[41]

For a time after Menefee resigned as editor, the *Canyon Cinemanews* passed from one editor to another: to Don Lloyd, then to Jan Lash and Peter Hutton (one issue: 71.2), to "guest editor," "red sky" (one issue: 71.3), then to Bruce Conner and Ben Van Meter (two issues: 72.1/2), Van Meter (72.3), Susan O'Neill (72.4), David Boatwright (72.5/6), and Al Saxton (73.1). During these years the comparative stability and consistency Menefee had brought to the magazine was lost, and individual issues varied a good deal in format and in feel. Then, for all practical purposes, *Canyon Cinemanews* went into a hiatus: from early 1973 until mid-1974 six issues went to press, but they contained little of interest. Finally, in mid-1974, when Diane Kitchen became manager of Canyon, she not only revived the *Canyon Cinemanews* but took it to a new level (see the introduction to section 3, "Revitalization," for specifics).

By the fall of 1977 Kitchen had transitioned out of the *Cinemanews* editorship just as—after years of discussion and debate—Canyon's distribution and exhibition separated. From mid-1977 on, Canyon Cinema distribution was run by Michael Wallin and Dominic Angerame. When Wallin left in 1986, Angerame became director and has remained in that position ever since. The *Cinemanews* (the name was changed from *Canyon Cinemanews* to *Cinemanews* in the 76.6 issue) was also in a transitional period. Mark McGowan took over the editorship from Kitchen and, after editing the July/August (77.4) issue with her and the September/October issue (77.5) by himself, filmmakers Henry Hills and Abigail Child, assisted by Stephanie Boris and Mark McGowan (now in charge of layout), shared editorial duties and took the *Cinemanews* into its final phase (though it would be revived, briefly, as the *New Canyon Cinemanews,* two decades later).[42]

The separation of Canyon Cinema from the San Francisco Cinematheque and the *Cinemanews* allowed all the energies of Canyon staff to be devoted to distribution and freed Canyon from the programming and publication controversies of the Cinematheque and the *Cinemanews.* Canyon did, from time to time, find itself embroiled in controversy, as, for example, when its members and directors began to question its exclusive focus on film. Now that so many filmmakers were also videomakers, shouldn't Canyon also be renting video? In general, however, the Canyon offices had increasingly become a place of business rather than a nexus for the Bay Area film community. Angerame and his colleagues did continue to make the facilities available to people interested in previewing films from the collection. Michael Wallin remembers that Godfrey Reggio came by one day in the early 1980s and arranged to rent and view dozens of films by Brakhage, Conner, Baillie—"all the big names. Money seemed no object to him.

A couple of years later, when I finally saw *Koyaanisqatsi* [1983], I realized he'd been ripping off ideas."[43]

During the 1980s Canyon Cinema distribution reversed the falloff of rentals that had happened during the 1970s. Following the production of a new, expanded catalog in 1982 (*Catalog 5*), rental revenues improved considerably. The total rental figures for 1980–1981 were $28,886; the year after the publication of the catalog, $42,567; and five years later, in 1988–1989, $69,619. This revival of Canyon's fortunes—as modest as it might seem, especially compared with the mega-revenues involved in commercial film distribution—went a long way toward stabilizing the organization and made possible continued first-rate service and more humane salaries for those working for Canyon. Until very recently Canyon's fortunes continued this modest expansion. Since the 1998–1999 fiscal year Canyon's gross income from rentals and sales has remained above $100,000; in 2001–2002 and 2002–2003, rentals reached all-time highs of $154,000 and $175,191, respectively.

No sooner might one have begun to grow complacent about Canyon's fortunes than a serious threat to the organization became unavoidable. Soon after Canyon moved its facilities to the Ninth Street Media Consortium building in 2002 (the other tenants at 145 Ninth Street include the San Francisco Cinematheque, the Film Arts Foundation, Frameline, the Bay Area Jewish Film Festival, and the National Asian American Telecommunications Association [NAATA]), rentals of 16mm prints fell drastically. Angerame is confident that this is due to the proliferation of DVD versions of avant-garde films previously available only as 16mm prints: "I noticed a considerable drop-off in Brakhage's rentals soon after the DVD of Brakhage's films became available."[44] Indeed, during early 2006, according to Angerame, Canyon was losing about $2,000 a month. To make matters worse, Bruce Conner, sensing that Canyon was in serious trouble, pressured its board to face the possibility of Canyon's having to go out of business, and to make the necessary plans to protect the films and member filmmakers.[45] When the board resisted, Conner withdrew his films from the rental collection—a major setback, since he was, like Brakhage, one of the most rented filmmakers distributed by Canyon. Various strategies for dealing with this new threat to Canyon's 16mm rental business are being considered. As this introduction is finished (April 2007), a long-range plan has not emerged, though a letter asking for contributions was sent to Canyon members and friends in 2006. In the report to Canyon filmmakers dated March 25, 2007, Angerame and Nathaniel Dorsky, president of the board of directors, announce that "Canyon Cinema is economically solvent"; they thank a number of donors for contributions and indicate that "during the past year, 2006/07 rentals have increased over the previous year." One breakthrough involves a new, more profitable way of renting films and DVDs of films to art museums for continuous loop projection (films that are on continuous loop receive a rental for each repetition of the loop).

One irony in Canyon's struggles is that the New York Film-Makers' Cooperative, Canyon's most obvious competitor (in addition to its being the organization's original inspiration), *was* able to become a nonprofit organization, under the name the New American Cinema Group (which had been incorporated in 1961), despite its remaining a membership organization. According to M. M. Serra, director of the Film-Makers' Cooperative since 1990, Marjorie Keller, then the president of the Film-Makers' Cooperative board, urged Serra to work at achieving nonprofit status: "We were turned down the first time: we had been in business for thirty years and they said, 'Why didn't you do this at the beginning?' So I went to the Volunteer Lawyers for the Arts in New York City, and Ralph Walters, a corporate lawyer, told me exactly what to do to prove that we *are* an artists' organization, artist-owned and artist-run, and that we provide an educational service. We needed letters of support from museums and colleges to demonstrate that our focus was education, but we put together a good dossier, and got our 501 C-3 status in 1993."[46] According to Angerame, "Every bit of legal advice we get tells us that it's just not possible to overturn an earlier decision by the IRS"; as a result, Canyon is not currently considering another application for not-for-profit status, though alterations in the structure of the organization are being considered.

One can only hope that Canyon is able to weather the challenge posed by DVD releases of 16mm films. The loss of this remarkable distributor would be a disaster for the field of independent cinema and for film history in general. But whatever does happen in the coming years, Canyon's founders, and the many people who have worked to keep it afloat decade after decade, can be proud: going on half a century after Bruce Baillie began to dream of a West Coast center for alternative cinema, the San Francisco Cinematheque (now under the directorship of Caroline Elizabeth Savage) continues to be one of the premier American showcases for a wide range of independent film and video, and Canyon Cinema distribution continues to offer first-rate service to avant-garde filmmakers from around the world and to those who program and teach their films.

2

In assembling *Canyon Cinema,* I have several goals. The most obvious of these, of course, is to draw attention to one of the few remaining distributors of films in 16mm (and, in some instances, 8mm, Super-8, and 35mm)—and arguably the most dependable such distributor in the United States. Without Canyon Cinema our sense of modern film history would be considerably poorer and this history itself, less accessible. Even at this late date—*especially* at this late date—as 16mm film seems, at least to some, on the verge of disappearing, Canyon can still serve as a model for those interested in seeing the vast and remarkable history of accomplished 16mm filmmaking and the possibility of 16mm exhibition safely to the next generation. Further, since Canyon has remained not only efficient and dependable but also solvent—even during periods of sluggish economy—it can provide a useful model for those interested in founding or reviving organizations dedicated to alternative art practices; hopefully, this book provides some sense of how Canyon has been able to remain a financially healthy organization for forty years.

The second goal of this volume is to make available general information and specific historical documents from the annals of Canyon Cinema and especially from the *Cinemanews.* The gradual evolution of this publication over a period of two decades provides an index of a volatile and fascinating historical period; and the wealth of interviews, essays, poems, drawings, photographs, film schedules, letters, announcements, and organizational minutes published in the *Cinemanews* provides considerable insight into many filmmaking careers and into the social and political contexts within which these careers developed. The *Cinemanews* also reveals general changes in the way in which independent cinema, and avant-garde film in particular, was perceived by the community that formed around it.

The following five sections of *Canyon Cinema* offer a sense of how Canyon developed over a period of twenty years and provide access to a variety of specific documents that have import not simply for this particular distribution organization, but for the history of independent cinema, and for film history in general. At the beginning, as the organization formed, those involved with Canyon saw it as essentially a community activity, both in the sense that Canyon was meant to serve a local Bay Area population and in the sense that those involved with Canyon considered themselves aesthetic neighbors, artists with common concerns involved in a common quest. This is obvious in the various letters, essays, and controversies charted in section 1, "Formation" and in section 2, "Incorporation."

Like any organization, Canyon was affected by a variety of social and economic currents. Its fortunes and effectiveness as an organization waxed and waned and waxed again, sometimes because of events beyond the control of anyone involved with the organization, and at other times because of the input of particular individuals associated with Canyon—as is evident in section 3, "Revitalization." By the early 1970s, the *Cinemanews* had become a leading nexus for news and thinking about what seemed to be an independent film movement, and the informal community dimension that was so obvious during the 1960s was giving way to an ostensibly more serious attitude toward the leaders of this movement. Increasingly, the Canyon Cinematheque was interested in presenting filmmakers whose cinematic accomplishments seemed particularly important, and by the mid-1970s, the *Cinemanews* was regularly presenting transcriptions of the lectures and conversations with filmmakers that took place at the Cinematheque. Section 4, "Intellectualization," reflects the expanded focus on individual, now-canonized filmmakers speaking about their work, as well as an expanded sense of the artistic community that independent filmmaking was part of. By the 1980s, as is clear in section 5, "Maintenance," the intimate, local energy that had created the organization and had generated its three-part service to the Bay Area had dissipated. The San Francisco Cinematheque had become entirely independent, the *Cinemanews* petered out, and Canyon Cinema distribution had become a well-run small business.

The formal organization of the five sections within this volume is rather unusual for a scholarly work. Of course, I want to provide something like an accurate historical representation of how Canyon developed and what it was like to receive that organization's newsletter as events were occurring. However, it has always been my belief that the duty of a film historian, particularly a historian working with a marginalized dimension of film history, is, first and foremost, to bring attention to the most crucial filmmakers and their work. As a result, rather than simply filtering what the filmmaker members of Canyon had to say about cinema in general and Canyon in particular through my own historical gloss, I have chosen to reprint a good many original documents and have organized them so that the documents themselves tell the Canyon story. Each successive section of *Canyon Cinema* includes a larger percentage of original documents—my way of moving readers from *my* sense of Canyon toward the plethora of voices that Canyon has always represented.

Each section of *Canyon Cinema* consists of a general overview, followed by a "portfolio" of documents. My hope is that my selection and arrangement of the materials included in the portfolios will allow the reader to gain a clearer sense not only of how Canyon functioned but also of what films were being rented and shown, where they were being shown, and by whom, as well as what some of the responses to these films were, inside and outside the community of independent filmmakers. Further, during the lifetime of the organization, particular individuals have moved to the foreground to address issues that seem crucial at

particular moments. In the portfolios I have tended to privilege letters and articles by and interviews with men and women who maintained their connection
with Canyon over a period of time, not simply by using Canyon as their distributor but by serving on the board, by writing to the *Cinemanews,* and by commenting on the history and the principles of Canyon in interviews. Bruce Baillie,
Chick Strand, Robert Nelson, Will Hindle, and Bruce Conner are the most obvious instances; they are the central characters in my Canyon narrative.

One further factor that plays a role in the arrangement of the documents
included here is a function of my interest as a film historian in montage. I have
ordered the elements within the portfolios so as to provide a rhythm of com-
monalities and distinctions, of themes and collisions that, I hope, will energize
the experience of the volume for those (perhaps few) who will experience
Canyon Cinema (or one or another particular portion of it) as an integral work
with its own particular energy and set of conceptual, narrative, and visual concerns. If it is recognized that one of these concerns is a form of scholarly entertainment, so much the better. One of the reasons Canyon has been as successful as it has is the high spirits and good humor of so many who have contributed
to the organization, and a book honoring and historicizing this organization
should incorporate that spirit. At one point during the evolution of *Canyon
Cinema,* Bruce Conner suggested that "At Canyon's Edge" would be a good
title; I agreed, thinking it might draw attention to this aspect of the Canyon history, and added the subtitle "The Life and Times of a (Wildly) Independent Film
Distributor." In the end, this title seemed a bit unwieldy and not entirely effective
in indicating to the prospective reader what the book's subject was, and I agreed
to go with the current title.

In the portfolios, I also attempt to provide a sense of the graphic variety
within individual issues of the *Cinemanews* and from issue to issue, without
allowing this book to become so cluttered as to be frustrating to explore. The
original *News* was a simple newsletter with no formal pretensions whatsoever,
and in many cases items were published without much concern even about
obvious typographical errors or misspellings. In time the *Cinemanews* became
somewhat more formal and less locally oriented, though it did continue to publish personal letters that were full of highly idiomatic language and punctuation.
Generally, I have been at pains to maintain the original texts with their "imper-
fections" so as to more fully represent the era and the sensibilities of those who
were contributing to Canyon and the *Cinemanews.* Obvious typos and mis-
spelled names have been corrected; and underlining for titles and emphasis has
been consistently changed to italics. When the *Cinemanews* editors overlooked
or created spelling errors in what were meant to be relatively formal essays,

Drawing by Robert Nelson celebrating the completion of *The Great Blondino* (1967) by Nelson and William T. Wiley.

these errors have been corrected; but when a contributor to the *Cinemanews* wrote in a highly informal, idiosyncratic manner, every effort has been made to remain true to that writer's intentions. While the format of particular items that appeared in the *Cinemanews* is often evoked, the format has been regularized to avoid needless clutter and distraction: for instance, the first paragraph of each prose item is not indented, while subsequent paragraphs are, regardless of how the original items indicated separate paragraphs. When I have inserted clarifications and notes within the documents included in *Canyon Cinema,* these have been placed in brackets. When indicating that something in an original document was handwritten, I have used "[hw]."

From time to time, I have provided some notation within the various reproduced items to clarify details that might otherwise be opaque to contemporary readers. I have worked to keep these editorial interventions to a minimum, relying for the most part on the context provided by the documents themselves to clarify what might otherwise not be clear to a contemporary viewer. Here and there, I have included photoreproductions of individual pages and/or covers, in some cases so as to be true to the effect of specific pieces, and in other cases, to give the reader a sense of how the imaging of the *Cinemanews* in *Canyon Cinema* has or has not translated the look of the original journal. In my introductions to the several sections of the book, as well as throughout this section of the general introduction, I use "the *Cinemanews*" to refer to Canyon's news organ, regardless of the name the journal had at that particular time. When I am indicating the source of a specific document in the portfolios, however, I have used the title of the journal as it appears on the particular issue in which the document was published. Also, *Cinemanews* issues appeared more regularly during some periods than in others, and editors used more than one format for indicating when an issue was published. As a result, in some instances, I provide the month and year of publication, whereas in others I can provide only the year and the number of a particular issue (e.g., 77.1 refers to the first issue of 1977, whenever that came out).

Hopefully, the documents reprinted here will allow the original writers to speak directly to the current moment and to issues that continue to confront people committed to alternative, critical forms of media. After all, a good many of the controversies, polemics, interviews, and poetic and graphic works included here are as relevant and interesting today as they ever were. The fact that *Canyon Cinema* historicizes Canyon should not obscure the fact that Canyon itself, and the field Canyon has represented and still represents, is very much alive. Ultimately, *Canyon Cinema* is meant simultaneously to enhance the historical record and to offer a potentially formative intervention into the current moment—an intervention that, ideally, might lead some readers more fully into the field of independent cinema and toward practical support of Canyon distribution through the rental of the films it represents, and other readers toward the kind of commitment characteristic of those who built and sustained this noble experiment in distribution.

There are, of course, dimensions of Canyon's history (and the history of the *Cinemanews*) that will not be evident in *Canyon Cinema.* Indeed, an earlier version of this project was twice the length of the present volume, and even *that* version was achieved only through the most heart-wrenching selection process. I have tended to choose contributions to the *Cinemanews* that *in retrospect* have particular interest: letters from filmmakers who have become major figures in the history of independent cinema, for example. As a result, other aspects of the *Cinemanews* and of Canyon are less evident than they might be. Especially during the early years, the *Cinemanews* was full of information about film series around the country; my selection has minimized the reader's sense of this. The regular focus in the *Cinemanews* on technical matters with regard to cameras and film stock and to shooting and editing is also not evident in this volume. There were a good many items relating to such matters, especially during the 1960s and early 1970s, including a piece on building your own optical printer (this appeared first in July 1967, then again in 74.4; see page 27), another on constructing homemade rewinds (72.1), and another on building an editing wall (72.3). In fact, there were enough of these how-to-do-it pieces to inspire at least one satire: Peter Feinstein's "DON'T MAKE REWINDS OUT OF OLD MEAT OR METAL GRINDERS when you can MAKE A STEENBECK OUT OF A WARING BLENDER" (in *Cinemanews* 72.3).

Although I have provided considerable illustration of the various kinds of graphic art published by the *Cinemanews,* there has not been room (or in some cases the opportunity) to include all of the most interesting contributions. For example, I have included a good many drawings by Bruce Conner, because of his longevity as an important influence at Canyon and his accomplishments as a fine artist; but I have not included the drawings and collages of other accomplished artists such as Patricia Oberhaus and Xeno Kung whose work graced *Cinemanews* pages. The July/August 1968 issue, for example, featured Oberhaus, who did the cover image and a sequence of nine drawings, presented as an inset on better-quality paper than the other items.

Photographs of filmmakers were regularly included in the *Cinemanews,* and I have included far fewer of these than I would have wished. Often, photographs were used decoratively, but in some instances the photographic image was a way of thinking about Canyon and of engaging in the debate about avant-garde

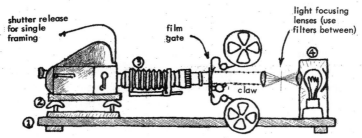

shutter release
for single
framing

film
gate

light focusing
lenses (use
filters between)

claw

①—Base board has length-wise groove for camera mount to slide for
focusing changing magnification. Another, cross-wise, for
projector horizontal alignment.

②—Camera mount raises and lowers camera by thumbscrew adjustment on
threaded shafts, stilt-like, stuck into slide base.

③—Extension bellows allows magnification range from 1:1 to 1:2, or 16mm
to 16mm up to 8mm to 16mm. We use 75mm C-mount lens.

④—Currently using GE 250 watt photoflood with screw base as light source,
a light gathering lens and a collimating lens to direct light beam
onto film.

Instructions for building an optical printer.

filmmaking. For example, the cover of the November 1967 issue features a portrait of Donna Kerness on location for Mike Kuchar's *Sins of the Fleshapoids*
(1965). The portrait, called "You'll Get Lost in the Folds of Her Cloak," was by
Lenny Lipton and, according to the *Cinemanews,* "is the first in a series concerning important film personalities omitted from Sheldon Renan's book *An
Introduction to American Underground Film* [New York: Dutton, 1967]." While
there were no immediate follow-ups to this "first," the first *Cinemanews* of 1969
included, on the inside back cover, a portrait of Lenny Lipton with the caption
"Canyon Cinema Presents Portraits of Filmmakers Series #1: Leonard Lipton."
This series continued in subsequent issues (on the inside back page) with Anne
Kish (69.3), Ken DeRoux ("Kenneth Royal DeRoux," 69.4); Pat and Loren Sears
(69.5); Lloyd Williams, and John Heinz (69.6), Stan Vanderbeek (69.7—no longer
on the inside back page), Ray Craig, Bob Greenberg, Richard Lerman, and Bob
Cowan (70.1), Patricia Oberhaus, Ron Finne (70.2), Freude Bartlett (70.3; see page
136) . . . [47] Photographs in the *Cinemanews* became an ongoing part of Canyon's
mission to maintain a community of avant-garde makers and a way of arguing
for a more inclusive canon, or no canon at all.

Of course, in addition to the distortions I have created in my choices of what
to reprint from the *Cinemanews* and from Canyon's files, this book will be
marred by simple factual errors, and especially errors of omission, since over

forty-plus years, hundreds of people have been involved with Canyon in one way or another. I have interviewed a substantial number of people, but there were so many more I wish I had had time and energy to contact. In a very few instances, individuals were not interested in speaking with me; for example, I am disappointed not to have had a conversation with Ben Van Meter. My guess is that in the coming years I will talk to many more whose input could have made this book more interesting and more factual, and I will have to hope that what I learn does not entirely embarrass my efforts here.

I can only offer my apologies to readers, and to those who remember Canyon and the *Cinemanews,* for whatever unfortunate distortions my choices have created. My hope is that what *is* here is valuable enough to compensate for my failings. If in time other scholars are drawn back to this historical moment—and to the films that inspired it—in order to provide correctives or further explorations, that will be very good news, indeed.

Writing/assembling a book of this sort is a long-term proposition. I began conceiving of *Canyon Cinema* in the late 1990s. In 2001 and 2002 I conducted interviews with people of particular importance to Canyon Cinema. During the winter/spring of 2002, I read the entire run of the *Cinemanews* and began to develop a clearer sense of what might be available; in the winter/spring of 2004, thanks to a National Endowment for the Humanities Fellowship I held from January through August 2004, I narrowed my selection and began the process of collecting the necessary permissions (in the current copyright climate, permission must be granted for every essay, letter, drawing, picture, and interview published), and continued to talk with people who had contributed to or worked with Canyon. The book's current balance of expository prose and document was negotiated during 2005–2006 (my thanks to Mary Jordan for her guidance and her flexibility), and the finished manuscript went to the University of California Press in June 2006 (I am grateful to Rachel Berchten, editor at the Press, for her suggestions and her enthusiasm for this project).

During the years I have been working on *Canyon Cinema,* I have had the assistance of a good many people. Throughout the process Dominic Angerame has been entirely responsive and helpful, providing information and useful documents, and endlessly answering questions. The Canyon Cinema board of directors offered financial support for the book in the form of a National Endowment for the Arts grant, part of which was used to support my research and writing. The board, however, consistently and entirely refrained from offering unsolicited advice on the volume and made no demands on me whatsoever.

From the early stages of researching Canyon Cinema, I had the invaluable assistance of Steve Anker, then Director of the San Francisco Cinematheque; Kathy Geritz, Film Curator at the Pacific Film Archive in Berkeley, which houses a collection of documents relating to Canyon Cinema; and Mark Toscano, who was Angerame's assistant from 2000 until 2003. Peter Thomas's research on Canyon's financial history was most useful. I am also grateful to Nancy Goldman, head of the Pacific Film Archive Library and Film Study Center; Steve Polta, Executive Director of the San Francisco Cinematheque from 2002 until 2006 (now Administrative Director); and Caroline Savage, the current Executive Director.

During the process of preparing this book, I had the opportunity to speak with a good many people, and virtually everyone I spoke with seemed happy to talk about Canyon and proud of their connection with the organization. Thanks in particular to Bruce Baillie, Robert Nelson, Bruce Conner, Larry Jordan, Ken DeRoux, Edith Kramer, and Jon Gartenberg.

Closer to home, my Hamilton College colleagues Sharon Britton, then Director of Public Services at Burke Library; photographer Marianita Amodio; my typist, Elizabeth Spaziani; and Professor of English Patricia O'Neill offered assistance whenever I needed it.

Notes

1. Recently, the traveling film series and now DVD collection, called "Unseen Cinema," has argued that what we now call "experimental" and "avant-garde" film is basically a continuation of the wholesale experimentation that characterized the earliest decades of moviemaking. For access to "Unseen Cinema," contact www.unseen-cinema.com. "Unseen Cinema" was the brainchild of Bruce Posner, who edited a catalogue to accompany the series: *Unseen Cinema: Early American Avant-Garde Film 1893–1941* (New York: Anthology Film Archives/Black Thistle Press, 2001). The Posner project is much indebted to Jan-Christopher Horak, ed., *Lovers of Cinema: The First American Film Avant-Garde 1919– 1945* (Madison: University of Wisconsin Press, 1995); the "Unseen Cinema" DVD was produced by David Shepard.

2. There have been any number of attempts to chart the early history of critical forms of cinema. Some of the more valuable of these include David Curtis's *Experimental Cinema: A Fifty-Year Evolution* (New York: Delta, 1971); Malcolm LeGrice's *Abstract Film and Beyond* (Cambridge, MA: MIT Press, 1977); Jan-Christopher Horak's anthology *Lovers of Cinema: The First American Film Avant-Garde 1919–1945* (Madison: University of Wisconsin Press, 1995); and Rudolf E. Kuenzli's anthology, *Dada and Surrealist Film* (New York: Willis Locker and Owens, 1987).

3. The San Francisco Cinematheque remains one of this nation's premiere exhibitors of critical forms of cinema (see note 5). Its schedules are available at www.sfcinematheque .org/.

4. For a history of early commercial distribution, see Charles Musser, *The Emergence of Cinema: The American Screen to 1907* (Berkeley: University of California Press, 1990);

and Benjamin Hampton's *History of the American Film Industry, from Its Beginnings to 1951* (New York: Dover, 1970).

5. Over the years, "avant-garde" has come to represent a body of films that, in a literal sense, may or may not be avant-garde, at least in the sense that they do something first; "experimental" is also common, though obviously some filmmakers do not like the term because they don't see their films as "experiments." "Independent film" has been co-opted by "low-budget" commercial filmmaking. And "alternative" is often useful, though many makers would rather see their films as valuable cultural contributions in their own right, rather than as alternatives to something else. My personal preference has been for "critical cinema," though this too seems to assume that the history of avant-garde film cannot exist in its own right but must offer a critique of conventional film. For anyone familiar with this field, the struggle for a moniker that will be satisfactory for filmmakers and those who see, write about, and teach their films is both familiar and pointless, given the number and kinds of film such a term needs to encompass. But we must call this wide world of cinema *something,* and for purposes of this introduction, I will use "avant-garde," with full awareness of the several limitations of this problematic but generally recognized term, though in particular instances I have found several of these other terms useful as well.

6. Horak, *Lovers of Cinema,* 5–15. Horak explains, "Earlier filmmakers [that is, American avant-garde filmmakers of the 1920s and 1930s] . . . thought of themselves primarily as film amateurs rather than as professionals. The professional was an employee in Hollywood, producing for hire a profit benefiting the corporate hierarchy, while the amateur was concerned with the cause of film art" (15).

The 1920s also saw what appears to have been the first important American film society, the Film Guild, founded and run by Symon Gould. At the moment, unfortunately, little is known about the Film Guild.

7. See Patricia R. Zimmermann, *Reel Families: A Social History of Amateur Film* (Bloomington: Indiana University Press, 1995), 71.

8. For an overview of the ciné-club movement, see chapter 3 of Richard Abel's *French Cinema: The First Wave 1915–1929* (Princeton, NJ: Princeton University Press, 1984). For a discussion of the American Workers' Cinema of the 1930s, see William Alexander, *Film on the Left* (Princeton, NJ: Princeton University Press, 1981).

9. Haidee Wasson describes a pair of film societies that formed in 1933 for the purpose of exhibiting films not shown in public theaters: the New York Film Society and Film Forum. The first of these was devoted to the exhibition of a wide range of independent cinema; the second, to the exhibition of films from the political left. Both film societies lasted less than a year, and neither seems to have had a distribution component. See *Museum Movies: The Museum of Modern Art and the Birth of Art Cinema* (Berkeley: University of California Press, 2005), 37–44.

10. For a history of Cinema 16, see my *Cinema 16: Documents toward a History of the Film Society* (Philadelphia: Temple University Press, 2002); and my *Art in Cinema: Documents toward a History of the Film Society* (Philadelphia: Temple University Press, 2006). See Cecile Starr's *Film Society Primer* (New York: American Federation of Film Societies, 1956) for a survey of the American film society movement during its heyday.

11. In her " 'Some Kind of Racket': The Museum of Modern Art's Film Library, Holly-wood and the Problem of Film Art, 1935," *Canadian Journal of Film Studies* 9, no. 2 (Spring 2000): 5–29, Haidee Wasson describes the founding of the film library at the Museum of Modern Art in New York and its move into independent distribution. See also her *Museum Movies.*

12. Brandon was not convinced that anything like a serious avant-garde film movement was beginning; in his *Handbook for Film Societies,* included in the 1950 catalog, he warns, "Avant-garde films—experimental films also may prove disappointing unless they are a def-inite interest of a particular audience, and in any case if they make up a full unrelieved stretch of two hours or so. There are some notable exceptions (which should be shown and encouraged), but many *current* experimental films made in the U.S. are specious and obscure and make little contribution to the exploration of the medium. . . . Very stimulating experimental work has been done in Europe, the U.S.S.R., and Great Britain, and in recent years some outstanding work has been achieved in Canada."

13. See Cecile Starr's comments in MacDonald, *Cinema 16,* 82–83.

14. Bob Pike, in his "A Critical Study of the West Coast Experimental Film Movement" (master's thesis, University of California, Los Angeles, 1960), 164. I am grateful to *The Most Typical Avant-Garde: History and Geography of Minor Cinemas in Los Angeles* (Berkeley: University of California Press, 2005), for David James's discussion of Pike's activ-ities (219–21). James also mentions Kenneth Anger and Curtis Harrington's Creative Film Associates, founded in 1948, an informal distribution organization that attracted a variety of filmmakers, including Oskar Fischinger, the Whitney Brothers, Jordan Belson, and Elwood Decker.

15. From the "First Statement of the New American Cinema Group," *Film Culture,* no. 22–23 (Summer 1961): 131–33.

16. The New York Film-Makers' Cooperative currently uses a 60/40 split, with 60 per-cent of rental money going to the filmmaker, though, according to current director M. M. Serra, a 50/50 split is being considered.

17. There is good work to be done on the history of filmmaker cooperatives in the United Kingdom and in Europe. In this country the best known of foreign cooperative orga-nizations is probably Light Cone, formed in 1982 by Yann Beauvais and Miles McKane. Light Cone began as both an exhibitor and a distributor, paying filmmakers in a 70/30 percent split, though, according to Christophe Bichon, who has managed the Light Cone collection and preservation projects since 1999, a 60/40 percent split is currently being considered. Bichon indicates that there are a good many distributors of independent media in Europe, among them, Lux (England), Sixpackfilm (Austria), Defilm Bank (Holland), Montevideo (Holland), Filmform (Sweden), Argos (Belgium), CJC (France), Heure Exquise (France), Arsenal Experimental (Germany), 235 Media (Germany), and Re:Voir (France).

18. The revenue split between Canyon and its member filmmakers has undergone peri-odic changes, depending on the particular financial needs of the moment. In 1973 the debt that resulted from the publication of *Catalogue 3* led to a 50/40/10 percent split, with 50 per-cent going to the filmmakers, 40 percent to Canyon, and 10 percent to pay off the catalog debt. Once the catalog debt was paid off, the ratio changed to 50/50. In 1977 the filmmak-

ers' percentage was raised to 60 percent, and in 1979 to 65 percent. The split remained 65/35 through the 1980s, and then, during the 1990s got incrementally smaller, until in 2001 it was changed to 50/50.

For a time, the Film-Makers' Cooperative was not reliable in returning the promised percentage of film rental money to filmmakers, though in recent years the Coop has managed to shed its bad reputation in this regard.

19. I certainly do not mean to disparage the good work of other American distributors of critical cinema. Both the Film-Makers' Cooperative and the Museum of Modern Art Circulating Film Library, the two most important distribution organizations other than Canyon that focus on critical forms of cinema, continue to provide very valuable services. Losing either would create a crisis in the field of independent cinema. But my personal experience over a number of years with these and other distributors, and particularly in recent years, has been somewhat less satisfactory than my experience with Canyon, in terms of both the quality of prints offered and the dependability of their arriving when scheduled.

20. Bruce Baillie in my interview with him in *A Critical Cinema 2* (Berkeley: University of California Press, 1992), 113–14.

21. Callenbach in *Canyon Cinemanews,* no. 76.2:7.

22. Bruce Baillie, letter to *New Canyon Cinemanews,* no. 95.1 (January 1995): 6.

23. Unpublished interview with Chick Callenbach, November 6, 2002.

24. Strand, "Chick Strand's Recollections of Canyon Cinema's Early Beginnings with Added Commentary from Chick Callenbach," *Canyon Cinemanews,* 76.2:10.

25. David Sherman in an unpublished interview, April 24, 2004.

Ken DeRoux, who worked at Canyon from 1969 to 1973 in a variety of capacities, was in charge of Canyon screenings for some years. During the period when Canyon's office was in the basement of Intersection, the Canyon screenings would take place upstairs in what had been a church; the seats, as DeRoux remembers, were pews. These screenings have much in common with those that take place now in some microcinemas, except that they were probably more volatile. DeRoux remembers an argument breaking out during one screening between Bruce Conner and another viewer who refused to be quiet: "Suddenly, I heard a commotion behind me, and turned around to see Bruce running out of the theater, and heard a man behind me say, 'He *spit* on me!' " DeRoux in an unpublished interview, January 6, 2006.

26. Rebecca Barton in an unpublished interview, April 24, 2004.

27. Barton and Sherman have recently moved to Bisbee, Arizona, where they continue to organize community screenings of a wide variety of films.

28. Ernest Callenbach in an unpublished interview, November 6, 2003

29. Jordan in an unpublished interview, August 12, 2003.

30. Baillie, in my interview with him in *A Critical Cinema 2* (Berkeley: University of California Press, 1992), 116.

31. Ibid.

32. The Canyon Cinema newsletter began as the *News,* and retained that title until the

October/November issue of 1964 (2.8), when it became *Canyon Cinema News*. The next change occurred in July 1967, when it became *Canyon Cinemanews,* which it remained through the July/August 1977 issue (77.4), at which time it became the *Cinemanews;* then, from January 1978 (77.7) through September/October 1977, the *Cinema News;* and finally, from November/December 1978 until the end of its run, the *Cinemanews*.

33. Baillie, in *Critical Cinema 2,* 117. Baillie also indicates that at first "Chickie Strand and I edited it [the *News*], and later Paul Tulley and I" (117).

34. Steve Anker, "The San Francisco Cinematheque: A Brief History," in the catalog *San Francisco Cinematheque: Four Decades of Film and Video,* published by the San Francisco Museum of Modern Art on the occasion of the fortieth anniversary of the Cinematheque in 2001.

In 1974 Vincent Grenier took over Cinematheque programming and began regular open screenings. According to Anker, "Grenier's one-year tenure, though brief, was extremely influential for the future of the organization. Under his leadership, the Cinematheque's curatorial vision expanded into the national and international arenas more firmly than ever before" (Anker, "The San Francisco Cinematheque," 3). In 1975 Carmen Vigil and Charles Wright took over from Grenier. When Wright left in 1977, Vigil remained principal programmer until 1982, when the Cinematheque board insisted he relinquish control of the programming—a result in part of a growing dissatisfaction among many Bay Area filmmakers with the Cinematheque's role in the local film community, and with Vigil's continued championing of those makers who had become part of the avant-garde canon in the 1960s and early 1970s. During the 1980s Steve Anker, working in concert with David Gerstein (who had become the Cinematheque's executive director in 1983—he remained director until 1994), oversaw Cinematheque programming, expanding the Cinematheque's range (in 1985, for example, Anker curated the Cinematheque's first all-video program) and visibility. Anker remained in charge of exhibition, after 1994 with Irina Leimbacher, until he left to become dean of the Film Program at the California Institute of the Arts in Valencia; Steve Polta took over in 2002. Once the Cinematheque split from Canyon Cinema in 1977, the history of the two organizations became and remained separate and distinct. Of course, when the history of American alternative exhibition is written, the Canyon/San Francisco Cinematheque will require a substantial chapter.

35. Unpublished interview with Lenny Lipton, c. April 2004. Lipton stopped making films around 1975 and turned to stereoscopic imaging. His company StereoGraphics developed the device that makes possible the 3-D imagery of the surface of Mars.

36. The sixteen-page catalog is identical in its listings to the *News* listing in the November 1966 issue. Supplements 1, 2, and 3 of *Catalogue Number Two* are paginated so that each begins where the previous listing leaves off.

37. Ken DeRoux was in charge of getting this catalog out.

38. *Catalog 4* (no editor is listed) appeared in 1976; a supplement ("made by" Philip Perkins, Warren Bass, Stephanie Boris, Janet Perlberg, Michael Wallin, and Gwin Graphics), in 1978; *Catalog 5* (by Dominic Angerame, Andrew Moore, and Michael Wallin), in 1982, followed by a supplement (put together by Dominic Angerame and Mary V. Marsh); *Catalog 6*

("compiled and edited by" Nina Fonoroff and Melanie Curry), in 1988, followed by a "Film/Video Supplement" (by Dominic Angerame and Melanie Curry), also in 1988, and another (by Melanie Curry and Amy Stewart), in 1990; *Film/Video Catalog 7* ("compiled and edited by" Melanie Curry and Heather Mackey), in 1992; and the most recent printed catalogue, the unnumbered *Film/Video Catalog 2000* (edited by Christine Metropoulos, designed by Kevin Barnard, proofed by Susan Vogel), in 2000. The Canyon catalog is now online at www.canyoncinema.com.

39. Unpublished interview with Larry Jordan, August 12, 2003.

40. Unpublished interview with Edith Kramer, June 8, 2006.

While the articles of incorporation make clear that Canyon "does not contemplate gain or profit to the members thereof" and is "organized solely for non-profit purposes" (article VII), the bylaws make clear that Canyon Cinema, Inc., was to be a membership organization.

41. *Film Culture,* edited by P. Adams Sitney and connected with the New American Cinema, Jonas Mekas, and what became Anthology Film Archives, also focused on this community, though *Film Culture*—as its moniker suggests—was, from the beginning, more scholarly and closer to an academic quarterly. Throughout its history the *Cinemanews* was resolutely nonacademic.

42. Though the same group of people were involved in producing the *Cinemanews* during 1977 to 1979, they functioned in somewhat different capacities from issue to issue. Issue 77.6 was edited by Henry Hills; Stephanie Boris was production editor, and Mark McGowan did layout. Issue 78.7 was edited by Abigail Child; 78.2 (there was no 78.1), by Hills, with Boris and McGowan in the same roles. Issue 78.3/4 was edited by Hills, with Child as assistant editor (again with Boris and McGowan in the same roles). Issue 78.5 lists Janis Crystal Lipzin and Joel Singer as coeditors, with Janet Perlberg the production editor and McGowan doing layout. For 78.6/79.1, Child was West Coast editor and Hills, East Coast editor, Perlberg was production editor, and McGowan did layout; for 79.2–4, Hills and Child were East Coast editors; Carmen Vigil and McGowan, West Coast editors, and Gail Vachon and Robert E. Galloway were co–production editors. In 79.5–6, Hills was editor; Child, East Coast editor; and Vigil and McGowan did layout.

43. Unpublished interview with Michael Wallin, January 21, 2006.

44. Unpublished interview with Angerame, May 22, 2006. *By Brakhage,* produced by Peter Becker and Kate Elmore for Criterion and released in 2003, includes twenty-six Brakhage films, including such frequently rented works as *Window Water Baby Moving* (1959) and *Mothlight* (1963).

45. Conner had become concerned with what might happen if Canyon were to go belly-up. Would there be enough money to pay for returning the hundreds of films in its collection to their owners? If Canyon accumulated debt, who would be responsible? Might those members whose films had earned the most be considered financially responsible for the organization's debts? Might films be seized and sold to pay off debts? Since the Canyon board could not deal with these questions to Conner's satisfaction, he felt he had no option but to withdraw from the organization he had been so important to for so long. Thanks to Edith Kramer for her insight on this issue.

46. Unpublished interview with M. M. Serra, May 26, 2006.

47. Subsequent Filmmakers' Portrait Series portraits: Bruce Conner, Jonas Mekas and Charles Levine, David Buehler (70.3); Maurice Levy, James Broughton (see page 141), Ulvia Alberts, Taka Iimura, Ben Van Meter (see page 64), Keith Rodan (70.4); Kurt Heyl (71.1); Bruce Baillie (71.2). The numbering stopped, but filmmaker portraits had become, and remained, a *Cinemanews* convention.

1 : Formation

The decision of filmmakers involved with Canyon Cinema to publish a newsletter was crucial to the evolution of the organization. The *Cinemanews* was Ernest Callenbach's brainchild, though the idea of a news organization serving the local community of filmmakers and film enthusiasts originated with Bruce Baillie. Of course, Baillie's idea was a *filmic* newsletter, and it did result in the production of several short films, but Callenbach seems to have understood that if Canyon were to function and grow *as an organization,* word of mouth and/or the sporadic production of cinematic news items would not be as effective as a regularly available publication. The rationale for the *Cinemanews,* originally called the *News,* was made clear in the announcement of the new publication in late 1962. The *News* staff—Ernest Callenbach, Alexandra Ossipoff, and Chick Strand in Berkeley, and Evelyn Bowers in Chicago—explained that their mission was to make available the "large amount of fugitive information about movies" not in general circulation. The announcement asks for items from filmmakers, distributors, exhibitors, teachers, anyone interested in the "serious" making, showing, and discussion of films, especially focusing on new or newly available films. The intention was to get information to subscribers quickly and democratically ("anybody who wants to get it must pay. There will be no gratis list, no exchanges"), and to be impartial: to represent "no critical or production clique"—other, that is, than those who were interested in "more than merely commercial projects."

The first issue of the *Cinemanews,* published in December 1962, provides a useful sense of the North American film scene at the moment when the new periodical arrived, as well as a clear sense of what the fledgling Canyon community considered important. The issue begins with a guide to film festivals, organized chronologically so as "to help film-makers decide how they can best gain attention for their work." Relevant addresses, the dates of the festivals, and an indication of whether particular festivals offered prizes or were noncompetitive are included. Two American festivals—the Independent Film-maker's Festival, held at Foothill College in Los Altos, California, and the Midwest Film Festival, held at the University of Chicago—are listed as "of special interest," largely because they focused on independent filmmaking. A separate item focuses on the San Francisco Film Festival; it ends with a query to readers: "What kinds of coverage of festivals will be of most use to you? Shall we try to concentrate on short films not well covered in the regular film press, for instance?" During the early years

PUBLISHED BY
CANYON
CINEMA

Editorial office:
2185 Acton St., Berkeley 2, Calif.

Alexandra Ossipoff, Editor

December 1962 $2.00 per year   (January 1963 issue will be Vol.I, No.1)

FESTIVAL GUIDE. A chronological list to help film-makers decide how they can best gain attention for their work. The following accept films from individuals rather than countries and appear to be the most significant at present (there are literally hundreds of festivals in the world). Dates vary slightly from year to year. Some have entry fees; most do not pay shipping. Entrance deadlines are normally many months before festival time. Those asterisked give prizes, but for shorts only; those marked # are entirely noncompetitive.

PUNTA DEL ESTE. (Organisateur Littmann, Country Club, Punta del Este, Uruguay.) Mid-January.

OBERHAUSEN. (Westdeutsche Kurzfilmtage, Schwarzstrasse 71, Oberhausen, Rheinland, West Germany.) Mid-February.

*AMERICAN FILM FESTIVAL, N.Y. (Educational Film Library Assn., 250 West 57th St., New York 19, N.W.) Primarily for teaching films. April.

CANNES. (Festival international du film, 25 rue d'Astorg, Paris 8e.) Early May.

MELBOURNE. (P.O. Box 20, Camberwell, Victoria, Australia.) End of May.

BERLIN. (Am Hirschsprung 4, Berlin-Dahlem, Germany.) End of June.

ANNECY. (Journees du Cinema, 21 rue de la Tour d'Auvergne, Paris 9e.) End of June.

SAN SEBASTIAN. (Palacio Victoria Eugenia, San Sebastian, Spain.) July.

MOSCOW/KARLOVY VARY (alternate years—1963, Moscow). (13, rue Vallilievskaya, Moscow.) July.

*VANCOUVER. (Hotel Vancouver, Vancouver, B.C., Canada.) July.

#MONTREAL. (5011 avenue du Parc, Montreal 8, P.Q., Canada.) Mid-August.

VENICE. (Mostra Internazionale d'Arte Cinematografica, Ca' Giustinian, San Marco, Venice, Italy.) Late August.

MANNHEIM. (Internationale Filmwoche Mannheim, Rathaus, Mannheim E5, West Germany.) Mid-October.

SAN FRANCISCO. (172 Golden Gate Avenue, San Francisco, Calif.) Early Nov. Note: The "Film as Communication" section, for 16mm films, charges $25 entry fee and does not seem worth it for independent film-makers.

TOURS. (Journees du Cinema, 21 rue de la Tour d'Auvergne, Paris 9e.) A festival entirely devoted to surveying the year's work in short films. This year 6 days instead of 5; using new theater (2 run simultaneously). Early Dec.

EDINBURGH. (3 Randolph Crescent, Edinburgh 3, Scotland.) End August--misplaced in list! A festival of documentary, but also accepts fiction films and some experimental work.
                              *****

TWO U.S. FESTIVALS OF SPECIAL INTEREST:

Independent Film-Maker's Festival, to be held May 10-12 at Foothill College, Los Altos, California. For information and entry blanks (due Feb. 1) write:

First page of the original issue of the *News,* December 1962.

of Canyon and the *Cinemanews,* film festivals were regularly listed and discussed by those who wrote items for the publication or who responded to these items with letters. Then, as now, festivals were seen as one, if not the, primary potential outlet for independent filmmaking, and the refusal of many festivals to include avant-garde and experimental forms of cinema created considerable consternation within the independent filmmaking community.

The original issue, which set the tone for several years of the *Cinemanews,* also included a listing titled "Distributors Interested in Short Films for Theatrical Release," as well as individual items announcing new catalogs of films available from Cinema 16 and from Brandon International, and the decision of Audio Films to distribute Brakhage's *Blue Moses* (1962) and four films by Chris MacLaine. The bulk of the individual items in the December 1962 issue, however, were dedicated to announcements relating to individual filmmakers and writers from a wide range of filmic terrains. We learn, for example, that Claude Jutra, "independent Montreal film-maker who helped McLaren make 'A CHAIRY TALE,' is currently editing a feature he shot this summer," and that McLaren himself "is currently at work with Grant Munro on a multiple-superimposition ballet based on musical forms [*Pas de Deux,* 1967]"; that "SASHA HAMMID's 26 CASALS films, produced by NATHAN KROLL for NET and edited by MIRIAM ARSHAM, are being shown one a week on New York's educational TV channel"; and that "KENT MACKENZIE has been working on TV films while trying to arrange distribution for his feature-length documentary on American Indians living in L.A." Virtually any form of film, other than Hollywood features, seems to have been of interest to those publishing and reading early *Cinemanews* issues. The first issue also announces the recent activities of author George Bluestone, the appearance of a new issue of *Film Culture,* the formation of the Catholic Film Center of Chicago, and Stanford University's decision to offer graduate scholarships in journalism, broadcasting, and film.

Early on in the *Cinemanews,* no special focus was reserved for Bay Area filmmakers, though each issue did provide items relevant to filmmakers working in the area and to Canyon Cinema itself. The first issue announces several films recently completed "at Canyon Cinema" and available from Canyon—including Baillie's *Have You Thought of Talking to the Director?* (1962), *Here Am I* (1962), *The Gymnasts* (1961), *Mr. Hayashi* (1961), and *On Sundays* (1961); Ernest Callenbach's *Varoom* (c.1963–1964); and Dan Mardesich and Charles Larson's *North Waterfront*—and the availability of "a cutting room for cooperative use by member film-makers" that included "shared, borrowed, and inherited equipment of sufficient sophistication to allow totally professional technical quality in the making of 16mm sound films." Stan Brakhage's move to 650 Shotwell in San

Francisco is also announced. During the several issues that followed, the format established in the first issue was maintained: generally the items included were brief and practical, despite the original announcement's indication that the *Cinemanews* might include "a certain amount of gossip, informal notes, jokes, and other miscellaneous materials."

By the May 1963 issue, there had apparently been enough curiosity about the nature of Canyon Cinema that the editors decided to open with "What *Is* Canyon Cinema???":

> *A vicious nihilist threat to the Established Order?*
> *A giant international syndicate of independent production?*
> *A secret society dedicated to the overthrow of all that is decent in American life?*

People do sometimes seem to be mystified, and we herewith present a brief summary of what Canyon is, more or less. —In a phrase, a floating underground theater also active in production. Bruce Baillie, in the summer of 1961, decided that if there were to be new films made, there must be a theater to show them and possibly help finance them. Since there is no place in the San Francisco Bay Area which seemed appropriate, he began showings in a backyard in the tiny town of Canyon, in the redwoods about 5 miles from Berkeley. Since then, Canyon Cinema has floated from a Berkeley cabaret to a restaurant to a private home, on a pad of hot air supplied by the city authorities, looking for a physical environment that would pull people together as an audience. During the summer of 1962 a new effort was made to find a place of showing that would meet the requirements of the fire, health, and other city regulations, and also serve as a studio. It turned out that there was no existing, available, private building in Berkeley which would meet these regulations. In September, however, a sympathetic student president of the University YMCA (Stiles Hall, long noted for its sympathetic support of dangerous causes) altered their rules to let Canyon book biweekly showings there. But the antiseptic campus atmosphere doesn't create the desired intimacy, so Canyon is now seeking a new place to show, in San Francisco.

Together with its program of showings, Canyon has acquired, by begging and borrowing, a variety of editing equipment, which is available for use by members and friends. (A moviola or comparable device is now being sought.) Since last summer, when this was brought together into one place, about a half-dozen films have been completed, and several are in production currently.

Canyon also, of course, publishes this NEWS, in an effort to get information circulating quickly to similar groups and persons all over the country. There is surely a possibility of such groups as Canyon in a score of American cities, and we hope that independent film-makers may gain a sense of common purpose and possibilities through reading of what goes on elsewhere.

By the end of 1964 some changes in the *Cinemanews* were under way. These included somewhat more focus on the now-burgeoning Bay Area film scene— the September 1964 issue includes an "Index of Filmmakers" working in the San Francisco area (nineteen are listed); and the October/November 1964 issue begins with an open letter announcing, "The CANYON CINEMA NEWS has now increased its coverage to include still photos (from both experimental and industrial films), a continuing index of film-makers, plus editorials, articles, letters, interviews, and statements about the New Film—thus adding to its regular coverage of news about equipment and film festivals, films in progress, and other cinema events." As if to demonstrate this new expanded coverage, the issue includes an extended essay by Saul Landau about the attempted suppression of Jean Genet's *Un Chant d'amour* (1952) by the San Francisco police department. Landau's essay, which opened the way for longer essays in the *Cinemanews,* remains an important document of the era and about the fortunes of a remarkable film.

The October/November issue of the *Cinemanews* also includes an announcement of a benefit for the San Francisco Mime Troupe to help with the costs of the trial instigated by the showing of *Un Chant d'amour* (at least one of these benefits involved another screening of Genet's film), a benefit for Kenneth Anger to be held at The Movie on Kearny Street, and several letters from filmmakers. Gregory J. Markopoulos contributed notes "after a trip across country lecturing, and finally meeting fellow filmmaker Jack Smith in Los Angeles to judge the filmmaker's festival [the third Los Angeles Film-makers Festival] with Michael McClure at the Cinema Theater." Larry Jordan describes an audience's reaction to a program of his films: "Sometimes they shouted applause (usually during the fast parts), and sometimes they booed and hissed and made jokes (usually during the slow parts)." And Bruce Baillie reported from the road during the process of filming material for what would become *Quixote* (1965). Letters from filmmakers would soon become a *Cinemanews* staple.

For a time the *Cinemanews* ceased publication entirely. No issues appeared from late 1964 until May 1965, though, for a brief moment, there seem to have been two publications: a Canyon newsletter and the *Cinemanews.* Bruce Baillie's editorial in the May 1965 issue indicates that regular publication was resuming. The reappearance of the *Cinemanews* confirmed the changes in the format and coverage that had begun at the end of 1964. The May issue includes two polemics on the new excitement about underground film, by a Dutchman, John W. Chr. Muller, and Marshall Anker—both of them unconvinced about the value of the new movement as an alternative to commercial cinema. The same issue includes another letter from Bruce Baillie on the road. Judging from this and other letters included in the *Cinemanews,* especially during the early years of the publication, Baillie and the others compiling the newsletter seem to have assumed that part of their function was to model new ways for a film artist to function in the world. Baillie, for example, seems to have seen himself as a wandering film-poet, someone aesthetically akin to Matsuo Bashō, the seventeenth-century Japanese haiku master, in his *Narrow Road to the Deep North* and other travel sketches.

The June/July 1965 issue returns to the issue of film festivals; included are excerpts from a series of letters solicited by the *Cinemanews* on the subject. The focus is on judges, who, Stan Brakhage argues, should be able to function as individuals rather than as parts of "a voting machine" (that is, as members of a committee or institution). There is also much concern in these letters with the difficulty of retrieving films from festivals without physical damage to the prints, especially in a repressive censorial climate. The suspicions about film festivals are nowhere more evident than in an article, originally printed in Jonas Mekas's column in the *Village Voice* (March 25, 1965) and reprinted in the *Cinemanews,* in which Gregory Markopoulos launches an attack on the Ann Arbor Film Festival, then in its third year, to which Ann Arbor founder and director, George Manupelli, responds. This was the first of a good many extended controversies that unfolded in the *Cinemanews,* and like several others, it reveals how filmmakers, driven by idealism and the presumption that as film artists they needed to confront complacency and conformity whenever they thought they recognized it, could underestimate the commitment and intelligence of others working to serve the field.

The *Cinemanews* continued to be largely made up of smaller items (announcements of films being completed, scheduled screenings, new publications, funding opportunities, and the like), but the indication, early on, that the *Cinemanews* would also include "a certain amount of gossip, informal notes, jokes, and other miscellaneous materials" was also, by the end of 1965, resulting in a variety of items that help to create a sense of Canyon as a kind of village with its own small-town newspaper. One item from the August 1965 issue provides information about breaking up dog fights ("approach one offending animal from rear, grab quickly—lightly, deftly—about the rear haunches and pull upward and away from opponent; swing him slowly to left or right. Other dog will cool down in a moment; meanwhile your dog will not be able to reach back and bite you. Works better with two guys. If people are around there are usually no dog fights"). Another indicates that smoked fish is available from Mendocino: "Inquire: Blackberry Tarts Div., Box 11, Caspar, California." And poetry was often included: the October 1965 issue, for example, included poems by Bruce Baillie,

Ken Burns, George Manupelli, and Esther Peterson. This small-town aura seems to have been largely a result of Baillie's influence, an echo of Canyon's earliest days, but this echo would continue to be heard in the *Cinemanews*. The "Blackberry Tarts Division," for example, would remain the nominal source for a wide variety of information for years.

Schedules for screenings of independent films or of film series that included independent films, in the Bay Area and around the country, were increasingly in evidence. Indeed, judging from the *Cinemanews* a change was under way: film festivals remained important but were, less and less, the primary exhibition venue for alternative film. Increasingly, the focus was on screening series that could feed the growing interest of some audiences for alternatives to commercial film and television. The January 1966 issue includes listings for the Gate Theater in Sausalito and Intersection, at 150 Ellis in San Francisco (screenings sponsored by the San Francisco Mime Troupe and Canyon Cinema), and at Firehouse Films in Minneapolis (Tom Olson, director). The September/October issue includes listings for the MIT Film Society in Cambridge, Massachusetts (founded and directed by Fred Camper), and for the Aardvark Cinematheque in Chicago (directed by Jeff Begun). In general, the *Cinemanews* had become both more national *and* more local: the focus of Canyon, at least as it was represented by the *Cinemanews,* was increasingly on the Bay Area independent film community as part of a national and international network of individuals and organizations with similar interests and goals. In October 1965, P. Adams Sitney reported on his trip to the Buenos Aires Exposition to present avant-garde cinema. A November 1966 item reviewed Willard Van Dyke's opening of a film exhibition of avant-garde film at the National Museum of Modern Art in Tokyo; the item indicated that of the films Van Dyke took to Japan, two—Kenneth Anger's *Scorpio Rising* (1963) and Robert Nelson's *Oh Dem Watermelons* (1965)—were stopped by Japanese customs.

The most important new development, however, was the announcement of Canyon's formalization of its distribution activities. The August 1966 issue of the *Cinemanews* indicated that Canyon had held some meetings in San Francisco in July to consider the possibility of a West Coast distribution cooperative, and asked "if anyone in the area knows a responsible person willing to work nearly full-time for a few months without pay, taking charge of the distribution part of the coop . . . answering phone, keeping accounts, shipping films, maintaining distribution correspondence, please send the information to the NEWS." Meetings continued after August: Tom DeWitt remembers a meeting hosted by Scott Bartlett at his studio in what had been the Reno Hotel, attended by Bruce Baillie, Will Hindle, Robert Nelson, James Broughton, DeWitt, and possibly others (phone conversation with DeWitt—now Tom Ditto—May 29, 2006). DeWitt himself produced a trailer for a benefit for the fledgling organization that he believes was held in late September or October 1966. By the November 1966 issue of the *Cinemanews,* the "Canyon Cinema Co-op Catalog Issue," the organization had been formed and was announced as follows:

> In its sixth year, Canyon Cinema felt the need to establish an independent film distribution office on the West Coast of North America to better serve the needs of film-makers and audiences in that part of the world. That facility came into existence on the 14th day of August, 1966, in the wake of the pioneer Film-maker's Coop and in this year of new Co-ops in London and Boston and rumored Co-ops in Chicago, Philadelphia, Austin, Rome and Paris. The San Francisco Co-op, ourselves, is known as the Canyon Cinema Co-operative.
>
> Canyon Cinema Co-op is, on one level, an organization of independent film-makers, formed to facilitate the distribution of their work and to advance the art of the cinema in all its aspects.
>
> On another level, Canyon Cinema Co-op is a federation of willing devotees of the magic lantern muse, consisting of artists engaged in the creation of 16mm film, 8mm film and other related light and image production media. The devotees have a policy of non-policy, and are subject to only the barest and most basic "procedures" for co-operatively distributing their films or informing likely audiences of their light-projection capacities.
>
> At any rate, the Co-op is a single, non-profit office to help a large number of individual film-makers distribute their own works, at their own prices and on their own terms and conditions. The film-maker receives 75% of the rental, the Co-op retains 25% for operating expenses.
>
> All film artists are invited to join the Co-op.

The terms of rental and sale, methods of payment and other specifics followed, along with an alphabetical listing of filmmakers already part of Canyon distribution and the films available for rental.

PORTFOLIO

Announcement of Publication of *Canyon Cinema News,* 1962

The Canyon Cinema News is the outcome of needs felt both by the staff of *Film Quarterly* and by the members of Canyon Cinema, a group in Berkeley which shows films and also makes them. There is, we know, a large amount of fugitive information about movies which presently circulates, when it circulates at all, primarily through private correspondence, formal and necessarily wide-spaced distributor announcements, and the like. We have in mind items about films that have recently been made; films that have become available — with their sources and prices and succinct descriptions; plans and steps toward such projects as the American Film Institute; news about special series such as those at the MMA, about seminars, classes, and other events; about trips taken by film people; about festivals.

Such news ought to circulate quickly. Canyon Cinema is therefore going to undertake the publication of an approximately monthly national news bulletin, of which this is a more or less typical issue. Its policies are:

1. To print *news items* submitted by film-makers, distributors, teachers, organizers of film societies and other exhibition groups, and others interested in the serious making, showing, and discussing of films. News should be sent in on 3x5 cards. It should be strictly news; the only editing which we will do will be to cut out plugs and to reduce length where needed.

2. To print the news *quickly and cheaply.* To do this we will use mimeograph, and there will be no fancy design, illustrations, or other frills. It appears that a $2.00 subscription should cover costs of about 12 issues.

3. To make the News *self-sustaining.* It is intended as a strictly service activity, for which anybody who wants to get it must pay. There will be no gratis list, no exchanges.

4. To be *impartial.* The News represents no critical or production clique. It takes no position on the worth of the projects reported through it, but intends to serve all aspiring film-makers and film-showers who are attempting more than merely commercial projects.

We also hope to include a certain amount of gossip, informal notes, jokes, and other miscellaneous materials, depending on space available.

All interested parties are urged to:

1. *Subscribe.* Send $2.00 to Canyon Cinema News, 2185 Acton Street, Berkeley 2, California. This is the only issue for which free sample copies are available.

2. *Send news*, on 3x5 cards (postcards are good) to the same address.

3. *Spread the word* to other film-makers, film-society members, etc.

We welcome suggestions, ideas, and criticism generally, and are eager to contact persons in the various areas of the country who can hunt around, especially in the early stages of the publication, for suitable news items.

At present the staff of the News consists of:

Berkeley: Alexandra Ossipoff, Chick Strand, Ernest Callenbach
Chicago: Evelyn Bowers (Docfilm, U of Chicago)
New York: (Persons interested please contact Miss Ossipoff)

—

FROM *CANYON CINEMA NEWS,* OCTOBER / NOVEMBER 1964

Saul Landau, Member, Board of Directors, S.F. Mime Troupe

AN ESSAY ON CENSORSHIP

On Arresting Movies (Not People) in San Francisco: "On Friday morning, the D.A. called and said 'You can come and get your trash!' "

The following is an account of the police action at the showing of Genet's film.

San Franciscans often refer to their city as the Paris of the West. It is a beautiful city, not yet destroyed (although on the way) by the modern land rapists, and it has a liberal aura, which includes an appreciation of Culture (opera, ballet, and that kind of 19th Century European stuff). Even the Police Department conducts itself in a civilized manner (in comparison with other American Police Departments,) but there are some things that even sophisticated San Francisco cannot accept.

I announced the first public showing of Jean Genet's movie *Un Chant D'Amour.* The squib in the San Francisco Chronicle, reduced from a full page press release, described the film as "dealing with homosexuality among men in prison." The movie theater, an abandoned church and the home of the S.F. Mime Troupe, was located in the Mission District, a Spanish-speaking neighborhood some distance from downtown. The operation had been open to the public, with performances, for two years, holding classes, showing movies, and performing plays.

The police has been to our Abandoned Church only once before, when we showed the films *Blonde Cobra* and *Flaming Creatures*, which had been seized in

New York. Two plainclothesmen arrived, identified themselves, and reported that they were investigating the film because of an anonymous complaint.

Blonde Cobra was on, and the sequence that had 15 minutes of blank screen with only the sound track had begun. The voice of Jack Smith, star of *Blonde Cobra*, droned on to a gray screen. One policeman fell asleep. They exited, commenting to us that, except for the remarks on religion, they couldn't see anything in the film. They apologetically said, "You know how some people are, but we gotta investigate these complaints when we get them."

On the screen, in technicolor, were bare buttocks with a dagger hanging out of them as Jack Smith said "Sex is a pain in the ass." Several minutes later, genitalia were flashing across the screen during the orgy scene in *Flaming Creatures.*

For the Genet Film hundreds of people waited outside to get into our tiny theater, many of them, as a newspaper account reported, prominent lawyers, artists, and architects.

The policemen couldn't get seats for the first showing, but four of them, including one very dark-skinned Negro, watched the second showing, and then methodically and efficiently "did their duty." One walked up to the projection booth and seized the film and the projector. He explained that "without the projector you couldn't show the film."

"You know," said one officer in a sport coat, "it's evidence." They explained that they didn't have to arrest us at this point, since they could arrest us later if the D.A. decided to prosecute.

I asked why they had seized the film. "Why," they said in unison, "the film is obscene and objectionable."

The policemen checked the wiring, the exit signs, the permit to operate, peering into the nooks and crannies of the Abandoned Church (at one time a Church, and either God or the congregation, or both, abandoned it.)

The D.A., John J. Ferdon; the Chief of Police, Thomas Cahill; most of the Inspector's Bureau, and all of the assistant District Attorneys saw the film at the Hall of Justice. The D.A. reported that he had not yet made up his mind.

The film was seized on Saturday night, and by Wednesday the D.A.'s were still watching the film. Marvin Stender, our lawyer, phoned the D.A. and was told that we could have the projector back and that no charges would be pressed; they would keep the film. Stender said no deal. Later, the D.A. said that he would give the projector and the film if we would not show it anymore. Stender repeated; no deal.

On Thursday Stender made it plain that we would sue the city to get back the film and the projector. On Friday morning, the D.A. called and said "You can come and get your trash." One of the D.A.'s told a reporter that the reason there would be no charges pressed was because they couldn't win in court.

We recall the trial of the poem "Howl" by Allen Ginsberg, and the trial of Lennie [Lenny] Bruce for saying "cocksucker" in his act, and the trial of *Tropic of Cancer*, and the trial of Ron Boise's sculpture, which was inspired by the *Kama Sutra*. In each case, the city lost and had been humiliated. Presumably they didn't want to try again, although each law enforcement official that we talked to had the same opinion of the film: it was "obscene, filthy, vile, disgusting, degenerate" — but it didn't arouse them. Not one of them had heard of Jean Genet.

The film, when we got it back, bore signs of heavy use — or misuse. Sprocket holes were torn, scratches and dirt smudges appeared on every frame.

But they didn't prosecute; they couldn't prosecute — not Jean Genet in San Francisco. But on the morning they returned the film, R. G. Davis, director of the Mime Troupe, was ordered to come before the Hall of Justice for a review of his permit to operate. The Troupe had announced that it was having a benefit performance which would include dancing and an art auction of some paintings by prominent artists in the Bay Area. Didn't we know, asked the Police Inspector, that we needed a permit to have a dance, and that a permit cost $100 and it was, of course, too late to apply for one now; and aren't we aware that one needed a permit to hold an art auction, and that took a week to obtain; and didn't we know, he asked, as he thumbed through the Police Code Book, thicker than the New York telephone book, that we had various fire and health hazards in the building?

R. G. Davis and I decided that we would show the Genet film again. We reserved a room for Monday night at the Sheraton Palace Hotel, one of the oldest and most respectable establishments in the city. At 2 P.M. Monday, the management of the Palace telephoned us to cancel the showing. The reason was that there were "too many calls in opposition to the film" and that we had not told the clerk who took our order for the room the nature of the film.

I replied that I had given her the filmmaker's name and the title of the film. We argued whether a contract on the phone is binding or not; I threatened to sue; he said it was too bad. I finally told him that if he did not permit us to show it, we would show it on the street right in front of the Hotel, since we could not disappoint so many people.

Two hours after the Palace canceled, the assistant manager phoned saying that he had reconsidered and we could show it after all. So we showed it, to approximately 400 people.

The Palace management obviously had the scars of the recent civil-rights sit-ins fresh in their minds — 1,000 people sleeping overnight in their lobby chanting and singing "We shall not be overcome." I was greeted with "You better behave yourself tonight, boy." They had also hired a Burns Detective to guard against whatever it was they were afraid of.

The showings went smoothly. Davis and I thanked the Palace for their cooperation. The next day we decided that we should show it again at the Palace. This time,
they refused to even consider renting us a room.

The next day I was informed by my supervisor at San Francisco General Hospital
that my services would be terminated at the end of the week because my "duties as
a medical social worker at General Hospital are incompatible with showing controversial films."

I found out later that the directive to fire me had come from the City Hall and
that the official excuse was "excessive absences." Since I had worked at the Hospital,
always as a temporary worker, on and off for several years, and since this was the sixth
time they had hired me, "Excessive absences" was a poor excuse.

Everyone — even the Hospital authorities who had fired me and the D.A. who
will not press charges — agreed that we have done nothing wrong in showing the
film. But "you lose your effectiveness by showing films like that," and, "what can you
expect of the hospital authorities; would you want some one who shows pornographic movies — I know you're legally O.K. — to work with the public?" In conversation even some of our friends refer to *Un Chant D'Amour* as a dirty movie,
although the entire Police Department watched the film and decided that no
charges would be pressed.

Another response — equally revealing — begins by stating that the film is no good
because "it didn't arouse me" or "it was poorly shot" or "the flower sequence was
corny." This approach assumes that since the film was not a good film there should
be no fuss; since it didn't arouse the viewer (at least that's what he says) the police
were stupid in seizing it — of course leading to the conclusion that if they felt the
film to be truly erotic, which it really is, then there might be a case. Ultimately the
liberal arguments come down to: "Why are you wasting your time showing lousy
films, when we need good organizers to defeat Proposition 14?"

Un Chant D'Amour is not a complex film, although it is ambiguous. It deals with
homosexual love and it shows men making love, caressing each other with erect
penises. It shows the difficulty of communicating love, or expressing true feelings
physically. It takes place in a prison, a microcosm of human existence. Is this the
real threat that Genet poses? Or is it the sado-masochistic relationship between the
prison guard and the prisoners, which produces sexual fantasies for everyone, these
fantasies finally merging with reality itself so that the viewer cannot distinguish the
real from the illusory.

No one quite knew how to deal with the film, with their concepts of pornography, with their image of the self, and with their easy-to-deal with cliches about
homosexuals and homosexuality. In this sense it was very threatening.

The homosexual viewing *Un Chant D'Amour* is doubly upset: on the one hand the secret rituals are shown on the screen before a mixed public; and on the other hand, the actual love making sequences, arousing in themselves, become intensified and disturbing by an ambiguity: the shots are fantasies, produced by the guard's beating of the prisoner, and the viewer is uncertain whether the illusion is that of the sadistic guard, the masochistic prisoner, or his lover in the next cell who is aware that the beating is taking place; or is it the illusion of all three?

Several heterosexuals confessed that they became aroused, and in the scene which shows the two prisoners making love in the field, one man admitted that he could not see any difference between the actions of the prisoner and his own response in making love to a woman. Other people admitted that the face of the hairy prisoner, weeping over his frustration at not being able to communicate with his lover in the next cell, aroused great compassion.

At the showings most of the audience left the theater silently; the conversation overheard was guarded and embarrassed. I myself found it difficult to talk about the film, and even more difficult to clarify and verbalize my reactions.

What would happen, I wondered, if this kind of film were shown in theaters and television? If someone could convince Madison Avenue that this stuff could be packaged right and sold as a consumer item? But first there would have to be a frank admission made by Madison Avenue for the 160,000,000 people it represents that pornography is fun, enjoyable, exciting, and arouses all but the frigid and eunuchs.

With all this admitted, the Genet film would still be upsetting, not because men masturbate, but because there is little else for them to do. When actors play with themselves it is natural; just as when one longs for another, or tries to arouse himself by squeezing the tattoo of a woman, or dances wildly in his cell with his penis dangling between his legs; all this is natural for men in any confined setting. A prison is the most easily understood confinement. Better to portray loneliness and frustration with than a room, a house, a park, or a city. But each man, and probably each woman, has experienced the feeling expressed on the face of one of the actors.

And the prison guard, the authority figure who confuses and confounds the simple communication of love, who spies on each prisoner, watching them masturbate, or dance, and himself getting aroused, this figure is in all our lives. He prevents one prisoner from grasping the bouquet of flowers which is swung from one cell window towards another. Only when this figure disappears, after he has experienced orgasm, produced by fantasies stimulated by his beating of the hairy prisoner, is the swinging bouquet caught and pulled slowly, carefully into the cell.

With this little ritual, sentimental if it were not in prison, the film ends, with the date scratched on the cell wall, a day like other days, perhaps; but what does time have to do with any of the fantasies or activities, or the frustrations that derive from the inability — whether in the form of a wall or another man — of men to consummate love for each other, for humans to express what they feel with all of their physical and intellectual capacities.

A penis can be drawn to illustrate dictionaries and medical books, and its qualities can be described, but to see one, in the hand of a man, or erect and pounding the wall between it and another man, this is threatening. And the cell wall itself, that blocks the lovers' desires, is it not the wall that we all encounter when trying to communicate to those we love or yearn for?

When this can be discussed in newspapers and magazines as well as in conversation, freedom of art will have achieved some meaning, for it will have acted as a force for the expansion of human consciousness, its most revolutionary function.

We won the free speech fight in that we have the film legally can show it. But what good is this right if no one will deal with the theme of the film? The one person who reviewed the film, in the San Francisco Chronicle, missed the point of the movie, called it banal, and implied that Genet missed a good opportunity to expose the brutality of French prison life.

If one can not admit that the film is erotic, that it deals with the essence of the human condition, the communication of tender feelings, the physical and emotional desires to touch, caress, give and take; if one cannot admit that human beings live with symbols, rituals, with sexual fantasies, sometimes produced by violence, and sometimes by disappearing smoke or a bouquet of flowers, if these basic questions cannot be dealt with, then free speech is meaningless. If a serious point is made and there is no one to answer it, or talk about it, or discuss it, or deal with it on any but superficial and misleading levels, then what is the purpose of speech at all, or art for that matter?

Part of the meaning of free speech is dealing with dangerous ideas. To denounce fascism or any doctrine is no great feat in the United States. No one cares. But to discuss one's own reaction to a film that touches all our inner lives, that questions our identity, and challenges our stated motivations, this is the revolutionary function of art and the artists. We have lost the true battle, unless we can force people to confront the ideas and images in *Un Chant D'Amour*, the sad song of love and life.

Freedom of art is the most important part of free speech, for it is ambiguous in that it deals (in this case visually, like our fantasy lives) with the emotions and feelings that are hardest to verbalize, that are the most painful. Not a homosexual nor a heterosexual that saw *Un Chant D'Amour* and allowed himself to see and feel honestly, came away without questions on all levels of his intellectual and emotional life. Is not the reaching, the swinging of the bouquet of flowers to the man in the next cell, the smoke rising and disappearing after a brief communication, is this not a symbol for all of us, for all our loves, and all our attempts to reach and touch tenderly, a man, a woman, a child? Is it not the search for freedom to live and love that drives these prisoners? And is not the guard, the uniform, the brutality and sadism that goes with the job, is this not anti-life in its most universal sense? The soapbox revolutionary cannot expose our nature in this way, and while his right to speak must be defended staunchly, is [it] not the artist's freedom of expression that must be crucial?

Un Chant D'Amour seemed to threaten so many people, many of whom had not even seen it, many of whom had never even heard of Genet, a chain reaction was set off of harassment by various agencies, private and public, liberal and reactionary. San Francisco, with its soft pastels, its quaint tourist sites, and its aura of liberalism proved to be provincial and repressive when its deepest cultural norms were attacked by so minute [a] silent film shown in a small theater in the Mission District.

—

FROM *CANYON CINEMA NEWS*, MAY 1965

Bruce Baillie
REPORT FROM ON THE ROAD, FILMING . . .

November. Setting out again from California, Mrs. Dog and I spent the first night outside Wells, Nevada. It got down to 20 below that night — we had two sleeping bags put together which we had to share. The next morning the car wouldn't start, the windows were ice. After we got started, we ran into a man who had been walking all night. He said he had learned from his father you had to keep moving when you were caught in the cold. We ate some good cheese and bread and headed north into Idaho.

Spent some time with Gene Dawson and his family in Pocatello, giving a show at the University — many good people are on the staff there — went to an old outdoor hot springs south of there, open all winter. Tried to ride a pinto mare, with camera — spent several hours trying to get a bridle on her — finally, she threw me and I didn't get a shot I had had in mind for several months.

Choteau, Montana . . . Getting colder . . . mountain men coming out of the Rockies on horseback; spent the night in a bar near the hotel — shot 2 rolls. Following an eagle in a storm one morning; shooting a basketball game; heading straight north to the Blackfeet Reservation around Browning.

Browning, Montana — Cardston, Alberta, Canada. The pass on the east side of Glacier National Park can be closed anytime by snow. Stopped at a bar midway, met three Blood Indians (part of Blackfeet nation), Talked me into going into Canada — spent evening with them. Next day, having found very little material to substantiate this section of the film, I ran into something at the last moment. Two old Blood gentlemen in a cafe gave permission to shoot and record them. My recorder kept stopping, but I finally came out with something editable . . . had to pay these men, of course, had only $15 to get me all the way to S. Dakota. I gave them what I could — promised to send the rest (which I did, by Christmas.)

On the way through again I had to take another road, across the reservation, because of ice and snow. Dog and I ran onto some mountain sheep that we took pictures of; we got some footage of a truck ahead of us (telephoto, 32fps), snow flying back toward us, great dark wheels spinning against the icy road — had to change film while driving with my knee.

On through S. Dakota, Christmas, Minnesota, Michigan, staying with friends, giving a few shows. Finally to NYC. Using all Double-X negative now for the last section. Was able in northern Minn. to photograph a pinto. In Ann Arbor I shot and recorded sync the Falcon Quartette, in a kind of special attitude, as though I had never heard jazz.

NYC. Conditions for financing independent film work are poorer than I expected. The Ford Foundation says they are not going to continue their grants; there is no agency, to my knowledge, with any interest in supporting film experimentation. The excellent contemporary film series — Oct., '64 — at the Gallery of Modern Art, set up by James McBride, has been discontinued. On the other hand, the Filmmakers' Cinemateque will soon have a permanent home — the Co-op is sending out shows. More film artists are moving around the country with their work and schools are instituting film depts., preparing, they say, to extend invitations to some of the film-makers to come and teach. Gregory Markopoulos had been to Pocatello the week before I arrived. Stan Brakhage was to arrive there a week after I left. They both are having showings here at the Cinemateque. Stan is touring colleges, I think raising money not only to live on, but also for a new film. Stanton Kaye is on his way here.

February 4 . . . Was able to smuggle my camera into the stock exchange today. Received $25 from home and bought 4 more rolls of film. Unexpected friendliness on the street; especially like it just south of Wall St. Yehuda, friend from the film school in London is taking care of me. With another Israeli friend, we were walking along the Bowery the other night. A dead-drunk man was jumped in front of us, by six guys who went through his pockets and threw him around a little. A few minutes later they came back and wrestled him down again and took off his shoes. He was helpless, so I went over and put his shoes on for him and helped him down to another block. We talked a little on the way. I asked if they had got anything from him — he had a face that reminded me of a sailor I had seen one night, who had floated in face-down into San Diego Harbor. He laughed all the way across the street. It was kind of like some of my films the way it came out.

The next day I had permission to shoot at the Catholic Worker during the morning free meal. The men protested, so I had to leave. I learned that the week before, a TV crew with 5 cameras, lights, smiles, suits, and ties, etc, had worked there for six hours without any trouble. Could be that people really prefer to believe in the establishment.

Met Ken Jacobs and his wife — Spent a nice afternoon in his loft putting a show of mine together. He has some good 8mm equipment around. I hope he [has] some luck finding money to keep working.

Cinemateque gave me a show Feb. 18 — then we headed back to Michigan to write letters for financial assists, finally leaving for California.

On the way through Iowa we saw the Sunday beatings in Selma on TV . . . headed north in a snow storm to Minneapolis. Leaving dog and car, I flew to Alabama with camera (borrowed the money). Spent Tuesday around Second March there shooting vital material for film.

California. No more chance to make the film than when I started, needing a thousand dollars to develop and workprint all this material. With some luck, through friends and laying on additional debt, I have sent the film to the lab.

In respect to the *form* of the new work, I have now released it from its original title, "QUIXOTE," and will not call it anything. Gordon Mumma of Ann Arbor will be doing the sound.

Thanks to everyone for giving me so much help of every kind.

—

FROM *CANYON CINEMA NEWS*, JUNE / JULY 1965

Gregory Markopoulos
DENUNCIATION OF THE ANN ARBOR FILM FESTIVAL [1965]

The film festival brochure stated that "movies" were to be shown March 11–14 at 7 and 9 in the evening in the Architecture and Design Auditorium. The brochure continued further: 'To encourage the work of the independent producer, and to promote the concept of the film as art, the Cinema Guild of the University of Michigan and the Dramatic Arts Center of Ann Arbor take pleasure in announcing the Third Ann Arbor Film Festival.'

Mr. Mekas had asked me if I would take his place at the Ann Arbor Film Festival due to other pressing business with which he was involved. I accepted and took the plane to Detroit, where I was met by Mr. George Manupelli, the chief organizer of the Ann Arbor festivals. That same evening the opening program of the festival was held. Prior to this I made an opening speech during which I said that all the arts were dead except film. The students accepted my comment. No one challenged it. One young woman asked, at one point during my informal discussion, 'Why are we unable to see these films?' I replied that it was mostly because of the incompetence of the individuals in charge of the film societies; and also because of such individuals' total disinterest in the film as film. I continued that such individuals treated the thought of the film on the same level as the commercial theatre owners and distributors. Curiously, later, after the end of the first evening's program, I was approached by two members of the Cinema Guild, who seemed amazed at the tremendous reception which the students had given to the films. Many had been turned away. This reaction reminds me of similar reactions of some foundations, who are surprised when projects for which they have given insufficient funds are completed and well received. At such times foundations recoil more bewildered than ever. Indeed, the accountants who are in charge of the foundations cannot fathom what has happened.

Chains on Time

The best received motion picture of the first evening of the festival was David Brooks' 'Nightspring Daystar.' One judge remarked that it reminded him of a Rauschenberg lithograph. 'Quiet,' by Robert H. Spring, was a hilarious spoof made in a morgue. Also, 'The Devil Is Dead,' by Carl Linder. Several people commented that this film was too long. What we fail to understand is that one of the privileges of the film-maker is to create a motion picture as long or as short as he feels. Certainly a spectator would never consider suggesting to a painter that he should use less of this or that color. There is a strange tendency — like the misinterpretation of 'camp' — today to fear that the average man, the masses, shall and shall not have their share of TIME. Man is become free, but he is not allowed to do with his TIME as he will. Leisure is promoted and chains have already been put upon TIME.

Certainly one of the highlights of the four-day stay in Ann Arbor was a showing of 8mm films. Later, when I was to request that these films also be included in the voting for prizes, I was more or less told that if the 8mm films were accepted, then next year the selection committee headed by Mr. Manupelli would have to accept 'all those 8mm films.' Apparently in the swamplands they do not consider 8mm as film. Another curiosity of the preselection committee became apparent the second evening of the festival. One member commented after having seen the films again in a proper auditorium with good projection: 'the films looked so different . . . on the wall they looked so insignificant.' That's how the New American Cinema, all the films of the film-makers across the country who are in love with the medium, blossom and will bloom on the surfaces, the old and new surfaces that are inevitable, in the new theatres for film across the nation.

No Understanding

During the four days that I was in Ann Arbor I had an opportunity to research the kind of reviews that the experimental films had received. As has happened elsewhere on other campuses, there was no understanding of the film as film. The general attitude was that in order to understand film, it must be given the meaning of literature, the meaning of painting, the dubious meaning of psychology or sociology, but never its innate meaning as film itself. Advertisements that purported to be devoted to experimental film programs would read like one which I found: 'Audience members who may be disturbed or offended by scenes representing the more extreme tendencies in experimental filmmaking are urged not to attend.'

Another work which was received with tremendous enthusiasm by the students was 'The Poon-Tang Trilogy' by Ben Van Meter. The satirical and marvelous surprise of the festival was Benjamin Hayeem's 'Papillote,' which was shot in the New York Stock Exchange. Nathaniel Dorsky's film 'Ingreen' was also roundly applauded. Many wanted to view the film again; they did not know what it was about. One of the grand faults of the festival: there were no program notes. Finally, the greatest horror of the film festival was a film made at New York University, 'It's Not Just You, Murray.' It boasted an Edward Kingsley Award.

Two 'Unworthy'

Late in the afternoon of the second or third day of the festival I learned that certain films had not been admitted into the festival because Mr. Manupelli's selection committee thought them unworthy of inclusion. Among these were Naomi Levine's lovely 'Jeromelu' and Jose Soltero's 'Jerovi,' another film on masturbation like 'Ingreen,' but more direct, and without the symbolism of 'Ingreen.' A part of the selection committee ran 'Jerovi,' and they were visibly shaken. One young woman immediately proclaimed it pornographic. 'What's pornographic about it?' I asked. No reply. Then I learned that this film was shown privately, at the home of Mr. Manupelli, the festival organizer, during a party with music which made it seem obscene. I considered it an outrage, in as much as the film-makers send their films to film-makers' festivals in good faith, and it is the privilege and responsibility of the organizers to respect the film-makers' efforts, finished efforts or not.

In the evening, having spoken to Mr. Manupelli and insisting that both Miss Levine's and Mr. Soltero's films be included in the festival, I met with the Greek poet Konstantinos Lardas. Prior to this I had seen last year's award winner, 'First Time Here,' by Richard Meyers [Myers], and also his latest film, 'Coronation.' Both films were theatrical in content, well made, but not deserving of the first prize — which 'Coronation' was later to receive. The truly remarkable film of the evening was 'Glass House,' by Lawrence Janiak, with its evocative soundtrack.

The Judges Meet

Sunday afternoon the judges met. One admitted being unqualified to judge the films. He did not understand Breer or Vanderbeek. Before proceeding with the problems of judging the films for first, second, and third prizes, I asked the judges for a short statement as to their attitude toward the medium of film. I should have resigned then and there. Film, for these judges, was unfortunately film which corresponded to the drafting table of the art department.

The judging of the films took place in the following manner: the films were read one by one and eliminated. 'Jerovi' (which I had managed to have shown) and 'Ingreen' were both thrown out, 'to make the judging easier,' since both were about masturbation! And so it went. But I remained until the moment that a point system was used to judge the films. I waited for the results and resigned on the spot. It was threatened that if I did not stay, the check issued for my expenses, meager though it was, would be stopped. Another selection committee member shouted, 'You have been contracted.'

I walked out of the house where the committee was meeting and left Ann Arbor. I had accomplished the showing of Naomi Levine's 'Jeromelu' and of 'Jerovi.' I later learned that these films were received very well. And much, much later I learned that even the 'Poon-Tang Trilogy' had received a prize of $50, even though more than half of the judges had said, initially, that it was devoid of content!

The results of the awards after I left were announced as follows: 'Coronation,' $250; 'Nightspring Daystar,' $150; 'Everybody Hit Their Brother Once,' $100; 'Papillote,' $50; 'Poon-Tang Trilogy,' $50. Honorable mentions to: 'Ingreen,' 'Fist-Fight,' 'Disintegration Line.'

'Sense of Censorship'

My wire of resignation sent to the Michigan Daily and president Harlan Hatcher read as follows: 'Sir: I have resigned from the Third Ann Arbor Film Festival as Jurist and Guest Speaker. I find its direction hardly of an international scope as advertised by Mr. Manupelli. I am further horrified that a sense of censorship should prevail during such an event, an event which is for the students and not to insure the showing of local films out of competition. It is to be hoped that a true festival of the film will take place under the auspices of more inspired management. I have since yesterday been waging a battle for the public showing of "Jerovi" by Jose Rodriguez Soltero. This afternoon the jury overcame the discontent of the pre-selection committee and the film has been entered into the festival. I take leave of your campus with a very interesting image which I beheld the other day near the Student Union — a young man talking to a tree. Sincerely, Gregory J. Markopoulos.'

George Manupelli

TO THE EDITOR: A few days before the Third Ann Arbor Film Festival was to have opened, Jonas Mekas called festival representatives to say that he would be unable to participate in the festival as guest-speaker and member of the Awards Jury as planned, but that not to worry, he was sending Gregory Markopoulos as his substitute.

In his March 25, 1965, Voice column, Mekas praised Markopoulos and then turned Movie Journal over to him for a report on the festival.

What followed in the way of distortions and untruths were grotesque.

The following is a partial answer to Markopoulos's Voice report:

When Markopoulos reached Ann Arbor, he was handed a freshly printed program listing some fifty films that had been previewed by the selection committee and were now scheduled for public screening.

Markopoulos asked if he might have a look at the 'rejects.'

He was advised that this would be perfectly in order, and that, in fact, it was a rule of the festival that the Awards Jury could overrule the Selection Committee and call up for competition any film it so wished.

No more was ever said about looking at 'rejections.'

Markopoulos then noted that the film 'Poon-Tang Trilogy' was scheduled to be screened publicly. He advised against this because of the film's content, adding, 'Even Jonas won't show it in New York.'

It was explained to Markopoulos that while the Awards Jury may add films to the festival roster, they may not delete them, especially for reasons of content.

Markopoulos also advised against screening 'Jerovi,' not only because of its content, but, because, in his opinion, it was not a very good film ' — the grass is too green.'

At the time, 'Jerovi' had not yet reached Ann Arbor and the rule which states that no film may be judged and eliminated from the festival while it is still in the mails was applied.

Another film that was expected, and one in which Markopoulos took a personal interest, was 'Jeremelu.' He was determined that this film should be awarded First Prize even though some doubt remained as to whether or not the film had been sent.

If any sense of censorship prevailed at the festival, as Markopoulos has repeatedly charged, it was his own.

If there was any unfair play to film makers, as he also charged, it was Markopoulos' predisposition to award 'Jeremelu' a prize without having seen all of the other entries.

Markopoulos opened the festival with a talk.

He announced that because he was replacing Jonas Mekas, he was, 'frankly' unprepared.

After reading film reviews from a Buffalo newspaper for a while, commenting periodically, 'Isn't that silly,' Markopoulos tested the much tried, 'All the arts are dead except film.' He then listed his own 'Twice a Man' as among the three or four 'masterpieces' of the 'new cinema' — the only living art.

It is interesting that the film 'Coronation' by Richard Myers, which was subsequently awarded the First Prize over Markopoulos' objections, repeated the theme ' — the king is dead! Long live the king! The king is not dead! — ' over and over until finally everybody was dead.

If the overflow opening night crowd was willing to accept the death of all the other arts, it was in no mood to have a new Catholicism outlined for them at the time ' — Let me tell you something about the Film-Makers' Cinematheque.'

After much shuffling, coughing, and other irreverent sounds and gestures by the audience, Markopoulos finally gave up the speaker's rostrum.

Markopoulos reported as one of the highlights of the festival the showing of 8mm films. He said that when he requested that these films be included in the voting for prizes, 'I was more or less told that if the 8mm films were accepted this year, then next year the selection committee headed by Mr. Manupelli would have to accept all those 8mm films.' He went on to say, 'Apparently in the swamplands they do not consider 8mm as film.'

The local 8mm films in question were in no way connected with the festival. Instead, the printed program publicized them, while a verbal announcement further encouraged attendance at the private screenings that were planned. The films were first-films by talented young film makers, and, at midnight, after four full hours of festival screenings, 250 persons paid a donation of 50¢ each to the film makers to see their works. Two of the artists involved were my own students and part of a class that I teach without compensation except for the success of projects such as the 8mm films and showings that impressed Markopoulos so much.

To one of the young film makers he said, 'Your film looks very much like the work we are doing in New York; why don't you send it to the Film-makers' Cooperative?'

The student asked if there was anything real about Markopoulos. Another answered that he was a 'Greek myth.'

The Ann Arbor Film Festival has always been interested in 8mm films.

The First Ann Arbor Film Festival included a section of 8mm films organized by Mary Ashley called the 'Second Annual World 8mm Home Movie Festival.' Works by now-forgotten uncles and dads were projected simultaneously onto six screens, stationed three above the other, and accompanied by an electronic music sound-track by Gordon Mumma.

As part of the Second Ann Arbor Film Festival, Cinema Guild sponsored a loft-screening of experimental films with substantial cash awards.

This year, the festival rules stated that competition prints must be 16mm, regardless of their original gauge. Since 8mm films were not 16mm films, and since they were not otherwise connected with the festival, there was no reason to consider them for awards, unless, of course, one wanted to consider all non-16mm films not connected with the festival for awards.

Speaking of 'swamplands' — on a Saturday night in New York City about a year ago, I paid $1.75 to see Markopoulos' 'Twice a Man.' It played to two other persons besides myself (one of whom — Robert Ashley — was sleeping) and the projectionist who gave it a standing ovation when the film was over. Rave reviews followed in the next issue of the Village Voice.

In contrast to this, about 1,000 saw 'Twice a Man' in Ann Arbor, but because of the large audiences, there was no telling how many people were sleeping besides Robert Ashley who attended each of the four screenings.

On the morning after the second day of the festival, 'Jerovi' reached Ann Arbor and was previewed later that day by several members of the Selection Committee along with Markopoulos who reported that they were 'visibly shaken.' He also claimed that Nancy Fallis of the Selection Committee 'proclaimed the work pornographic.' The word actually used was 'picturesque,' and when Markopoulos asked, 'What's pornographic about it?' she responded, 'I'll bite, what is?'

Since all the members of the Selection Committee were not able to attend this pre-screening of 'Jerovi,' no decision was (could be) made regarding its competition status. It was here, however, that Markopoulos reversed himself and indicated a strong preference for the film. Perhaps it was he who was 'visibly shaken.'

Late that night, as a member of the Selection Committee who had not yet seen the film, I screened 'Jerovi' in my house. Some friends were present and a most unfortunate incident followed. Noting that the film was without a soundtrack, some-one put on the Beatles' 'Mister Moonlight.' The playing of the record did not make the film seem obscene as Markopoulos reported. Quite the contrary was the case. Nevertheless, Markopoulos was right to complain.

'Jeremelu' was lost in the mails but was finally located shortly before the seven o'clock show on Saturday, the third night of the festival. The post office was kindly unlocked and the tiny film discovered under a postcard.

When Markopoulos arrived for the competition screenings that evening — late, thereby missing several competition films — he flatly pronounced that if 'Jerovi' and 'Jeremelu' were not screened at the festival, he would resign.

During intermission, he loitered with Greek poet Kostantinos Lardas, thereby missing more films.

Aside from Markopoulos, the Awards Jury was composed of Annina Nosei, an Italian critic of avant garde art whose brilliant articles have appeared in numerous international publications; Marvin Felheim, who brought experimental films to Ann Arbor 20 years ago; Doug Rideout, a respected producer of educational and documentary films; and Hilton Cohen whose 'Space Theatre' was performed at the Venice Biennial, 1964.

The jury met on Sunday afternoon to preview the seven o'clock show and to come to some decision regarding awards so that the award-winners and highlights of the festival could be announced and replayed at the nine o'clock show, the last program of the festival. (Up to this point, the jury screened films at the same time they were shown publicly.)

Because 'Jerovi' had still not been previewed by the whole Selection Committee and because 'Jeremelu' had arrived only the night before, the jury was asked if it would take over the normal functioning of the Selection Committee. The jury accepted this responsibility, and, after seeing both films, voted to include them in their deliberations and to screen them publicly. One member of the Awards Jury voted against accepting 'Jerovi' into competition because, among other reasons, he thought it 'prudish,' but the majority vote was respected.

Now, having seen all of the official entries, the jury began its deliberation.

When it became apparent that 'Jeremelu' was not about to receive the First Prize, Markopoulos resigned from the festival. When invited to make whatever remarks he might wish as part of the last show of the festival, as Pauline Kael had done the year before, Markopoulos declined with, 'I'm not Pauline Kael.' He then threatened everyone saying, 'I'm going to tell every film maker I can reach not to enter your festival, ever!'

One member of Cinema Guild did suggest that he might want to stop payment on checks issued Mekas as a result of Markopoulos' performance at the festival. In the same sense that Markopoulos had advised the opening night audience, 'If you don't like the films, ask for your money back.' The student was, in effect, asking for his money back on Markopoulos. At any rate, the differences between Kael and Markopoulos are obvious enough.

Now out of sight, Markopoulos sent a telegram of resignation to the President of the University of Michigan and to the school's student newspaper. This action must have at least surprised the President, since the festival is not connected with the University. In his telegram of resignation, Markopoulos wrote that the direction of the festival was hardly international, as advertised.

The festival brochure states simply that there are no restrictions regarding country of origin. It is Markopoulos who is advertising the festival as an international event. Even so, several European nations have expressed interest in an exchange program of experimental films with the Ann Arbor Film Festival next year.

Markopoulos went on to say, 'I am further horrified that a sense of censorship should prevail during an event which is for the students and not to insure the showing of local films out of competition.' If any sense of censorship prevailed, as I have already noted, it was Markopoulos' own. His attempt to have 'Poon-Tang Trilogy' and 'Jerovi' eliminated from public screening are the cases in point. Too, the festival is not for students. It is for film makers of which I am one. Local films are introduced to the festival only after all the competition films have been scheduled, and, even then, only if time remains and it generally does. Even so, a large time-block is kept open for late arrivals.

Markopoulos ended his telegram by saying, 'I take leave of your campus with a very interesting image which I beheld the other day near the Student Union — a young man talking to a tree.' Neither the tree nor the young man realized they were being watched.

—

FROM *CANYON CINEMA NEWS,* OCTOBER 1965

George Manupelli

ON HIS BLINDNESS

The pink Albino, wearing slitted glasses
To protect him from the glare
Traced the monster's footprints in the snow

At length, the footprints grew smaller and smaller
And the depressions increasingly more shallow
Following some mathematical principle of depreciation
They disappeared entirely

Not being a scientist, the Albino could not understand
But he realized that he was suddenly alone
     in the Himalayas
     without food or drink.

2 : Incorporation

Canyon formally incorporated on February 20, 1967. The organization's purposes are made clear in the articles of incorporation: "(a) The specific and primary purposes are to establish and operate for educational purposes an organization which will conduct classes and workshops in the preparation and production of high quality non-commercial cinematic works of art, and which will promote the making of high quality cinematic works of art of a non-commercial nature. (b) The general purposes are: 1. To promote the distribution of high quality cinematic works of art to the public. 2. From time to time to make available to the public at free showings or at low cost, the films produced by its members and other films which are made available to it by members of other similar non-profit organizations." The articles stipulate that there will be four "directors of the corporation": Lawrence C. Jordan, Benjamin Van Meter, Robert Nelson, and Bruce Baillie. The articles were signed by Jordan (president) and Earl E. Bodien (secretary). The "By-Laws of Canyon Cinema" include sixteen articles that stipulate the particulars of how the organization will function. Both the articles and the bylaws are at pains to make clear that Canyon Cinema is "A Non-Profit Corporation"— indeed, the articles indicate quite clearly that "this corporation is organized exclusively for educational purposes and no part of any of its net earnings shall inure to the benefit of any member." Nevertheless, as the years went by, the State of California and the Internal Revenue Service would make clear, again and again, that in fact, as a members-only organization, Canyon was not *legally* a nonprofit entity, even if, in fact, the organization made no profit from the rentals of the films it distributed.

The July 1967 issue of the *Cinemanews* announced that Earl Bodien had resigned as manager of the Canyon Cinema Co-op and that Edith Kramer was taking over that position (Roy Ramsing would continue to be a part-time assistant). "Earl," the announcement indicates, "has, almost singlehandedly, built the Co-op into a viable and functioning center for film distribution and information for the West. The Directors of the Co-op seem interested in providing for the filmmakers' needs without succumbing to the fuck-you attitude of commerce, so things should continue in the way that Earl began them, with Edith and Roy providing continuity." Bodien had run the distribution operations from his living room at 58 Verona Place in San Francisco; Kramer would soon be running the distribution operation from an office in the basement of Intersection for the Arts

Portrait of Ben
Van Meter, from
Cinemanews (70.4).
Photographer unknown.

(incorporated in 1965, Intersection is one of the oldest alternative art spaces in the Bay Area) at 756 Union Street in San Francisco. Larry Jordan and Robert Nelson remodeled the space for Kramer.

By the late 1960s, Canyon had become an established, if financially marginal, organization, and the *Cinemanews* was increasingly important both as a general source of practical information for independent filmmakers and programmers and as a place where filmmakers could communicate informally about the films they were making or hoping to make and about their difficulties and concerns in seeing their films into the world. The personal tone of the periodical remained, as did its informal design. For years it would remain common for members of Canyon to write to the *Cinemanews* to keep readers abreast of their activities; their letters provide a sense of the lives of these young men and women as they worked against the odds to produce a cinema they could be proud of.

In general, however, while personal letters and informal items continued to enliven the pages of the *Cinemanews,* the newsletter increasingly revealed that Canyon was part of an international movement, and that its distribution and informational activities were functioning as models for a far-flung readership. Taylor Mead wrote from Rome on December 31, 1966: "Thank you for your brochure. I didn't know so much was taking place nowadays." In 1968 the Japan Film-Makers' Cooperative—whose directors were Takahiko Iimura, Kenji Kanesaka, Tyushin Sato, Nubuhiko Ohbayashi, and Donald Richie—wrote to announce that it was distributing avant-garde films, "under the same 75/25 split in effect as at the NY and CC Co-ops." Readers of the *Cinemanews* must have enjoyed the Japan cooperative's warning that "we are against any censorship but to remind you Japanese custom would not allow to enter any of such scene: cubic hair and sexual organ." The May-July 1968 issue of the *Cinemanews* also included a report from the Australian independent group UBU describing its various activities in distribution and exhibition and offering a "Hand-Made Film Manifesto," which argued that the best way to provide an alternative to commercial filmmaking was to craft one's own films by hand—an idea ahead of its time: in the 1990s and the 2000s many filmmakers have turned to hand-crafted filmmaking. In January 1969 Intermedia Film Cooperative announced its formation in Vancouver, British Columbia. And Basu Chatterji wrote from India to let *Cinemanews* readers know that Film Forum "is the largest film society in India. It is doing good work, in its own limited ways, and has a membership of 2800 . . . ," and to request information about Canyon's activities.

With increasing frequency, Canyon filmmakers whose success had allowed them to go on tour with their work reported at length on what they had learned from their activities. Some filmmakers provided lists of men and women in the United States and in Europe who were interested in hosting filmmakers or who had bought prints of their work. In the September/October 1967 issue Bruce Baillie supplied his "Prejudiced Guide to Film Festivals." And in the January/February 1968 issue Robert Nelson reported on the now-legendary Brussels Festival, as well as on a Swedish proposal to develop an archive for New American Cinema (an essay intercut with a set of surreal "miscellaneous notes"). The Brussels Festival stands as one of the high-water marks in the production of an international avant-garde cinema, and Nelson's report is not only reasonably thorough but sometimes embarrassingly candid in a manner that is typical of the not yet politically correct late sixties.

The *Cinemanews* became the place where filmmakers could voice serious concerns over how their films, and independent filmmakers, were treated by exhibitors, distributors, critics, and others, and from time to time, voicing these concerns created controversies that played out in the pages of the *Cinemanews*. By the late 1960s the high hopes of the middle part of the decade, when young men and women could still imagine sustaining lives and careers as avant-garde filmmakers without thinking about anything but making art, had begun to wane. Money for making films and for maintaining a life was increasingly a source of frustration; and one by-product was a tendency to be suspicious of business organizations that claimed to be supporting the field. Robert Nelson's "Open Letter to Film-makers," attacking what he saw as the decadent commercialism of Robert Pike's Creative Film Society, was typical of this attitude. It instigated an impressive response from Pike, who was to become a regular contributor to the *Cinemanews*. Given the desire on the part of some filmmakers who were involved with Canyon to fight for a cinema that was produced without any concern for the marketplace, that was *pure* in some deeply moral sense, anyone interested in running an organization that actually turned a profit could look like a corrupt businessman rather than an ally. Pike's intelligent, practical response to Nelson's attack must have helped put this into perspective for other Canyon members. Nelson's subsequent response to Pike in the September/October 1967 issue—"In reply to Robert Pike's reply to Robert Nelson's open letter to film-makers: I think Robert Pike is cute"—suggests his embarrassment.

The marginal financial health of the avant-garde film world also created controversy among those who were in charge of what seemed to be the most established organizations in the field. The February 1967 issue of the *Cinemanews* included a request from filmmaker Tom Chomont, who was then managing the Film-Makers' Cinematheque in New York City: "Tom Chomont asks that film makers, in order to keep the Film-Makers' Cinematheque alive, allow him to use at least one of their films this year (and following years if possible) without payment. The Cinematheque is in great danger of closing because of debts, and it is hoped that a series of benefits can be scheduled for early March. Write him at 125 W. 41st St., NY 10036." The following issue of the *Cinemanews* included a response from Bruce Conner, arguing that if the Cinematheque could not be run efficiently, it was not up to Canyon members to subsidize incompetence. No response was immediately forthcoming, but when Conner reconfirmed his attack on the New York Cinematheque in May 1969, in a letter to the board of directors of the New York Film-Makers' Cooperative, Jonas Mekas responded to Conner in the *Cinemanews,* firmly but with good (and diplomatic) humor. Unmoved by Mekas's defense, Conner reconfirmed his sense that the Film-Makers' Cooperative and the Film-Makers' Cinematheque were incompetently, even corruptly, run, and he has remained suspicious of Mekas's activities ever since. The Conner-Mekas interchange made enough of an impact that Ed Emshwiller wrote to both the *Cinemanews* and the *Filmmakers' Newsletter,* hoping to resolve the conflict in the interests of the field, calling for "Peace, brothers, peace!" Not surprisingly, even Canyon itself was not entirely free of the suspicion that it was a corrupt business. Ken DeRoux remembers that at some point during the late 1960s Jon Jost was so suspicious that Canyon's books "were being cooked" that for a time Jost "camped outside the Canyon office in his Volkswagen bus to keep an eye on us. We liked Jon, but he drove us crazy" (unpublished interview with DeRoux, January 6, 2006).

One of the strangest controversies that developed in the pages of the *Cinemanews* involved several Chicago organizations competing for the local avant-garde film audience. On October 25, 1966, Jeff Begun of Aardvark wrote to inform *Cinemanews* readers that after an arrest for showing Shirley Clarke's film *The Connection* (1961), which had been banned by the Chicago Film Censor Board, Aardvark had moved to Second City, where it had scheduled a series of Monday evening screenings (the Censor Board had also rejected, then approved on appeal, a series of avant-garde films, including Robert Nelson's *Plastic Haircut* [1963] and *Oh Dem Watermelons*). In April 1967, Begun wrote to announce that Aardvark's new catalog was out (according to Begun, Aardvark was distributing around two hundred films), that the Second City International Short Film Competition was under way, and that Aardvark had a new address, and to tell Canyon readers about another censorship problem: "Big furor in Chicago over film censorship. A group showing films at the Wellington Congregational Church was busted last week for showing Tom Palazzolo's film, *'O,'* without a permit. Police said that we filed a complaint, which is nonsense. What makes it even more ludicrous is that the film has been cleared by the censors, we have a permit, it's available to anyone who wants it, and the police who made the arrest knew all of this."

In the July 1967 *Cinemanews,* John Heinz wrote to explain how he had been working with the Hyde Park Art Center offering a film series that had become so popular that it had to be moved to a nearby theater: the series had included Barbara Rubin's *Christmas on Earth* (1963), Ben Van Meter's *Poon-Tang Trilogy* (1966), and Genet's *Un Chant d'amour.* Heinz indicated that on opening night at the new theater, he had received a call from Jeff Begun tipping him off that the police were planning to bust the screening. After the screening was canceled, Heinz contacted Sergeant James Murphy, "Grand Inquisitor of the Motion Picture Review Section," who told Heinz to go ahead with his screenings but in the future to bring films in for prescreening and licensing. Heinz learned what Begun already knew, that when a film was licensed, potential screening organizations paid a fee that entitled them to exclusive use of the film, though, if they wished, they could sell the rights to others. Since *Oh Dem Watermelons* was one of the films Heinz planned to show, and since it had already been licensed by Aardvark, his group had to buy the rights from Aardvark: "The Aardvarks, by getting permits on every film that they show, are building up a monopoly on the underground film in Chicago."

Frustrated with the complex procedure of either getting licenses from the censor board for each film or contacting the licensee for each film, Heinz moved his series back to the Art Center's sculpture room: "Before our last showing—the films of Ben Van Meter—I got another call from Jeff Begun who politely inquired if the films were going to be licensed; I told him I hadn't decided yet." Two weeks after a successful (unlicensed) screening, Heinz got a call from Sergeant Murphy: "Someone—he refused to say who—had told him that *POON-TANG TRILOGY* had been shown in Hyde Park after it had been refused a license 'And now this other group is complaining,' he said." The other group, Heinz realized, could only be Aardvark: "Nobody else is cooperating with Murphy." In a short note to the *Cinemanews,* Begun denied that he had filed a complaint against the Community Arts people and claimed that the Chicago newspaper reports had been inaccurate.

In the August 1967 issue of the *Cinemanews,* Charles Willoughby Smith, who had set up the Community Art Foundation New City Film Group, wrote that when its April 12 screening was stopped, the film confiscated, and an arrest made, the resulting press coverage resulted in Mayor Daley's sending a letter to the city council, suggesting that the Chicago censorship ordinance be revised to exempt showings connected with religious or educational institutions from the requirement of obtaining permits (licenses). The revisions were passed. A couple of days later, Smith was in San Francisco, where he saw Begun's denial that he had had anything to do with a complaint. "The day after the arrest," Smith explains, "a CBS newsman, Bill Curtis, asked me what my reaction was to the people who filed the complaint. He had a tape with him on which the Corporation Counsel (Ray Simon) said that 'Aardvark complained.' . . . And that is where the Chicago papers got their 'inaccurate stories,' baby, from the man who takes complaints & sends the cops. . . . 'Like, if we burn each other, where we gonna end up.'—Lenny Bruce." On August 16, Begun wrote to the *Cinemanews* that it would be possible "to argue the New City Film group thing for months, but neither Charles Smith, John Heinz, or Aardvark/Second City are trying to screw anyone, so you'll hear no more about it from us."

A similar though less elaborate controversy developed when competing groups attempted to bring American avant-garde film to Japan. In the September/ October 1966 issue of the *Cinemanews,* Takahiko Iimura, who was visiting Harvard University at the time, wrote to let Canyon know that he was touring with some Japanese independent films, and that in Japan the Second Independent Film Festival was being planned for the coming December (the first had shown films by Stan Brakhage, Carl Linder, Robert Nelson, and Donald Richie, among others, including Iimura himself). In 1969, Masanori Oe, Kenji Kanesaka, and Jushin Sato wrote as representatives of the Japan Filmmakers' Co-op to say that the Sogetsu Film Festival (aka the Film Art Festival Tokyo 1969) was a corrupt enterprise, despite Iimura's involvement, and that Canyon should not be involved with it. Early in 1971, Tyushin Sato of the Japanese Underground Center in Tokyo wrote to say that "a few ugly people tried to get hold of the management" and had sent letters to the United States defaming Iimura and the Sogetsu Art Center. Sato had resigned from the Co-op, having "never experienced such an embarrassing situation in my life," and started the Japan Underground Center to distribute the work of Japanese independents. He reported that Iimura had returned the American avant-garde films he had brought back to Japan from America, rather than let the three "schemers" have control of the prints, and requested that American filmmakers trust the Japan Underground Center with their work.

Many of the controversies that erupted in the pages of the *Cinemanews* were a result of the somewhat paradoxical situation avant-garde film and the institutions interested in distributing and exhibiting it were finding themselves in by the late 1960s. On one hand, this new cinema "movement" had developed a substantial reputation; even mainstream magazines included features on it, and a number of its more outrageous partisans had become notorious. Yet, despite the increasing awareness that these films and filmmakers existed—an awareness that had created, for a moment in the mid-1960s, increasing revenues for film rentals and filmmaker appearances—the field was becoming as financially marginal as it was well known. Indeed, throughout what some scholars have seen as a golden age of American independent cinema, the financial fortunes of those committed to this cinema were never more than marginal. These financial concerns begin to show up in the *Cinemanews* in the February/April issue of 1968, in a letter from Loren Sears, bemoaning the disappointing turnout at a recent Canyon Cinema meeting: "The Co-op survives," Sears explains, "only because Edith [Kramer] and a few others put out far more than is reasonably their job. . . . The financial statement for 1967 is groovy: $22,000 gross rentals. But the Co-op 25% amounts to something like $5500. After rent, office expenses, part time office helper, etc., it's rare when Edith's $75/week salary can be paid in full. In other words, we survive because Edith gives."

The difficulty in finding the funds to pay Canyon's single full-time employee her humble wage would become a motif in the minutes of Canyon board meetings published in the *Cinemanews*. In the meantime, Canyon tried various ways of improving its financial situation. Phil Frucht, who did accounting for Canyon

(Frucht worked for nothing, because of his commitment to the organization), had suggested that Canyon change its 75/25 split of rentals and take a larger percentage of the rental moneys. The board resisted this change, though as the years went by, changes in the percentages were made (*Catalog 3* indicates that the filmmaker/Canyon split was 66/33 percent; the fourth catalog, 60/40 percent; the fifth, 65/35 percent; the sixth, 65/35 percent; the seventh, 65/35 percent; and since 2001, when Canyon moved to a more expensive rental space, the split has been 50/50 percent). Other suggestions included having the more successful filmmakers raise their rental rates, working to make previewing films by critics and possible renters easier, and creating a "Blue Plate Special" list of rarely rented films, available at a discount rate. Nevertheless, one of the first orders of business at subsequent board meetings continued to be addressing the injustice of Kramer's salary, to which the board regularly added small raises (sometimes in the face of Kramer's resistance).

From time to time, despite Canyon's marginal finances, the board and membership would try to flex their muscles, but generally this led nowhere. In 1969 the January issue of the *Cinemanews* returned to the issue of film festivals, publishing a "general statement about the need for a film-maker/festival contract." This general statement was a result of suspicions that filmmakers were not receiving just financial compensation from the many film festivals that were now exhibiting avant-garde work. So many festivals seemed to be springing up that Canyon members were concerned that free festival screenings were cutting into their already marginal rentals. The board, in the name of the membership, drafted a set of rules that festivals would need to abide by: the Film-maker's/Festival Contract. The rules included: "1. The Festival agrees to pay rental of $1.00 per minute for each public showing of films"; "2. No entry fees will be paid by the film-maker to the Festival"; "3. Deadline for film arrival at the festival must be no earlier than *one week* before the opening date of the festival. Films must be shipped back to film-maker during the first possible day after the last screening."

Responses to this set of demands on the part of Canyon filmmakers and others were quick in arriving. The February issue of the *Cinemanews* included a letter from filmmaker Bob Cowan, who saw the nine rules as unrealistic and extremely one-sided: "The festival organizers seem to have been left out of the discussion entirely." The following issue included a letter from Mary Jo Malone and Carol Duke, Bellevue Film Festival cochairs, expressing their agreement with Cowan and explaining that had the rules been in effect during the previous festival (Robert Nelson had been the juror), the festival would have been financially wiped out. Despite Lenny Lipton's claim in the same issue that the filmmakers "seem to have won" the battle with film festivals, and that the idea of festivals paying rentals for the films they showed, rather than giving prizes, would become the norm (and would result in festivals becoming noncompetitive), little seems to have come of the Film-maker's/Festival Contract.

At times, keeping Canyon afloat created considerable strain for board members. In the third issue of 1972, for example, the *Cinemanews* published a set of letters under the title "Shit Hits Fan." These letters were instigated by a comment in the minutes for the January 15, 1972, board of directors meeting, relating to the publication of a new catalog (*Catalog 3*) for which Canyon had borrowed from the filmmakers' rental account. The question now was how to pay this money back: "It was suggested that the Board of Directors who disappeared after leaving this economic mess be contacted to help raise the money by donating their time to work at the Cinematheque. Nobody present wanted to ask Bob Nelson, Scott Bartlett, etc. to do this. Soo . . . back to miasma." The suggestion, subsequently attributed to Bruce Conner, created a brief furor, including letters from Nelson, Scott Bartlett, Freude Bartlett, and Ben Van Meter, who explained,

> We could have borrowed $4,500.00 from a bank but that would have tied up the filmmaker's account as collateral *plus* costing us a very high interest rate. Since the balance of the filmmaker's account has not fallen below a figure of $14,200.00 since February 1971, we felt that we could safely borrow without danger of being unable to meet our commitments to the filmmakers. We also have a plan for paying back the loan within six months. (See minutes of last Board meeting—this issue.) We all felt that not getting out a catalogue is much more a threat to the co-op than borrowing the money from ourselves and we were quite pleased with us for having thought of it. If you can think of a better way to finance it, we will be quite pleased with you too.

In the end, Conner apologized to Nelson and the others, but warned,

> Whenever there is a real problem at Canyon it is very difficult to find someone responsible for it and capable of solving the problem. The staff always says that they don't do nothin but follow orders and that they are underpaid and the Board of Directors should solve the problem. I was not present at the first meeting of the present Board of Directors when it proposed and passed that $4,000 should be borrowed from the Filmakers Account to pay for the catalogue. I do not agree with this method of paying for the catalogue, but, no other plans had been organised previously which would have set aside the money from rentals for the catalogue. I think it is very thin ice indeed and it is the same reason why UBU and FILM CANADA and other film groups have gone under . . . by spending the filmaker's money without his consent.

Despite early struggles and periodic infighting, however, by the end of the 1960s there was no question that Canyon had grown important to the field of independent cinema. Its distribution operation was functioning with reasonable efficiency, and the *Cinemanews* was increasingly being used by filmmakers for the publication of essays and other materials that had an importance well beyond the Bay Area film scene, and even beyond the American film scene. By the end of the 1960s there was also a sense, especially among some of those who had played a formative role at Canyon, that in the successful establishment of the organization and in the evolution of the field it served, something important had been gained, but something else, equally important, had passed, or was passing. Robert Nelson sounded this note in the *Cinemanews,* first, in a report he wrote on judging the Bellevue Film Festival, and subsequently in an attempt to decide how he himself was now thinking about Canyon. Others close to Canyon provided their own assessments.

Conversation with Edith Kramer, July 2001

(Kramer became director and senior film curator of the Pacific Film Archive in Berkeley, California, in January 1983; she retired in July 2005)

MacDonald: Robert Nelson and Bruce Conner agreed, in totally separate conversations, that when you were at Canyon, you did all the work, but that you'll never admit you did anything.

Kramer: [laughter] Oh, I'm not so shy.

I find I remember the most fun things or the most ridiculous things from that time, and a lot of the day-to-day just goes out the window. I didn't become involved with Canyon Coop distribution until I came to the Bay area from Eugene, Oregon, over the holiday season at the end of 1966. Canyon had just incorporated that fall. I know they had had a big benefit screening in San Francisco.

When I arrived, the coop had been officially named. I think the bylaws, the letters of incorporation—all that legal stuff was completed. There was a legal entity for distribution, and there were actually films to be distributed. Jonas Mekas agreed to publish the first catalog as an insert in the New York Filmmakers Cooperative catalog. So we had copies of that insert to send out. We were grateful to Jonas and his colleagues because at that time we didn't have a mechanism for making Canyon known.

MacDonald: How did you find your way to Canyon from Eugene?

Kramer: I was teaching art history at the University of Oregon in Eugene, from 1962 to 1966. The Art History Department in Eugene was not in the Humanities

Division of the university, as it usually is; it was a department within the School of Architecture and Allied Arts: painting and sculpture, graphics and design and ceramics—and art history. That meant I was part of an art-making environment, as opposed to a standard academic department. I'm sure that had a lot to do with what I did.

I had gone to Eugene with an interest in film—I've always had an interest in film. And in Eugene I had a certain amount of freedom in terms of teaching. As low person on the totem pole, I had to teach more general courses than the senior faculty, but I could add things if I was willing to take on the work, so I started teaching film history as part of art history.

MacDonald: That's very early to be teaching film history.

Kramer: Yes. I was teaching myself as I was teaching the students. The students were very enthusiastic, and they also wanted to *make* films. There was one faculty member in the Allied Arts who years before had made some films and had some technical expertise. We scrounged 8mm cameras and maybe one 16mm camera.

I showed the films to the students; we talked about films; and we practiced making films. Very crude, but it was history and process rolled into one.

MacDonald: Did you know about experimental film at that point?

Kramer: There was a film society. I got involved with that. I had heard about what was going on in New York, and I remember ordering *Flaming Creatures,* which was banned at that time so you had to get it secretly. Leslie Trumbull at the New York Coop sent me the print in a brown paper wrapper. I told people that we were showing a film and that we could get in trouble, and I arranged to have students guarding the door.

Oregon has always been a very interesting place: you can have simultaneously the most radical, free-spirited sorts of things *and* the most conservative and oppressive. At that time, there was an organization called, I think, Oregon Moms or the Mothers of Oregon. It was superconservative. They had started a campaign against what they thought were inappropriate books in the schools. They sponsored a public burning of Ginsberg's *Howl* on the steps of the student union. That was the conservative side.

But there was also the student awakening, a revolutionary spirit, drugs—a mirror of what was going on in Berkeley. I was young enough to align myself with the students who were revolting. I was from the East, where things were freer, and I was kind of shocked at the repressiveness I had walked into, and wanted to fight back. Showing experimental film was part of that.

I had been teaching early experimental film—what went on in the twenties in the U.S. and in France—as part of my film history course, and certainly saw experimental film as part of film history. But then, at some point, Chick Callenbach and Bruce Baillie came to town and showed some films. I know they showed *Oh Dem Watermelons;* I'm pretty sure we saw *Castro Street,* and I think Conner's *A Movie.* It was a short program.

I was completely fascinated by what I saw. Chick was very articulate about what was going on, and Bruce was very inspiring. It made a terrific impression on me. I linked that with what I was reading and hearing about what was happening in New York—and by 1966 I knew I wanted to get out of Eugene, that it was time to move on.

I loved it in Eugene, but felt very isolated and needed the stimuli of a city. I also knew I had real limitations on my academic abilities, that I would never be able to maintain a faculty position. With a master's degree I could never go further in academe. And I knew I was not going to be a deep scholar; I was not going to publish. My chair was urging me to go back to Harvard and finish my Ph.D.; he said he would give me a leave and hold my job for me. But I knew I had no patience for that. I didn't even think I had the intelligence for it. It just wasn't me.

So the writing was on the wall. I'd been very lucky and had enjoyed teaching, but it was time to do other things and to find out what I *could* do next. And because I was very curious about what Chick and Bruce had shown and said, I thought, "Well, the closest big city is San Francisco—it's not New York, but obviously things are happening there." I already knew about the Art Institute, and I thought, "Maybe I'll take some filmmaking courses; then I'll understand more about what people are doing." So I came to San Francisco in January of 1967 and enrolled in Robert Nelson's class in filmmaking at the Art Institute, and also in a class in still photography.

I was very blunt with Robert: "I'm *not* gonna be a filmmaker. I just want to see what I can learn." The other people in Bob's class—Roy Ramsing, Michael Wiese, Steve Arnold, Al Wong—did go on in filmmaking, making and teaching. I was the only nonfilmmaker in the class, and it was obvious. I mean, I knew I was out of my element: I just wanted to learn what it was like to make a film. I needed to understand the process. So I worked hard, but I knew I wasn't talented, wasn't an artist.

So I went through the course, made my little 8mm films, and a few months later, I was looking for some kind of part-time employment—so I could pay the rent—and I was having a hard time figuring out what I could do. I was teaching some adult education courses at UC [University of California] extension, but that didn't pay very much. One day, Bob asked me if I had any time to volunteer at the

Coop and could I type. I said, "Yeah, not superfast, but I can type; I even know a little bookkeeping." So he asked if I would go over to the Coop, which at that point was in the Bodiens' apartment south of Market, and help them out. Earl and Mary Ann Bodien were officially managing the distribution business, but either they didn't have the clerical skills they needed or they weren't interested in doing clerical work.

So I went over there and sat at a desk and typed up the letters and answered the phone, and filled out the order book. It was very simple—you didn't need to be a business genius or anything. There were so few films that the process was very basic: you get an order; you confirm it; you send out the confirmation; you send out the film; you make a record; you get the check and deposit it—an idiot could have done it. But I could type and I could keep records (you'd never know it to look at my office now!). But *then* I had a filing system; and everything *was* neat and tidy.

I remember that working there was my first experience with cockroaches! And you couldn't get rid of them. I just had to do the work with them running over the desk and in and out of the drawers.

Sometime in the late spring, Earl, who was from somewhere in the Midwest, announced that he wanted to go back to see if it was better to live there. The Bodiens were having some problems—I don't know what they were—and things weren't easy for them; it wasn't easy for anybody then. Certainly there was no money to be made as the manager of the Coop. The Bodiens' apartment was slated for urban renewal anyway, so there was no sense of permanence.

So after Earl went to the Midwest for an exploratory visit, he and his wife decided to pick up and go back to where they were from. That left me alone. I'd finished my course with Nelson and still didn't have a job, so the board asked me if I would assume the responsibility for the distribution business, and they would pay me a salary. So I officially became the manager. Don Lloyd volunteered to be the bookkeeper and help me out. And I think Roy Ramsing was doing film inspection. This is where I get foggy. It's hard to remember who helped with what.

So I was manager, and by the time we got kicked out of the Bodiens' apartment, the board had negotiated with Intersection, which was part of Glide Memorial Methodist Foundation, to get a little space in the basement of 756 Union Street, a defunct church. All the people on the board came in and, in a day or so, put up Sheetrock and framed a little office in the basement, where we moved all the films and my desk and the files.

When we lost the ability to stay at Union Street, Nelson was able to negotiate with the Art Institute to have the screenings there; and I moved the distribution cooperative to a warehouse in Sausalito. Nobody wanted to leave the city, but I couldn't find office space that we could afford: we could only pay twenty dollars a month rent! I found space in an architect's office in an industrial building in Sausalito; she rented us half her office at twenty dollars and then later, thirty dollars, a month.

I'd been living in San Francisco, but I didn't have a car, so I looked for a place in Sausalito and moved over there. But it was difficult. People were upset that I'd moved the office; it wasn't that they couldn't get to Sausalito—most of them had cars—but they felt Canyon had to have a San Francisco presence. I was saying, "Fine! Find us a place we can afford that will be able to accommodate more films, and we'll move back."

MacDonald: Was Canyon growing fast? We're talking 1967–68–69.

Kramer: It had a spurt. Partially it was because there were so many filmmakers visiting San Francisco. The East Coast people were coming out; *everybody* wanted to come out—for the right reasons and the wrong reasons. There was a great deal of activity and craziness and some good things, all mixed up—the music scene, the film scene, poetry. Whenever filmmakers came out, we encouraged them to put their films in the Coop, and they were happy to do that. And because we had screenings, there was a venue for bringing audience in and creating more interest in the films and filmmakers. And more and more people were renting the films.

MacDonald: Were you also involved in the *Cinemanews?*

Kramer: Yeah, but that *was* a cooperative thing. [laughter] Bruce Baillie's *mother* in Berkeley would slave away, typing it up. You'd collect all of the articles and items, and different people would volunteer to mimeograph it, and then we'd have collating parties. Everybody would come in, put the issue together, and get it into the mail. It was a social event. I don't remember when one person stopped doing it and another person started, but somebody always took the leadership role to make sure it got out. Mrs. Baillie, and Emory Menefee for a long time, and Lenny Lipton.

There was a lot of energy in the *Canyon Cinemanews,* but no real organized publishing process. Things happened because, even if people were grumbling and had arguments, they worked together. It certainly wasn't that everybody got along—sometimes there were furious fights, and insults and all of that—but the fact is, people *did* get together to make things happen. There *was* that kind of energy and commitment. You could count on people coming together to do things.

And it was fun. As I look back on it, I remember being worried about the money: sometimes you couldn't write paychecks. But then money would come in and you'd pay the back salaries. There was a lot of pro bono work. A proper CPA, Phil Frucht, donated his time to do the taxes. He's still my accountant. Phil was very sympathetic to what artists were doing, and to anything antiestablishment, and he volunteered his time.

MacDonald: Are there specific moments that stay in your mind as quintessentially Canyon?

Kramer: There was a lot of socializing at Canyon, which was very pleasant and sweet. I got to be friends with people. When we were in the basement of Intersection, there was a little kitchen. I'd get supplies, and people would drop by for lunch. I'm not much of a cook, but I'd make grilled cheese sandwiches, and variations on grilled cheese sandwiches, or tuna fish sandwiches. I remember P. Adams Sitney coming out to visit, and being amazed. He called me a "den mother," or something like that. But it just seemed to me that this was my home, so why *wouldn't* I invite people to have something to eat?

I remember giving Carl Jacobs away as a door prize because he didn't have a place to live. He had come out from New York, film in hand, and had his film shown at the Cinematheque at Intersection on Union Street. At that time, Anne Severson and her daughter April would give away a door prize at the intermission, and I said to Anne, "There's a filmmaker who needs a place to stay, and there's no more room on my floor; let's give him away!" So we did; he went home with some couple. Carl ended up moving to a houseboat in Sausalito. We became very close friends; he'd come to my apartment to use the bathroom and shower, because his houseboat, basically a raft with a hut on it, had no plumbing. I always left food in the refrigerator for him—chocolate pudding.

Ultimately he went back East and ended up becoming a therapist, and I lost track of him. But not long ago, I got a call from New York, asking if this was the Edith Kramer who had given him away at intermission at the Cinematheque—the most embarrassing moment of his life, except for his bar mitzvah. [laughter]

MacDonald: Knowing Robert Nelson a bit, I've always assumed that he was a primary spirit at Canyon, though I know Baillie was important too.

Kramer: By the time I was on the scene, Baillie was a distant force, kind of like Papa sending us letters. Occasionally he was there, but generally he was more detached—but always writing, sending things. Nelson and Conner and Larry Jordan and Lenny Lipton and Ben Van Meter—I saw them *a lot*. They were very present. Some I got closer to than others.

Lenny Lipton was a technical genius, and his willingness to share what he knew with other filmmakers was tremendously important. He built a homemade

CINEMA NEWS
presents
THE MIRABILE DICTU AWARD
to
EDITH KRAMER

for her years of service to the
independent film community

Canyon Cinema Cooperative
San Francisco Museum of Modern Art
Pacific Film Archive

I have heard of the lady, and good works went with her name.
—Measure for Measure, III, 1

Edith Kramer, honored by Diane Kitchen and Gunvor Nelson in *Cinemanews,* 80.3/4/5.

optical printer—and described the process in the *News:* this liberated filmmakers from being technically dependent. Tom DeWitt and Scott Bartlett were like that too: brilliant technical people who could teach others how to do things. That sharing was an important part of the period.

And Emory Menefee was marvelous, a Rock of Gibraltar for us.

You spent so much time in the job that your friendships developed out of it. Of course, I was new to San Francisco, and the people I knew from Canyon were my first friends in the area. I became very very close to Larry Jordan's wife, Patty, the photographer, and their daughter, Lorna. Patty was an earth goddess, the most supportive, giving, loving woman. She wanted to take care of me, and make sure I ate well. In this den of mostly egocentric artist types, she was very much the caregiver and was always reaching out. I spent a lot of time in their home.

MacDonald: Are there particular crises you remember?

Kramer: Money. There were very difficult moments. Every time you knew you had to move, or might have to move, or the rent was going to go up, was a crisis. But the really serious crises came after I left Canyon.

I was there at the easy time, the optimistic beginnings, where the spirit is at its highest and you're not discouraged. I didn't have to deal with the stuff that comes later, when you've reached a certain critical mass and can't conceive of *not* surviving. I'd joke with Bob Nelson, "You know, we're an organization created by the members, to serve the members by doing this function, so if we become incapable of fulfilling that function, we can just commit suicide as an organization." We were both amused by that. Later, when you get institutionalized and are supporting a staff, *then* you have the necessity of keeping the organization going, no matter what. I was preinstitutional. Yes, I gave Canyon some order and some respectability by being responsible, by doing what had to be done, and properly. But I left before it got to be too much of an institution.

MacDonald: Also the collection of films distributed by Canyon got larger and had to be creating new problems, like what do you do when most of the rentals are of films by a small percent of the makers?

Kramer: That was already clear early on. There are always films on the shelf that are not going to be moneymakers; some don't rent at all. It was obvious to me that the money coming in regularly was going to be from rentals of Conner and Nelson and George Kuchar and Lenny Lipton, and a bit later, Scott Bartlett and Tom DeWitt. Twenty-five percent of the membership was going to pay the bills.

MacDonald: In retrospect, it's impressive that the stars didn't just create their own small, exclusive distribution organization; it might have been profitable.

Kramer: I don't know about *that.* Remember, the Coop was nonexclusive. Some of the best-known filmmakers had their films in distribution elsewhere: in other coops; in commercial distribution through Audio-Brandon and the Creative Film Society; Pyramid picked things up. And libraries started buying prints—public libraries, college libraries, even high school libraries.

MacDonald: How long were you at Canyon? What did you do when you left?

Kramer: I wasn't there very long. I started in 1967 and left in 1970, or at the end of 1969.

Afterward, I didn't do anything for a few months—I didn't quite know what I wanted to do—and then I was offered a job at SF MoMA, in the old building, to take charge of a regular film program. Their occasional film presentations had been done through the educational department; films were chosen by a committee of members. They asked if I would take programming on as a paid job, and I agreed, so long as it no longer involved a committee, so long as I had sole responsibility. I worked there for two to three years. Then I went to Europe for a few months, came back, and got a job teaching at UC-Davis: a faculty member was on sabbatical, and they needed somebody to teach a basic course in film history. Then the person on leave extended his leave, and I stayed there for a year and a half.

And then I came to PFA—at the end of 1974 or the beginning of 1975—as Tom Luddy's assistant. Sheldon Renan was the founding director. He had brought Tom in as programmer. By the time I came on board, Sheldon wanted to leave; and Tom would become director, so it was really Tom who hired me. My specific assignment was to do the avant-garde programming and to buy a collection of avant-garde films for the Archive, and to be general assistant to Tom.

I'm a cynical New Yorker. And even during the most optimistic of moments in the sixties, I was *never* a California dreamer. But I did love the notion of collective, cooperative work. In my *heart* I always wanted that to work; but my *mind* was totally cynical. I knew intellectually that there were moments when these things could flower and people would get behind them, and that in time the honeymoon would be over. I love the moment when people have their idealism, but I also know it doesn't last, at least not for most people: it's there's for a time and then you get more practical.

I'd look at filmmakers who had these visions of the future—they were going to change Hollywood: "People are going to realize that *this* is what film is!"—and I'd think, "Dream away." I never believed we were going to change the status quo. Yes, obviously the mainstream cinema has appropriated what the Canyon filmmakers did—absolutely. We were seeing the appropriation right then, day by day, in advertising and in mainstream cinema. You can look through the Canyon records to see who rented what; the films didn't just go to teachers or little cinema clubs, they were seen by people in the business.

Also, the CIA and the FBI rented some of our films. In the sixties organizations like ours were suspect, and so all of our activities were closely monitored. And what filmmakers made was monitored. We were on lists. It was all part of the government's surveillance of antigovernment elements. It was perfectly reasonable. Why *wouldn't* they monitor us?

When I was at SF MoMA doing the film series, an FBI agent came to me, showed me photographs, and asked me if I recognized anybody. Long hair, beads, tie-dyed clothes. I said, "No, but why are you asking me?" "We want to know if these people are frequenting your audience; you're showing certain kinds of films that we think the people we're looking for are likely to attend." And I said, "Well, they look like everybody else; I haven't the slightest idea if they come to the films I show or not." They were looking for the Weathermen. And I realized, they're not looking just at *us* for showing or distributing or making; they're looking at our *audiences!* It was all part of the climate of those years.

Amazingly, we weren't paranoid; the authorities were—but we knew we were on the high road. It was a moment when a lot of people were encouraged to reinvent their lives, to experiment and create new possibilities. It didn't seem to matter so much if you failed; you could do something else. You weren't required to succeed. That sense of possibility and lack of a fear of failure stay with me.

I've always had both an idealistic side and a cynical side. I love to see people working together; I love to see people volunteering, rather than having to get paid. I love to see that spirit of creating your own jobs and your own ways of doing things. I love the notion of change and rebelling and starting something new. I think it's healthy. Of course, people *do* keep reinventing the wheel—see, that's my cynical side. But my idealistic side thinks, "Oh, yes, but that's OK, it's *their turn.*" I had my turn, and it was delicious.

PORTFOLIO

FROM *CANYON CINEMA NEWS*, FEBRUARY 1967

Bruce Baillie

LETTER FROM CHAPALA, MEXICO, JAN. 24 OR SO

Much coming in thru eye holes here, little going out — tho I even try to "memorize" ways to get my robot-like flesh and blood form to expel all these stimuli — all this loveliness and serpentine violence — I cannot.

Yesterday I bought 6 rolls of Kodachrome in Guadalajara, for $1,035.00 Mexican dollars. I also had a steam bath & shot some more in the huge common market there. The girls in food booths throw meat and radishes at men passing by, saying "Psst, Psst, fish? white fish? beer? — hey —"

Here, in Chapala, I have vague hopes of being admitted into a family, where I can have a pad in the corner, & where on identical lovely mornings I can practice my lust through my camera. Otherwise I will get crazy and have to be sent home by the authorities.

Tulley & I still working on the long B&W film, which appears to be shaping into a combination of movie and literature, kind of the way Robbe-Grillet & Resnais worked together, only not visually so strong, or stylized, or interesting.

I got picked up by 4 rich people the other eve., the lady in the front of the Mercedes making the invitation. I had *no* $ in my pockets — they said I was their guest, they liked beatniks. We got to Guadalajara — the 2 ladies had to be let out because they were incapacitated by brandy and pessi. We rode all over town — I took 8 pp. of notes for a possible 35 mm film. They let me out at 3 a.m. with 10 pesos 45 miles from home.

—

FROM *CANYON CINEMA NEWS*, MARCH / APRIL 1967

Bruce Conner

LETTER FROM SAN FRANCISCO, FEBRUARY 18, 1967

In the February issue Tom Chomont requested that film makers, in order to keep the Film-Makers' Cinematheque alive, allow him to use at least one of their films this year without payment.

I recently presented two programs of my films at the Cinematheque and discovered some defects in the organization which are responsible for this:

1. The projection booth is open to all comers. $3,000 worth of equipment has been lost in 6 months.

2. Programs are poorly publicized. The listing of programs in the Village Voice presents the program for one week starting with Wednesday. Most copies of the Voice are not on the stands until Thursday.

3. Tickets are sold in the lobby. No one takes tickets. Ticket purchasers wander through the lobby and go into the theater when they wish to. Anyone who does not wish to buy a ticket can wander the lobby and go in without being bothered. Film-makers, friends and relatives of the Cinematheque walk in free. The theater appears to hold a couple of hundred people.

The Cinematheque guarantees the film-maker a minimum of $25. The Cinematheque deducts expenses of $120.00 from the gross sales.

I was informed that my program was very well attended and it was necessary to look closely in order to see any empty seats in the auditorium. It appears to be unusual to have such good attendance at the Cinematheque. After the performance I learned that there were only 93 paying customers at $1.50 which equals $139.50. Deduct $120.00 from this amount and you discover what the more commercially successful evening at the Cinematheque can net you for two programs of films.

If the Cinematheque can not re-organize their method of presenting film I would suggest that film-makers expect the Cinematheque to pay straight rentals for the films they show, which is what a film society in Keokuk, Iowa, the National Council of Churches, or the CIA would have to do.

—

FROM *CANYON CINEMANEWS*, JULY 1967

Robert Nelson
OPEN LETTER TO FILM-MAKERS, JUNE 12, 1967

The co-op system for distributing our films that started with the "Mother" organization in NY and which is now becoming an international network, gives us our only real hope of remaining independent and receiving fair treatment for ourselves and our films. Our youth and idealism can keep us free from the disease of commercialism. The commercial world has a list of priorities: money at the top, we and our films at the bottom.

Last year I made the mistake of selling to Robert Pike prints of some of my films (Robert Pike, director of Creative Film Society, Van Nuys, Calif.). For various reasons I became unhappy with the arrangements and one month ago I tried to buy

Cover of July 1967 *Cinemanews* (film take-up reel as Buddhist Wheel of Life?), designed by Mary Ann Bodien; the opening item in the text of this issue is the announcement that Earl Bodien "has resigned as manager of the Canyon Cinema Co-op. Until he and Mary Ann leave for Wisconsin in August, she will handle bookings, etc. After that, Edith Cramer [Kramer] is taking over as manager, with Roy Ramsing putting in part time."

them back. I offered to purchase them one-at-a-time, whenever I had enough money. I offered to pay him the same price as he had paid me and to honor all outstanding bookings — with the rental money from those bookings going to him. In effect, he would have had the films and all rentals free from the time he bought them until I bought them back. He refused to sell me back my films under any conditions.

I also learned that he was in the habit of "renting" (as he calls it) stills from films he distributes. I wrote and asked him not to "rent" or sell any stills from my films. Yesterday I found out that he had gotten paid for the exact duplicates of stills that I had sent to Playboy Magazine (for their recent article on Underground Cinema).

> (from Playboy, June 9, 1967) "In reply to your questions about payment for the two stills used in the April installment of 'Sex in Cinema,' first of all, we returned your prints to you with a letter to the effect that they were not used. This means that we did not reproduce from the pictures submitted by you. The two pictures used from OILEY PELOSO THE PUMPH MAN and OH DEM WATERMELONS, that is the two pictures from which we actually reproduced, came to us from Robert Pike and Gideon Bachmann. In my original letter to you regarding payments, I stated that it was our policy to pay for all published photographs from those which you would submit to us. Unfortunately, we did not actually use your pictures in the layout but pictures from Pike and Bachmann which duplicated those you sent us."

I have never heard of Gideon Bachmann and I have no idea how he got his hands on stills from my movies. I do know how Pike got *his* hands on them.

The following quotes are from correspondence that I have had with Robert Pike regarding purchasing prints from me for his distribution. I think the quotes speak for themselves. I hope that they say something to you so that you will not be blinded, as I was, by double-talk and the need for money, and thereby put your films in the hands of business people who, despite their protestations, always place money first. Don't betray yourself or your films. The co-op system hasn't lost sight of us . . . *we* are the co-op.

> (from Robert Pike, CFS, March 31, 1966) "I am writing a series of articles on film for various local magazines. For an article on the current experimental film scene I need provocative stills, as many as possible."
>
> (from Robert Pike, CFS, April 18, 1966) "As for why I won't pay full purchase price for films when I buy them outright, there are many reasons, all valid: (1) The CFS library and volume of business is relatively small; therefore, I can't afford to lay out any more money than absolutely necessary; (2) Most distributors offer sales discounts to other distributors; almost all of the films in our library purchased outright from other distributors and/or individual filmartists were purchased at a dealers discount; (3) When representing a film for sale as well as for rental we have to utilize

our rental prints for free purchase previews, tying them up for weeks without receiving any remuneration for our time and trouble. This is offset by the discount we received when purchasing the prints. Virtually all distributors receive their rental prints at a discount when representing the films for sale as well as rental."

(from Robert Pike, CFS, May 14, 1966) "Regarding your films, in each case I felt that the heavy hand of an editor was needed to eliminate what I considered overly repetitious material and overly long sequences. In my opinion they will not stand the test of time as polished works of film art."

(from Robert Pike, CFS, July 27, 1966) "As for rental and sale prices, naturally I will be consistent with your rate, as I have no desire to undercut you. Our only difference seems to be that I allow two screenings during the one day for the basic rate, rather than one. I charge an extra 50% for 3–5 screenings over a one-day period."

(from Robert Pike, CFS, May 6, 1967) "Therefore, in answer to your inquiry: no, we do not sell stills from your films. We *do* rent them."

Your films are made of love. Don't put them into the hands of people who are in the business of selling love.

— R.N., *June 12, 1967*

Bruce Baillie
LETTER

My studio moved to parents' — me living in little grove trees, temporarily, day-day, with tall girl who is friendly. Have horse over wire fence next place/neighbor's. . . . She is Valentina, named with the making of my nice new film, *VALENTIN DES LAS SIERRAS* — all stuffed away in middle of being done. Can't find way, place, reason, to be in way, place, reason to be continuing what I am doing. So in middle of having not even a pair of pants again (last bought in Ft. Bragg, wore out in Mexico, oh not so long ago (sounds like old man in "Q.")). — and in middle of woods and in middle of time, I run into (today) another one to make, a second "show leader" — to intro. shows . . . other was naked in stream, etc. — ever see it? Banned in Stockton. Anyway, of me getting off horse, picking up recorder, talking — then going on to introduce all the current people and creatures in my no-life — winding up with serial-type summary of charac's., with titles under each, of name — tech. well known to each of us. I think I'll do it. Meantime, am out of forest one day, doing bus. — using type. — going Seattle — U. of Wash. — by airplane tomorrow to be famous one day only. Then back and do leader for one wk. while trying to circle in on that elusive threshold landing place where I'll be doing — as I visualize — my already shot and rec. films, just waiting for me like babies to make.

—

FROM *CANYON CINEMANEWS,* AUGUST 1967

Robert Pike

REBUTTAL TO ROBT. NELSON'S "OPEN LETTER TO FILM-MAKERS"

In the last issue of Canyon Cinema News, an Open Letter to Film-makers from Robert Nelson was printed in which Nelson attacked the Creative Film Society and all other experimental film distributors — except the NY and Canyon Cinema Co-ops — as being commercial organizations who "are in the business of selling love." The gist of Nelson's Letter was that only the Co-ops give a damn about the welfare of the filmartist and that all other distributors are merely interested in the money they can make from the filmartist's work. Nelson went on, quoting letters out of context he had received from the Creative Film Society, to infer that the CFS was a typical example of a cold-blooded commercial distribution organization.

Such an attack is both unfair and untrue. Moreover, it is typical of the modern generation of filmartists who believe that the history of film-art began in 1960 with New American Cinema and the Co-ops, and that before them there was nothing.

To place the Co-ops and New American Cinema in their proper perspective, once and for all, and to correct the injustice done by Nelson to the other experimental film distributors, I welcome this opportunity to answer his Open Letter completely and objectively.

First of all, I think it is necessary to explore the true history of the "co-op" in relation to American experimental film history; as contrary to Nelson's inference, co-ops did exist prior to the present one founded by Jonas Mekas.

The first distribution of national importance regarding experimental films in this country was done by the NY Museum of Modern Art in the early 1940s. It was through their distribution of the experimental films produced in the 1920s and 30s that Kenneth Anger, Curtis Harrington, Jordan Belson, Harry Smith, James Broughton, Sidney Peterson, Frank Stauffacher and others received their orientation and enthusiasm for experimental film production, exhibition and distribution. As a result, Anger made FIREWORKS, Harrington made FRAGMENT OF SEEKING, Broughton and Peterson made THE POTTED PSALM, Belson made IMPROVISATION #1, etc. It was at this time that Maya Deren and her husband, Alexander Hammid, were in Los Angeles making MESHES OF THE AFTERNOON and AT LAND, returning ultimately to NY, where they finished them and exhibited them successfully at the Provincetown Playhouse.

As a result of these activities, Anger and Harrington formed the first distribution co-op, Creative Film Associates, through which they distributed their own and other filmartists' work. However, being more interested in film production than distribution, their organization was not a lasting one. In the meantime, in NY, the Provincetown Playhouse showings were so successful that they were taken over by Amos Vogel who — like Jonas Mekas — had recently come to this country from abroad, filled with enthusiasm and vitality. Maya Deren went back to producing films, while Vogel continued her work in exhibiting them. He then set up Cinema 16 as the first major American distribution organization specializing in experimental films.

In the meantime, Frank Stauffacher convinced the SF Museum of Art to begin a series of festivals in 1946 entitled ART IN CINEMA. This series, which lasted until his untimely death in 1954, was as influential in stimulating experimental film production during its time as the present Co-ops are today. Stauffacher also distributed current experimental films through the SF Museum. When he died, many of these films were distributed by Kinesis in SF, then Film Images in NY, where most of them are today.

By the late 1950s, there were essentially only three American national distributors available for experimental filmmakers: Cinema 16, Brandon Films, and Film Images. Each required exclusive distribution in all media for 5–11 years, with the filmmaker depositing 3–5 prints at his own expense, along with his master printing materials, in return for 50% of the profits. Because these contractual terms were so difficult to accept, the Creative Film Society was formed in 1957, offering terms as varied and liberal as the present Co-ops, but offering the usual 50% of profits to the filmmaker, or the alternate choice of purchasing its rental prints outright. The CFS became the primary distribution source for John and James Whitney, Jordan Belson, Bruce Conner, and many other West Coast filmartists.

In the early 1960s, the present Co-ops began forming, offering the filmmaker an unprecedented 75% of the profits, with the more recent entry, Aardvark Films, offering 66 2/3%, and the most recent entry, the Canadian Film Co-op, offering the more realistic 50%.

Because of the tremendous current interest in New American Cinema — primarily due to the effective drum-beating of Jonas Mekas and the notoriety of such films as FLAMING CREATURES, SCORPIO RISING, COSMIC RAY, and THE CHELSEA GIRLS, experimental filmmakers have the mistaken notion that everyone but them is getting rich quick on their work. Unfortunately, this is not the case at all. Some exhibitors are making a small profit. Some distributors are making a small profit. And even some filmmakers are making a small profit. But the profits, in relation to the expenses, are too small to be exciting. I know of no exhibitor or distributor specializing in experimental films — including the Co-ops and the Filmmakers Cinematheque — who are making enough profit to warrant subsidizing experimental film work on even a modest scale. And believe me, if the potential profits were there, it would be good business for distributors and exhibitors to advance money on such projects!

At best, a little money is being advanced to aid in the completion of films. SCORPIO RISING was completed on CFS equipment with the aid of CFS and NY Co-op money . . . with no strings attached. Bruce Baillie, one of the heads of the Canyon Cinema Co-op, has expressed his gratitude to Willard Morrison of Audio Film Center, one of the current leading "commercial" distributors handling experimental films, for Morrison's unstinting financial aid when no-one else was willing to lend a hand.

If Nelson's accusations were well-founded about all experimental film distributors other than the Co-ops being cold-blooded vampires, sucking the lifeblood out of the filmmakers they represent, then it would stand to reason that no experienced film artist would deal with them, as the Co-ops offer 25% more profit and less rigid terms. But let's look at the present situation: Stan Vanderbeek, Ed Emshwiller, and Robert Breer are three of the leaders of the NY Co-op, yet each of them is also represented by Cinema 16. Vanderbeek is also represented on a percentage basis by the CFS, Emshwiller is considering representation by the CFS on a percentage basis, and Breer is willing to sell rental prints outright to the CFS. Robert Nelson, Bruce Baillie, Larry Jordan, and Ben Van Meter are leaders of the Canyon Cinema Co-op, yet Nelson, Baillie, Jordan, and Van Meter are also represented by Audio Film Center — a competitive "commercial" distributor in the same city! Nelson, Van Meter, and Jordan have also sold rental prints outright to the CFS. And Nelson has sold prints to Aardvark Films as well. Other strong Co-op supporters include Carl Linder, Stan Brakhage, and Kenneth Anger. Yet Linder also works on a percentage basis with the CFS, while Brakhage and Anger have sold rental prints outright to the CFS.

While it is theoretically true that the Co-ops in offering filmmakers loose contractual terms and 75% of the profits are the most tempting distribution representative, the other — "commercial" — distributors must also be offering something substantial if they can continue to represent this country's most outstanding filmartists at the lower rate of 50%.

What can these so-called "commercial" distributors possibly offer that keeps Emshwiller, Vanderbeek, Conner, Breer, Nelson, Van Meter, Anger, and so many others willing to split their distribution between them and the Co-ops? Could it be possible that these "commercial" distributors are not quite as cold-blooded as Nelson infers? That they might just possibly be as interested in the welfare of the filmartist as are the Co-ops but are merely going about it in a more businesslike manner? Could it be possible that even though they offer only 50% they also offer more efficient service to their customers? Whatever the reason, suffice it to say that the top filmartists in the country are convinced that such a reason (or reasons) exists.

Now, what about Nelson's other gripes. One of his major personal beefs was that after selling rental prints outright to the CFS, we refused to sell them back to him when — one year later — he wanted to buy them back. As far as I'm concerned, this was merely a case of Nelson's wanting to have his cake and eat it too. He had a choice of selling prints outright to the CFS or depositing them on a percentage basis. He preferred the quick, easy profit of outright sale. A year later, when those profits were long gone, Nelson realized that the CFS rental prints on which he was making no further profit were competing with the Canyon Cinema Co-op prints on which he was making 75% of the profits. He therefore decided to try to buy back the CFS prints in an effort to eliminate the competition — so that he could have the greatest profit in the long run. A straight business motive, in our opinion, which was refused for the same reason.

If Nelson's reasons had been other than purely business, if he had needed to withdraw his films completely from circulation for legal reasons or to enable him to sell them outright for a large profit, we would have gladly cooperated. In the past, we sold back our rental prints to Bruce Conner and John Schmitz for such reasons on a purely voluntary basis. But for Nelson to expect the CFS to sell him back his prints just so we could be eliminated as business competitors to the Canyon Cinema Co-op was a request we had to consider in the same light as it was being made. And for that reason his request was denied.

I think it is a good time to discuss briefly for the benefit of new filmmakers the advantages vs. disadvantages of selling rental prints outright. It you want a fast profit, or aren't sure that your films will rent well, or need money, sell prints outright to a distributor such as the CFS on a non-exclusive basis. You will still be free to have the Co-ops and other distributors represent you on a percentage basis. On the other hand, if you have confidence that in the long run your films will rent well, deposit prints with as many non-exclusive experimental film distributors simultaneously as you can, as each distributor has his own share of loyal customers; thus, your films will ultimately be rented to the greatest number of people.

Nelson's next gripe was that the CFS had rented a still from one of Nelson's films to PLAYBOY, cutting Nelson out of the rental fee for the same still he submitted to them. Nelson made quite a point of inferring that the CFS policy of renting film stills was a typical example of cold-blooded commercialism. Maybe yes; maybe no; it depends on how realistic you are. Every film distributor has as one of his basic functions the promotion of the films he represents. For this promotion work, he normally has a set of stills on each film he distributes. These stills are used to service requests from magazine and book publishers as well as his regular customers who may need them for display or publicity brochures. The distributor has a choice of supplying the stills free of charge or for a charge. Since the distributor has to pay the cost for making up duplicate prints of the stills, I feel it stands to reason that he should charge for their use except in certain instances where the prestige exposure warrants free cooperation. Otherwise, if the stills are provided free of charge to every requested user, the distributor would be besieged with requests for them, just as he would be for his films if he allowed them to be used free of charge.

The case of PLAYBOY was an unusual one, and had Nelson merely informed the CFS that he had also submitted his own still copies to them, we would have automatically forwarded the rental fee to him. Instead, he chose to write an Open Letter without even bothering to first inform us of the situation.

Nelson's final gripe with the CFS is a rather curious one, yet it should be dealt with, as I believe it reflects upon the whole attitude of his Open Letter. In one of the out-of-context quotes he referred to, taken from a letter to him from the CFS, he quoted me as writing: "Regarding your films, in each case I felt that the heavy hand of an editor was needed to eliminate what I considered overly repetitious material and overly long sequences. In my opinion they will not stand the test of time as polished works of film art."

Presumably, by quoting that portion of my letter to him, Nelson was inferring that the CFS was not a good distributor because we found his films to be less than perfect. Of course, the CFS does differ in its distribution policy from the Co-ops in this respect. If we do not feel an experimental film is up to our quality standards, we will not represent it. The Co-ops feel that such quality decisions should be left entirely up to their customers and therefore are willing to distribute every film offered to them. I see nothing wrong with either policy and feel there is a valid place for both. Nelson, it would seem, disagrees.

In quoting from my letter out-of-context, Nelson, however, omits several important points. First, he neglects to mention that in spite of my criticism of his films he was perfectly willing to sell prints of them to CFS anyway. So it would seem that at the time my letter was written to him, he accepted the criticism in the spirit in which it was intended. Second, while Nelson's out-of-context quote was accurate on a word-for-word basis, it hardly gives the correct impression of the overall exchange of thoughts, which went like this:

(CFS) "My reaction to your films, unfortunately, is what you had anticipated. Either I am behind the times, you are ahead of them, or the times call for vast differences in viewpoint as to what constitutes finished motion pictures. Be that as it may, again let me wish you congratulations on the enthusiastic response to your work which you have been receiving, and continued success in your filmic endeavors. While I may not agree with a film-artist's approach to his medium, I support his efforts in spirit, so long as his work is produced with sincerity. For this reason, if I can be of any help in any way in the future, don't hesitate to call on me."

(NELSON) "As for your not liking my films, well you're certainly not alone. Yes, it is true, I have received a great deal of enthusiastic response and the films have been very successful . . . but despite that, there have been many many people, like yourself, that haven't liked them . . . I think that whatever 'popular' appeal that they do have, doesn't necessarily make them 'good' films. As a matter of fact, as we both know, it may be the opposite. The really good films are not always easy to respond to or like and are not usually 'popular' with any audience. You speak of 'sincerity' and perhaps there lies the key to your response to my films, because they are, in many respects, insincere. From the beginning they are conceived insincerely and with many of them as they proceed they become more insincere until finally, when completed, they are almost totally insincere (this varies with different films . . . but only slightly)."

(CFS) "Regarding your films, I must say that each had certain very memorable moments and/or ideas. I got quite a kick out of the girls on the swing and the sequences with Ron Davis in OILEY PELOSO; I thought that OH DEM WATER-MELONS was a potentially great idea; and PLASTIC HAIRCUT could have been good modern avantgarde stuff. But in each case I felt that the heavy hand of an editor was needed to eliminate what I considered overly repetitious material and overly long sequences. If OILEY PELOSO and PLASTIC HAIRCUT were each cut down to their best 7–8 minutes and WATERMELONS cut down to 5 minutes, I think they'd become classics comparable to THE LEAD SHOES instead of just shocking New American Cinema that appeals to today's "hip" set but — in my opinion — will not stand the test of time as polished works of film art."

(NELSON) "I think you have hit the nail on the head this time, i.e., the Test of Time! If I can be forgiven for stretching a metaphor, I think that my films have gotten a quite 'good grade' on a daily quiz . . . or at most a midterm. By the time the finals come around, I will have failed . . . failed the Test of Time. It's like the 'big talkers' who come on strong in the beginning, but have nothing to say when the chips are down. Those with polish go unnoticed in the beginning but their truth eventually proves stronger than a hundred big mouths. Five years from now, anyone that remembers WATERMELONS will probably do so with a sneer."

Was Nelson being sincere in his letters, or were they just a "put-on"? By the same token, was he being sincere in his Open Letter, or was it, too, just a "put-on"? It doesn't really matter which. What does matter is that Nelson's accusation that distributors other than the Co-ops are "people who are in the business of selling love" is neither true nor fair. If his Open Letter is a "put-on," then it should be put down.

—

FROM *CANYON CINEMANEWS,* SEPTEMBER / OCTOBER 1967

Bruce Baillie

BRUCE BAILLIE'S PREJUDICED GUIDE TO FILM FESTIVALS

from the 8 & 16mm independents' ("new Amer. Cinema," etc.) point of view, keeping in mind that the festivals change from year to year, with new management,
changes of attitude or regulations:

> R– Recommended
> O– Okay
> N– Not recommended until further notice.
> AN– Absolutely not recommended until further notice.

R   Sogetsu Art Center, Tokyo, Japan (first year, Nov., 1967) See details this
      issue of NEWS. They are making a strong invitation to new American &
      new Japanese film-makers. We recommend everyone send current or past
      work not recently shown before.

R   IVth International Experimental Film Festival, Brussels, Belgium Dec.
      1967.

R   1968 Ann Arbor Film Festival (& tour). With the following exceptions, if
      they are included next year (which can be stipulated on entry forms):

> AN   Sacred Heart College, Newton, Mass. (see above).
> N   Mills College (festival held in obscurity).
> N   San Francisco Museum of Art.

R   Montreal International Film Festival.

O   New York Film Festival.

O   Oberhausen Festival.

O   16mm Festival at Annecy, France.

O-R   Bellevue Film Festival, Bellevue, Washington. Held first time with consid-
      erable success (i.e., arc proj., good adv., in good spirit) this past July.

O   Vancouver International Film Festival, Oct. Special invitation this year to
      "exper." film-makers. Not given R because of "European" type attitude in
      past. May be good this year.

N   Tours, France.

N   Mannheim, Germany.

N   Cracow, Poland. In spite of the good film situation in Poland, the Cracow
      International Short Film Comp. still represents traditional European
      stiffness.

N   S.F. International Film Festival, "film as Art" comp. (16 mm). Although this festival is often managed by an excellent group of film people (different each year), its policies originate from indifferent, ignorant business people who consistently make the basic error of not referring to the *source* (film-maker) for what is needed in this special aspect of the SF festival. We are sorry to make a non-recommendation, in the light of hard work & honest interest on the part of this year's Film as Art Comp. directors — who took over only after basic policy had been established ($25 entry fee, etc.).

N,R   Independent Film-Makers Festival, Foothill College

> N — for Independent film artists
> R — for college & univ. film-makers & students' work — documentary, etc.

General recommendations: Include 8mm in U.S. festivals. Provos in Holland start film festival. See May issue for advice on setting up festivals.

—

FROM *CANYON CINEMANEWS*, NOVEMBER 1967

Emory Menefee

Book Review Section: AN INTRODUCTION TO THE AMERICAN UNDERGROUND FILM, by Sheldon Renan. E. P. Dutton Paperback, D-207. $2.25.

This is the first book on "underground" movies to be written, so some of its shortcomings can be passed by on this reason — a lot of work went into this book, and it's unreasonable to expect everything to be there. It is unfortunate that the word "underground," with all its dark hint, has to be the one most favored by those publicizing independent films — though there is no adequate substitute (a lifetime NEWS subscription to whoever discovers or invents the proper term [in the following issue of the *Cinemanews* Menefee would include this item: "The name came in a flash: UNDEPENDENT — for the independent underground. And for the "sexploitation" opuses, same name except spelled Undiependent. — em"]). Into the book itself, one finds that there is some tendency toward personality cultism: considerable space given to a few film-makers and a selection of the rest relegated to listing by name in a couple of paragraphs. A little less non-essential prose in other parts would have left ample space for a line or so about most of the film-makers now working, maybe just a mention of a film or two, whether working in 8mm, favorite hobbies, etc. But to me the most serious problem of Renan's book is that it really isn't *about* the films; that is, there is little attempt at all to evoke any really critical opinion. This is a crucial problem that desperately needs attention, with hundreds of films being made every year and all kinds of attempts being made to promote them.

Nobody close to the independent film scene can find the book wholly satisfactory, but it will be of great value in film classes and as a rough guide to fairly inexperienced viewers, which is no doubt its intention. The perversity of the subject is perhaps best shown in the excellent chapter on expanded cinema, probably the most difficult to write. Anyway, everybody interested in film should have a copy of AN INTRODUCTION TO AMERICAN UNDERGROUND FILM: there are sure to be a few things in it he didn't know.

—

FROM *CANYON CINEMANEWS*, DECEMBER 1967 / JANUARY 1968

Will Hindle

LETTER

Wild '67. After years of timidity, hoping to earn a living and also keep the true and pure love that went into *PASTORALE* and *catholicam* I split open. Out came the rust and frustration called *29:MERCI MERCI.* A rude, polyleveled, much-hated non film that took four Ann Arbor Tour prizes and then was signed for a year long national tour. Wild '67.

FFFTCM came next in mid-'67 and was a crackling about-face. Violently pro life . . . pro being, pro go, pro the right to search for and attaining of work. Not meant to be distributed but a Lenny Lipton review brought it out. More than one person has seen it to be orgasm-istic. In his new book R. Pike of Creative Films calls it a statement on "male masturbation." Wild '67.

CHINESE FIREDRILL is 90 per cent filmed. Color. About 30 minutes. Filmed on a set built in a warehouse in downtown S.F. Outside of some Baillie footage in the early '60s this is the first time I've allowed anyone to be my cameraman . . . had to, I was in the picture. Set up positions, angles, pan pace and limits, etc. Can't praise William Hunter and John Schofill enough. Took direction beautifully, accurately and with a sensitivity and enthusiasm they themselves said they'd never before felt. Many people (another first time) in the film but briefly as gashes of memories or visions. Centers around the malestrom in a room/cell/universe inhabited by an Hungarian-Gypsy type. Disjointed. Editing will take it even farther out. Wild '67.

My association with NET/ITV/KQED is waxing very good. Fine film people down the hall like Allen Willis, Blair Stapp, Seth Hill, Jan Graham. Have my own separate ITV Film Department. Hope the budget soon allows the bringing in of additional good people. Have contracted to bring the coming Ann Arbor Tour to KQED in conjunction with U.C. and S.F. State showings. Manupelli in hearty agreement. Will try to get my weekly color series far enough ahead at the station so that I can go ahead with the production of a rather definitive show (or shows) concerning Art and Experimental Films. To be shown at AAFF time. Want to show film makers, to hear them at work or just resting. Approaches. Results. Integrity and/or devotion. Hardships. Rewards. Budget may afford some New York Scene shooting, probing. Certainly the S.F. area makers will make it and that includes the unheralded. Distributors, perhaps critics. Wild year.

—

FROM *CANYON CINEMANEWS*, JANUARY / FEBRUARY 1968

Robert Nelson
THE BRUSSELS FESTIVAL

Gunvor & I finished a hectic week at the Brussels festival. Here is a list of the prize winners, films I liked, & a short general survey:

Winners of the Brussels festival:
Grand Prize, $4000: WAVELENGTH, Michael Snow.
2nd Prizes, $2000 each:
     SELBSTSCHUSSE, Lutz Mommartz.
     GRATEFUL DEAD, Robert Nelson.
     To Ake Arenhill for his TV graphic research.
     To Stephen Dwoskin for all his submitted films.
3rd Prizes:
     WARUM HAST DU MICH WACH GEKUSST?, Hellmuth Costard.
     HUMMINGBIRD, Charles Csuri and James Shaffer.
     FOG PUMAS, Gunvor Nelson and Dorothy Wiley.
     ENTRETIEN, Michel Thirionet.
     SELF-OBLITERATION, Jud Yalkut.
International Federation of Cine-Clubs special prize to THE ROOM, by Mordi
     Gerstein.
Selection Jury prize to ALTISONANS, Karl-Birger Blomdahl.
Age d'or Prize to THE BIG SHAVE, by Martin Scorsese.

Films that I liked (not in any order):
MAE EAST, 5 min. B/W, Cassandra Gerstein, 250 Riverside Dr., NY. Sensuous
     fruity big nubes. Split screen 4 images. Music by Rolling Stones.

ERLEBNISSE DER PUPPE, 11 min. B/W, Franz Winzentsen, Hassenhöhe 35, Hamburg 55, Germany. Animated photographs. Surreal/funny. Girl with elephant legs tramps through some weird places.

MAKE LOVE NOT WAR, 11 min., Color, Ben Van Meter, 605 Grove St., San Francisco, Calif. One of the best films of the festival. Ben's "river of images" really flowing smoothly . . . carries you in a rubber raft over the rapids of joy.

DAVID HOLZMAN'S DIARY, 72 min., B/W, Jim McBride, 224 Kane St., Brooklyn, NY. A guy films himself (his diary) for days until his Eclaire and Nagra are stolen (faked but almost believable). Some really great moments. Touching portrait of a fucked-up self search.

WEEKEND, 19 min., B/W, David McNeill, 39 rue du Repos, Brussels 18, Belgium. Nice romp through a world full of Rube Goldberg devices, then to a jungle trek, then to paradise . . . good/comic.

1933, 4 min., Joyce Wieland, Box 199, Church St. Station, NY 10008. Strange magic worked by simple associations.

DAS GESICHT DER ALTEN FRAU, DIE SUPPENTERRINE, VRENI KELLER SPRIGHT UND DER POPO DER MADAME, 30 min., Color, Klaus Schönherr, Birmendorferstrasse 511, Zurich, Switzerland. Swiss head film . . . good.

UNSERE AFRIKAREISE, 12 min., Color, Peter Kubelka, Film-makers' Co-op, 175 Lexington Ave., NY 10016. A *great* film, to be seen many times.

WARUM HAST DU MICH WACH GEKÜSST, 3 min., Color, Hellmuth Costard, Hasenhöhe 35, 2 Hamburg 55, Germany. Fine 3 min. film . . . naked lady carries camera around, photos herself, then puts camera in drawer.

SELBSTSCHUSSE, 6 min., B/W, Lutz Mommartz, Schlesische Str. 98, 4 Düsseldorf, Germany. Great spirited simple self portrait. Winner of one of the $2000 prizes.

CONVERSATION, 13 min., Color, Clive Tickner, 62 Clarence Rd., Wood Green, London N 22. Almost motionless . . . periodically bursts into action. Still pic is of two girls, one close, one distant . . . would make a fine wall hanging movie.

COLOR ME SHAMELESS, George Kuchar, Film-makers' Co-op, 175 Lexington Ave., NY 10016. Another great Kuchar epic.

JüM JüM, 9 min., Color, Werner Nekes, Brüderstrasse 5, 2 Hamburg 36, Germany. Jump cuts of girl on swing to heavy percussion. Works on your mind.

GEOGRAPHY OF PERSIA, 4 min., Color, P. Adams Sitney, Film-makers' Co-op, 175 Lexington Ave., NY 10016. Simple poetic/girl in tub/2 screens.

THE BED, 19 min., Color, James Broughton, P.O. Box 183, Mill Valley, Calif. 94941. Broughton calls it a "Baroque Raga." A playful & gripping survey of everything that happens in bed.

SELF-OBLITERATION, 24 min., Color, Jud Yalkut, c/o Film-makers' Co-op, 175 Lexington Ave., NY 10016. Yayoi Kusama, a crazy Japanese chick puts dots on the whole world. Dots move into psychedelica which moves into orgy. Smooth transition.

THE BIG SHAVE, 5 min., Color, Martin Scorsese, 920 Palisades Ave., Union City, New Jersey 07087. On track is Bunny Berigan's "I Can't Get Started." Pop film man shaves goes into bloody blood orgy.

ASSA 1, 6 min., Claude Coin, 36 Chaussée de l'Étang, 94 Saint-Mandé, France. Neat mixture of childrens drawings, man running, and pixilated images. Nice film.

IL MOSTRO VERDE, 28 min., Color, Paolo Menzio and Tonino Debernardi, Lungo po Antonelli 17, Torino, Italy. Italian horror movie 2 screen psychedelica with Taylor Mead and Allen Ginsberg.

BOLERO, 15 min., Color, Albie Thoms, c/o Ubu Films, 54 George St. Redfer, NSW, 2016, Australia. Music Ravel's "Bolero." One track for 15 min. down an empty street to a girl that's worth it. Majestic.

WAVELENGTH, 46 min., Color, Michael Snow, P.O. Box 199, Church St. Station, NY 10008. One crude zoom in a room for 46 min. BOLERO above is polished and fine compared to WAVELENGTH . . . yet the spirit and roots to the nervous system are much more present in WAVELENGTH. BOLERO could give you courage but WAVELENGTH changes your life. It was the Grand Prize winner at Brussels and for once I agree with the jury.

NR 4 [No. 4 (Bottoms)], 80 min., B/W, Yoko Ono, c/o Connoisseur Films, 54 Wardour St., London W1, England. 365 asses walking away from camera (close up). Every kind that you can think of. Great movie.

A short General Survey of the Festival:
Tits: 90 (different pair)
Asses: 412 (counting Yoko Ono's NR 4)
Pussy (not lips): 73
Pussy (lips): 9
Balls: 39
Cock (limp): 48
Cock (semi-limp): 22
Balling (fake): 16
Balling (real): 0

Robert Nelson
THE SWEDISH PROPOSAL FOR NEW AMERICAN CINEMA,
AND SOME MISCELLANEOUS NOTES

Since no one else is doing it, and since they're posterity minded, the Swedes are stepping out with a program to develop an archive for New American Cinema. The independently-produced films of the NAC stand the highest risk of getting lost and the Swedish Film Institute is putting up money to preserve them (starting with the modest sum of $5000).

> Take your suitcase . . . lengthen it. Do a good job so that bad seams won't embarrass you in bus stations, and so that it will be strong enough to withstand rough handling by men of commerce. You will probably have to re-center the handle. Use whatever tools you have around you. If it seems too difficult, or if you have a short attention span give up. Do whatever you like, it makes no difference.

A summary of the Swedish Film Institute's activities might be helpful here. The SFI is a foundation run by a board of directors. One half of the directors are appointed by the Swedish government, and the other half by the SFI. Each year they take in, and dish out, 3-½ million dollars. The money comes off the top of all ticket sales in Sweden (10% of ticket purchases of *all* commercial cinema goes to SFI). Sixty percent of that money goes to prizes for Swedish films and to grants to cover production losses on quality films that are not commercial successes. (The biggest prizes go to the producers of big box-office films, i.e. the producers of films by Bergman, Sjoman, etc.)

> As you allow yourself to become weaker and weaker, decrease the resistance of your natural-born dimmer. As rapidly as you can, build up your tolerance to Light and Din. The Din should be constant. As for the Light, you should hardly be able to open your eyes unless you're wearing dark glasses. Once a year, of necessity, buy darker glasses. Enter the unknown with all of your increased weakness and useless armor. If you are unable to do this willingly, don't worry about it . . . do exactly as you've always been doing. If you must work on your zest and innocence loss, attack them from behind as though they were some faded crepe paper that you once loved.

The other 40% is spent on the SFI school and on the SFI activities. The school has a two-year curriculum. There are approximately 40 students (20 accepted each year) who are trained in the methods of conventional theatrical production. All those accepted get free tuition, free materials and money to live on. Each student studies a special field of motion picture production. Presently, there are 6 students studying to be directors, another handful studying to become producers, cameramen, lighting and grips, etc. In other words, they're training film-makers to use conventional forms of theatrical production.

You've probably, at one time or another, tried to touch the face in your mirror. A cold tipped hand has risen up to prevent you. . . . Fair warning! Don't touch! Check often the side or your jacket that has button holes, the part in your hair, etc. If all is ok, they should remain on the opposite side from the strangers in the mirror. This is a simple and fairly reliable check on your well-being. Refuse not to suffer not.

The archives restore and preserve films. They preserve all current Swedish films, as well as going into the past to find, restore, and preserve the old Swedish silent films. They also buy and exchange film classics with other archives. They presently have about 3000 titles. (I was told that most European producers are helpful and cooperative with the SFI archives, but that American producers are difficult and paranoid about depositing prints in the archive. For that reason, few of the 3000 titles are American films.) To do all the archive work, they have good professional equipment and technical experts. The facilities will be even better when the new archive building is completed (presently under construction).

Find a Christian denomination that doesn't hang crosses all over the place, that doesn't focus on the crucifixion, and whose collection bearers don't wear black. Remember that it is the pupils of your eyes that should be dilating, not the irises. This process is normally automatic and you should not have to give much attention to it.

Stone them not, for these are the first to kill Christ everytime/where he returns.

The SFI archives will start with $5000 to buy original NAC material. They will make inter-negs or dupe negs that will be preserved in the archive. They will not strike prints or screen the films. They will not distribute the films. In certain cases, prints will be made for other archives or for whatever non-commercial purpose the film-maker wants . . . but *only by agreement with the film-maker.*

This February the NAC Traveling Avant Garde Film Library is coming to Stockholm. A selection of films for the SFI archive will be made at that time. The film-makers will be contacted and from those who agree to the proposal, a total of $5000 worth of original material will be purchased. It is a start.

Next year they will have additional funds and they are interested in organizing a show from Canyon Cinema, so that they can see West-Coast films, and to make a selection for archive preservation. There are already several West Coast film artists represented in the program that will be shown in Sweden in February, but not enough. If we're interested in presenting such a program, it will mean finding someone with time and energy to organize the project.

The interest in NAC is high here in Sweden. They've shown all of the NAC films that they've been able to get their hands on. I've shown some of my films at the Swedish Film Club in Stockholm, Uppsala University, Göteburg University, and

I've had several invitations from other parts of Sweden (that I've been too lazy to accept). In Stockholm, about 400 people attended my showing, and both of Stockholm's daily newspapers wrote reviews treating the whole absurd business as though it was something very serious.

> God-damn your eyes, everyone.
> Everyone, God-*damn* your eyes.

[Editor's note: In the original presentation of this essay, there is imagery to the left of the indented passages: a series of five rectangles, each divided in half. On the left side of the rectangles are drawings of a woman, who is seen in increasing close-ups that focus first on one eye, then on a "sparkle" in the other; on the right side are a series of texts: "throw away everything you ever knew about going to the movies."; "an art form for today's generation . . . it's what's happening."; "a completely new way of seeing and feeling."; "expanded cinema . . . a totally new experience!"; "Flower-Power . . . it goes beyond Psychedelia"]

—

FROM *CANYON CINEMANEWS*, APRIL / MAY 1968

Will Hindle

LETTER FROM SAN FRANCISCO, APRIL 1968

Too bad. KQED gave the Establishment Delay treatment to my two 30-minute films-on-films, to have been presented around AAFF time here. Bosses that Be let my program idea sit on their desks since last December. Now "suddenly found," all was rush and budget and where and feet and spinach! This is prime method of defaulting on an agreement without responsibility of actually having pulled out. Simply make it impossible at the last minute for me to produce anything worthy of the occasion. Hard to believe this station would pull that old ruse, but it turned out to be very much the Establishment.

Should I ever get ahead on money will try to do it on my own . . . a definitive film on our Art form and its artists. Better that way anyway. Film artists (of which there are really very few . . . "making films" doesn't automatically qualify one as an artist in that field at all) have to maintain as much control over their works and its presentation as is possible. Have to hang in there until our art is finally recognized (sans exploitation) for the violently beautiful, powerful and prohibitively expensive expression it really is. Hang in there. It will come.

Help Canyon Cinema as much as possible . . . showings, the News, et al. It's the sweetest thing going for us today. Really. Ask to help. No strings. For real.

Viva the memory of JFK, MLK, Mal X and all those striving minds now torn from their skulls by a society which still does nothing about this freedom to kill.

Peace and Subtlety, brothers. The virility and integrity of your work is enough to show them the way. "FFFTCM" speaks of our right to fulfillment and to work, the awakening, the Reach. "29 MERCI, MERCI" is the illustrated rust that comes when the human element is allowed to idle. CHINESE FIREDRILL is the embodiment of the anguish borne of shamed love, shamed expression. A once-free soul shot down, haunted. So endeth the frigging lesson.

Robert Pike

NOTES FROM THE CREATIVE FILM SOCIETY:
PROS AND CONS OF THEATRICAL BOOKINGS

Ever since New American Cinema became synonymous in the minds of moviegoers with sex-oriented films such as FLAMING CREATURES, CONFESSIONS OF A BLACK MOTHER SUCCUBA, COSMIC RAY and CHELSEA GIRLS, the interest in this type of underground cinema has been on the upswing. First to take boxoffice advantage of the situation was the Art Theatre Guild with their weekly Saturday midnight showings at the Cinema Theatre in L.A., then the Presidio Theatre in S.F., and finally a total of 23 (now 20) theatres in their nationwide art house chain.

More recently, individual movie houses across the country have begun installing 16mm projection equipment in order to take advantage of this new trend. In most instances, these are former sexploitation houses, such as the Uptown Theatre in S.F. and the Cedar Theatre in Minneapolis, who were losing their audience as interest in sex-violence features continues to wane. In a few other instances art and quasi–art houses who had run CHELSEA GIRLS decided to stick with comparable products so long as their audiences would support it.

In any event, for the first time in the history of experimental film-making, the demand for film-art and pseudo film-art has expanded from the normal nontheatrical market into the larger — and more lucrative — theatrical market.

The advantages of these theatrical bookings are: (1) money . . . for the first time a film-maker can not only recoup his out-of-pocket production costs, but particularly if his films contain a female nude as a visual element, can even earn a modest profit; (2) prestige . . . with the added exposure of theatrical bookings, a film-maker can rise from total obscurity to the limelight in a matter of months. As a result, it is quite conceivable that as the interest in these films, and film-makers, continues in theatrical circles, the most popular film-makers will be in a position to gain the ear and interest of the major studios for future projects. Andy Warhol, as a result of the boxoffice success of CHELSEA GIRLS, was already approached by Universal for this reason. Kenneth Anger, Ed Emshwiller, the Kuchar brothers, and Will Hindle are others who similarly, should they wish, could find financial support from the movie "Establishment" for their work; as could any newcomer to the scene who is able to produce a film as commercially exploitable as SCORPIO RISING, RELATIVITY, HOLD ME WHILE I'M NAKED, THE SECRET OF WENDELL SAMSON, and FFFTCM.

The disadvantages of theatrical bookings are: (1) wear and tear on prints . . . a one week booking at a theatre can do more damage to a print than a dozen normal non-theatrical single screening bookings, partly because most 16mm theatre size projectors are poorly designed and scorch, scratch, and rip films in a way that almost negates the monetary advantage of the longer playdate; (2) lack of respect by the exhibitors — and projectionists — for the physical prints and the subject matter, which adds to the sloppy handling of the films, as well as the psychological linking of New American Cinema with sexploitation.

The CFS has been dealing with an increasing number of theatres during the past year; and in fact is the one and only experimental film distributor assigned to provide emergency substitute programs to the various theatres connected with the Art Theatre Guild's Underground Cinema 12 series. As such, we have been directly concerned with this problem of theatrical bookings for some time.

For those film-makers who object to having their films shown at theatres where the previous bill of fare was sexploitation, my answer is that these audiences are usually comprised of white collar professional men who can appreciate good examples of film-art as easily as bad examples of sexploitation and therefore should not be denied the opportunity to be oriented in this area. A typical example of this was a recent program at the Classic Theatre in L.A., which runs a two hour program consisting of one hour of "beaver" (girlie films in which pubic hair is visible) and one hour of experimental films, with approximately 1/3 of the experimental films utilizing nudity or erotica. Included in the experimental film portion of the program were POON-TANG TRILOGY and TRAGICOMEDY OF MARRIAGE as the sexy film-art, plus Pat O'Neill's 7362 and other "tame" experimental films (7362 is a beautiful abstract film made over a 3 year period). When the exhibitor returned this program of films he expressed the audience's and his own satisfaction with it, and particularly singled out 7362 for praise. Obviously, therefore, while the audience came looking for sex, they were equally capable of appreciating non-sex when they saw it.

A more serious objection to theatrical bookings is the wear and tear on the prints involved. In the past, some film-makers demanded that their print be replaced by a new one at the theatre's expense if it were scratched or damaged in even a minor way during a booking. While a few theatres, particularly those involved in the Underground Cinema 12 series, were willing to bend over backwards to keep the film-makers happy in this respect, it is realistic to assume that the majority of theatres will not act accordingly unless major damage has been done to the prints. Moreover, distributors are usually too busy to be able to catch minor damage such as scratches when inspecting films day after day. Therefore, the film-maker is forced to make the decision of either refusing to allow his prints to be booked theatrically or to accept the fact that the increase in rental income via theatrical bookings will be almost balanced by the increase in print damage. The ideal solution — from a practical standpoint — in my estimation is to set aside prints for theatrical use only, with the realization that these prints will be reduced to poor condition; while keeping the good prints reserved for non-theatrical use where more critical attention is paid to the films. Unfortunately, however, most film-makers are not financially in a position to have two separate sets of prints; so this solution is not always feasible. Moreover, when all of the theatrical prints are booked and a new theatrical booking presents itself which could be serviced by a non-theatrical print, the temptation is great to utilize it for the profit involved.

Another problem that has arisen with the increase in theatrical bookings is the advisability of non-exclusive distribution representation over exclusive representation. While I believe that non-exclusive representation is the best answer for a non-theatrical market, as each distributor in a major city has his own share of loyal customers and is therefore in a position to obtain rental bookings that no other distributor can get, so that, ideally representation by a separate distributor in N.Y., Chicago, L.A., and S.F. would give the film-maker the best possible coverage for his work; in the case of theatrical distribution it is far better to give exclusive distribution rights to one national experimental film distributor. In this way, the distributor is in a position to demand the highest possible rates for the films, as the exhibitors have nowhere else to turn if they want to show "Underground Cinema."

Of course, charging the "highest possible rates" does *not* mean charging totally unrealistic rates which would make a profit for the exhibitor a risky gamble. It means finding the rates which are high enough to please the film-maker while low enough to please the exhibitor. In this way, instead of an exhibitor apprehensively trying an "underground" policy for one week because of a too-high rental rate, he can enthusiastically try a six-week policy, with a good chance of making it a permanent one.

In addition to finding a distributor who is realistic about the rates he charges, an exhibitor is looking for a distributor who is thoroughly reliable in terms of servicing the playdates — with prints in projectable condition — and one who is in a position to immediately confirm playdates for his films, without first having to gain approval from each of the film-makers involved in terms of location and rental rate. After all, the exhibitor treats the film medium as a business and expects the distributor to be in the position of treating it similarly. He has no time to do otherwise.

While the theatrical use of experimental films has its disadvantages, I firmly believe that they are outweighed by the advantages, particularly in terms of raising the production of film-art from an extremely expensive hobby, financially, to one that at least can now be maintained on a self-supporting basis.

A film-artist still can't make a living out of producing experimental shorts . . . but neither can a commercial film-maker do so by making regular theatrical shorts. However, today it is possible for an experimental feature to be sufficiently profitable to provide a good income for the film-artist, as evidenced by CHELSEA GIRLS . . . or so we are led to believe by the reports of the film's success.

The picture isn't totally clear yet in terms of the future of film-art; but for the next year or two it looks brighter than ever.

More Notes about Theatrical Bookings
Recently, the Creative Film Society has been renting programs regularly to the Uptown Theatre in S.F. for week-long runs. This theatre is part of a chain to which the Rivoli Theatre in Seattle also belongs. We noticed that various titles rented from us by the Uptown Theatre would appear later in ads run by the Rivoli Theatre, such as: THE THIRD BANQUET, CHINESE FIREDRILL, etc. When we questioned this from the booking agent who handles both theatres, we were told that the Rivoli wasn't really playing these advertised titles, was actually playing programs of untitled "beaver" films, but that to look like an underground house was copying advertised titles used at the Uptown.

We pointed out that this was false advertising, etc. Later, however, we caught the Uptown duping some of the films they rented from us, including: VOYAGE OPTIQUE, HOMAGE TO EADWARD MUYBRIDGE, and CELERY STALKS AT MIDNIGHT. This made us wonder whether the Rivoli was merely advertising titles they weren't playing or whether they were advertising titles of prints that had been duped by the Uptown and forwarded to Seattle (and other theatres in the chain). Needless to say, we are investigating. In the meantime, watch out for these theatres!

We also had been instructed to provide six weeks of feature length programs for the Esquire Theatre in Cambridge, Mass. after they had originally scheduled six weeks from us earlier and then cancelled at the last minute. On this second series, they claimed they didn't receive the first program in time to show it. They showed the second; claimed the police closed the third after one night; and cancelled the remaining three programs. When we got back the first three programs, we found that they had arbitrarily used part of the first and part of the second program as one total program. They had chopped up a couple of prints through sloppy handling. And are slow to pay for everything. MORAL: Put this theatre on your D list, too.

—

FROM *CANYON CINEMANEWS*, MAY / JUNE / JULY 1968

News from the Australian Undependents

. . . Ubu has issued a HAND-MADE FILM MANIFESTO, 1968, which is of some interest:

1. Let no one say anymore that they can't raise enough money to make a film — any film scrap can be turned into a hand-made film at no cost.

2. Let photography be no longer essential to film-making — hand made films are made without a camera.

3. Let literary considerations of plot and story no longer be essential to filmmaking — hand-made films are abstract.

4. Let no more consideration be given to direction and editing — hand-made films are created spontaneously.

5. Let no media be denied to hand-made films — they can be scratched, scraped, drawn, inked, colored, dyed, painted, pissed-on, black-and-white, or colored, bitten, chewed, filed, rasped, punctured, ripped, glued, stuck on to, stuck in to, burned, burred, bloodied, with any technique imaginable.

6. Let written and performed music be rejected by makers of hand-made films — let hand-made music be created directly onto the film by any technique of scratching or drawing, etc., imaginable.

7. Let no orthodoxy of hand-made films be established — they may be projected alone, in groups, on top of each other, forward, backwards, slowly, quickly, in every possible way.

8. Let no standard of hand-made films be created by critics — a film scratched inadvertently by a projector is equal to a film drawn explicitly by a genius.

9. Let hand-made films not be projected in cinemas, but as environments, not to be absorbed intellectually, but by all senses.

10. *Most of all*, let hand-made film-making be open to everyone, for hand-made films must be popular art.

Barry Spinello
5144 Miles Ave., Oakland, Calif. 94618

LETTER TO JOHN SCHOFILL

We spoke briefly a few weeks ago about the 'sound track' of my new film. After a great deal of experimenting over the past eight months I've established a large set of drawn symbols that produce distinctly different sounds when passed through the photoelectric cell of the 16mm projector. For instance: [here Spinello includes tiny markings that look like ellipses, colons, series of short vertical lines of increasing/decreasing size]. Electronic music is composed and drawn directly on the film. Rhythms, more complicated than it [is] possible to produce via the human nervous system directly on percussive musical instruments can be planned and drawn on film once the necessary symbols and spacings have been learned. The audible part of my film consists of patterns and rhythms built of these sounds.

The visual aspect consists of framed (as opposed to frameless animation) drawings in color done directly on the film. I've designed and built extensive equipment to facilitate this type of drawing — a twelve foot long table with tracks to hold the film and delineate each frame, with a parallel rule built in. This enables me to use templates, long rules, French curves, airbrush, etc.

In addition, words flash on the screen, sometimes for subliminal effect for a single frame, sometimes longer, forming verbal passages.

I've tried to make, as directly as possible, a film that utilizes sight, sound and verbal meaning in a totally integrated way. Since all three of these (sight, sound, verbal meaning) are composed and recorded simultaneously and directly on the film, it has been possible to synchronize the three to the very last frame. The three are totally welded together, and inseparable. During the fastest passages of the film, the audible and visual directly interact twenty four times per second.

Except for the more recent McLaren, and the extremely elementary attempt of Peter Kubelka (ARNULF RAINER), I don't know of any film that has this type of sound-visual integration (where the sound and visual are initially conceived as a unit, and built together, frame by frame). The film is ten minutes long. It has been extremely well received by the very few people who have seen it. It was shown at David Hilberman's animation class at SF State College (in half-finished form) and was well liked by both the class and by Prof. Hilberman. Mario D'Amico, Italian critic and visiting professor at the University of California in Berkeley, has chosen it as an example of current American painting! It is to be in the annual International Art Festival at Palermo, Italy, in December 1968. (It will be given its world premiere at the Berkeley Film Festival on May 29.)

I got into this type of film making in a round about way — ten years of musical training in the NYC school system, privately, and as an undergrad; a B.A. in '62 from Columbia College in English literature with an emphasis in writing; Architectural drawing and painting for two years in Architecture School in Columbia until '64; and then three years painting in Florence Italy and other European centers. About a year ago I realized that my previous interests could be combined in a single art form. Since then I've been working toward this end. My wife and I came to Berkeley in August '67, and I've been working on this film here since September. It represents at least 1400 hours on the drawing board.

Lastly, I would like to mention that my film is not passive. I don't expect that it can be watched passively. It is my brain, and for ten minutes I expect (I hope, if the film is successful) that the viewer's brain functions as my brain. The title of the film is SONATA FOR PEN, BRUSH AND RULER.

Robert Pike
NOTES FROM THE CREATIVE FILM SOCIETY

I'm delighted to recommend Canyon Cinema News as the best clearing house for information about films, festivals, filmmakers, distributors and exhibitors, of all the publications available on the underground film scene. In the last issue there was my article lamenting on the duping problem regarding the Uptown (and presumably) Rivoli Theatres, and in the same issue a letter from Ulvis Alberts of Seattle commenting on the films he (she?) saw at the Rivoli. From the publication of Ulvis's letter I was immediately able to ascertain that the Uptown had duped GUMBASIA, LOVE IN, FAT FEET, and COSMIC RAY, in addition to the films I had personally caught them duping. Armed with this information I can now begin following whatever legal course of action is best suited to the problem. I shudder to think of how many CFS prints must have been duped during their exhibition at the Uptown; but as soon as I check further with Ulvis, and determine which S.F. lab did the duping (it was a lab that uses metal tabs for timing purposes), I'll be able to notify the respective producers, and we can all jump on the exhibitor's back and let him know what for.

In the meantime, I would be interested in having more people utilize the News for commenting on the pros and cons of both the Aardvark boys and the Bell&Howell film operation in Chicago.

Thus far, John Heinz and a few others have all said negative things about Aardvark. In the last issue of the News, Jeff Begun of Aardvark (who has continually poo-pooed Heinz and the other detractors) called for a show of hands from those producers whose films are being handled by Aardvark and who are happy with the way things are going. I'd love to read about producers being satisfied with Aardvark, as it would ease my own mind considerably about this organization. My own experience with the Aardvark boys has diminished from a pleasant, enthusiastic one to an extremely pessimistic one during the last year. I initially assumed their problem was the result of growing pains; now I'm in doubt as to whether it's a lack of organization or a lack of integrity. As of the beginning of May, 1968, they still owe the CFS for rental bookings dating back to March, 1967. They still owe Jim Whitney his award money for LAPIS from the 1967 film festival they held. And their so-called quarterly reports to the CFS on films we have given them for sub-distribution leave MUCH to be desired, both in terms of promptness and clarity. If they'd only sit still and be counted, it wouldn't be so bad. But as John Heinz pointed out in an earlier complaint, the faces at Aardvark keep changing from month to month. First there was Jeff Begun, Howard Cohen, and Paul Gonsky running the show, with Bernie Sahlins of Second City their shadowy angel. Of these three, Begun was busy as a student at Carnegie-Mellon University in Pittsburgh; Gonsky was a travelling accountant; and Cohen a friendly but (according to them) relatively disorganized businessman. He was later replaced by John Hofsess, who is now back in Canada. He was replaced by Ron Taylor. The main problem seems to be that no one is minding the store. If other producers are being sent intelligent, prompt quarterly reports from the Aardvark boys, let it be known, please. We need a good underground distributor in the mid-West, but until the Aardvark boys shape up, I've stopped recommending them as such.

As for the Bell&Howell distribution operation, I'd love to hear from producers who have been paid their share of the rental profits. On paper, the B&H thing looks great. They advance print cost for as many prints as they need; they (supposedly) also advance half the producer's profits immediately for a guaranteed 100 bookings per year. I'd like to see a show of hands in the next issue of the News as to how many producers have received their profit advance from B&H and how many have not.

My own dealing with B&H was at the very outset of their operation, when the shadowy Bernie Sahlins appeared in town to try to soft-soap me in a sophisticated hard-sell way into letting him take all the CFS films for B&H use. He promised the moon; producers' discounts at Wilding lab (just purchased by B&H); extraordinary profits; etc. I immediately took two steps backwards from anyone who made such fantastic promises, many of which he later contradicted in the same conversation. But to test his integrity, I ultimately gave him a print of Jane Belson's film, ODDS & ENDS, on a lease basis, requesting an advance payment of $100, plus $2 per booking. Sahlins took the print back to Chicago with him, requesting that I mail him the lease agreement. I did, and eventually received a check for $100 . . . but no signed copy of the agreement or any subsequent accounting of the film's bookings. In the meantime, the name Belson was used in their promotion of a package featuring California filmartists, with the omission of a first name giving the possible impression that Jordan, not Jane Belson was the filmartist in mind.

The main thing to determine, however, and the News seems to be the best place to determine it, is whether the majority of filmmakers are satisfied with their dealing with B&H.

—

FROM *CANYON CINEMANEWS*, AUGUST / SEPTEMBER 1968

Bruce Conner

LETTER, AUGUST 6, 1968

Shame on Canyon Cinema for the CANYON CINEMA ACHIEVEMENT AWARD to Stanley Kubrick for 2001. The shame is not for the award itself but for the reasons stated in the award. 2001 has the fascination of a precision machine working and is important in the technology of film-making, but to say that it does "completely justify the work of every independent film-maker, because without these to work from, and $10 million, 2001 could never have been made." I cannot understand that statement at all. MGM produced the film as they produce every other film: it is a company made movie and is not "independent" in any sense of economics and *is* under the control of the bankers of MGM. It is the most corporate movie production that has been presented as any I have seen. I think that the "justify" in your statement must have some reference to the quality of a few sequences in the film that show a definite reliance on techniques that have been developed in independent films in the past. If you think this should flatter the film-makers then you are incredibly naïve. Artists have been plagiarized, exploited and used as tools for centuries and for them to become independent would be to rebel against their being used, not to beamingly admire the exploitation. Black artists have been exploited by white men this way for a long time: Uncle Tom applauds the white man's minstrel show.

Another aspect of the award is the grandiose statement, perhaps influenced by current political oratory, "truly described as the 'best film ever made.'" I would say it is far from that. It is very impressive technical product and I made an effort to see it twice. I have seen Dreyer's PASSION OF JOAN OF ARC a dozen times and could see it another dozen times in this lifetime. I can think of many films I have seen almost as many times and I would feel the same way about them. I don't care about seeing 2001 again.

The dialogue has the quality of pablum and the only characters with any personality in the film are the ape-men at the beginning sequence and the computer, Hal. The main part of the film is a hymn to technology and dehumanization.

Computer techniques were used in the making of the film and there is probably not one shot that did not utilize some aspect of such thinking. I consider it unfortunate that the creative energy that went into this movie was only able to be utilized and produced with masses of technical equipment and immense budgeting *because* of basically unemotional, and therefore 'safe,' format of the concept. The other movie to be produced by the same company with as large a production cost would surely take the form of familiar trickery of emotional puppet-masters as dishonest as you have grown to expect. The success of 2001 involves Kubrick's skirting this problem of morals and ethics and, instead, presenting a product of equations. Kubrick uses art in an excellent manner. The multi-channel, full-range taped sound of well-written music is one of the most impressive things about 2001. The "psychedelic" light pattern effects, liquid chemical projections and the altering of color negative hues and intensities of aerial landscape photography is allowed the full advantages of the lab facilities and 70mm image quality. Process shots are beautifully accomplished. Technical aspects of front projection for the Dawn of Man shots will change the quality of films made in Hollywood in the future. The variety of mechanics used to simulate weightlessness are intriguing even though some of the demonstrations of altered gravity have the appearance of being performed by rote: the performance does not go beyond the effective demonstration of mechanics. The design of space equipment is a welcome change after all the space vehicles designed by Cadillac that have been prevalent. Despite all the technical aspects of 2001 I still cannot see it as the best film ever made. It may be the best for this year for a big budget movie. For creative development of unique kinetic patterns and images, the star-slot sequence still cannot compete with the mini-budget OFF-ON by Scott Bartlett and friends. I could envision a much more prodigious application of $10 million, with more meaning, than is in 2001.

[Emory Menefee's response:]

In replying to Bruce Conner I don't intend to open a polemic on a question of taste: some (myself included) think 2001 unsurpassed, others despise it. However, I think some of the other parts of Bruce's letter need a response, lest too many others also misconstrue the content of the overly short remarks in last month's News, in which the Canyon Cinema Achievement Award for July was given to Stanley Kubrick. The statements in Bruce Conner's letter based on the use of "justify" are stirring but irrelevant, since it is only his interpretation which alludes at all to "exploitation" and "flattery." Film-makers, nearly all, are constantly trying to justify their labors by putting their work in distribution or otherwise on view before others. The idea of the artist being completely independent and rebellious is a pretty one, but just cannot be valid in the case of film-making. Like it or not, undependent filmmakers are almost totally dependent on technology, and are mostly just using its products. They are working *outside* the technology because they haven't the money to go at it on their own, nor enough support and interest by the technological hierarchy to be brought in and allowed to explore. It is this aspect that makes 2001 so important, I think, and what justifies the lengthy struggles of film-makers to get where they are (art-wise, independence-wise, money-wise, or any other-wise). The film demonstrates in a most spectacular way that it is possible to subsume all kinds of emotions in a non-narrative framework. There have been a few attempts to do this before in commercial films, and we all know the undependents have been doing it for a long time, often in a totally non-narrative way. Usually the undependent films are episodic (or whatever the non-narrative analog is), and short. My accolade to Kubrick is for, besides making a superb flick, recognizing that there is a true non-narrative cinema possible on a commercial scale, and that it can be a massive emotional vehicle every bit as strong as the cinema of Dreyer. (Obviously not every scene in 2001 is this way, but a lot of it is.) I am certain that as a result of 2001 and similar high-budget films, the undependents will be allowed more freely to create *inside* the technology — still remaining undependents and not sellouts. A final word about exploitation, etc.: when an undependent film-maker (a film-maker who, among other things, doesn't have to kiss anybody's ass) builds onto the body of film-art and makes a film that is good, we don't call it plagiarism and exploitation. So why shouldn't an ass-kissing studio director be allowed the same luxury, provided he has imprinted his film with his own ideas, as Kubrick certainly has? It is not justifiable to say that just because an artist makes money with his work that it is exploiting something.

Robert Pike

[NOTES FROM THE CREATIVE FILM SOCIETY:]
THE STORY OF A CLOSET CINE-DRAMA . . . OR . . .
FROM ISOLATION TO IMMORTALITY

Once upon a time there was an obscure but talented filmartist named Dan McLaughlin, who worked quietly as the animation cameraman at UCLA and produced works of film-art in his spare time.

One day he decided to explore — and simultaneously disprove — the theory that if you combined the world's greatest art with the world's greatest music you'd automatically end up with the world's greatest film. So he loaded up his car . . . a small foreign job . . . with ten pictorial books on the history of art (which was the number of books his car could hold), and he took them home.

During the next few days, he leisurely photographed the drawings and paintings in the books, one page at a time, allotting two frames per page (with the exception of the *Mona Lisa*, which was photographed for twelve frames), until he ran out of pages and film. Next, he synchronized the footage to the beginning of Beethoven's Fifth; titled his effort GOD IS DOG SPELLED BACKWARDS or 3000 YEARS OF ART HISTORY IN 3-½ MINUTES; and put it in his garage.

GOD IS DOG sat quietly on the shelf for two years, until one day in the UCLA Animation class a girl raised a question about theory. At that point, McLaughlin smiled a quiet smile. "If you'd like," he said softly, "I'll show you a film that knocks a hole in theory completely." The girl's eyes widened to match her areolas. "Oh goodie!" she exclaimed. So the following week GOD IS DOG was taken down from its shelf, dusted, and driven to UCLA, where it was quietly shown to the wide-eyed girl in the darkened projection room.

Our story might have ended then and there, with GOD IS DOG relegated to its spot on the garage shelf; but as fate would have it, someone else viewed the film in that darkened projection room that day: Bob Epstein, a UCLA staff member responsible for programming the Royce Hall film showings. Impressed with GOD IS DOG, he asked permission to include it in the next Royce Hall showing. McLaughlin, surprised but pleased at this unexpected bit of enthusiasm for a film he felt was essentially a put-on, acquiesced to Epstein's request.

And so it was that the film had its premiere public showing at UCLA's Royce Hall, which resulted in its being criticized as a paganistic short by some irate faculty members of that venerable institution.

It also resulted, however, in a theatrical midnight booking at the Regent Theatre in Westwood, and a non-theatrical daytime booking at Chino High School (where the print was chewed to death by the projector).

Undaunted, McLaughlin next sent a new print to the 1967 film festival at Foothill College, where the film won critical acclaim and a print sale to Loyola University.

Events began snowballing as the film was then accepted for showing at the 1967 New York Film Festival at the Lincoln Center and the 1967 London Film Festival. Write-ups appeared in every conceivable publication; and demand for the film began to accelerate — sometimes in spite of its "paganistic" title. The film became so popular, in fact, that one of the giant American distributors, Contemporary Films, Inc., an organization that normally only represents shorts on a veddy veddy exclusive distribution contract basis, agreed to merely purchase one rental print for each of their three offices when McLaughlin refused to terminate his previous distribution with the Creative Film Society just to hand over all rights to the giant.

Things reached a peak in the early summer of 1968. Tommy Smothers was putting on a new hat in his career: producer . . . as he took over the reins of his Summer Brothers Smothers Show. For the first show of the series he needed something special — to fill an existing 3-minute spot. Mason Williams, co-head writer and all-around talent, suggested pairing a far-out flick with his fast-rising recording of *Classical Gas*. The Creative Film Society, who had answered a similar need on the Andy Williams Special with Jim Whitney's film, LAPIS, was contacted. Films were screened; and the winner: GOD IS DOG.

For a cool $750 the Summer Bros. had a hit on their opener. Mail and phone calls poured in. Ad agency men marvelled at the secret "McLaughlin technique" of animation. The Ted Bates Agency in NYC bought a print of GOD IS DOG just to analyze how it was done. The Smithsonian Institute in Washington, DC, bought a print for similar reasons. And people demanded a list of all the paintings and drawings used on the exciting film spot they had seen on their tube.

Knowing a good thing when they had it, the Summer Bros. decided to repeat the film — this time throwing in Mason playing his piece live, for good measure. And another $500 was passed to the smiling, quiet McLaughlin. Meantime, Warner Bros. Records, Mason's recording company, wanted to re-title GOD IS DOG as CLASSICAL GAS, give Mason credit for the music and McLaughlin credit for the visuals, and send out the new version as a promo film for Mason and his record. Would Mr. McLaughlin accept another $500 for this simple, quick use of his film? McLaughlin smiled and debated. His other sleeve was being pulled anxiously by the managers of the Smothers Bros., who were debuting as executive producers on the Summer Bros. Show and needed as much prestige as new execs as they could muster. How would McLaughlin like their blowing up GOD IS DOG to 35mm and having them release it T-H-E-A-T-R-I-C-A-L-L-Y??? Of course, again it would mean re-titling the film as CLASSICAL GAS and giving Mason-boy credit for the music . . . but a THEATRICAL RELEASE!!

No-one seemed to be aware of the fact that GOD IS DOG had, without the benefit of Mason's music, made it on various film festivals, theatrical and non-theatrical rental, and been sold to colleges, libraries and museums throughout the country. And McLaughlin, after trying to explain in his own quiet way that the film did, in fact, have a previous existence, just shut up temporarily and waited for the warm wind to die down. While the execs continued to buzz around his head, yelling words like MONEY! FAME! PRESTIGE! He began planning his next project, a series of films for IBM in which he was to be given carte blanche as to budget and running time, as well as content. He had merely to illustrate filmically certain abstract theories in whatever way he felt would be most effective. — A choice assignment for any creative filmartist.

The ending of the story of GOD IS DOG is still to be written. But at this point in time it is amusing to watch the excitement over a film that sat ever so quietly on a garage shelf for two years.

—

FROM *CANYON CINEMANEWS*, 68.7

Robert Nelson

SOME THOUGHTS ABOUT THE BELLEVUE FILM FESTIVAL
TWO WEEKS AFTER JUDGING IT

The language, the passing of information that the New Cinema gives us, the fantastic charge of a new thing that's meeting us somewhere between the screen and ourselves as we sit watching the film, this has already been established . . . with a force and direction that's now unmistakenly valid, unmistakenly important in the history of cinema. A language *has* been developed, a new poetic language . . . But the fact is that this new-wrought film language is beginning to seem repetitious. The freshness is gone (or going) and it looks like nobody knows where to go from here. The pieces look more finished, more competent . . . and more familiar (easier to take). The most interesting films were the ones that took some new risks. The question is how to go on, how to charge the movies with new meaning. Now that the call "Come on in, the water's fine" has been heard by all, it doesn't take that much courage to jump in. We've passed that stage. The problem now is to find the films that wade out into deeper water. There don't seem to be very many.

Sitting here now, a couple of weeks after I judged the Bellevue Film Festival, it seems to me that the 25 hours of films that I watched were more disappointing than appointing . . . despite the fact that there were lots of good movies to look at.

The scale that goes from demanding that the film work on you regardless of your resistance to it, to the total participation with any given visual experience that confronts you, is a broad and confusing one. Those that have visited paradise know that it's really *all* o.k., why not just get to "it" on whatever's there. That, in essence, is the new sophistication that hip audiences are expected to bring to the movie shows. You can't make something without revealing yourself, all revelation is beautiful, therefore all films are beautiful. The basis of that hipness is a soul-stance that before few, and now many, know how to get to. It's a spiritual, as opposed to worldly, esthetic position (roughly stated). The difference between the old esthetic stance and the new is that before, people sought out art stuff asking "show me my soul" . . . and now people seek it out saying, "let my soul suck on whatever you've got there brother" . . . or, at worst, the most suspicious ones say, "let me demonstrate my soul on your movie" (or other art stuff). This is all o.k., and a necessary liberation, but we don't have to abandon one for the other. The real depths of the soul will never be plumbed and the liberation is a new prison. The spiritual messiah, the next coming, has to be followed by a worldly messiah. When everyone finds out that God is alive, they've got to find out that He's dead. When they find out that He's dead, they've got to find out that He's alive. There is a place to stand where your weight is equally distributed on both feet, one planted firmly in worldliness (money, death, energy produced by conflict, antichrist, politics, society, body) and all the fine and beautiful things therein, and the other planted firmly in spirituality (life, God, energy flowing *through*, love) and all the fine and beautiful things therein. We are both things and maintaining equilibrium is risky touchy.

So it's now time to begin being tougher and asking more than we're getting from the New Cinema. "Show me a new place in my soul. If you can't, I know how to groove on what you've got, but shit man, I can do that on *anything*." It seems to me that the best film-makers have been giving us that all along, and they'll continue to do so. Their films are harder to recognize because the things revealed are unfamiliar and also because even asking for it is getting to be a lonely position. It's still a lonely business messing with art. (Parenthetically, for the same reasons described above, I was unhappy about receiving a prize for my GRATEFUL DEAD at the Belgium Festival in that THE GREAT BLONDINO didn't get that recognition. With its successes and failures, BLONDINO *is* a film. The GRATEFUL DEAD was easy. BLONDINO was a personal, esthetic and social risk.)

Judging the Bellevue Film Festival I responded to the films that did "that" (all "that" talked about above) the best. There weren't many . . . and I wish that the ones that *did* do it, did it more.

The Grand Prize of $1000 went to David Brooks for THE WIND IS DRIVING HIM TOWARD THE OPEN SEA. Brooks didn't content himself with refining the established vocabulary, but took a harder risk. He tried to make an abstract poetic document and contain it in a refined, carefully crafted, structure. His film has a vibrancy and liberated technique (the "looseness" is not fabricated, but it occasionally borders on that . . . and if the film is flawed, it comes from that slightly self-conscious snazzyness). Many of the shots were ones that couldn't be retaken, yet he never "cinched-up" or lost his expressive style. The images were beautiful, nearly lyrical and always evocative.

Second Prize of $300 to Bob Cowan for SOUL FREEZE. A tough film, in the best sense of the word. The images, the composition, and development are all rough and crude. It's as though any image, even if it's only somewhat right, will do as long as it's going to carry the ideas and get on with the poem. This kind of toughness about putting his stuff together adds to the film's force and vitality, and to its meaning. There are no apologies for its design or photography. The film has a force and power that will finally knock out of the way any prejudices one might have about techniques.

Third Prize of $50 to Ernie Gehr for MOMENTS [now called *Morning*]. This movie reminded me of WAVELENGTH. Simple elements (pulsing light from in front and from behind a window). Made magic.

Third Prize of $50 to Larry Jordan for THE OLD HOUSE, PASSING. Jordan's best film. It's a poetic narrative. He stepped out to pick up the pieces of narrative film and reassemble them into new forms and new meaning. Sustained mood through beautiful photography and photographed gestures that never let you down or go.

Third Prize of $50 to Lenny Lipton for SHOW AND TELL. A rich neat film with funny stuff in it. Very few (not enough) funny movies in the festival. Lots of them that were supposed to be funny were so cute or otherwise awful that I kicked them out of the festival altogether. This one, like Cowan's SOUL FREEZE, Broughton's THE BED, Nauman's VIOLIN FILM #1, Bartel's THE SECRET CINEMA, Gebhard's A NUMBERS RACKET (and to a lesser extent Ed Seeman's ELECTRIC CIRCUS and REHEARSAL) was full of humor that was neither self-conscious nor laughing at others, but full of pathos and feeling for humanity. Really funny things leave something deadly serious and beautiful that echo like after images in your mind.

Third Prize to Edward Owen for REMEMBRANCE. Owen's films (REMEM-BRANCE and TOMORROW'S PROMISE, both of which were in the festival) are rare esthetic experiences that are accomplished works in the style of Markopoulos. It's impossible to ignore the artistic level that Owen achieves but I find myself con-stitutionally and ideologically against what these films represent (particularly TOMORROW'S PROMISE, Malanga's ALLA RICERCA DEL MIRACOLOSO, all the works of Markopoulos . . . and to a lesser extent Owen's REMEMBRANCE) because I believe that they are essentially reactionary cinema. They are of and about the lack of being. The films and the people in them are sucking on the past and cherishing the pollution of the YET (past, present, and future in the all-together). They are not enough about The Horror, but a staving off of it with charisma and rit-ual. Like finely wrought beautiful pieces from the devil, their magic is essentially evil. REMEMBRANCE somewhat escapes this condemnation because it is ame-liorated by the subject matter; older people whose presence and being are too pow-erful to be destroyed. The presence of life is too strongly etched in their faces to be relegated to the past. (Malanga's ALLA RICERCA DEL MIRACOLOSO escapes by a fine thread of humor that is nearly but not altogether invisible.)

Third Prize to John Schofill for X-FILM. Beautiful rendering of film images and technique. The images are modern but the notions are classical.

Third Prize to Ed Seeman for ELECTRIC CIRCUS, REHEARSAL, and SEX PAINT AND SOUND. Three good short jazzy spiffy movies of, about, and around The Mothers of Invention. Psychedelic, but with some humor which makes them personal and separates them from the ever-growing dirge of psychedelica that in three years has gone from far-out to *ad nauseam.* . . .

Will Hindle

LETTER, SEPTEMBER 10 [1968]

The trip by car to Putney and back may have torn a hole in my hull, the breadth of which I have yet to realize.

Gashing through day and night air, I looked through that windshield at mile after mile of human struggle. Urban renewal and dying faces.

The heat and many days must have dinned fatigue down to my molecules the last week of travel. When I got to Blythe at the Cal border it was 110 or so. Mid-late afternoon. Motor groaning, hot air past my legs from the vents. Tan-white glare. And some miles out from town toward L.A., in the very epicenter of this earth-heat and pure desert came a speck fast beside the road. At 75 mph all I saw clearly were the eyes briefly scanning mine . . . in permanent squint against the brightness. A face, a little bit of hair under a covering of cloth, a small form, a dress, a blur of suitcase . . . and then she was suddenly miles behind. I re-played the video in my head and saw that she was baked, wizened, old, bent. The clothes were shredded, the suitcase bound with rope.

My car had run off the road and I brought it to a stop in the bed of a dry gully. I was going into shock. My eyes were putting out great drops but I was not crying so much as dying. I could hear a polyglot of words coming from me in a voice and pitch I didn't know I had.

I was able to turn around. To put on dark glasses. To find her back there. To drive her to the next town. To see her entire back covered with blisters that would pop if she leaned back. To lift her things to the sidewalk and into the shade. To grab whatever was in my wallet and run after her. To look away. And to curse myself ever since for having bought-out of her life with whatever happened to be in my wallet.

FIREDRILL is a living thing. Much of it bashed and clanged around me on the road, amplified by the very confines of the car, the van, the cell, the room, the universe in which I moved. . . .

But what I really remember about Flaherty's Putney is that woman who wanted to know the name of the coffee houses in SF where we all go. Wanted to say "A no-name hole by the waterfront when it fogs-up." Instead, shattered her a bit by saying the back of my van there in Vermont was the first place Nelson, Conner, Bartlett and I had ever sat down together. Actually Conner was sitting on the portable chemical toilet so maybe this voids the whole thing. Specify glossy or matte.

About the Chicago Co-op. The big piss-off is that out of all the names in this world they came up with CCC for initials. Ron and Tom are for real. If you can afford to leave your prints with them until the co-op takes root it would be a good thing, I think. Miss Sloane of Bell & Howell phoned while I was there and talked of how she and Baillie had become "pen pals." That, the 98-degree weather, and my gift bottle of Yippie Oven Cleaner will always say "Chicago" to me.

Most Mysterious Cities Seen Along The Way: Charleston, W. Va., Kansas City, Mo., Taos, N.M. . . . If you dig Tiburon and Virginia City kneaded into the shape of a giddy pueblo cluster try Taos. A spa for hide-away TV script writers. See Famous Les Doux Street! Probably got its name from famous Indian lesbians who teepeed there. Isn't that the way Orinda-Moraga got started?

About the American Film Institute: Don't be afraid of their application form. They're new. They're running cautious . . . Want to learn, to know . . . so *tell* them in that "narrative letter" clause. Don't bother to be academic, they're not. Psychedelic snow jobs won't work either. Too many good heads read the mail for that. They want to know about *you*, your for-real quotient, how much crap you've put up with in order to see your ideas through, and the color of your adrenalin should they put some money there. I understand their distribution clause is a bit stringent because they need as much control as possible to do it. Even that might be relaxed. For tie-wearing types (with keen taste in secretaries), they've come a long way in nine months. Sic transit, Gloria.

[Editor's note: The 1968 Robert Flaherty Seminar, mentioned in paragraphs 1 and 7, was held in Putney, Vermont.]

Bruce Baillie

LETTER, "AUGUST, BEGINNING OF SEPTEMBER" [1968]

We are listening to PARADE on tape. From the Picasso, Massine, Cocteau, Auric ballet of 1917 — a short piece was in CASTRO STREET, with the RR engineer. Breakfast, hot sun. Eggs and green onions on homemade bread toast. Angel our mailman just came up the road with the film we have waited for to resume shooting on QUICK BILLY.

Tulley, Charlotte and I are making some "Acmeplays," on high contrast positive film. This one is a western. We are doing all the acting, with make-up, costumes, artificial lighting. 3 photofloods quite close to actors, fl.9. Becomes really too grainy at this f-stop, but we still like the quality. We are translating our ideas back to early dramatic, silent cinema. There is an unique rhythm sense when using intermittent written material between pictures. We may go on this fall and winter doing a group of these films. BILLY will run about 9 min. and probably will be avail. in the catalogs next month or so by itself. If we do more they will all go together. I can't predict what or how much work will get done these days. I have put FEETFEAR aside for awhile in homage to this new sense of fun.

I wanted to suggest that the newsreels, via NY, be made available if possible through our cooperative distribution channels. So that there might be a continuing supply of immediate information — document, poem — flowing within the most effective channels available to us. Encouraging film programmers to ask for "the news," whatever newsreel might be at whichever co-op on the show date. I would further like to encourage film-makers and non-film-makers to send film and tape material into this channel: formal films, abstract, dramatic, documentary. Informal material, as shot. Poems. Descriptions of the most minor events in yours or others' lives: eating toast in the morning . . . what Morris said while he was shouting from the crapper. News.

Commitment? (ref. to film-maker's recent letter in NEWSLETTER): More than a deliberated act by the socially-politically conscious man. It is too a commitment to the socks you put on in the morning. The smile you see in the mirror of your belly if you don't get hung up with any idea whatsoever as to who/what you are supposed to look like. Commitment to self is total commitment, the egotism of THEATRE.

I also wanted to report how bad all the labs are. We have got to work toward setting up a few labs of our own. I sometimes wait months for a print of QUIXOTE from Western Cine in Denver. A recent print omitted B-roll through one section, they skipped one frame at the head of ea. scene on another sect. They did another for me free; very lovely print. But it had 3 or 4 sprocket breaks and an unintended fade-out, fade-in. I can't get credit somehow at General in Hlwd. I get really weird explanations about film dirt, etc. from local labs. I have spent one entire year now attempting to obtain a satisfactory printing master for 2 color films. If anyone knows a good lab, please let me know via this paper.

Finally, I guess, I wanted to tell you what a good film course we had up here at the Mendocino Art Center. I plan to send a summary later on from the daily program I more or less kept up, usually *after* the day's class.

Couple more notes: I want to invite film groups to show QUIXOTE again this year. Ask for the revised print — there will be a couple of good prints around this year. I think the film will have some pretty specific value to people now, after 2 or 3 years.

We had a really good showing in class of John Schofill's FILMPIECE FOR SUNSHINE — near complete wrap-up of viewer and viewed.

Michael Stewart's short CONSEQUENCES excellent film. Going to see the 8mm blowup of THE GRAY UNNAMABLE this wk.

Wrote to AFI on tail of Will Hindle's efforts in S. Barbara where they seemed to become aware for the first time that there exists a whole revolutionary cinema in our country, for the most part I believe existing within the cooperative organization. There might be a more direct relationship between the AFI and ourselves — indeed, the absence of such a natural relationship would not be unlike the disparity between People and the conventional political institutions. It had also been suggested to the AFI that we are already in possession of an effective structure which is in immediate continuous contact with film-makers' needs — methods for distributing production funds, from beginner all the way along to established artists.

—

FROM *CANYON CINEMANEWS*, 69.1

Will Hindle

LETTER

She napalmed my breakfast shielding the whites of the eggs with her body to keep them slippery cold. Then she went over and blasted a member of an underprivileged minority group for falling asleep, face down, in a cup of coffee she had fresh killed that very morning. I guess I'll always remember her that way.

Fall dawn in North Beach. Wet. Alive. All day and all night and dawn alive. Still wide awake and up in Union Street. The Sun? Holocaust in the West? No. There was this violently big billion kilowatt bulb sticking out and over and down from the façade of Canyon City Coop. I grinced and lavered to the door hoping for a film fix. A splice job. A mylar maybe. Anything. Big light, empty house. Nothing but the electricity meter going inside saying gimme some white front.

Lavered some more over Russian Hill and fecuddled left to my street. And old Cataffo on the corner there doesn't seem to know that the S.F. "Film Festival" is not real. Old millionaire suffering humanity-gap problems hinting head on that no kiss on the behind, no couple *hundred* dollars donated. No lettum up on stage to hand couple hundred personally to strange art-types, no give *anything* next year. BoomBoom on chest . . . "Better than New York Festival, than any festival ever elsewhere as well too because this festival here is the only festival to make a profit." Big sad thing, this thing.

I would recommend a fertile boycott of this S.F. "festival" were it not for the fact that I am boycotting boycotts. Keep putting your mind together on film . . . keep work good and you and true. And send that singing star thing of yours anywhere you see fit to send it. Song it to the people. Hope to win a prize, break into the cash. But if not your statement, your stroke is no less magnificent. If you need the money and the recognition keep going outward as long as you can stand it . . . Until that time when you feel you have the strength to endure the Full Quiets.

The water/swim film [*Watersmith*, 1969] is being born these nights and mornings.

John Lennon

FAN LETTER TO BRUCE CONNER

[Editor's note: Bruce Conner included the following note with this letter: "Once I sent a print of LOOKING FOR MUSHROOMS to John Lennon and some cards that Mike McClure and I made. Enclosed is reply that I received from John (I suggested a fan letter). Please to print this because I'd like someone else to know how pleased I was to receive."]

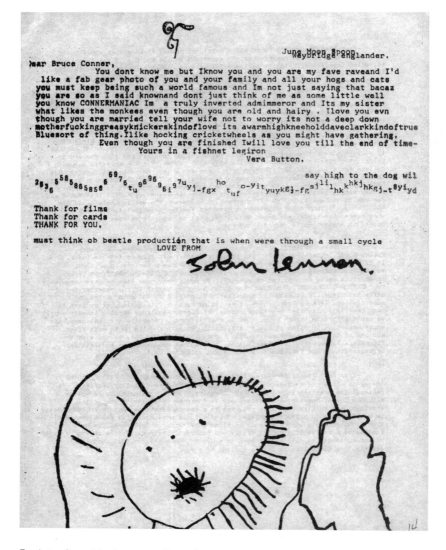

Fan letter from John Lennon to Bruce Conner, from *Cinemanews*, 69.1.

—

FROM *CANYON CINEMANEWS*, 69.3

Barry Spinello

LETTER FROM OAKLAND, CALIFORNIA

I have recently completed an 11 minute film-painting entitled *SOUNDTRACK*, made without camera or sound equipment of any sort, using a variety of audio-visual film-painting techniques I am developing. I would like to address this letter to the absorbing and very pertinent problem of the relationship between sound and sight in film.

May I refer the reader to the first three pages of John Cage's *Silence*, written in 1938, before the magnetic tape recorder was available. Cage speaks of a "new electronic music" to be developed completely out of the photo-electric cell optical sound machinery of film. Any image (his example is a picture of Beethoven) or mark on the soundtrack successively repeated will produce a distinct sound with distinct pitch and value — different from the sound and value of any other mark. The new music, he says, will be built along the lines of film, with the basic unit of rhythm logically being the frame. With the advent of magnetic tape a few years later and the enormous advantages it has in convenience and speed (capacity to record and play back live sound, and erase) the filmic development of electronic music initially envisioned by Cage was completely obscured. Composers now work with tape. Had tape never been invented, undoubtedly a rich new music would have developed via optical sound means. Composers would have found ways to work with film.

I think this is the point we are at now. Film and music have gone their separate ways so that the only conciliation of the two seems to be — in one form or another — in "synchronization," namely: an existing musical passage to which film is composed; or an existing film sequence to which music is composed. This is really choreography of one art form — technology — thought sequence — to another. Undoubtedly beautiful films have been made and will still be made by this process, but to my mind, it's not what true audio-visuality can be. The synchronization process (even when both music and visual are made by the same person — but separately) is like two people closely collaborating to write one story — with one person providing the verbs, the other nouns. Why not an audio-visual mix that is conceptually a unit?

According to L. Moholy-Nagy, writing in 1947: "Only the inter-related use of both sight and sound as mutually interdependent components of a purposeful entity can result in a qualitative enrichment or lead to an entirely new vehicle of expression. . . . To develop creative possibilities of the sound film, the acoustic alphabet of sound writing will have to be mastered; in other words, we must learn to write acoustic sequences on the sound track without having to record real sound. The sound film composer must be able to compose music from a counterpoint of unheard or even non-existent sound values, merely by means of opto-acoustic notation." (Moholy-Nagy, *Vision in Motion*, N.Y., 1947) My film-painting *SOUNDTRACK* is a descriptive record and anthology of several technical ways of doing just this.

During the first half of *SOUNDTRACK* the carefully composed and modulated sound-painting on the sound track is redrawn, frame by frame, on the image track, so the viewer, instant by instant, literally sees what he hears. The images here are black ink (Pelican Ink, series K; Grumbacker Masking Ink) against clear leader and are primarily compounds of dot and line, which are drawn with mechanical drawing pens (Rapidograph, Acetograph, Leroy): sizes 000 through 8. Treble tones are made by scribing very close, thin, evenly spaced lines into a previously opaqued section of the soundtrack. A Linex cross-hatching tool helps produce these lines rapidly. Pitch is controlled and modulated by basing drawn symbols around the module of the frame. For example: a size 5 Leroy drawing pen consistently will fit 5 dots in the space of a frame, thus giving a constant, predictable pitch; while a size 6 pen will consistently draw 4 dots per frame, thus giving a different constant predictable pitch, etc. Rhythms are built by spacing sound particles on multiples of the 2 frame series (2-4-8-16-32 frames); or 3 frame series (3-6-12-24 frames) and combinations of both. One passage in the film counterpoints these two series directly against each other, simultaneously.

The type of painted symbol necessary to produce a given sound becomes clear to the viewer after subsequent screenings. As it happens, the visual images in this section are very reminiscent of one of the most familiar (but little realized) images of the mid 20th century — in its variations the broken line down the center of the highway. With practice in image-sound interpretation certain visual experience (kinetic-sequential-rhythmic visual experience) can be interpreted through imagination as sound experience. When seen from a moving car fences, trees, posts, and always the dots and lines of the highway divider take on rhythmic sounds as one imagines what they would sound like if passed through the photo-electric cell of the projector. This type of experience could be relevant as film-composers search for primary bases for image-sound relationship.

The second half of *SOUNDTRACK* makes use of a most amazing filmic building material I happened upon in the fall of 1968.

Acetate self-adhesive screens and tapes (Zip-o-tone and Mico-tape being two brand names), cut to size to fit on the sound track, yield instant sound of controlled pitch, for any duration, in many different sound qualities (as many as there are patterns). Multiple sounds are built by arranging multiple layers of tape. These tapes produce extraordinary images in black and white or solid colors, when used on the image track as well.

With acetate tapes and the direct-drawn methods described above, a viable, inexpensive, readily accessible, alternative array of building materials, free of costly technological gadgetry, which in some cases favors spectacle at the expense of thought, is available to the film-composer, with which the new problems of audio-visual composition can be directly approached. In a subsequent letter I would like to discuss what I'm finding some of these problems to be.

—

FROM *CANYON CINEMANEWS*, 69.4

EXCHANGES

Bruce Conner

LETTER TO THE BOARD OF DIRECTORS OF THE
NEW YORK FILM MAKERS COOPERATIVE, MAY 16, 1969

Dear Sirs:

A couple of years ago I showed my films twice at the NY Cinematheque to more than 400 people. I was to receive 75% of the gate. Only 93 people had paid and then $125 "expenses" were deducted leaving a balance of about $23 for two shows. The projectionist showed up an hour late and then set up, sound levels, focus etc all had to be done while the audience was in the hall. No projectors were in the booth when I got there. I had requested an 8mm projector which would run at 5 frames a second and offered to carry one all the way from California if they did not have it. They said they had it. They did not. Later I received a letter. They had the gall to ask me to let them run my films free of rental. Then they asked me for a discount. I said no. I told them to rent them from the Coop at the same price that a struggling film society in Newark or Boulder, Colo. would have to pay. The Coop rented them at a discount. Leslie Trumbull refused to collect the difference of $120 and wrote that I was being disagreeable about supporting a worthy cause. He later implied that the discount was a decision of the Board of Directors. This is contrary to all agreements between film-maker and the Coop that I have ever seen whereby the rental is not to be lowered without film-maker's Okay.

I think that the Cinematheque performs a disservice to the film-maker through the mismanagement and ineptitude of Jones Mekas and the fact that he is also a Director of the Coop constitutes a conflict of interest. The Coop has displayed favoritism towards an exhibitor at the expense of the film-maker. The Coop does not serve the interests of the film-maker anymore. I am withdrawing my films permanently from the Coop and I recommend that all other film-makers do likewise.

Jonas Mekas

LETTER, MAY 20, 1969

To the film-makers, about Bruce Conner, and other things

I'm afraid this letter won't be very rational. You see, finally Bruce got me. Finally, I'm getting fed up. I have been hearing from Bruce for three years now. He keeps kicking me whenever he feels so, just for kicks. Being a farmer, I'm very patient. And I have said on a number of occasions, that an artist is right even when he is wrong. I stand by my statement. I also state (I'm lifting my right hand) that Bruce Conner is an artist. But one thing is RIGHT or WRONG and another thing is BULLSHIT. And I've had enough of Bruce Conner's Bullshit. I don't want to go into any serious discussions here on any of Bruce's points, touched in his letter to the Directors (and in his letter to the Canyon Cinema News, a good year ago). He knows all the facts himself. He is not interested in truth. He is neither lying nor playing dumb: he is only bullshitting. It's O.K. when he writes such letters to me, I can take plenty of crap without opening my mouth. But when he wants all film-makers to believe his bullshit, then I say there is a limit. As Buddha once said, There is a limit even to bullshit. There are things with which one shouldn't bullshit. Bruce knows what the Cinematheque does, what kind of screenings it holds. But he likes to play a game of literal interpretation of the word "theater," whenever it suits the whims of his bull-shitting. He speaks (or dreams) about "more than 400" people who attended his show, a hyperbole which is beyond understanding of anyone who has seen the size of Cinematheque's theater. He knows damn well that the house was scattered. He knows damn well that his screening wasn't announced in advance, it was an impromptu event — Bruce knows that he came to New York on a different business. Since Bruce was coming to our town, and he had all his films with him, we thought it was a very sound and nice idea to see his films, no matter on how short a notice. He also knows very well that he was paid a full rental, but he speaks about $23! For that one, myself, being a farmer, I'd like to kick him in the ass. He may need a good spanking more than anyone else. Anyway, we held a show, to honor our guest, but our guest turned out to be a greedy bullshitter. The Cinematheque's policy has always been the same: whenever a film-maker wanted to have his own show, he had to take the chances. But even when he lost, the Cinematheque paid all expenses and at least a $25 minimum. But whenever we planned the screenings ourselves, whenever the film was booked from any of the cooperatives, a full rental was always paid. Which, really, is not such an easy thing to do, as anyone who has seen the size of New York avant garde film audiences knows pretty well. Just to give you some indication: the San Francisco retrospective alone, just the month of May, has cost the Cinematheque over $4000 in rentals. One last thing: There is a disease that could be called the "free-audience-paranoia." New York film-makers got over it somehow, but it took some time. Ron Rice had it. He went over it. Jack Smith had it. He went over it. Many other notable artists had it. There was a famous LeRoi Jones and Living Theater case. They all went over it. Harry Smith, by the way, never had that disease: he lets everybody into his screening, he invites people from the street. The way Bruce is raging about it, one may think, that those few, those three or four (really, seldom more than three or four) who get in free, are some kind of enemies or something. So what, if the poor soul has no money to buy a ticket? You ain't going to become rich with his buck. You should be worrying about the rich people not coming and not paying — why worry about a poor soul coming and not paying? If he wouldn't come in free, he wouldn't come at all — so what would you do with those empty seats, make curry? And then, it happens to be so that those poor bastards that you are so mad about are film-makers. And we made this rule four years ago that no film-maker will be asked to pay — they need their money to buy film. And we are sticking to that rule, no matter what Bruce or anyone will say. Surely, Bruce, you don't want to profit from other film-makers? Poets profiting from other poets? in cash? Phfui that I'd do such a thing. So, where was I? I would like to sound very angry. But I can't. As I said, (quoting Buddha again), my anger doesn't last longer than a fuck. And then, I'm closing the Cinematheque screenings anyway. There will be some, but very very few. I ran out of money. Debtors on every corner. Holes in the shoes. I had enough. I'm changing my address. Here it is, if anyone wants to write or reach me: Bellevue Hospital (Dept: Dngrs), New York City.

P.S. One serious footnote is needed to conclude this matter. It has to do with terms "theatrical" and "non-theatrical." Bruce is misleading (or bullshitting) in his letter, where he talks about "discount." He implies that the Cinematheque was screening his films with discount. Which is not true. The Cinematheque paid full rentals whenever it screened Bruce's films. What he means, is that the Cinematheque didn't pay MORE than the regular rental: the way Bruce sees it (or pretends) the Cinematheque is a commercial theater and has to pay special, increased rate (I have no idea how and to what figure he would come; usually, in a theatrical situation, operating on the Cinematheque scale he would get only a small fraction of the regular rental). And this is the area of real confusion. This is the only question worth serious discussion by the Directors of the Co-operatives, and by all film-makers. It comes to defining what a "commercial" rental (screening) is and what a "non-commercial" screening is. A so-called University film society non-commercial non-theatrical screening can be bigger and more commercial than many a commercial show. Etc. That's why one can go only by individual cases. And that's why, at one point, when this question arose concerning the Cinematheque screenings, the question was brought before the Director's meeting. It was agreed, that the Cinema-theque screenings do not fall into the category of the "theatrical" "commercial" screenings, and the Secretary of the Coop was advised about it. In short, the deci-sions, whenever a question arises, can be made only by the people who know the "theater" in discussion. We in New York we'd have to trust the opinion of the Canyon Cinema Cooperative concerning the showcases and theaters on the West Coast, and the West Coast has to trust the decisions of the New York Film-Makers' Cooperative. There is no other reasonable way of working this out. When one "signs" the agreement with the New York (or any) Coop (that is, when one places a film for distribution) one accepts automatically all the policies of that Coop, which are supervised by the Directors. That applies to Bruce Conner. (To the rational part of him, I mean.)

Bruce Conner
LETTER, MAY 27, 1969

Film-Makers' Cooperative Catalogue, page 4:

> SPECIAL RATES: Rental rates are a compromise between the needs and expenses of the film-maker (our first concern) and the budget of the viewer. As a matter of policy, all requests for special rates must be submitted for approval by the film-maker.

From a letter by Leslie Trumbull, Sec'y NY Coop, dated 9-17-68:

> Rentals to the Cinematheque have been made on the basis of full rate for the first projection, plus half rate for each additional projection, or evening. The five show-ing rental of 9 FILMS BY . . . was made on the following basis:
>
> $60 for May 22
> $30 each for May 23, 24, 25, and 26 = $120
> Total charged and received $180

Full rental *was not* paid by Cinematheque. This discount was unauthorized and the NY Coop owes me $120.

. . .

Dear Canyon News:

I just this moment (visiting Canyon Cinema) discover Jonas letter calmly and per-suasively honoring me as the straw [that] broke the monkeys back. This is the first time Jonas has ever replied to me and he has neglected to direct it to me. I regret that his private party is over and I regret that I was ever invited. I have run film societies for years and lost money and always paid film-makers in advance the full rental. I had always thought the function of such presentations was to help the film-maker in the only way that counts, with the means to make more films and a return gift to acknowledge his work. I have always found the money to go to movies instead of eating when I had to. Jonas has been involved in promotion of the most inept homosexual drivel to come out of New York. He has glamourized it with the work of the truly fine film-makers like Brakhage and others. He has been more interested in playing public relations than presenting films in the best possible context.

Sincerely, Bruce Conner

P.S. The full rental was not paid by the Cinematheque. The first days rental was paid and each days rental subsequently was discounted and I have a letter from Leslie Trumbull acknowledging that this is true. The Cinematheque did not pay full rental which would be charged to any non-profit or commercial rentor. The Coop should, like Canyon Cinema Coop, inform the film-makers of any change in policy which would affect them. Any distributor should be expected to fulfill his agreements and change them only with mutual agreement. Shirley Clarke was present at the farce the night my films were shown and she can corroborate what I have said in my letter to the board of directors. The balance at the evening end was $23 for what I was told was a very successful audience attendance and so I received the minimum of $25 and at Shirley Clarke's urging I received another $50 from another source. The film program of two showings does not add up to full rental of the films. Jonas has a habit of changing the rules or neglecting to give the information in its fullest. All of the things he takes for granted that I should have accepted gracefully were presented to me after the fact. Since we had agreed to divide the gate, as agreed beforehand, I did not have my friends allowed in free of charge because I would be taking money from the Cinematheque by doing so. The deduction of $125 was not presented to me as a fact of the agreement until afterwards. The auditorium holds more than the 80 or so people who paid and there were two showings. Jonas should remember that it was his friends who gained all the advantages from the Cinematheque and that his policy of free entry could not be so unpleasant to the film-makers who can take advantage of it all the time: Jack Smith, (late) Ron Rice, Harry Smith, etc. who all live in NYC. NYC has millions more potential audience than Boulder, Colorado except that the Experimental Cinema Group at the University of Colorado which I started there 12 years ago still exists and has an audience and, to my knowledge, pays more rental and presents films under better conditions than the Cinematheque, which came much later, has ever attempted.

—

FROM *CANYON CINEMANEWS*, 69.5

Ed Emshwiller

(cc Filmmakers' Newsletter)

LETTER

Reading a recent series of charges and counter charges prompts me to comment on something that's been bothering me more and more the past year or so. It seems to me that our filmmaker-family quarrels, which can be helpful and useful, have grown rougher than is good for us. By that I mean more and more often people are trying to close one another down, asking boycotts of this festival or that coop, etc. Jesus, if it keeps up, soon we can all retire to our respective attics and bolt the doors. I can't imagine a situation with as many people involved that wouldn't have plenty of fights, with or without justification, but what bugs me is all the pressure politicking that seems to be increasing, especially in the way of people trying to wipe out, through group action, the efforts of somebody they don't agree with. If you don't like the way some guy runs a festival or distributes films or exhibits them, O.K., you can argue with him about it or refuse to deal with him or go and do it better yourself, but I don't see why his efforts have to fit some formula any more than all films should be made according to one school. It's one thing to warn fellow filmmakers of what seems to be dangers in dealing with somebody or some outfit, it's another to launch a crusade to destroy them. What with misunderstanding, mixups, muddles any group of people get into, we don't have to go around calling each other monsters of evil design.

And since my writing hand is loosened up this far, I'd like to sound off on a related topic, the economics of personal filmmaking. I think a lot of the family fights I mentioned above are due to the fact that personal filmmaking is damn rough financially. It's my bet that about the only guy, if any among us, making enough money just from the sale and distribution of his films to live and make movies is Andy Warhol. Everybody else has to supplement film income with a job (teacher, lecturer, cameraman, carpenter, etc.) or hand-out (grants, independent income, working wives, etc.) or some combination of both. I also bet that just about every one of us would like to earn enough from our personal films so we wouldn't have to spend time getting the money elsewhere to make them. Obviously nobody, film-maker or distributor, is getting rich on these films. I figure on an average it takes about five years for rentals to return my out of pocket costs on a film to say nothing for the time spent. That's hardly a business proposition. And that's just the point. We're not in this because we're businessmen and if we were businessmen we wouldn't be personal filmmakers any more than we'd be poets. I don't believe in getting into a balance sheet bag over personal films. If we do, or are forced to, then we get up tight in all the classic conflicts over money and who needs that?!

The way I see it, a lot of accusations thrown around result from the tensions of the relative poverty of filmmakers whose handiest scapegoats are their brothers. It's an old, sad story.

Peace, brothers, peace!

—

FROM *CANYON CINEMANEWS, 70.1*

Stan Brakhage
LETTER

Subscriptions to the NEWS were solicited from filmmaker-members last issue via a mimeographed note stapled into complementary copies. Following is the response elicited from Stan Brakhage:

To Whom:
I feel badly about writing this: but you asked for it (i.e. note on yellow paper): I, no, don't want to support Canyon Cinema News — just can't, honestly, "subscribe" to it in any sense . . . just can't get myself to send you a couple bucks even for 'old time sake' or some-such.

Every issue that arrives does *tempt* me to read it: but when I *do* begin to read, I get so discouraged by the "funky commercialism," the doting on "Festivals," and (in general) the drift of film-maker attitude *away from* anything to do with any possible Art of the Film that my day has often been ruined by the dim-lit of your publication.

The basic spirit-attitude of Canyon Cinema News, these days, seems *to me* to be about that of a Mad. Ave. PR man's dream of being a film artist on the West Coast: maybe that's because West Coast film-makers are tending too much to dream of themselves as Mad. Ave. P.R. men? — I dunno!; but I *do* know that, for instance, competition is destructive force on Art, and that Canyon Cinema News smacks its paper lips over aesthetic-batting averages as surely as if it were Sports Illus . . . and flips its page-self over technological gimmicry as surely as Dress Designer convention.

Please don't bother me with it anymore.

Sincerely

—

FROM *CANYON CINEMANEWS*, 70.2

Will Hindle

LETTER FROM ALABAMA, JANUARY 1970

Wrote something for the News after returning from two months in Midwest and East last fall. Must have misplaced it getting ready to come here. Concerned how badly films are being projected all over country . . . bad proj threading, sound weak or left off entirely, and lights left on; a travelogue in some high school class stands a better chance.

Have a great and deep respect for Jordan Belson who has fought alone against these bad showings for so long. But many must act together — to monitor, to boycott if necessary — to halt this destruction of film, from sprocket holes to mood. For certain filmers, the making of films represents long dedicated hours, months, even years per film plus every cent not spent on feeding baby's face. Low-threshhold-quality showings blunt, if not kill, our ability to share, and totally deny the audience its ability to receive.

Jon Jost

Box 803, Felton, Calif., 95018

I LOST IT AT THE MOVIES
OR ELECTRO-VIDEOGRAPH INTERFACE MEETS MR. NATURAL

Reading the (#69–7) cinemanews I came across Vanderbeek's Confessions of a Technocrat & something kicked me, saying speak up: Equal Time. Stan sold out to MIT (major defense and industrial research center). He sold out to IBM (maker of pleasant little black boxes for aiming napalm and other exotic chemical mixtures). But Stan is too preoccupied having fun with his new toys to notice. He loves to talk with those computers: to play with those video-tape machines and to indulge himself in a steady diet of celluloid. But Stan doesn't worry (he's "opto-mystic"). He's got lots of company to chant with him — "sink or swim in the new era of technology and humankink . . . no turning back from the tools and the tools that make the tools." Ah yes, no turning back. (An implied "forward": Progress is Our Most Important Product!) & so the chorus goes, with Fuller (and Fuller's carbon-copy protégé, Gene Youngblood of the LA Freep [Los Angeles *Free Press*, for which Youngblood wrote]); and McCluhan [Marshall McLuhan] & Stan Kubribeek & Scott Bartlett & legions of others, all of them in harmony singing their Hymn of the Technocrats. Over on the "art" side they have a tendency to be bearded, hairy and bizarre (a stock brokerage) but no matter the affectations, they are still technocrats no different than the head of IBM, Dow, Joint Chiefs of Staff, or indeed, the very President himself. They all join together in their quick trot to the new temple, white robed priests in hand, off to the lab to check up on the latest videographicinterfaced electronic toy. The uptightwhitecollar smiles and shells out to his freak companions sure in the knowledge that they'll manage to wrench some "poetry" out of the works. Now the IBM straight knows damn well he can use that artistic hype to push over his new toys so of course he turns to Stan (Vanderbeek or Kubrick) or another like him and says, here, play with these. End result: 2001 or Moon 69, it doesn't matter much, the message is the same: technocracy is good for you — technocracy is the door to your soul, whether via a little chemical manipulation (officially disapproved of in certain forms these days) or electronic audio-visual saturation (or both). Unfortunately these technocrats are too busy doing flip-flops and loops and feedbacks to take any notice of what they're really playing with. Even worse, the very persons so busied with the technocratic gimmicks have a penchant for mumbling mystic utterances about One-ness & Being &c: Technocratic Zen!

10 Notes of Advice for the Technocratic Mouthpieces

1.) Stick your head out of the air conditioned lab and breathe in deeply. (Cough involuntarily.)

2.) Look at the yellowbrownorange sky. Feel it in your eyes.

3.) Take your clothes off (as you are often prone to do) & go for a swim with the oil soaked birds, dead pelicans & whales. (Or, as many of you profess to be prophets of sorts, go walk across the waters. If you try Lake Erie maybe you'll make it.)

4.) Eat some food. Enjoy the spicy tang of DDT, the extra nitrates and all the other free additives. (Sorry but you can't really grow organic foods: the water, the earth, all of it comes supplied, gratis, with an abundance of additives, from strontium 90 on down, whether you want them or not.)

5.) Think of your beloved computers, video-tape sets, 16 channel tape deck multiple screen media mixes. Now think of the immense technological base required to produce all these toys: the mines, the steel mills, the chemical processing plants, factories; the vast transportation system needed to connect all of these together; the administrative bureaucracies. Think of working on an assembly line, sticking tab A of transistor M-922-b onto printed circuit B-1A. Take a vacation in Gary Indiana or in Detroit.

6.) Pause for a moment &, since you've built up a habit, fondle your computer for a minute. Now repeat steps 1,2,3, &4. Now try to connect smog, water pollution, the ecological damage (many species of sacred creatures gone, many many others going fast), the artificial food (as an aside you might note that the use of nitrate fertilizers while resulting in short range bumper crops in the long run exhausts the soil & renders it sterile: the love you take is equal to the love you make) — think of all these things and of the many other, to use one of the favorite words of your aero-space pals, "fallouts" of the technology which you so passionately praise. In case you don't get the hint, there is a connection. Surprise, surprise.

7.) Think of all the raw materials required to produce your favorite toys. And all the raw materials required for the technological base needed to produce that ("the tools that make the tools . . . "). Now look at a globe. Notice that it is most definitely FINITE. That it only has so much oil, so much iron, so much copper, earth, water, air. That it is an extremely complex and delicate mechanism, one that the technology you so admire has already severely damaged, & should it persist, will render unfit for living organisms (like yourself).

8.) Think of all the aforementioned. Now think about IBM, Bell Labs, MIT — the entire technocratic/industrial/economic/political/cultural combine. The one that seduced you, bought you, sells you, & is fucking you. Think about how you are fucking yourself, fucking your friends, fucking your environment, fucking the world — all in the most unloving way — just so you can play interface games with your video-computer technocratic gimcrack. Think about the man who is thoroughly convinced that he actually needs a combination transistorized AM-FM radio-electric toothbrush (with spray-pick), built in cigarette lighter & emergency flashlight. Now draw a parallel between this obviously sick man and yourself. Draw it because there is one: an addictive consumer, no matter how esoteric, is still an addictive consumer. Mad Ave is proud of you.

9.) Decide whether you prefer Life or short-term technocratic fun & games.

10.) Choose a side and get ready to fight because there's a big one in the works. And as Eldridge says, "Either you are part of the problem or you are part of the solution." And right now you are part of the problem.

While I am not a particular partisan of the man, there is a quote from Mr. Mao which spells things quite clearly:

"In the world today all culture, all literature and art belong to definite classes and are geared to definite political lines. There is in fact no such thing as art for art's sake, art that stands above classes, art that is detached from or independent of politics."

IBM = MIT = USGOVT = CORPORATECAPITALISM = TECHNOCRACY = VIETNAM = DEATH. The class which consists of technocrats, no matter what garb they come in, is anti-ethical to life. Mister Vanderbeek, and those of similar inclinations are members of that class. Vanderbeek = MIT. Heads up.

POWER TO PEOPLE/FUCK MACHINES

Freude and Adam Bartlett ("F.P.S. [Filmmakers' Portrait Series] #16"), with Adam's birth certificate, from inside front cover of *Cinemanews,* 70.3.

—

FROM *CANYON CINEMANEWS*, 70.3

Bruce Baillie

LETTER

Dear News,

A few reports. You must have lost the one I sent from on the way back to Texas at Christmas, about a girl in a green shirt, shades pulled along the freeway, and so on.

Quick Billy is coming along. I have spent the time since December re-shooting at home in Houston: front projection, 7255, super (Kubrick) 3-M screen and half-silvered mirror. f-2-f-4, 1000W lamp, 3" lens, reversing original in projector for correct frame orientation, #80 filter. Non-sync @ 24 fps, my Bolex and the B&H projector, no flicker problem. If one unit speed changed, flicker more or less in terms of ratio, e.g., 1:4 speed change gave every fourth frame black, resulting in jerky effect, or flicker. Now A-B-C-rolling the entire three parts, including the final one-reeler, entitled "Quick Billy," which we announced for separate release last year. It turns out *Feetfear* will include this dramatic film as a conclusion. The entire work — about an hour long — will be called *Quick Billy*. I should be finished by July, this year. Am working my way out of Houston now, into Part III. When this done, will head West again, stay in Camarillo near LA, work with timer at Consolidated Labs. Hope to visit Brakhages on the way.

Finally Chose Consolidated because they consistently exhibit correct *film-handling* methods, if nothing else. Also, I know their machines work. The risk here is with the big labs' tendencies toward mechanized work: automatic color correction, etc. I would continue to have all my work done with Multichrome and Palmer in SF but sometimes need more varied effects lengths and like to set this film up at a lab that can make an interneg.

Let me skip around with different things of general interest or concern: Back to the method gradually evolved for Q.B.: I don't know how good it's going to look, since I haven't seen a composite of my many months of homework . . . a natural job for electronics — a day's work at the future video console is taking me about one year of awkward, long-winded, many-phased effort. The re-shooting has been essentially one-roll matting (with my hands) — put together more in the memory than by any mechanical, or even simultaneous visual device. My first workprint dates to about two years ago. Now I am making my first run-through over the light table, A-B-C-ing . . . which will give me a composite workprint. If it *looks* okay, I'll go on, in California, with corrections, etc. — more orthodox editing, using this 2000' workprint composite. Then it all goes back for another silent work-print, unless I feel I can make it over the table at that stage. Then the track, etc. A long, clumsy mixing job, the only way I could finally figure it . . . my own primitive tools as usual.

What else? Hindle's right about projection around the country, it's abominable. Took a new print up to Canada — stood by the projectionist. Huge scratch down the middle. Had it Vacummated at the works as well as Tough-Coating it myself. Sent it on to a show in France anyway. The same here at Rice. Machines that don't work, or a loss . . . of contact of some sort, between persons involved — the guy who runs the projector, this person, that person, running around to put on a show — somehow it falls apart — very easy, happening everywhere. A good visit with Gene & Carlene Dawson up in Regina, Saskatchewan — 5 days — pool tournament in their basement. Charlotte hitched across from B.C. — went on the Quebec.

Internegatives: One solid year of energy spent via Bell & Howell Films, Chicago, several years ago — their lab, Wilding Inc. — trying to get a reasonable interneg of *Castro Street*. Always pure *pink* — over and over. Finally a correct, normal version. Then pink prints again. Lab & I both gave up. Multichrome made me an optical EK master composite. A little dark, good part of original sparkle gone, but okay for a while. Perhaps same method, same lab, could be better another try. 3 tries @ opt. master for *Tung* resulted in an excellent piece of work. Just spent 4 months with Cine-Chrome, Palo Alto, interneg for *Quixote:* their film-handling (at least shipping) procedure extremely and apparently consistently bad: shipping originals and prints on cores in paper envelope containers or ordinary flat cardboard boxes. Weeks spent in the mail, final pos. print. REA strikes NYC — mail very slow — lost for a week at Mus. Of Mod. Art shipping room, etc. Arrived scratched, probably from lab projection. Paid for anyway, since interneg itself pretty good: good timing job there, other times very good. Low level sound seemed to distort. They don't seem able anymore to pay attention.

A clear thought on internegatives: recent good offers from museums, etc. to begin making internegatives for some of our films. It is my thought that the first internegatives should be made to allow continuous print circulation. Therefore, they must be made at a given lab and retained there for printing. The preservation motivation comes second, I think, where the interneg is permanently stored at a museum. Many of our films (nearly all of mine, for example) need good internegatives made before any more prints can be drawn from them. Before this can be done, as far as I am concerned, there is needed:

An agency, secretary, whatever to do all the *business* involved.

Definite knowledge of a good lab.

Money to pay for the work.

(The filmmaker to furnish the original materials and necessary lab information. The answer prints to be approved by the filmmaker, wherever he might be at the time.)

We used to make up a lot of things in the *News,* that's why it felt good in those days. Things are more scattered now days — whenever there's time — all the emptiness needed — you can put together good things. When you've got too many things to do it all comes out the same. It needs all the highs and lows, the ups and downs of an open life. I guess you can send those into the *News* yourself . . . if we can always depend on a few good people to be there to put it together. The last issue looked pretty good — good enough to keep it coming, I think.

from some notes:

- absolute excellency, I want to know
  my davenport
        is going full speed all day.

Canyon Cinema Board of Directors' Meeting Minutes

Sometime around the end of April the directors and office staff of Canyon Cinema Cooperative met. These are the minutes of that meeting. Present were directors Emory Menefee, Lenny Lipton, Loren Sears & Roy Ramsing; manager Jan Lash, & staffers Ken DeRoux & Don Lloyd. The scene opens in room 220, Industrial Center Building, Sausalito, overlooking Gate 5 of the yacht harbor:

A breeze whisked the curtain aside as it entered the open window, circled the room and left as it had come in, taking the ragged tail of the curtain & about 14 tons of cigarette smoke with it. Out there beyond the jaunty sailboats tugging at their moorings, beyond the golden spires of the bridge, even beyond the whitewashed apartment hills of the city — somewhere out there waited the 200 or so members of this now famous cooperative. Waiting for the outcome of this high-level confab.

Ken returns from the Big G supermarket with beer & chips. Don & Loren chat quietly in the corner, Roy slouches on the couch. Jan sits in the leather upholstered arm chair Edith had vacated, at the desk Edith had vacated, feet propped up on the writing extension, giggling. We await the arrival of Emory & Lenny from their homes in the East Bay. Ken paces the floor looking for an opener. Jan giggles.

Outside, a car door slams & a strange squeaky noise is heard treading the flight of stairs. Everyone looks up, knowing well the sound of Lenny's Space-shoes making their way up the freshly painted steps. The door bursts open & in squeak Lenny & Emory. Coughing, the latter relights his pipe, nods hello & a volley of greeting is exchanged all around. We are now all assembled, save for Ben Van Meter who had just returned from a fund raising trip to LA & had gone on home to rest.

The agenda, prepared by Don & Loren, is completed after a brief discussion with the two late arrivals. A President is appointed & the meeting begins. "Would you like a beer?" Ken offers and begins trying to find the opener again. Jan leans back too far

& just catches herself before nearly falling backwards into the filing cabinet. "Yes" answers Emory, lighting his pipe. We all applaud Jan's skillful save. A breeze ruffles the papers on her desk, throwing a few of them into the wicker basket at its side. Someone's beer has dribbled onto the agenda & the president gets up to find a paper towel before proceeding. Jan leans back & giggles as the assembly breaks into little enclaves of discussion during the pause. "Where are the corn chips," inquires Loren. Ken points. Roy's eyes follow. Lenny passes the sack. Don sits watching the ant colony which has taken residence in the potted plant on his desk. Emory looks ten years younger now, without his beard.

Idealism is a thing of the past. We are now preoccupied with a business, with office expenses & salaries, renter relations & marginal income. The weight of these matters hangs heavy in the voice of each as we speak to the situation at hand. First one, then another is heard only as the crunch of a potato chip and guzzling of beer break the thread of thought weaving itself around our heads. Roy, always quiet & contemplative, clears his voice to speak. Emory nods & lenny arches an eyebrow as the President gives floor to Roy. Across the floor march rows of tiny ants, leaving significant patterns in the dust.

Loren suggests these may have something to do with the problem & gets down on his hands & knees to watch more closely the hexagrams as they form behind the advancing oracle. This causes Ken to step over him as he goes once more in search of the opener. Don comments on the patterns these two are making and relates them to those of the ants. Jan coughs in the rising dust and nearly falls backward into the filing cabinet, accidently kicking the open beer bottle off her desk into the wicker basket at its side. A wave of beer foam & dust engulfs the army of prophecy making its way across the floor. We take this to mean the end of the meeting. "Peace" crys Lenny. "There is no peace" mutters Emory, "only Struggle." "24 Frames Per Second" exclaims Roy. "Fate" Ken whispers. And a cloud of earth tones rises before us in the center of the room, lifting Jan to the ceiling before gently placing her in the filing cabinet.

The beer soaked agenda rests in the wicker basket beside Jan's desk. She & Ken have painted the wall behind the bookshelves a bright, cobalt blue which seems to generate a light of its own. Cartons of catalogues & new supplements line the opposite wall. A beam of sun light thrown in under the curtain illuminates the dance of a million microscopic dust particles. If one were to freeze their motion, all that has ever happened in the past, and yet the future, everywhere, could be read.

L. Sears
5/20/70

—

FROM *CANYON CINEMANEWS*, 70.4

Arthur Cantrill

RIGHT BACK TO THE BILLABONG

Two experimental films, BILLABONG & THE GREAT BLONDINO, are the first of a group with which the National Library has begun to rejuvenate its study collection, and the action of the censor has raised the whole question of the value of study material which is not protected from the tampering of the Customs Department.

BILLABONG by Will Hindle is an 8-minute film poem on the corrosive effect of loneliness in an American west coast Job Corps camp. The scene which caused the trouble is a fleeting 3-second shot which impressionistically suggests masturbation. You need to be alert to make it out: few at Mr Chipps screening in Canberra on Monday last week spotted it, even when the individual frames were projected.

Nelson's earlier WATERMELONS was refused entry by the censor when it was brought out by the Museum of Modern Art in 1968. BLONDINO is a 43-minute film which Nelson made with William Wiley as a dedication to all who live "at great risk for the beauty of it."

The Australian censor gagged over a shot of a girl in a car swearing — ironically one of the very few lines in the film, and, in fact, almost inaudible. It wasn't heard by the Canberra censor when it was first screened: he referred it to the chief censor because a shot of Blondino stroking a rhinoceros horn worried him.

The two films are in the first group of five to be acquired — the others are SIRIUS REMEMBERED by Stan Brakhage, BREATHDEATH by Stan Vanderbeek, and WATTS TOWERS by Gerald Varney.

There is a strong case for a government-financed collection of new cinema to compensate for Australian isolation from the Mainstream of American and European experimental work. Nobody is suggesting that the elusive Australian film industry should be solely engaged in turning out experimental film — but there is no doubt that an interplay of ideas and techniques is essential for a healthy film culture.

Certainly something is needed to lift Australia out of the billabong of world cinema.

Below is a quote from Hindle's programme note on BILLABONG which could just as well be a description of certain aspects of the Australian cultural sensibility.

"Many aspects of the self are often drawn off to one side, allowed to stagnate and go unattended. Visions narrow, Horizons cloud over with inactivity and frustrations and apartnesses. But life is still there with all its needs and love and trials. And pale fantasies abound . . . tapping directly the energy it needs from an untutored life-force. Stagnant. Yet just beyond these confines lies a giant moving sea."

Scott Bartlett
57 Harriet, San Francisco 94103

getting it off my hope chest dept.
film work
epic assemblage
butterfly collected pieces of 3 years
documentary driftwood fifty years old
transparent sculpture of 9 months
distillation from 10,000 puzzle pieces
trace of INDUSTRIALIZATION template
fm fire to fire
history intersections & concentric storys
worktitled "THE END"
master a & b roll original
was erased chemically early in june 1970
by film lab's permascratchremoval machine
fantastic
beat the devil w/forged irony

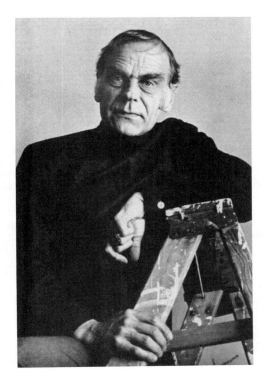

Portrait of James Broughton
("Filmmakers' Portrait Series
#22"), from *Cinemanews,* 70.4,
by Andree Ferris.

Robert Nelson

LETTER

[Editor's note: Nelson's essay was preceded by an epigraph from Bob Dylan: "Right now I can't read so good/Don't send me no more letters . . . no,/Not unless you send them from/ Desolation Row."]

For some reason Canyon Cinema isn't an alive vital organization. It's "back" a little bit. It's not out in front where things are at. There is no longer any prestige involved in being a member. What it *meant* to be associated with CC a couple of years ago has been denigrated by what everyone seems to believe to be the naturally short evolution that things have these days.

When I agreed to be a director, I did it knowing that my own image of Canyon Cinema had diminished and that caused me to feel a certain ambivalence about the job. I didn't know if I had my heart in it (I didn't). Why not just let it go on with its slow disintegration?

At the last directors' meeting Bruce Conner pointed out very clearly that CC is in deep trouble. The look and feel of decay is everywhere in the structure. We got a financial report and found out that rentals are down and on a downward curve and that expenses are up and on an upward curve. We haven't the money for the much needed catalogue supplement, let alone the money for a comprehensive new catalogue that should be in the works. We've got debts, etc. The whole thing could fold in a minute.

Bruce Conner's sharp focus on many of the Coop's problems allowed me to see it much more clearly in my own terms. That focus plus my own dilemma about whether or not I even wanted to get into it, made me consider more carefully if CC is really valuable or not. Is it valuable?

I realized after some thought that the coops (not just Canyon but the other few coops precariously surviving in the world) are truly post-revolutionary organizations. They are the best models that we have for organizations that can service people without exploiting them (and in our case, service *art* and *film* as well). The coops are the only place — *the only place* — that will accept any film without any kind of discrimination or judgments on content, who made it, why, or how. Mostly we have films that couldn't get in anywhere else . . . films that wouldn't be distributed by anyone else. Most of the 800 films that CC distributes could not be seen by the public, except for the fact that the coop exists (and many films that are now very well known owe a deal of their success to the coop).

It's truly an egalitarian organization. It's completely open to people. The membership *is* the Coop. Already we have a four year history (modeled after the NY Coop which is 10 years old) of operating under the guidance of principles that people are dying in the streets to attain! We have 800 political films (the representation of human values over commercial values automatically puts a political cast on things these days). We have 800 films that are mailed to colleges, universities, film clubs and theatres all over the country . . . and these films have an effect wherever they are shown. Any filmmaker that has travelled around the country and talked with people knows how true it is. The point is that these films represent a kind of humanism, they represent it and express it in every aspect from the effect of the films on the screen to the fact that they are in the coop. The hundreds of screens glowing with this 20th century folk art represent an extraordinary communications feat, because of the mounting resistance, repression and censorship that exists in all the public media.

Most people these days, it seems, like myself, are in some kind of dilemma about finding a place to insert themselves, to activate their energies to work for the positive values that are everywhere threatened in the world. In front of us is an organization that breaks from the model of exploitation for capital gains. It is designed to serve all of the people involved with it as well as servicing art and film. It serves the public in the dissemination of vital information, the free expression of people.

For those anxious to put themselves into something worthwhile and humane, I suggest the coop. All you have to do is support it in work and deed and, for the occasional times the members are called upon, with your energies. If CC is really doing something worthwhile then the energy to perpetuate itself should naturally flow from the organization. To the extent that we're ignorant of its value and to the extent that we're victimized in our own heads by our capitalistic heritage, we may choke off that energy. If CC atrophied for those reasons, we would suffer a genuine loss. At the moment it should be at the front of things, it would instead lie dying. I think that we'll be able to tell soon.

—

FROM *CANYON CINEMANEWS*, 72.1

Bruce Conner
LETTER

People keep asking if I have a new film. Until I got a Ford Foundation Grant seven years ago I was an artist who had made two short movies. Afterwards, I was a film-maker who incidentally made sculptures, paintings, assemblages, drawings, prints, etc. I was an "established film-maker." I resented that piece of paper that usurped the kingdom of the artist in favor of the film-maker.

Except for that grant all my films have been produced by myself. Style and form of the films were determined by the economic (therefore the technical) limitations of my own pocket. The films were basically a mime or a dance of pictures accompanying sound. Picture and sound are independent of each other but they relate to each other. My pocket wouldn't let me go beyond this style into synch sound. For ten years my personal income has been less than $4,000 a year (there's 3 of me) and sometimes less (none) except for 2 years I got rich. All other income went to making films, prints, painting, etc.

I've never been able to buy synch sound equipment, blimped 16mm camera, etc. after working with a camera and editing bench for ten years. In the last 4 years I've been rejected 3 times by Guggenheim Foundation, twice by AFI and more than that by commercial (& educational) T.V. Entry to commercial films is blocked by Bankers (the money) and Unions (the job). The films I wanted to make these last 4 years didn't happen and they won't now because they should have been made then and not now. I haven't used my old style equipment for several years so I'm selling it. It is no longer important to have synch sound or make the movies I planned. Thoughts about movies I want to make are turning off. Film-maker goes into hibernation.

The artist returns.

Chick Strand
LETTER

My dears,
Dedicated to pleasure seekers is rum pie . . . 14 Ritz crackers — smashed. one cup sugar, 2/3 cup pecans, broken up pretty small, but not crushed . . . mix all of this together in a fairly big bowl. Beat 3 egg whites until stiff, add ½ tsp. baking powder and some vanilla, then gently fold the egg white mixture into the dry stuff. Put into greased, floured 9" pan, bake at 300 for 30 min. Top with real whipping cream to

which you have added lots of rum, or cream d'cocoa, or whatever you like. If you can wait to chill it, do it, if not, so what. Do whatever you want with the left over egg yolks. Bruce Baillie makes some really fine pies . . . with grapes (seeds left in), geranium petals, whole wheat flour and wine to moisten. He recommends the Lusk Hotel in Lusk, Wyoming, or is it Montana, never mind, that whole area is nice in early summer.

I've been asked to comment on the old and new Canyon Cinema. Bruce started it years ago . . . held showings outdoors in Canyon . . . projected on an old sheet and had popcorn. Later he got together with Paul Tulley and they began showing features along with independent films at an anarchist café called the Bistro San Martin. People came. It was decided to get some dumb lady to do the correspondence and paper work . . . I volunteered. We thought that we would run out of independent films in a few months . . . but we showed films for five years at various places, always one step ahead of the law . . . something about running a business without a licence. We asked for $1 donation, and were always in the hole. We began a film workshop in Chick Callenbach's basement, and Chick had the idea for the Canyon Cinema News. We all worked very hard. One summer Chick donated his back yard, and we sat next to Strawberry Creek watching Gilbert Roland as Zorro. Times have changed . . . and we have had to change.

John Jost
UNDERGROUND MYTHS AND CINEMA COOPERATIVE REALITIES
(SOME CONCRETE POLICY SUGGESTIONS)

Contrary to one of the dominant myths of the Underground, film isn't some tantalizing presence unattached to the worldly problems of money, politics and labor. Nor is 'art.' Nor are those self-proclaimed genius/artists who occasionally give vent in these pages to their pious disdain for all things 'commercial.' Nope, all of these things are just like so much bullshit — as the periodic crises of the coops attest. Like it or not, film and art, and even filmmakers (whatever their disclaimers), are up to the neck in a complex interrelationship with economic/social/political factors that frequently could give a shit less about one's supposed sensitivity, artistry or budding genius, or about the imagined sanctity of 'art,' or even about your latest theory of film. With utter indifference the latest recession in the economy brings a drop in rentals, or an audience subjected to the umpteenth fit of adolescent 'self-expression' goes to sleep and doesn't come back until next week. In one fashion or another hard reality intrudes and the wistful theoreticians of the underground get a kick in the ass: the coops flounder, filmmakers can't get their print costs back, and the newsletters are swamped with a lot of whining. But whining is a bore and it doesn't help.

Some Dirty Proposals Aimed At Solvency
(Keeping the Truth in Mind)

The policy which governs the coops is openly idealistic: no censorship; any film is accepted for distribution. Despite the verbal winds of some underground propagandists this means the coops end up carrying a lot of shit. Admitted the coops — made up of member filmmakers — are loath to concede this. This makes the problem all the more difficult: witness the uproar when it was suggested that non-renting films be returned or charged a storage fee. However we would do well to set aside our sentiments and take heed of Mr Natural on the Last Supplement cover: He who shits in the road is going to find flies on his return. To a great degree the flies have come to roost on the coops: it is only natural that someone renting a film from a coop and getting a turd for his bother is going to think twice before he comes back for more. For all the theories devised to prop up the anything-goes policy, he had to sit there and watch some would-be artistic ooze slip by while his audience walked out. Since, like Hollywood, on a random basis, most underground films are just so much junk, this kind of renter's blind-man's-bluff is detrimental to the coops as a whole: the renter once burned is going to start looking elsewhere. And believe it, there are a lot of people who rent films in large quantities who simply will not book from coops because they are afraid they'll get junk. There is, however, a possible solution, and one which would not require a policy change from the coop.

(Previews)

In order to eliminate the five card stud game the renter is presently forced to enter, the coops could arrange for previews for bookers. This would let the renter know what he was getting, thus getting him off the situation in which the odds are against him, or that in which he is forced to 'play safe' with the handful of 'names.' Because the logistics and costs of allowing individual previews are plainly more than the coops could support, it is clear that preview showings would have to be for groups. This is common practice among commercial distributors, and while it requires some hassle, it is a hassle which to a large part would be happily borne by the would-be renters themselves — film freaks all. The scheme might go like this: coop asks filmmakers if they will/won't allow their films to be previewed. (Figure out why you wouldn't want yours previewed for yourself.) Then the coop, either through a willing member or through soliciting a heavy renter (through an announcement in the catalogue, newsletter, or by direct mailing), would arrange a series of regional preview showings, locations determined by known rental patterns. Those responsible for such a regional preview would have to obtain adequate facilities. Once that was assured the coop would announce, well in advance, a date or dates in a mailing to the area involved. The mailing would explain the reason for the preview and ask if the party would/would not attend, and, if he would, what films he would like to preview. Of the list this acquired, all, or as many as possible would be shown. If the number were simply too large to handle, those receiving the most requests would take precedence. Through this means the coop would relieve itself of any selective bias. If well organized, such preview showings could result in an appreciable increase in coop rentals.

(Packages and Bulk Rate Discounts)

Another factor which discourages rentals is that coop films are rather high priced relative to other films on the market. This is often blamed on the supposedly difficult economic straits of the independent filmmaker — a problem largely created by the filmmaker's attitude towards both his audience and the inescapable 'business' end of filmmaking. If more attention were given to both these things rentals could be increased a great deal, and, as a result rental fees could be lowered. There are two methods immediately available to accomplish this: one is to offer a discount for package bookings, the other a discount for bulk rentals.

In the case of the package discount, after receiving the filmmaker's agreement, the coop would offer say a 25% or 30% discount to persons who book a feature length — say 80 minutes or more — program for showing on a single date. This would encourage bookings of this sort, and the discount can be afforded because the operational costs of providing such a program are considerably less than if the same amount of film were dribbled out in separate bookings. The discount would be split 50/50 by coop and filmmaker.

In the case of the bulk rate discount a percentage reduction — say 25% — would be offered to those who booked, in one order, 80 or more minutes of film to be shown individually on separate dates. In this case, since the coop's costs are not cut as much as with the package, the filmmaker would absorb $2/3$rds of the discount and the coop $1/3$rd: i.e., the filmmaker accepts the greater burden in trying to get his film rented more often. This kind of discount would encourage the booking of more films, perhaps especially to renters who regularly book features for whom the drop in rental fees might allow the addition of a short to each program.

(Publicity Incentives)

A major drawback of the coops is that, beyond the catalogue, they do not provide any publicity push. As is well understood in the film business, good PR can make a trashy film box-office and lousy PR can kill a good film. The same is true of the underground, and to a large degree it is precisely those who have hustled their work who get good rentals, regardless of the quality of that work. The coops (meaning everybody who has a film with a coop) would do well to provide some incentives for those who can get themselves together enough to do their own PR. It is, after all, the people whose films do rent that make the coop possible at all. One way this might be done is to offer the coop's mailing list and use of the coop 3rd class mailing permit to anyone who shows up with a PR mailing — though he should do the address pasting and pay the costs of copying the mailing list. If there are any other ways in which the coops could help the filmmaker engage in PR activities, they ought to do so.

(Idealism That Doesn't Work Is No Idealism At All)

The operating principles of the coops, being idealistic, necessarily have a tough go of it when confronted with the less than ideal realities which we face. As much as possible should be done within this idealistic framework to make the coops viable, or else, finally, it will mean nothing since the coops will collapse. To that end members ought to remind themselves that it is a *cooperative* that they are part of — which is to say they ought to think of what is good for the collective body rather than what appears good only for themselves. I.e.: engage in a little self-criticism — is a film really good enough for public distribution? has a film become dated? does a film rent or is it just taking up space in the catalogue and shelves? are you helping the coop by your presence or are you just a dead weight? These kinds of questions are at the core of what a cooperative effort means — if coop members can't seriously confront these things for themselves (rather than having it dictated) then surely the coops will fail . . . and most deservedly so.

(A Minor Postscript)

The coop should, as a flat matter of policy, refuse to accept any prints which are in poor condition (badly scratched, lots of splices, etc.), and should automatically return worn out prints. If someone rents a film in poor condition he thinks that's what the coop dishes out and he'll not be back so eagerly — don't mess it up for everybody else.

—

FROM *CANYON CINEMANEWS,* 72.2

Bruce Conner

EIGHT DRAWINGS

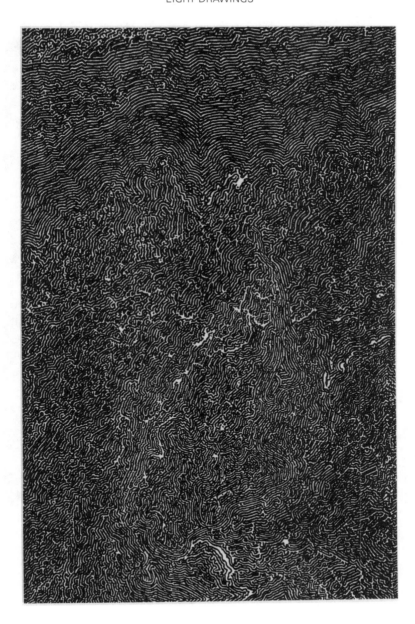

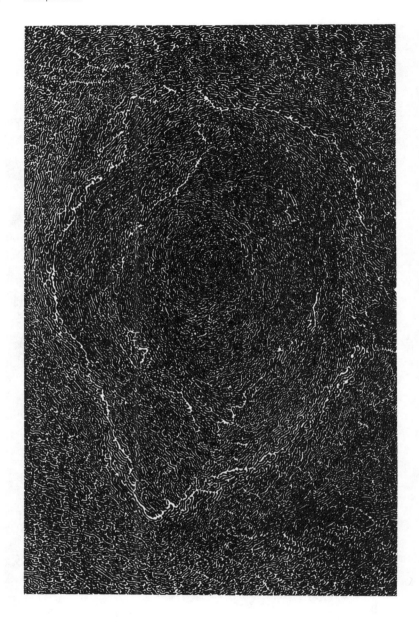

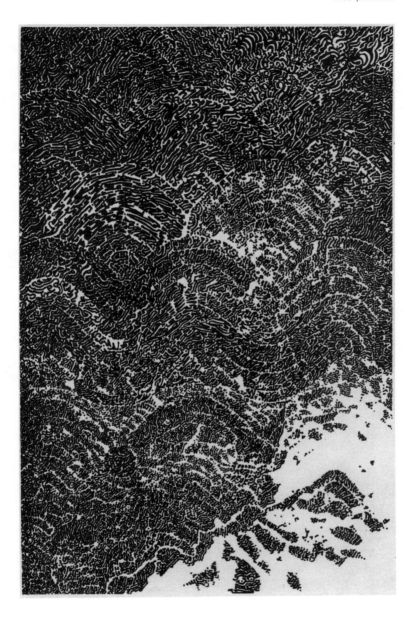

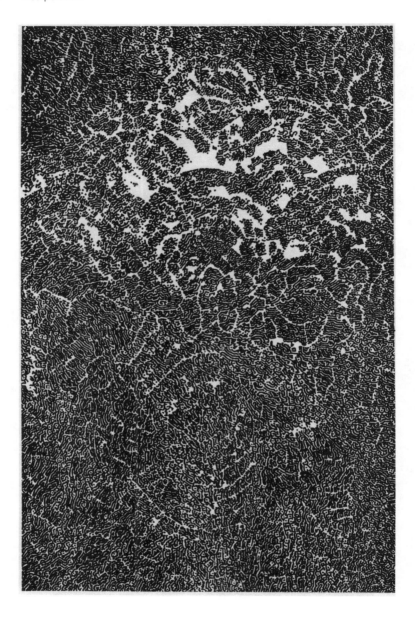

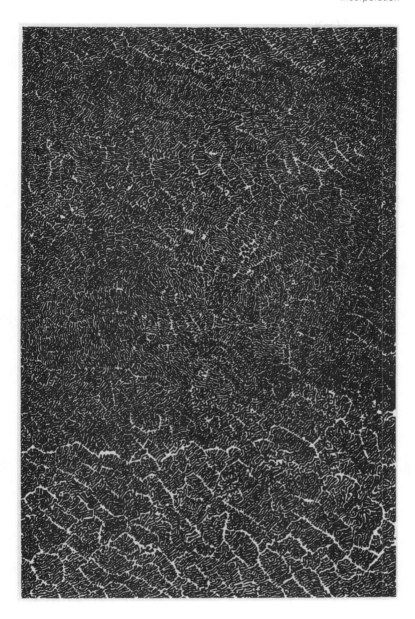

Don Lloyd

WHATEVER BECAME OF CANYON CINEMA CO-OPERATIVE?

When Earl Bodien started as our first manager in 1966, he had no idea what the Co-op was going to become like. Nor did anyone else. 'Business' was so light and the films were so few that he was able to handle each rental on a personal basis and inspect the films himself. For a while, each renter would receive a two or three paragraph letter from Earl concerning his or her rental. Earl had a talent for knowing who to trust and who to extend credit to, and where to draw the line to stop bending over backwards; this of course established a very good reputation for us. The 'Co-op' was still going to be an equipment co-op and filmmakers' workshop. (We actually did have an 8mm class taught by Bob Giorgio for a short time.) The business began usurping more and more of Earl's time and it was no longer something he could operate in the small room in the front of his apartment as something he could take care of every once in a while as he happened to pass by the room, like watering plants. His wife Mary Anne helped for a few months and finally Earl just had to leave. Film handling was turned over to Roy Ramsing. At that time all I knew about bookkeeping was enough to tell Earl to "save everything" and I would add it up at the end of the month. One of the last things he mentioned to me before leaving was that he thought Canyon Cinema ought to get an offset printing press, an idea that was about three years ahead of time.

When Edith Kramer took over the managership, she brought to the Co-op a substantial foundation of office lore without which we would never have been able to handle the independent film 'boom' of '68–'69. That put us right on our feet, expecting more of same (which hasn't come yet). Roy passed the inspecting job on to Ken DeRoux in November of '67 as a less than part-time job. Ken's perfectionism alone might have turned it into a nearly full-time job had not the steadily increasing inventory and volume of business kept him too busy to take such pleasures. He did somehow manage to maintain very high standards, and this, combined with Edith's always being there, working whatever number of hours were needed to get the job done, established firmly our positive reputation.

One by one, our other aims were pared off. Perhaps the basis for much of this was the long-coming realization that were we *not* going to be supported by big grants from the sky, that business was *not* always going to be skyrocketing, and that all expenses *would* be going up, especially taxes. The quality and amount of work that needed to be done was beyond anything you could reasonably ask a volunteer to do. As a result, non-staff participation in the Co-op had to decline. Tasks became more specialized so that it was more work to show somebody how to help you than it was to do it yourself. Efficiency became important. The role of the board of directors as spiritual representatives of the body of filmmakers became less and less relevant as

Canyon

Directors'

Canyon Cinema board of directors' meeting, from *Cinemanews*, 72.3.
This image was a centerfold.

Cinema

Meeting

the body of filmmakers became less and less cohesive. We didn't need general direction toward our 'ultimate aims' so much as immediate direction toward keeping our head above water.

When Jan Lash took over the managership in April of 1970, she had just come from a job as editor-typer-programmer-layouter of the KPFA Folio. KPFA is listener supported radio and the monthly folio communicates to all of its subscribers with articles, interviews, and the program for the month. So the first thing she met head on here at the office was the gap between the Co-op and its members that had developed from our survival patterns. Jan proceeded to de-centralize. Edith and our CPA, Phil Frucht, had been teaching me a little more bookkeeping all along, so I took over more and more of the financial matters, and Ken broadened the responsibilities of our 'shipping dept.' as well as taking care of the Cinematheque which Edith had run out of the office before. (Loren Sears was the manager during the interim. He had tried to develop a local circuit for the Cinematheque which could have done much to support the office, but the timing just wasn't right and there weren't enough people involved to make it work. Loren was responsible for pulling together over $300 from the filmmakers as a retirement fund for Edith.)

Jan always wanted to work on the Cinemanews to stimulate a more supportive exchange between the Co-op and its members, but her responsibilities as manager made her stick to 'survival' essentials such as the Double Supplement to the catalogue, and to making the office more efficient, and also, when Ken quit in November '70, breaking in new help, and finally running the Cinematheque (for free) since last June to help pay for the monster catalogue coming up. We had a run of short-term employees in 1971, filmmaker-members who were taking an active role like Peter Hutton and David Boatwright as film inspectors and Paul Lawrence as secretary and Dagny McClosky as secretary. We had hired help for Catalogue #3 and things got rolling on it only slightly behind schedule, but when the tremendous proportions of the job became apparent, it fell back to the office to get it out.

Ken DeRoux returned in November of '71 to take on the managership of the office. Jan is presently in semi-retirement (which means full-time at home instead of in the office) doing the catalogue which requires a mess of talents and a lot of energy, and which will be a fantastic book, furthering our reputation into the realm of professional. She and Dennis Tremalio will continue running the Cinematheque until the end of May, at which point they are expecting a baby and Jan's retirement will perforce be complete.

Ken has hired Gene Kenney as film inspector and Susan O'Neill as secretary, and I'm still here (though now on half-time basis) and the board of directors (see below) is becoming more actively involved.

—

FROM *CANYON CINEMANEWS*, 72.5/6

Peter Hutton

c/o Mifsud, G.P.O.
Box 2716, Bangkok
Thailand

LETTER FROM BANGKOK

In Pattaya with Misfud halfawake in slowmotion Asian dream floating on the Gulf of Siam. Bangkok engulfed in Thai futurism with the embellishment of military dictatorship. Little men wearing guns like wristwatches, Pattaya 100 miles south, empty bungalow slow tropical rhythms and Misfud's saxophone. A car just drove by so fast it speeded up my heartbeat.

I'm still spaced from the abrupt transition of time and spatial elements — like a minor astronaut in an experiment we've just watched a massive army of red ants transport a giant dragon fly and wing across the floor. Tomorrow is "Low Krathong," a Buddhist celebration, the people float little boats and temples on the rivers and in the sea, they are decorated with flowers and candles. Maybe the ants will float the dragon fly. Heartbeat back to normal. I've started some filming but am uncertain of ASA's. . . . Film goes to Australia for processing, 3–4 weeks, but we're trying to locate something closer, projectors are expensive to rent ($20 a night w/attendant). Busy improvising viewers. Maybe we could use P. Feinstein's article on making a Steenbeck from a blender. I'm contemplating going to work in Sandpiper Lounge w/ Dragon ladies and slow fans, if so I'll be able to stay for sometime.

The *sounds* here/hear are amazing. Wild birds lizards chinese gong music the final touch to hypnotic Asia gone slightly mad.

I hope to hear from you soon . . .

Much love . . .

—

FROM *CANYON CINEMANEWS*, 73.1

Ken DeRoux

CANYON CINEMA, WHAT NEXT?

Canyon Cinema is now well into its seventh year of operation as a film distribution co-operative. It has maintained its initial concepts of accepting any film submitted for distribution, with the filmmaker retaining all rights to his/her film and to its presentation; and is organized in a way that the governing board of the Co-op is elected from within the filmmaker membership.

Seven years out there may be a certain amount of bemusement among the founding fathers and mothers that it's still around and even some feelings that maybe there's not any reason it should be. But some think it should. There are still ideals, both jaded and unjaded. Some filmmakers know exactly why they're in the Co-op. Others have no idea. Most are in it for the money and some just have to put their film somewhere. At any rate, the Co-op continues to serve a real purpose, providing both financial and moral support to independent filmmakers.

There are a few things that have changed in these seven years, most notably the percentage and the energies of the people involved. Canyon's percentage split of gross rentals between the filmmaker and operation expenses has just recently changed; from $66^2/3\%$ to 50% for the filmmaker from $33^1/3\%$ to 40% for the office, and 10% is being paid back to the cost of publishing the recent catalog. When the catalog is paid for, the percentage should revert to 60% filmmaker, 40% Co-op.

This percentage change is perhaps reflective of the general economic situation in the country and the increasing cost of living. It *is* related to the fact that rentals have dropped from the high point of 1968–69 (which now appears to have been a "fad" period for "underground" films) to a rather low, sometimes up, sometimes down leveling off place; which when down, leaves a very small margin for operation. Canyon has always taken a generally passive stand towards promotion (partially because of lack of funds), and waited for the renter to come to us. In addition it has been the policy not to promote one film over the other, which as a rule, means not saying anything. This policy grew out of the early FOUNDING concern for protecting the rights of the filmmaker, and to get away from judgmental practices. But there is a growing awareness that this doesn't rent, or goes somewhere else, and rather than "your" film renting instead of "mine," nobody's does. There is some reluctance to change this policy for fear of opening up a Pandora's Box, but it probably will be changing, although time will tell to what degree. The Co-op office has always offered programming assistance and tips on new films to the customers it was on a friendly basis with. It's just time that the service was allowed to come out into the open and be of more use.

The Directors have expressed a desire to more actively promote or advertise the Co-op films. So far this has been restricted to getting the catalog sent out to a larger number of potential renters and whatever free publicity we can get in magazines. As (or if) money becomes available, other types of promotion should be thoughtfully considered. The Canyon Cinema News should be used more directly as a tool for publicizing specific films in the Co-op. (As has been said many times before.)

To a lesser degree, the inflexible rental rates have probably contributed to the present economic situation too. The rates are high, and this is probably why almost all rentals are to schools and other funded operations. This is a difficult problem and goes hand-in-hand with the economics of making short films independently. There would be some advantages though, to a policy of allowing discounts in certain cases, without the need of getting the filmmaker's specific approval; rather, the Co-op should have a blanket approval for these situations.

For the Co-op, as it is, the catalog is its primary asset. It is the only way in which we advertise the films and most rentals result from the listings in the catalog, the balance of rentals coming by word-of-mouth (where would we be without word-of-mouth?), promotion by individual filmmakers or occasional mentions in magazines and newspapers.

But since the catalog is so important, a corollary is that it is an increasing liability, and may indicate the need for some changes in Co-op structure. For one thing, the increasing number of films listed and the thus larger catalog has made it impossible for the Co-op to pay for printing from its percentage of rentals. For the foreseeable future, catalogs and supplements will have to be paid for by pro-rating the expense among the filmmakers according to space. The increased number of listings also poses an additional problem, especially with regard to potential renters who are unfamiliar with the films. The sheer volume of titles, combined with the myriad styles of description and lack of "subject" categories tends to discourage a lot of these people. (These are often people who may have liked a certain film and wonder if there are any others of a similar kind, or people who are unfamiliar with "underground" films but would like to rent something "different").

Canyon now has well over 1000 "different" films, and new ones are presently coming in at a rate of something like one every three days. This could obviously get to be a problem. For several years there have been discussions at Board meetings about devising some kind of system of categorizing the films in the catalog in order to assist renters, but no one has yet been able to figure out how this might be done. Recently the Board has brought up the possibility of limiting the number of films in the Co-op, perhaps by some kind of natural selection whereby any film would still be accepted, but if it didn't rent, for instance in two years after listing, it would be sent back. It seems very likely that a system something like this will have to be adopted, or we will run the risk of collapsing under our own weight.

Reassessment is in the works. The needs and positions of the membership have changed over the past years. In addition there is quite a bit of cloudiness among the members as to what their relationship is to the Co-op: what the Co-op can do for them and what it can't, what they need to do in order for the Co-op to do what they want it to, and what they can do for themselves.

Canyon, while maintaining its filmmaker oriented policies and ideals, should begin to temper them with a better understanding of the renters' role in distributing film. With some thought and some money the Co-op can continue to be a viable alternative to the too-often-discouraging pitfalls of commercial distribution.

3 : Revitalization

During the years when Diane Kitchen was at the helm of Canyon Cinema (she arrived in 1974, left in 1977), the nature of the organization changed in a variety of ways. Kitchen made efforts to remedy what seemed to be the deterioration of Canyon's distribution business. The long-discussed separation of distribution from the nonprofit sectors of Canyon took place (with some serious misgivings on the part of some members, including Bruce Conner): the Cinematheque, now housed at the San Francisco Art Institute, became a separate organization, and the *Cinemanews* became a different kind of publication. Kitchen seems to have been well aware of the small-town spirit that had been so important to Canyon early on, and she worked quickly to revive something of this spirit in what were clearly changed circumstances.

When Kitchen arrived, the annual income from Canyon distribution had been falling for several years, from a high of $54,000 in 1969–1970 to just $28,000 in 1972–1973—a drop of more than a third. Her commitment to reviving the distribution operation, which resulted in Canyon's fourth major catalog, did not bring the organization back to the boom moment of the late 1960s; in fact, judging from the numbers, Kitchen's efforts do not seem to have had any impact on Canyon's business—despite Kitchen's assumption that the more renter-friendly *Catalog 4* (published in 1976) would be a major improvement over *Catalog 3*. Canyon's income was $37,000 the year Kitchen arrived (1973–1974); it fell to $32,000 in 1974–75, to $30,000 in 1975–1976, and to $26,000 in 1976–1977 (the worst year in Canyon's history), and was up slightly, to $32,000, in 1977–1978. Canyon distribution did continue to operate effectively and efficiently, and this may have kept the organization from folding altogether, but a clearly positive change in Canyon's financial health would not be evident until the 1980s.

Kitchen was successful in her attempts to reenergize the *Cinemanews*, which by late 1973 was publishing virtually nothing of interest and had lost any clear sense of identity. Under Kitchen, the form of the *Cinemanews* was regularized: each issue was printed on 8½ by 11 inch pages, stapled together, and although the covers of successive issues varied considerably (the name of the journal also changed again: beginning as *Canyon Cinemanews* and becoming simply the *Cinemanews* as of the sixth issue of 1976), the feel of the periodical became more predictable. Each issue was approximately the same length; the front and back covers included photographs of filmmakers (many of which were part of

165

George Kuchar on the set he designed for Larry Jordan's *The Apparition* (1976), from *Cinemanews,* 74.4.

what was called the "Filmmaker Portrait Series"), stills from films, and artwork by Canyon members. Kitchen was able to create a consistent look for the *Cinemanews,* without sacrificing its antiestablishment feel: each issue included a range of typefaces and page designs, though certain typefaces and page designs were reserved for particular kinds of information, so that considerable variety was created with a minimum of confusion. In a subtle way Kitchen even emulated the self-effacing, community-oriented spirit of Baillie and Menefee, who generally did not list themselves as editors in the *Cinemanews,* even though the names of the staff were indicated (their self-effacement seems overelaborate; surely readers should know who is responsible for the issue of a periodical they are reading); after the first three issues in which she lists herself as editor, each subsequent issue "was put together by Diane Kitchen."

Kitchen was a hands-on editor who understood how important the newsletter was to the local filmmaking community, to Canyon distribution, and to the field in general. She was able to expand the intellectual dimension of the *Cinemanews* without losing the sweetly anarchic tone that had energized the magazine during the first years and then under Menefee's and Baillie's editorship. A wide variety of news items, brief essays on film-related technologies, letters, poems, drawings, and photographs continued to find their way into the

Cinemanews—plus an imaginative variety of contests and other features designed to remind *Cinemanews* readers that they were part of a small but vital and high-spirited community. The November/December 1975 (75.6) issue indicated that entries "for the *Canyon Cinemanews Malapropism Contest* are now being accepted at Room 220, Industrial Arts Bldg., Sausalito, CA 94965. Prizes will be announced." The May/June issue (76.3) presented the winners. First place went to Tony Reveaux for "Kenya Cinnamon Ooze"; second place to Richard Lerman for "Can Yon Cinema Lose?"—though I have been laughing about Freude's silly "Can-you-sit-on-my-shoes" for decades. A Canyon T-shirt design contest (won by Bruce Conner) followed.

The cover of the March/April 1976 (76.2) issue includes three photographs of an early Canyon event in Chick Callenbach's backyard and "Chick Strand's Recollections of Canyon Cinema's Early Beginnings, with Added Commentary from Chick Callenbach." This appeal to the roots of Canyon and the *Cinemanews* was confirmed by the regular inclusion of letters from Canyon stalwarts and various forms of "neighborly" interchange. Bruce Baillie continued to make contact with *Cinemanews* readers in brief notes; early in 1976 (76.2) he reported in from Vermont: "Dear Folks and all good friends. I do miss you in exile here in the east . . . but this week reprieve. Vt. lovely, not crowded. Much snowing. Good small group, like family, here at Dartmouth. Ray Foery is teacher and filmmaker. Vladi Petri [Petric] (Mus. Of Mod. Art) just here, good man" [76.2]); and in July, from Bard College:

> Dear folks, the Billy Bish school of Integral Media continues ["Billy Bish" is one of a number of characters Baillie uses], day to day, students welcome. Never know where it'll be the next day. Current seminar focusing on survival in the tropics of the Hudson River valley in summer, while staying ahead of the administrators (of an institution wherein one might be temporarily obliged to perform his/her labors). In between, somehow, squeezing out the birth of that miraculous *song* which defies, indeed transcends all of man's mundanery. —Pvt. Bruce Baillie, summer '76 from the cellar of Ward Manor, Rm. 96, Bard College, Annandale-on-Hudson, NY 12504.

And Chick Strand wrote, "Dear Friends, Nice cool weather here after the hot desert winds that brought everyone on their knees to the edge of lunacy, but I've remembered that sick bears eat ants . . . it's always feast or famine here. Work continues on BLESS ME, ULTIME . . . slow but sure . . . so all is well" (76.4). The January–February 1976 issue reported that "Pat O'Neill had a cerebral hemorrhage and underwent 10 hour brain surgery. He is having a miraculous recovery, is out of the hospital and is convalescing at home"; and in the May–June (76.3)

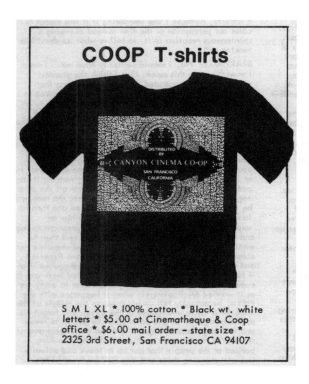

Canyon T-shirt with Bruce Conner's contest-winning design.

issue, O'Neill himself wrote to say, "Things are going along OK down here in sparkle city—the doc's did a good job and I can walk, talk and see and digest my dinner! Only problem left is that I can hardly *read!* Words look strangely unrecognizable, but that seems to be improving. Thanks a lot, everybody, for the cards and encouragement! It was good to know I have friends in Sausalito I haven't even met!"

In at least one instance, confusion between the feeling of community maintained by the *Cinemanews* and the actual community of those who worked at the Canyon office resulted in some embarrassment. In the spring of 1976 Will Hindle wrote from Alabama during his long convalescence from an auto accident in the fall of 1975, in a hopeless mood, to indicate that he was planning to have a will drawn up: "I have gone as far as I can. But at least I might be able to make a will that would help others. . . . I already have Canyon Cinema down as second beneficiary of my annuity, my mom coming first (but my death might kill her). And I thought I would do the same with my land and equipment and build-

ings here." He asks readers to let him know if they have any response to his letter: "I am virtually alone during this attempt to recuperate and some form of
answer/rapport/conversation would be of much help in guiding me. . . . 'Post
accident trauma' is what they have called it, but I feel it with the violence of hell."
In July 1976, after a late June letter during which Hindle seems to have completely recovered (*Cinemanews,* 76.4), and after seeing the *Cinemanews* issue
(76.3) with his earlier letter, he describes discovering "this thing I had written
under medication way last spring to the CCC office people, only; and there it was
all hanging out. . . . If you'll forget that pitiful pack of words I'd appreciate it.
Think moss. Think go. Think fall, gall themselves and gash gold vermilion; think
dappled dawn drawn falcon. So the small rain down can rain" (*Cinemanews,*
76.4).

The *Cinemanews* continued to be a general nexus for sharing information of
many kinds. The September/October 1976 issue included a plea from Jean
Peraino at the United Farm Workers of America national headquarters in La Paz,
California, requesting a copy of the Canyon catalog, and (since "to put it rather
mildly, there isn't a heck of a lot to do here") inviting Canyon filmmakers to visit:
"Should any of you there ever have occasion to be in this neck of the woods,
please make it a point to stop and visit for awhile. Just announce yourself at
the checkpoint and ask for myself, or someone on the film committee." The
November/December 1976 issue included a letter from porn star Harry Reems
and the "Harry Reems Legal Defense Fund." Reems had been arrested and found
guilty of being involved in a "national conspiracy to transport interstate an
obscene motion picture":

> In January 1972, I participated in the filming of the controversial sex movie DEEP
> THROAT in Miami, Florida, by accepting a one-day acting role. I was paid $100
> and signed a contract relinquishing all artistic, marketing and distribution rights.
> In July 1974, I was arrested in the middle of the night by FBI agents and subse-
> quently extradited to Memphis, Tennessee. . . .
>
> . . . the Prosecutor contended that under the conspiracy laws, all actors, writ-
> ers, directors, technicians, film processing employees, even location owners are
> liable for prosecution if the final product is later found to be against the law.
>
> Thus, anyone who worked on a film ruled obscene after it was completed
> could also face charges years later, thousands of miles from the filming location,
> and under laws applied retroactively. Artists, sculptors and their models may be
> liable after they sell their work . . . any time, anywhere, if found obscene.

Kitchen also provided expanded space for reports on filmmaking activities in
other nations. For example, Lyle Pearson contributed interesting reports from
Palestine and India.

Kitchen seems to have been one of the first to recognize that the events hosted by the Cinematheque might have a life beyond one evening's presentation. In her second issue as editor (September/October, 1974), she included "Peter Kubelka at the Cinematheque, October 3, 1974," a transcription of the discussion that followed a presentation of Kubelka's films. Interviews with Stan Brakhage, Chick Strand, George Landow, George Kuchar, and other luminaries were included in subsequent issues. Some of the interviews and discussions that were published in the *Cinemanews* during these years were reprinted from other sources, though the majority were recorded in the Bay Area and first published in the *Cinemanews.* For the portfolio of documents that follows, I have selected only conversations and interviews that appeared first in the *Cinemanews,* and, in particular, interviews that seem to have had particular relevance and resonance for the Canyon community.

The shift in the focus of the *Cinemanews* toward particularly accomplished filmmakers was one dimension of a more general change that was taking place in the sensibility of those who had a serious interest in avant-garde film and in the self-perception of those who identified themselves as avant-garde filmmakers. By the 1970s a number of filmmakers had produced substantial bodies of work, and an audience for this work had formed in locations across this country and in Canada, Europe, Japan, and Australia. Not surprisingly, more and more filmmakers were beginning to take themselves seriously as professional film artists; and increasingly, the audiences interested in their work (including many subscribers to the *Cinemanews*) were seeing these filmmakers as significant figures whose thoughts about their own films and about cinema in general were not merely interesting or useful but *important.* Throughout the Kitchen years, the tone of the *Cinemanews* remained comparatively informal, but increasingly, this informality was a means of contextualizing the reports and interviews that were becoming the focus of the periodical. A column by a "Commodore Sloat" (I have not been able to identify who this writer actually was) that provided amusing letters satirizing the increasing canonization of particular filmmakers, along with the publication of poems by James Broughton, who regularly made light of serious issues, helped to maintain an unpretentious tone. When Kitchen left Canyon and the editorship of the *Cinemanews* fell to others, the trend toward a more intellectually serious periodical continued. By the late 1970s much of the intimate feeling that had characterized the *Cinemanews* up through the mid-1970s was gone and had been replaced by different forms of "intimacy"—pieces of experimental writing and new expressive forms of reviewing, for example.

The portfolio that follows my interview with Kitchen includes several transcriptions of discussions with filmmakers at the Cinematheque. In my presentation of these discussions I have remained true to what seems to have been an assumption on the part of many of those connected with the *Cinemanews* and the Cinematheque: that the best transcription is the most literal, the one most precisely true to the voice recording. As a devoted reader of the *Cinemanews* during the 1970s, I was hungry for the filmmakers' insights, but even at the time, I found the literal transcriptions of these interviews—some included every "uh" and "mmm," every vocal hesitation and misstep—annoying and fundamentally misleading, since in our experience of a conversation we tend to ignore vocal detritus the same way we ignore accidental scratches and dust when we watch a print of a narrative film. I have come to understand the literal transcriptions published in the *Cinemanews* as a defiantly anti-illusionist device that was meant to render the interviewees human in ways that many interviews tend to hide. And, of course, these unedited transcriptions *were* characteristic of the informal, "no-bullshit" attitude of many of those involved with Canyon. I have reprinted discussions with filmmakers in the manner of their original publication. Especially since most of these interviews are relatively brief, the frustrations caused by their style are overweighed by the filmmakers' insights—and in one or two instances we are reminded, precisely by the *Cinemanews* method, that some brilliant filmmakers are virtually incoherent as public speakers.

Some readers may be aware of my series of interview books, *A Critical Cinema,* published by the University of California Press. The interviews in those volumes are the result of considerable manipulation of the taped recordings I make with filmmakers: that is, I assume that the tapes, and my careful transcriptions of them, are the raw material out of which, over time—and in concert with the filmmaker—I can fashion a conversation that will represent what the filmmaker and I see as the essential ideas and experiences informing and relating to particular bodies of film and video. Finished *Critical Cinema* interviews generally bear little resemblance to the original recordings. My desire to make interviewing filmmakers a component of my research and my particular approach to interviewing were, in part, a direct result of my reading the interviews and post-film discussions published in the *Cinemanews* during the 1970s.

Conversation with Diane Kitchen, March 2002

MacDonald: Your editorship of the *Canyon Cinemanews* was a bright moment in the history of the journal, and I've heard from more than one person that without you Canyon itself might have disappeared.

Kitchen: I don't know . . . it may well be.

MacDonald: When did you first become involved with Canyon?

Kitchen: This morning I drew up a hazy outline of my involvement—hazy because when I moved to Milwaukee from San Francisco, I gave the Cinematheque a lot of the paperwork from those times. What I do know is that I started sometime in 1973. I was hired to do what they called in those days "the booking." This meant that when orders came in for film rentals, either by phone or mail, I would scope out how long it would take a film to get where it was going and how long it would take to get back, type invoices, and take care of that process.

MacDonald: Were you already a filmmaker at this point?

Kitchen: No, when I was hired by Canyon, I didn't know *anything* about film— but I wanted to; that's why I got involved.

I had stumbled into various Canyon Cinema screenings, without knowing what Canyon was. My friends and I would say, "Well, some of those crazy films are showing over at Intersection; let's go see what they're doing tonight" (Canyon screenings were held in the basement at Intersection, which was housed in a former church in North Beach, a short walk from the Art Institute). We'd go, and, despite our lack of any frame of reference, we'd enjoy it—sometimes, and sometimes not. It was just part of the San Francisco scene.

I was a student at the San Francisco Art Institute, in painting and sculpture, and after graduation, I hit the road and took a ten-month journey. When I got back, I needed a job. I was painting and working in clay—but I was also thinking, "Wouldn't it be nice if the painting was large, mural-sized, had lights behind it and things moved" [laughter].

But, no, at that time, I didn't know about film. There was no film department at the Art Institute when I was a student, though I learned later that Bob Nelson was getting one started.

So after this long journey, I was broke and scrounging around for a job, and thought, well, if I could get a job doing something around film, I could at least start learning a little about it. A friend, Susan O'Neill, was working at Canyon as the booker and was about to quit. She said, "You should take my job." And I did take it. The job didn't pay very much—probably minimum wage.

When I started, I saw that there were a number of ties between Canyon and a large, loose affiliation of people, many of whom were, or had been, connected with the Art Institute—artists in San Francisco who were working in various media. Peter Hutton was a member; I had become acquainted with him when I was a student and knew that he was doing something with a camera. And Anne Severson had presented a couple of those programs we had gone to at Intersection. She had been my first-year humanities teacher. Around that time I heard she was filming students standing nude [*Riverbody,* 1970], and then later that she was aiming a camera at women's vaginas [*Near the Big Chakra,* 1972]. So I guess I did have some frame of reference.

When I arrived, Canyon was in transition; all the people who had been running it had decided to leave at just about the same time. In those days, Canyon had a staff of three: a manager, a booker, and a film shipper who shipped the films out and inspected them when they returned. Rene Fuentes-Chao was the new manager, but I'm forgetting the name of the guy he hired to do the shipping [Adolfo A. Cabral]. I do remember that I would give him directions about how to ship a film, and he wouldn't want to do it that way because he thought he could save money by shipping the film another way, and so films wouldn't get to the screenings on time. That resulted in a lot of angry phone calls from renters. Rene didn't know avant-garde/experimental film at all—even *I* knew more than he did. He really wanted to be a distributor of international feature films. An opportunity hadn't come along yet, so he had taken the Canyon job. He had such an elaborate personal life that he put a separate phone line in for his personal phone calls.

Anyway, his was a rather unorganized system of managing poor Canyon Cinema, which, I saw pretty quickly, was not in good shape. It felt like things were on the downturn, and I thought, "Oh, *this* is why everyone quit!" Our board meetings were full of gloom and doom. Rentals had gone down.

A new catalog had come out in 1972, before I got there. The catalog had been organized so that all the filmmakers could design their own listings. Now, it's always been, and still is, Canyon policy that filmmakers *describe* their own films; but in *Catalog 3,* they were doing the graphic design as well as the written descriptions—a freewheeling idea that was fun in the abstract, but that made for a rather confusing catalog.

At this time, the office was located over in Sausalito in a rambling World War II prefab building right by the docks. We were on the south end of the second floor and had good light. We shared the space with an architect; on the floor below us were sailmakers; and throughout the three floors of the building were small businesses and artists' studios. Different filmmakers would drop by to bring films in or to take films out, or to check on things, and you got to know people.

I got to know Gunvor Nelson, who was coming off a relationship and was moving back to Muir Beach. She had a spare room in the back of her house, and she asked if I wanted to rent the room. I don't know if you've ever been out to Muir Beach, but it's a very beautiful area, and rural, with no commercial development at all. I decided to take her up on the offer.

109

Pages designed for Canyon rental catalogs by George Kuchar *(Catalog 3)*, Ben Van Meter *(Catalog 3)*, and Adam Beckett *(Catalog 4)*.

VANMETER

<u>THE NAKED ZODIAC</u>

PISCES 5 min. Rental $9. Pur. $100.

ARIES (Not Available)

<u>AQUARIUS</u> 5 min.
  Rental $9.
  Purchase $100.

<u>CAPRICORN</u> 6 min.
  Rental $9
  Purchase $110.

<u>SAGITTARIUS</u>
  (Not Available)

<u>SCORPIO</u> 11 min.
  Rental $15
  Purchase $250

<u>LIBRA</u> 6 min.
  Rental $9.
  Purchase $110.

<u>TAURUS</u> 10 min.
  Rental $15
  Purchase $225.

<u>GEMINI</u> 6 min.
  Rental $9.
  Purchase $110.

<u>CANCER</u> 5 min.
  Rental $9.
  Purchase $100.

<u>LEO</u> 6 min. Rental $9.
        Purchase $110.

<u>VIRGO</u> 11min. Rental $15.
        Purchase $230.

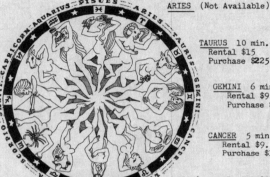

Astrological figure and character studies in the nudie genre'. Originally an 80min.
work in 12 parts each featuring a different young lady. I have divided the film into
twelve separate short films and am offering ten of those for exhibition this year.
All segments of The Naked Zodiac use complete nudity. Some are more erotic in content
than others. Scorpio is the only explicitly sexual scene, although Libra and Virgo
seem to arouse a good deal of p-----t interest. None are hardcore porno and no over-
lit clinical photography is used. These films are most suitable for a college age
audience, perhaps used as a serial (in any order) on a continuing film series. My
favorite reviewer's comment about THE NAKED ZODIAC is the following:

"VanMeter has a Rubensque appreciation of flesh."
                                    Stanley Eichelbaum S.F. Examiner

<u>VIVID COLOR 3D NUDE MODELS</u>

Color 15 min. Rental $15 Purchase $300.

Colored lights and lovely ladies.
Snatches of great beauty.

<u>THREE OLD NUDIES</u>

B&W Silent 9 min. Rental $9. Purchase $110.

This is a found film vintage about 1925?
Includes THE FIVE BARES, SHE PUT HER FOOT
IN IT, & PEEKING TOM. Very innocent and
amusing.

Gunvor was interested in what was going on at Canyon—not necessarily wanting to be heavily involved, but interested—and I told her that I didn't think Rene was all that appropriate for Canyon. I described how he and his boyfriend were always having big emotional turbulences and how the red, personal phone was always ringing. She didn't like what she was hearing, so she called Bob [Nelson], and they and the other board members got together and decided it was time for Rene to go.

I remember the board meeting that was held to discuss what to do next. People were dispirited, and here was another crisis to deal with. Bob Nelson said, "Let's close Canyon down and send everything to the New York Coop." That's how far things seemed to have sunk.

There are certain moments in the history of an organization that are a barometer of the state of that organization. One of these moments happened just after I had been hired, when Rene was still manager. One day, Michael Stewart, who was a filmmaker living in Sausalito (he had films that were renting), comes into the office with his dog, and the dog immediately goes over and pisses on a big box of catalogues. I remember thinking, "Even the *dog* knows the state of this organization!" [laughter].

I liked the *idea* of what Canyon Cinema Co-op was (it was called Canyon Cinema Cooperative in those days, even though it may not have been a true cooperative in terms of how the law defines cooperatives), the fact that anyone could put their film into the collection and that Canyon tried to give as much of the rental as possible back to the filmmakers. It seemed to me that Canyon was worth trying to save. And I thought it made sense to have one organization on the East Coast and one on the West Coast, because at that time, there *was* East Coast filmmaking and West Coast filmmaking. Films from the East tended to be much more structural and theoretical, and films from the West, much more wild and woolly.

They asked me if I wanted to be the manager. I didn't want to work full-time, because I was trying to find a camera and get involved in other things. But I saw that it was either now or never to try to help Canyon out. I took on the role of manager, though I didn't like the title, "manager"; I didn't want hierarchy in the office. It didn't seem healthy, especially since we were struggling.

Diane Levine was hired to do the booking. She'd worked as a production assistant on a Larry Jordan film, a feature with actors [*Hildur and the Magician*, 1969], and came recommended as being an organized and good-hearted person. We had already hired Wolf Zimmermann to do the shipping. He was a student at the Art Institute.

I wanted everyone to take equal responsibility, and that's why we didn't have titles. We needed to have real cooperation in order to make Canyon work. And commitment: we were all working part-time, probably for minimum wage.

A system had been set up long before, but hadn't been followed. So we just started trying to get things in shape. I got into the books and saw that finances were bad; correspondence was going unanswered; when films were damaged, the people who damaged them weren't being charged and we weren't getting replacement footage from the filmmaker—all kinds of important stuff hadn't been done. There were stacks and stacks and stacks of films that hadn't been cleaned or inspected for a *long* time. The four-hundred-footers were in piles three or four feet high on a bench, and when a film had to go out, it would just be pulled out of the pile, inspected real fast and sent off. It was a big mess.

I hadn't really worked in an office before and didn't really know what I was doing, but most of it just needed common sense, and we learned as we went. I do know this: if it hadn't been for the filmmakers whose work rented a lot, and who tended to leave their rentals in Canyon for long periods of time, we wouldn't have made it.

Wolf started going through the stacks of films and inspecting them, regardless of whether they needed to be shipped out, and did a *great* job. And when things got going a little better, various people would come in and do nice things to help out; slowly it felt like more of a community was starting to build. Later, when Wolf left, we hired Larry Huston to do the shipping and inspecting. He was a film student, also from the Art Institute, a capable and easygoing guy.

I always wondered if *Catalog 3* was a problem. If people called and asked for a catalog and you sent it out, you didn't hear from them again. Meanwhile, a lot of new films were coming in. I thought we needed a new catalog, but there was no money. The filmmakers certainly weren't going to want to pay for another one; they'd just finished paying for *this* one.

MacDonald: So what did you do?

Kitchen: I had heard that Jonas Mekas had helped the New York Coop with an NEA grant, and I knew that the New York Coop, like Canyon, did not have non-profit status. Mekas had funneled the money to them through his organization. So I called him up and told him the situation. He said, "You can use my group as a conduit for a grant," and that's what we did. We wrote an NEA grant and received it, through Jonas, to do the catalog. This was around 1975; the new catalog came out in 1976. It took a while to put together, because we didn't have any equipment. It was pretty much done by hand. But at least we could pay for the typesetting and the printing. The filmmakers paid for photos if they wanted them.

So all these various things were happening in tandem—including getting the *Cinemanews* going again. The old board members were starting to cycle off; the same few people had kept things going for so long—and they were tired. We went out into the Canyon community and appealed for new people to become involved.

Running the Cinematheque was another aspect of Canyon. For about a year after Rene left, the Cinematheque was run by Vincent Grenier. He was good at programming, but left the other work to the office to handle. When Vincent moved to New York, the two people who applied for the job were Carmen Vigil and Charles Wright, and I can still see them sitting there on the couch, which was probably an old car seat with one of those East Indian bedspreads thrown over it. Charles was quiet, but seemed likely to be very careful about keeping track of things; and Carmen was outgoing and ebullient; and I thought, "Well, maybe they should do it together; what one doesn't have, the other does." After they left, we talked about it: "Why not see if they'll *both* take it." And they did. And that seemed good, because especially at the beginning, they nurtured each other. After a while Charles moved to New York, and Carmen took over at the Cinematheque. Carmen wasn't real good organizationally, but by this time, there was a system: Charles had set things up pretty well.

The main problem once things were a little bit stabilized was that it was becoming so expensive to run the Cinematheque. Carmen increased the number of visiting filmmakers, and paying honorariums and film rentals was costly. This was a chronic problem. It seemed logical to look into becoming a nonprofit organization. Those were the golden days for nonprofit formations because of the National Endowments for the Arts and for the Humanities. As out of the loop as I was about a lot of things, I did know that. At some point I started looking into nonprofit status, and we talked about it at board meetings, and I learned that in the past Canyon had tried at least twice, maybe three times, to get nonprofit status for the Coop, but hadn't been successful.

I went down to the law library to look up what exactly "nonprofit" meant, because none of us really knew. The statutes spell it out pretty clearly: no one can make a profit from your service. And at Canyon any filmmaker who has a single rental makes a profit, so that was that—very simple. There was *never* going to be a way to get nonprofit status for the *distribution* arm of Canyon. The *exhibition* arm might be eligible, but only if it was separate from the distribution. And so we began working to separate them.

The Cinematheque has been nonprofit since 1977. Not everyone has been happy about the separation, but at least both organizations have survived.

MacDonald: What has made some people unhappy?

Kitchen: I guess it has to do with the fact that, compared to the Cinematheque, Canyon, the distributor, has always had a lower public profile. The Cinematheque has a more prominent public personality because it brings people together; it sponsors screenings of people's films and has a certain rapport with a wide range of filmmakers and with an audience. The Coop is just for renting out films—nitty-gritty, not glamorous work.

Anyway, I said to myself, "Stay long enough to do the catalog and finish the nonprofit application." I was certainly interested in seeing Canyon and the Cinematheque continue. And if the organization hadn't split, it is possible that Canyon would be long gone, because the financial situation was dire. If not everyone has been happy, all I can say is that there was no one else there doing the work, so the job got done the way the person who was there thought was the best way to do it.

MacDonald: One problem, of course, is that unlike other distributors, Canyon has always had a policy of not promoting any particular film or filmmaker.

Kitchen: That's part of the framework of the organization. All along, there have been a few filmmakers whose work has rented enough to make it possible for those whose work does not rent as much to have a place where they can keep their films in distribution. When I was at Canyon, it was clear that without Gunvor Nelson, and Bob Nelson, and Brakhage, and Bruce Baillie, and a few others, it would have been very difficult to keep things going. This was just simple economics.

Actually I was kind of thrown for a loop when I saw *Oh Dem Watermelons* [1965]. We had six or eight prints that were out *constantly,* and I thought, "I've got to see this film!" I have a kind of goofy sense of humor myself, but when I finally did see it, I wasn't sure what the big deal was. Not that I didn't appreciate it, but I thought, "Six or eight prints? Out *all the time?*" In those days, I was trying to envision the context where the films were being shown. I didn't know why some films rented so much and others never rented. As I saw more of the films and came to know something of film history, I understood it better, but I also got a sense that there were some places that just rented the same things all the time. Also, there were trends that would come and go.

When women started making more work, the same three or four films by women—all having to do with eroticism—were going out a lot. That stopped when that trend ended.

But to come back to *Oh Dem Watermelons: now* when I see the film, I'm much more amazed by its audacity than I was then.

MacDonald: In addition to your other duties at Canyon, you became involved with the *Cinemanews,* which had a nice period early on, then crashed and burned for some months, until 1974 when you took it over. You put filmmaker portraits on the covers—first, Storm DeHirsch, then, Peter Kubelka . . .

The photograph of Peter Kubelka, the way it *should* have looked on the cover of *Cinemanews*, 74.5.

Kitchen: Oh, that terrible picture of Peter Kubelka!—it was *such* an embarrassment. The actual picture was fine, but we were using the cheapest printer in San Francisco; it was all we could afford. When we finally saw the cover, it was too late, and the guy wouldn't reprint it.

MacDonald: Early in 1975, the *Cinemanews* starts to have its own look, and more substance. You begin mixing graphic formats in interesting ways, and so on. And you also used the *Cinemanews* to build a sense of community. For twenty-five years I've been laughing about the contest for readers to come up with a malaprop phrase that sounded like "Canyon Cinemanews." I still remember Freude's contribution: "Can you sit on my shoes."

Kitchen: [laughter] An image that sticks with *me* is the photo of Edith Kramer milking the cow. Freude got hold of the picture and found the quote to go with it.

MacDonald: Your last regular issue as editor of the *Cinemanews* was 77.4—except when you stepped back in with Gunvor in 1980 to do one issue.

Kitchen: Yes, our reactionary issue.

MacDonald: I assume you were reacting to the Abby Child and Henry Hills period of the *Cinemanews?*

Kitchen: [laughter] Well, to a kind of New York stuffiness.

MacDonald: Those issues that Hills and Child were the ringleaders of were important in a different way from your issues . . .

Kitchen: Oh, definitely, definitely. I celebrated what they did. I was so glad that *someone* had come along who was willing to *do* something. And the *Cinemanews* needed to grow and mature.

In that issue you refer to, Gunvor and I felt we *had* to reprint one article that had been in a previous issue ["New York Cut the Crap," by Gary Doberman]. It had appeared in such small print that you practically needed a magnifying glass to read it. The whole thing, the article and the tiny print, seemed so pretentious to us at the time that we decided to reprint the article, but make it *so* small that you *couldn't* read it. For us it was a dada moment. We were laughing the whole time we were doing that issue.

MacDonald: Your primary involvement with Canyon ended with the new catalog in 1976?

Kitchen: Yes. I had left the office to do the catalog, and Shelley Diekman took my position and worked with Diane Levine. *Catalog 4* came out in 1976—with the manila yellow, William Wiley cover (that was the color of the paper he did the drawing on). I quit after the catalog was done.

I also wanted to finish the nonprofit process. One problem was coming to an agreement with everyone as to what the address was going to be, which became a political issue. I really didn't care, so long as the process happened. We ended up using Carmen's home address on Head Street. He and Susan were married then. I've always been very fond of Susan, so I felt comfortable with that, but some people may have felt that the Cinematheque shouldn't be too connected with Carmen.

The hardest thing was finding a name for the new organization. I remember asking *everybody* what they thought. We had lists of names, and we finally agreed on the Foundation for Art in Cinema, which Edith Kramer suggested, based on the old Art in Cinema series that Frank Stauffacher had done at the San Francisco Museum of Art in the forties and early fifties.

I shouldn't forget to mention the help that came, once again, from Jonas Mekas. He was very supportive of our efforts and gave us a copy of his own bylaws and articles of incorporation to use as a guide.

The Cinematheque did not get nonprofit status right away. I don't remember whether it was the State of California or the Feds who wrote back and said, "Well, we know who *you* are! You're the same people trying to sneak this distri-

Cover of *Canyon Cinema Catalog 4*, with drawing by William T. Wiley.

bution organization through." I called the guy and explained that there was nothing sneaky about it; it was in the papers we submitted that this new organization
was a complete break from Canyon, with a new board of directors, a new
address, a new bank account, new everything. So he relented and sent a few
questions asking how the Foundation for Art in Cinema was going to be organized, and I sent back a few answers, and finally nonprofit status came through.

When I left, we had a big party at Carmen's house. It was very touching; people had taken up a collection, and they presented me with a check and a really sweet letter. I was totally surprised because for me this had all been a labor of love.

Some years later, things started to break down at the Cinematheque. I'm not sure exactly when it all broke down, but I got call saying that there were problems, and did I want to be on the board. I hadn't become completely disconnected; I had been going to some Cinematheque shows, but I wasn't paying much attention to the organization itself, so the call came as a surprise.

At this point the board was Warren Sonbert, Nick Dorsky, Larry Jordan, and Shelley Diekman. We started having meetings, and it became clear that Carmen was no longer doing a good job. He and Susan had divorced, or were divorcing. Things were turbulent for Carmen. When I saw what the books looked like, I could see the problem was serious.

The final straw for me was when I heard that Carmen had left the mailing list on the bus. The mailing list is your lifeblood; that's who gets the calendar. If you're so distracted that you leave the mailing list on the bus, I'm sorry, but there's no more forgiveness. Even so, we all had a strong attachment to Carmen as an individual, and we were very grateful for the service he had done. He had been very energetic and loyal to the Cinematheque for many years. He'd brought people in and expanded the reach of the programming so that it became international—he'd done *a lot*. So we had some deep discussions about the situation, and it came down to one meeting at my kitchen table. I said, "Listen, I found out that Carmen left the mailing list on the bus. That's *it*. I love Carmen as much as anybody here, but he has to go." Nick was, "Awww, I don't know," and Warren too. But I said, "Too much work has been done to let one person take it down, and that's what's happening."

In the end, we all agreed. It wasn't fun and it wasn't happy. Carmen and I had gone through a lot together as Canyon people. But it had to happen.

We started scrambling around for Carmen's replacement, and at some point we learned that Steve Anker had moved into town. All I knew is that he had gone to school in Binghamton, and that he had helped Michael Snow on a film [Anker worked on Snow's *"Rameau's Nephew"* . . . (1974)]. That sounded good to me.

Steve was very leery about the job. He met each of us and was very cautious. We begged him, and eventually he agreed. Steve's story would take many chapters to tell, because he had the helm for so long and expanded the Cinematheque in all kinds of ways.

Scott, I know I'm forgetting so much.

PORTFOLIO

FROM *CANYON CINEMANEWS*, 74.5

Peter Kubelka at the Cinematheque, October 3, 1974

Question: What is the title from of the "Arnulf Rainer" film?

Kubelka: The titles are always the compromise in my films. All were commissioned films, which started out mostly as an attempt of a compromise by myself and then after the film was finished it usually ended with disillusions with the people who commissioned it. But I still gave the title as a thanks to whoever sponsored it. So Arnulf Rainer wanted a film about himself.

Q: Is there any reason you don't use subtitles?

K: I use the words not just as a vehicle for the meaning of the word. What I use, what you hear, is spoken language, what I call "real language" which has almost nothing to do with written language. So written language you can translate, not real language. By real language I mean, as soon as a person talks, the talk is a part of this person as much as the face is. It expresses the actual mood of the person, the character, the upbringing and so on. It is something completely different from the words which actors speak. Actor words are like . . . artificial milk. It's not grown. But a grown real language comes out of a person, like the smell; you cannot change your smell on purpose and you cannot change what your language gives away from you. When you see and hear the film you get all these meanings, you get the moods. The only thing you do not get is the actual meaning of the words, which of course is a loss. But there is no way helping this. You have to learn the language.

Q: About the black and white film, "Arnulf Rainer," to me it's an antifilm.

K: It's just the opposite for me. It's the essence of cinema. I went back to the four most simple and essential elements, which is light and the absence of light, and sound and the absence of sound. My film is my articulation. It goes upon you and you have been preconditioned by other people who have formed you before me. So the concept you have been geared to, sticks at this time still stronger to you than what I gave you here. My code gets into a decoding office with you which is geared to other codes. You have to be living very near to the reality of the person of whom you accept an articulation.

    Cinema is not as cold, as untasting as it seems. It is not so living as a violin is living, or as a drum is living. It is cold, it's iron, steel, celluloid. But there is sensual taste in cinema which you can see most in my films in the Rainer film. The "Arnulf

Rainer" tastes different in every projection. No film varies so much because there the taste of the projection comes to be. It tastes different as to the room.

Q: Is there a specific structure in the sound of "Arnulf Rainer"? At times it is very melodic, the repetitions.

K: Yes, it has a completely balanced structure. It consists of 16 even parts. I worked two years on this film and it was in a way a development of a musical form where I did not decree things but I discovered things. Such as you discover musical rules. I came upon fact, such as you can have let's say, a positive or a negative in time, of a certain form. It's an exact structure, there is nothing random in it. . . . The sound was what is called white noise. It is the nearest to white light containing all frequencies and I chose it for that. I just wanted sound; least specific.

In "Unsere Afrikareise" everything was recorded on this journey, all the music. It's nothing made afterwards. No sound mix. Straight cuts. The whole film is tailored, hand-tailored.

I worked mainly with 35mm because there was no 16mm filmmaking in Europe at that time. I like very much to handwork. When you have 35mm film in your hand, that feels really good. It fits in your hand and when you hold up an image you see what the image is. Then you have what's very important, the space between the frames where you can make a splice. Film is made in the head too. The Africa film was made with a workprint with a negative in black and white. That was all I could afford. I didn't have a color workprint.

I always wanted shortness. I wanted speed. But one other reason my films are short and compressed is the absolute lack of any money . . . most of the films are handmade without having access to an editing table or projector.

Q: The third film I noticed it looked like a label. Could that possibly have been a commercial job for a commercial?

K: Yes, that was done for a beer factory. The name of the factory is "Schwechater." This film maybe illustrates best these two components of outside pressure and my own wish. My ambition was to make the greatest visual adventure that anybody had ever seen. And this film was my great breakthrough in terms of energy. Because here I broke the old rule that film is moving. The wrong concept. Film is not moving. Film is the projection of still frames. And the possibility to imitate movement on the screen is the weakest part in cinema. The strongest is that I can give you a different visual information each 24th of a second. This is what happens in this film.

Q: Do you think the filmmaker should be interested or have control over distributing their own films?

K: I for myself will never work for a producer. And I will not sell any rights to my films. And I will not give exclusivity to anybody. I will not be a product in the hands of businessmen. I make films so they can wait twenty years, you see? I'm not dependent that I'm released next week. Friends of mine, filmmakers who have tried to work with producers, their life is sheer misery. So the best way is the co-op. The only way. And also a co-op which is conducted on different economic principles than the commercial cinema. The commercial cinema is an industry. It aims at bringing back the invested money. It aims only for the broadest public. The commercial industry puts so much money in publicity. Now all attempts to channel independent films into a commercial system has not made money for the filmmakers. There was a long attempt in New York, it was called Filmmakers Distribution Center and they tried to bring films into cinemas. And it didn't work because a film only makes money when it runs for, I don't know, for twelve weeks, in a sell-out crowd. The two-week run is already a loss. There is not enough public for us. And there is nothing wrong with that. There is not enough public for Bach either.

So the co-op, what does the co-op do? The co-op does not make publicity, which is completely right. Because the publicity goes by word of mouth, by books, theoretical books, and by the Canyon Cinemanews or whatever. The co-op system gives practically all of the little money that comes in to the filmmaker without spending for nonsense. The co-op that's a system which is economically feasible, and this system only, will in the future keep us alive.

—

FROM *CANYON CINEMANEWS*, 74.6

Will Hindle

RECUPERATING AT HIS FOREST PLACE IN THE
MOUNTAINS OF NORTH ALABAMA, SEPTEMBER 1974

An untraceable beast took a nip at me this summer and set off the mandatory Pasteur anti-rabies vaccine treatment . . . from 14 to 21 shots, one a day, back and forth across the belly. I guess it isn't really mandatory. You can die in slow agony if you want, I suppose.

The shots aren't much better than rabies themselves, but at least you can walk away. Makes my third Pasteur go-round. The amassed pathologists at the University of Alabama Medical School (28 blocks) in Birmingham smilingly proffered that after this series I might well be immune to hydrophobia. During that initial emergency examination I had about the only "pleasure" I was to have for some months. Usually I think of definitive things to do and say seconds after it's too late to do them. But as one intern stepped forward, working his way through the amassed specialists and nurses sprayed white and pompous for the day, his face and head came very very close to the small bite marks on my arm. It all seemed the right thing to do. I rose up slightly and barked in his ear. Many nurses came unglued, their little college hats askew, their little upsidedown watches bobbing around on bahzooms brought to full alert. One of the Viennese-type doctors turned gray and sickly, the circle exploding backwards. The intern slammed backwards into one of those sterilized and enamelled cabinets, totalling it.

Had to take a medical leave of absence this quarter. And in quiet forests there comes a great surge to wax waldenesque.

Between stomach cramps and assorted dry-heaves, I sat on possible moraines in dappled shade. And on a certain afternoon, I thought a great thought. It was Thursday, I remember. The thought escapes me now.

I have felt for quite some time but I figured it to be a personal stigma. Things have changed and not all for the good . . . and a lot of people can't see it or won't. The teaching of film, the personal film, is a new phenomenon. The avant garde of this genre went "into" film from the hip or heart or soul. Few had rigid, formal schoolized "training." The personal film *was* very personal. Poverty of equipment was the natural state of things and we improvised and from the improvisations (our mistakes, even, if you will) came a vast splay of individual approaches and insights and expressions. Things have changed. I used to make a little film and then stick it in a drawer. I'd never heard of a co-op and there were only a few to hear of.

Majoring in English I found the diploma just the right size to line the spoons and fork's drawer with. I was a gardener, and I sailed the south seas on a schooner called *Wanderer* out of S.F., and I sorted bills for Pacific Gas and Electric. I did a lot of things but I never put what I loved out in the market place. I saved, then filmed out of pure joy and feeling. It was nothing to make an A/B/C — rolled master on a single gang re-wind . . . mainly because I was never told you had to have a four-gang re-wind. I soared on wings of sheer ignorance. Like the bumble bee (whom engineers have proved aerodynamically unable to fly) I didn't know I couldn't, so I did.

Film is now taught, for the most part, as a giant, many-tentacled thing. The student is almost immediately exposed to intricate requisites and an explosion of patented machines promising infinity of expression.

If someone were to hand you a bevy of light-weight precisioned motion picture equipment and say, "There it is out there, the entire world . . . go do it." How far do you think you'd get. If the "Business" route didn't kill you first, the infinite variables would. Man and filmer need to feel, know, and love some *one* thing, well, deep. You can't do justice to anything, including yourself, not to mention love and understanding, on the fly.

At the risk of sounding like *Kung Fu*, allow that person a hard won smattering of basic, even hand-wound, equipment, a fairly steady side job, and seek of him (or he seeks of himself) the properties and essence of a single square mile of earth and sky and water. You will find a personal art emerging. Paradoxically, imposed limitations (as opposed to limitlessness) tend to free you. Tends to give a firmer grasp. Tends to let you truly see. A quickly-passing blur of "everything" shows you nothing. On film, it might evidence itself as first "quaint," then pitiful fragmentation.

Allow the filmer an even smaller quadrant and the ratio of peace and knowing increases.

Perhaps the violently miniaturized circuitry of a proud "Hal" or computer might revel in its singularly effortless and feelinglessness of binary procedure, but man must pause in order to personally function. That little bit of devilish poverty the avant garde of the personal film felt was its time of birth and knowing. It's practically impossible to avoid in a land of gross exploitations (the land of incinerated joplins [Janis Joplin, who died in 1970, was cremated]), but once you embrace "popularity" and *seek* "acclaim" and recognition as motivation, you have turned your back on the only love film and you can know.

"Classes" in film now, often, are celebrated by men and women who themselves had nothing to begin with. Their love affair with film was pure "need," pure fulfill-ment . . . almost as if had there been no film they would surely have invented it with bare hands. Yet some of these people start their new students out six feet above firm ground. Rules, laws, advanced pieces, grafted side effects . . . the roar is deafening and a dream can die of it. They preach the scope is "infinite" and yet growing, enigmatically.

Yet some teachers today are inflicting just such weaknesses on their students. And in some cases, students infecting other students with their own dilemma. Students come to study from the "masters" how to climb the expression ladder, yet the teach-ers teach from their own current levels . . . as if they themselves had started out so "well" equipped. The art is in the head, in the fibers. Why some of these gentlemen and gentlewomen persist in crippling their charges thusly is not readily explainable to me.

Some departments actually feel like folding if they don't have a steembeck (is that spelling right?) editing table! And other schools pride themselves on having at least three for the new filmer's use. All you have to do is reach over and unplug all those dazzling devices and said student can't operate.

The current "inflation squeeze" or "depression envelope" we're experiencing could be a great boon for films and filmers. I've told university audiences I've vis-ited . . . as I tell my own classes . . . [at] the university . . . to take small steps, *very* small steps first time out. Get to know that busy little picture box and its small circle of accoutrements before you start to run. It's not only prohibitively expensive to start out running but, often, what gets shown on the screen is a hit in the head. Nothing, if anything, of the vision comes across. And, too, don't populate your first efforts with casts of thousands . . . maybe not even two or even one. Share your fumbling early moments quietly in this love affair in the solitude of that which is awaiting you to learn, the camera. And try not to crank out action and insight in a smoke screen of zooms. Do not get restless over the fact that you must care for the camera *totally* or else no picture at all. Like anything else in the world, first/small things first.

With cutbacks everywhere there is now a perfect opportunity for those who learned and did with a minimum of equipment to now share those true and honest beginnings with their students . . . because that's where their students really *are*. Not up there in the beguiling glare of advanced decay, but back there where the good teacher once was . . . with just his head and love and hope to go on. And the teacher should tell, too, that jobs are not waiting for the graduate in film. Accepting an "offer" right off the bat (should one actually occur) would turn personal growth and fulfillment into mere labor, just working for money . . . not for the joy of filming. 'Cause employers (TV news, local TV commercials shot in city park, industrial promotion films, etc.) of this genre pay you to keep your mind closed and obedient, not open and growing. A marriage, a baby or two . . . and you can never go home again. Oh, you rap when a "great shot" gets into the current project but you know full well inside it was a fluke, not procedure.

A very good man in San Francisco used to give me pointers now and then ("What's a degauser?, Mr. Jones."). He started out with nothing but sheer imagination and energy. To pay for his planned personal work he rented a large building and put in a sound stage fitted out with kitchenset and living room set — all for income commercials. To pay the rent on the building, to pay the insurance, the salaries for people used in the making of commercials, the office help, the punch-button phones, the better home requisite for the big man filmer . . . they all took an ever spiralling need for more and more of everything. He never even had the chance to look back, once. Not one creation of his very own ever got made. That early-on crossing of wires shorted out every bit of what was him and his. He became a servant, not a lover, of film.

The student should, *must* be told that as with any other fine arts student, there is no waiting, hands-out-to-accept-him world out there. He and she must make that world themselves . . . and that means a lot of doing other things to pay the rent.

It is a vast uphill matter even at my own school, where I was asked to come to teach film as fine art, to get across the idea that film demands much . . . Most especially at first . . . and gives nothing until *you* get *your* head straight. The camera and emulsion are neutral, so to speak. Impatience, lack of respect for foundation and precision, coupled with high dreams of monetary reward and critical acclaim are instant anathema.

Friend Baillie (jeeze, since 1958!) writes he requested of his school permission to "teach" the film experience via a method of zen. Film people will live, eat and go about their learning in a packet of activity separated from other departments and classes. It promises to truly deal with personal discipline and basics . . . without which ain't nothing' gonna be done. My deep love and best wishes to him for this only-way he won out of school officials. May it flourish, but quietly, never to be exploited. And may schools everywhere be able to somehow stop their nervous twitching and ego scenes.

We're going nowhere, folks, until we learn and know that it is not the measure of what we can get, but what we can do without that gives us strength and self fulfillment.

With schools everywhere pushing "innovation" and "advanced research" in order to gain grants and stay alive, this must sound disgustingly naïve. I did not wish to offend.

Love,

—

FROM *CANYON CINEMANEWS*, 75.2

Stan Brakhage
REMARKS FOLLOWING A SCREENING OF *THE TEXT OF LIGHT*
AT THE SAN FRANCISCO ART INSTITUTE ON NOVEMBER 18, 1974

I have believed for many years and come to believe more and more the older I get that the art is given as a gift through persons' urgency. And that the responsibility of the artist is to be personal enough. That this gift, this that he or she could not arrive at along a train of logical thought can just come to exist along a line of . . . shaping itself according to the extent of the maker's experience and no more. That is, that it not pitch over into ego or that a maker begins to shape him or herself according to cleverness or whatever. Certainly there is no work that more confirms me in that sense than *The Text of Light*. For me it is most clearly of all things a gift given to me to make. I really have found only two things to say about it that illuminate what I was involved in; one is almost as a prayer bead or a constant reassurance I returned to Johannes Scotus Erigena's "All that is is light." Secondly, William Blake's "To find a world in a grain of sand."

Q: How did you make it?

Br: I was trying very hard to make a portrait. I am getting involved in portraits. I have known a man since high school and he subsequently became a multimillionaire. So for years we were separated in that way that millionaires and artists are separated. Finally we overcame that separation, and as this is an art school I think this is a valuable piece of information how we did it. I declared to him that I would never under any circumstances accept any money from him; and in such a firm and full way that he knew I meant it. Then we could be friends. To a man with a great deal of money, a poor man is a bottomless pit. So from that point on it became very interesting, the relationship, because his world was totally distinct from mine and was quite a mystery. In fact the American businessman is a real bogeyman. So along the line of doing the Pittsburgh trilogy on police, hospital, and at the morgue, I was determined to get a portrait of an American businessman if possible, and that it would be a rare opportunity, and that here was someone I had known since high school and there was a chance. So I was trying to photograph him in his office and he, terribly embarrassed, was blowing great clouds of Cuban cigar smoke and obscuring everything and I was failing. And it was interesting because I had a macro lens on, which I was using as a kind of distance lens. It has a bellows. And I was failing and the camera slumped forward and the lens bent sort of with the bellows and it seemed hopeless. But I have the habit to always look into the lens before moving the camera. So I looked and saw what seemed to me at first a forest. And I thought, my god, where is this coming from? And looked more close[ly]. And I called my friend around and he looked and was astonished and then I looked again and it had changed and a stream was running through it. Then I saw that the lens was pointed at his ash tray. So I began taking single frames of his ash tray. And he is so lovely a man that he accommodated this. In fact he's so witty a man that he invited people to go on with conference meetings on business and I went right on photographing this ash tray. His office also is such a location and construction that it has sun all day long. He has windows all round, from dawn to sunset there is wonderful sun pouring into this office. So I just began moving from window to window in this office, and Helen, his secretary, got very excited and brought other pieces of glass; which at first, only not to hurt her feelings, I set kind of around the ash tray. Then I noticed that if I touched [the] very outermost piece of glass out here, it very often changed what was in the ash tray. And then someone brought in the grand . . . so proudly, brought in a crystal ball. And this I put in the center of the ash tray. And there was finally a collection of very fine crystal all around the ash tray, and sometimes a little bit in the ash tray, and this way and that way and the crystal ball, and all this was in the sun of course, just shined beautifully and I went on clicking away, most of the film a frame at a time throughout that summer.

Once I remember somebody came to a business conference and they walked through the room and he said to Gordon, kind of very, "What's he doing?" And Gordon without a break in stride just said, "He's photographing our ash trays." This began to help him in business because people became so confused and disturbed at what was this mystery that he had the business edge on them. So it worked out fine for everybody. Except I made one error which I must point out. I became so obsessed with this ash tray that I bent over all summer and ruptured one, possibly two disks. And anyway it was worth it.

Q: I saw you one of the last times you were here and you were showing *The Act of Seeing with One's Own Eyes*. And before showing it you said it was nothing to be afraid of, it was only about light hitting objects and bouncing back and seeing it with your eyes. And I was interested in why after using light in such a very exquisite, definitive way you wanted to use it in a way that was so unarticulated, that was so abstract.

Br: Well, she is telling me in the form of a question that she thinks my film is unarticulated with respect to light. And I must disagree, that this film is called *The Text of Light* because in that ash tray I found a way to create an equivalent of many behaviors of light that I have observed, that are not recognized by science, and in fact I suppose would be considered mad by some of the less generous scientists of our time. But I will name a few that therefore, that because they are not recognized by science we are not trained to observe; and not very many people have seen these, though some have.

I have seen that before a rainstorm there are light-like streaks that come down through the air that are metaphors of rain though they are not wet. In fact have held my hand and some of them come through that hand with no sense of moisture and of course the fact that the streak goes right through the hand is itself clear that it's not raining. And then rain will follow. And because I live in a place where many clouds pass over and most do not rain, I had a way to check myself. Could I tell within 30 seconds to a minute if it was going to rain or not and invariably I could because always, if that cloud was going to rain, it was preceded by these light-like . . . they would be streaks as if you would see a tiny streak of light or spark in a dark room only they would be bluish. Though they could be yellowish also. Those are interchangeable colors anyway, optically. They could be yellowish.

Then I have seen light-like phosphorescence move horizontally along the ground, as a wind. And I have seen it pool, as if a pool of phosphorescent image. Then I have seen sometimes that streaks shoot up from these pools or from the very ground. Again light-like and ephemeral like a phosphorescence in daylight which makes shapes, shapes of plants. And I have seen this quite a bit in the spring on just dirt and I have seen a similarity of plant grow up in this place. I have seen as Kirlian photography almost touches on now, and maybe does, I have seen leaves spark or emit a spark-like emanation at their edges that are offshoots directly of the veins within that leaf, and therefore as that leaf then grows, do create a metaphor previous to the actual extension of these veins. These things I have seen, one, because I have been involved with seeing all my life and I'm really open to seeing all there is when I'm well. Two, because somewhere along the line I realized something that was constricting my sight in this pursuit: which was my training in this society in renaissance perspective — in that form of seeing we could call "west-ward-hoing man," which is to try to clutch a landscape or the heavens or whatever. That is a form of sight which is aggressive and which seeks to make of any landscape a piece of real-estate. In fact the irony that we have so named property our Real Estate demonstrates the western limitation. I would like to see science make a check of the eyes, of the musculature of eastern peoples, let's say as distinct from ours. I believe it would be quite distinct. This search for this form of grasping sight has created a powerful musculature to permit that. And too as is necessary to permit us to drive on these throughways [thruways] and to move with this mobility among these constructions supportive of that renaissance perspective.

Well, that pursuit is wonderful in itself, and it is of course my native pursuit, but on the other hand it has the problem that it is exclusive of all other kinds of seeing. So what I'm trying to get at, in order to see these things, I have to be in an extraordinary relaxed state of seeing. Then all other kinds of seeing become immediately possible and of great involvement with the light of course. And I believe, not only do I believe with Johannes Scotus Erigena that "All that is is light," but I even think that a wonderful thing has happened in our time and passed almost unnoticed. That a dialog beginning with him and reaching a public prominence in the 13th century in the writings of Grosseteste . . . Dig that name. The first man whom they tried to put down with the name Bighead. So he picked it right up and made them understand that it was so. And then later Duns Scotus and then of course Francis Bacon who is better known . . . who came and tidied up a whole lot of things and therefore is better known. But this brilliance of these Light Philosophers, English philosophers, who because of their feelings stated in words that: *thought was illumination.* I mean the last run down of what they did, is in the comic strips when somebody's supposed to have an idea: they make a lightbulb. But they felt their thinking was electrical or light-like. Now hundreds of years have passed and finally an enormous construct of science which would seem to be antagonistic to such thinking has permitted Niels Bohr and Riemann and of course Albert Einstein to prove, within that structure, that matter is still light. Light held in a bind. So what this ash tray permitted me to do was to photograph equivalence of things seen and processes of evolution, of ephemerality of light taking shape and finally taking a very solid seeming shape. Along the line of exactitude. On this level, it's even pedantic.

Q: I was wondering if you actually saw the spectrum through the viewfinder, through the lens?

Br: Yes, I saw very much what you saw on the screen, only it was better of course. Because in the meantime it has passed through . . . only what Eastman Kodak film would accept has been taken down, only what the lab didn't botch has been left on the strip. Then it similarly has had to pass through an interneg, and finally come to a print. So if you enjoyed this, then go look in an ash tray, or something. Because it's much better. How it's been able to pass through me so that it can be called a "Text," is that I have been true to my appreciation of light operating in every day life in these fashions, that is preceding matter. I even believe it precedes animal motion. But I have not seen that enough to be sure of it. But I believe that there is a form or at least certain kinds of gestures are preceded by a flash of light-like emanation. I mean this is very exciting to me, in fact it's . . . you see I've been reading Johannes Scotus Erigena and his later "echo," Duns Scotus, since Ezra Pound gave them to me at 18 or something. But it seems we are so trained in this society to read something and keep that quite separate from the living experience. So I thought it was wonderful but I didn't believe it. And then finally I came to see. And now I have had, through this ash tray, the opportunity to present an equivalent of it. And if you think about it, this is the most normal film in the world. Because here I am with a macro lens, which is a piece of glass here, and one stuck way out here, or several. And they are never more than an inch or two away from a crystal ash tray which is surrounded by other glass, so where does the lens end? That all could be considered a lens which is photographing the sun; and that's all that makes these shapes on the screen. And that's very exciting.

Q: My question has to do with what you said earlier. You said it had to do with a relaxed way of seeing and I was trying to get back to what you are now saying about seeing the ash tray. In my mind it seems the relaxed way of seeing comes about through the high excitement way of seeing.

Br: Well, I would agree with you because I don't, by "relaxed," mean placid. And I avoid the word "meditation" because it has certain Eastern connotations which in this society are usually misunderstood. So we need another word. What I'm doing in photographing this ash tray for instance, I'm sitting for hours to get 30 seconds of film. I'm sitting watching what's happening and clicking a frame, and sitting and watching, and further than that, I had shot several hundred feet and they seemed dead. They didn't reflect at all my excitement and emotion and feeling. They had no anima in them. Except for two or three shots where the lens was on a tripod, pressed against the desk, had jerked. Those were just random, but that gave me the clue. What I began doing was always holding the camera in hand. For hours. Clicking. Waiting. Seeing what the sun did to the scene. As I saw what was happening in the frame to these little particles of light, changing, I would shift the camera very slightly. If you want to know how slightly you have to realize I was never photographing in an area bigger than this 4th fingernail. You couldn't tap the camera. It had to be moved by a quivering attention of the hand. That took maybe 13 or 14 moves over a period of ten minutes. Then to get that in mind: what *it* was doing and changing and how *I* was dancing with it had to be extended in memory; one, how that would come out at 24 frames a second and two, as to, was the dance real?

And all the time I was doing this I had to have a friendly argument in my mind with Jordan Belson who I knew would hate just exactly this. He would say, Oh wonderful what it is, but why is it jerky? Or why not centered? Or, you know . . . And to hold myself together I would say, No, Jordan, it has to be this way. So I, I owe him very much. He sustained me in that way a beautiful argument can, because it was very much in his territory. I mean this film is very much on his side of the street.

Though there is another man I want to mention. That the film is dedicated to Jim Davis. I suddenly one night had this overwhelming feeling . . . I got mad . . . because someone had written an article on many people working with the so-called abstract film, which term I don't believe in anyway. But they had not mentioned Jim Davis; and he has always resisted being mentioned. It is true, he's a very shy man. He had lived all his life, the last 20 years at 44 Wiggins St., in Princeton, N.J., very ill with diabetes and with a lot of back trouble and in bed the last decade. With his great constructs before him, so that from his bed he could photograph whenever his constructs created a light pattern that seemed real to him, refracted light. He was literally the first man who had shown me refracted light in film. So I called him up and asked him if I could dedicate the film to him. And I was surprised that he didn't say no; but I'm so glad I did because he was dead a week later. Almost totally ignored. So he is someone to be looked at now that he's dead.

Q: I just want to follow that up . . . I think that most people are part-time film makers. And it's the moment of high excitement in which you realize you've got something there. As I watched this film, for example, I have very severe night blindness, as I watched this film I began to realize how important this night blindness is to me.

Br: Oh yes, wonderful.

Q: I was able to see a lot of things I never associated with that. It's the high excitement of the moment of capturing something which is so critically important to pass on to people. It's not to analyze in a philosophical way.

Br: Yes, I appreciate that: only it depends on how you use information. I mean, most people misuse philosophy worse than any other discipline in this time. And yet, I am very deficient in reading philosophy. Part of that, I was pre-prejudiced that this was the dullest area on earth by a series of very dull teachers. And only a very dear friend, Forrest Williams, who happens to be here tonight, has maybe saved me; and I would like to pass on to you, in philosophy you can find the most practical information in the world. You see, this line, "All that is is light" as translated by Pound and threads its way through the *Cantos* — many thoughts have moved along this line as if it's a very solid string. So it led me to the possibilities of this film. Now you say other people in the room want to make films and what will lead them? I don't know because that is truly a personal matter. And that's what excites me. Because it took me all these years to realize I could never be anything but personal. So then I had to ask myself, What did I think I was being those other times? Well . . . I thought I was being a good boy, and behaving myself, as I had been trained to do, and was continually encouraged for it, in fact threatened by every institute I've passed through. Be it school or job or whatever. And of course constantly by the overwhelming power of the government that is . . . I mean . . . the only contender left in the newspapers for equal space with the government, however stupid it becomes, is the sports field. And both of them move inexorably like a Chinese water torture against any concept of person. Sports move against it by putting the whole emphasis on teamwork to destroy the concept of play.

Someone asked me recently, Why have you struggled so hard to see and ended up so different from your neighbors . . . or something . . . who do you think you are? I said quite truly, To save my life! I knew they were trying to kill me and so when I first knew this I developed asthma at one year old. Which gave my mother a lot of other things to do. She was trying to use me because she had adopted me to save the marriage; and I'd failed. So she had for her efforts a child constantly wheezing. Then I moved to protect my skin surface — I was very fat, so I was again buffered against all this use as much as possible. Then I developed sinus trouble which shut off the nose. Earaches, glasses. Get the picture? By the time I was six . . . I escaped sports because I developed a hernia. The problem was that life wasn't worth living with all these tactics. So the next thing to do was get it all together and stop all this disease. In this society I think, for many, illness has been the only way to get through. And it may be one reason I have this back problem at this moment. Because the pressure is very heavy on me at this time. This may be. And if so, that's great because then I'll come to terms with it and find some other way and get rid of that too.

It has been — what I'm trying to say is that it has been a desperate struggle to keep alive. And to keep alive to me meant that I had to be personal, which is all that I could be. But then, having said all that, I want to say also, persons also wish to be social. So then the social inclinations come out. Like, I can understand that persons want to drive on the right side of the road or the left side so they don't run into each other. And I understand also of course, finally came with great difficulty, to beginning to understand the miracle of loving another. And that was very hard with this route that I took. That may have a lot to do with why I am an artist. And by "artist" I mean someone who makes things under/in trance. Things which can be looked at over and over again, or experienced over and over. Will last. Otherwise you can throw out the term "art" and I don't care. And I think I came to be able to make that because I had, was so locked in, that I was exploding with things. With feelings and thoughts that I wanted to get out. Then the way to get them out was the same as, I mean . . . Morton Sobotnick visited recently and told me that he thought the birth of music was the scream.

Two things: the scream goes to a greatest pitch that it can, but one cannot sustain that scream. So then the tone would drop away down low to provide a bass which can be held forever. Then a scale is established in between. My sense of it was that it began with the heartbeat which was overwhelming. That some man, woman, creature had to beat upon the chest to get it out, and stamp on the ground and then found a hollow log and then stretched skin over it. And you could send it for miles. So it's always that real . . . the need to get something internal exteriorized; and whatever the exterior is can only be an equivalent. Then people start listening to their own screams and their own heartbeats. Then to me, that's the point. I fear people getting hung up over art. That is, getting excited about art and just looking at art. To me, always an expression made out of such desperation and taking such a form, and leaping beyond what that person himself could arrive at; that is being informed by what you can call the muses, or god, or the angels or the subconscious, whatever you like. But something in the work process comes through, that I am not capable of thinking along the line of thought. It seems as if it comes from elsewhere, it does not seem as if it comes from me. But it only comes when I am being the most personal that I can be. Where I tell a story that's more unique to me, a unique story like something happening to me that nobody ever heard of [here, an accidental elision in the text of Brakhage's remarks occurred; the missing text was included in *Cinemanews* 75.3; I have put the missing text in bold parentheses] **(happening to anybody else,** then I know more that I am a person. And that's a very strong string for the conscious, the angels or muses to play upon.

It's caused me an awful lot of trouble, and made me very lonely that I see light behaving in ways that not very many other people see. And the ash tray, and this force that moves through such an experience gave me a way to exteriorize that. So I am very grateful.

Q: What about these flashes of light; do you ever see gestures, flashes of light, is that in the film itself?

Br: No, it's not photographable.

Q: Is this in mind?

Br: No, but that is an interesting question. What part of these visions are feedback fantasy, which is always just a mix, or an Irish stew of memories actually? So the mind can project out of the memory pot all kinds of mixes that do not directly reflect a creature you'll see on earth, but . . .

Q: What I'm talking about, is if you were in this last state you are talking about, would you be able to see what kind of mood I was in?

Br: Well, if I were relaxed and in my home, and able to relax to that extent and see, maybe. I do see auras, is that what you mean?

Q: All the time?

Br: Well, no. I have to drive on the freeways and make a living and so on. And I'm subject also to these ordinary pressures . . . and the world as it is. Which socially is, in my opinion, awful. I really feel that the human animal is up against the most intensive drive ever, to stamp out any sensibility of animal life. And, ah, oh people being persons. And I do feel it's so serious that I think the last public surfacing of persons is through the arts. And of course now, having been unable to starve out the artists, now the government is moving to create, ah, institutes to quote help the arts, end quote, and which will, to some extent, do that; but I am very fearful of what the intent is in) the long run. There is a greater fear, among those who rule, of The Arts, than there is of any political opposition.

Unfortunately, it is not that there are twelve dirty old men in Washington trying to destroy us all; it is that there are [is] in most people, through a cultural inheritance, an automatic wish to be governed and to govern others. And the government, they are the anchor down, if you like, of this proclivity. And the arts, artists in this century seem to make the only stance against this. And they do this not because they are wiser or braver or anything, but simply because no one has ever figured out how to make *a thing that will last* without being desperately personal during the making. So that's the struggle. And you could either regard it as very sad that you live in this time or very interesting. I do one or the other depending on whether I think I'm going to make it or not.

Really, I mean it's wonderful to live. And what worries me the most is that so much of the time I don't want to live, and so then I try to figure out why. Why not? Or for instance one of the prominent forms is that I go to the movies about twice a week. Now why? That's just an escape. And what could be more ridiculous when life is so short anyway to spend a lot of time and money and effort escaping. Then of course I get clues, like when I'm on a lecture tour and have to go to the faculty cocktail and it goes on and on and on. Then I stumble back to my motel in Pough-keepsie late at night and I'm desperate for the Tonite Show.

Q: It seems that your films might be short flashes of light, flashes of mind, inspiration, almost a separate personal eye seeing all these things on the ground, and then how do you structure something like that that seems to almost inherently tend to a short film, how do you structure a long film?

Br: Well, I exhausted everything I know. That's again as to why it's called *The Text of Light*. There are [a] certain number of extensions of light taking place that I have seen. So I exhaust all those I have seen, within a construction that gives me a sense of the whole world. And in fact to me on one level the film really can be seen very much as if exploring an alien planet which is very similar to the one we live on in many respects. Once I had exhausted . . . the ash try had metaphored for me and I had exhausted all that I had seen elsewhere, then I stopped shooting. And ordered that like a text, you could almost say an alphabet from the simple to the more complex, from the horizontal to the vertical, from meshes of light just come clumping, making triangles of mountain-like shapes through to finally what appears to me as a whole forest of trees, little flowers first, and finally gigantic trees. And that's one level of the film. Again, it was to structure it in a whole world sense and so there's also, there's a four season structure to it which cycles again and again. There's a day and a night. There's all that I know and all that's most familiar to me. Then too, that I was very moved by the symphonic form. I've always believed film is most close to music of all the other arts. It came quite naturally into four movements.

Q: You had answered it in a sense in what you just mentioned about the symphonic form and I was wondering whether at the start or somewhere involved in the middle of the film whether you have any connections to music or sounds per se because you bring up the scream, etcetera . . . and whether the editing or the pace at which the chops either increase in rapidity or decrease, give you any kind of musical sense of sound forms.

Br: In terms of the second part of your question, they don't increase or decrease just like that. There are increases or decreases but I can't say that's true as an overall form. But yes I'm very much involved in music, I listen to music and I mean not just as background, but I sit or lie down and listen to it when I'm home, two–three hours a day. It may be sheerly coincidental because I don't see any direct ties, but I was very involved in Schubert's Ninth Symphony while working on this film.

Q: Have you ever associated sounds with color per se?

Br: Yes, there is a melodic line constantly going through all the work as of the last decade. And I do think of shifting changes and tones, in most films a very cordial melodic development; and I'm very concerned with that. That's how I feel film and music are the closest — they share tone. Tone I take as seriously in film reaching toward music as Messian does in music reaching toward color.

Q: I was struck by how you get an almost simultaneous feeling of looking at something of extreme magnification and looking at something at great distance.

Br: Ah . . . I'm very happy that you have that vision of it because that is a very important one to me. I never did want to disgrace the ash tray or the event by just using it. Also I was very happy, Michael McClure was sitting next to me and he turned and he said, "Was it all one animal?" And I was a little stupid because of the occasion of the show making me a little nervous so I paused and I said, "Well Michael as you have to leave and won't hear the lecture after, I should tell you it was all shot in an ash tray." And he replied so beautifully, he said, "Ah, then I was right it is all one animal."

Q: When you say that the film sort of made itself you're really talking more about availability. Availability to listening or lending yourself to process. Have you used any tools and disciplines, drugs, meditation, psychoanalysis — that have increased your availability to those kinds of things?

Br: No I haven't because I'm afraid of them, though some have made use of these things. Some very fine artists. Each to each his own. For myself I have very much avoided any drug taking. Except for one, I'm a nicotine man and I chew tobacco. And I chew it a lot. And I don't meditate. I really want these qualities of seeing or recognition of the world around me, and this ability to make an equivalent of something I've seen on film, to last. I want these things to arise as naturally as possible. For instance when I most look at hypnogogic vision (that is what I see when my eyes are closed, which I think has a great deal to do with this film too) is when I have insomnia.

Q: I wasn't able to see any superimpositions in the film, are there any?

Br: No, there are no superimpositions in the film at all. There's a couple images that look like it but what they really are are slight changes of focus which in this mesh of light just create a totally different scene.

Q: Why didn't you use music to add to the contemplation in this film?

Br: Well because it would distract and be redundant and cut back seeing. All sound that does occur in sync, or intentional relationship with music, does diminish sight. So I've always thought of it — that you have to pay a price when you use a sound. And there are very few people that estimate that rightly. One of the greatest, THE greatest in my opinion is Peter Kubelka who really knows how difficult it is to make a sound film. You cannot take for granted that you just have a picture and a sound to go with it. Not at all. And I never felt a need for sound. Though I'm not against sound, as my praise of Peter and James (Broughton) ought to make clear. And Kenneth Anger, all three of whom work with sound in absolutely magical and incredible ways. But for myself I have moved along the line of the silent film which has a very special discipline; and I do that because of my own necessities to see certain particularities that tend to get blurred if accompanied by sound. Or, I have found no way to keep from damaging by any relationship, sound. On the other hand, I have just finished a 20 minute sound/sync film, the first sync film I ever made. And I'm very excited about it.

Q: With what you've said about the unconscious and implications of the muse and so forth, and that's where your ideas come from, I'm wondering if you can talk about editing. I'd like to know how you determine the length of each shot and the order.

Br: As to editing, I don't like the word any more, because it seems to imply the lord-god newspaper man with the green eye shade who takes all the reports and writes The Truth. Which of course is always a lie, then given to the people. Ah . . . the most horrible thing about journalism is that it's forgotten the origin of its name: "journal," that the newspapers were born out of private journals. That is, those persons who did attend the ball or saw the fire. And always just because of laziness I'm always wishing to have the unedited film. Twice in my life it's been given to me. But generally it comes back, the footage from the lab, and it betrays immediately to my looking that there are sections where the attention of the shooting of the photographing has dropped out or diminished. Or there are, also, I'm sure, sections that would be fine if I later could have the sensibility to see them clearly.

So my consideration is always to try to see what the film says and to study it in a sense and let it tell me, and then through the subconscious, if you like, to arrange the material so that it has the most of the impulse of the moment of photography in the final film as possible. Now in some works I am able just to take the work and drop out those sections where the attention was *not* at the moment of photographing; was too willful let's say. But at other times, certainly with this film, I am caused to arrange shots all over the place. As I . . . the problem is to, first of all, get the first shot. Once that seems to stand out as a beginning from looking at all the material, then what comes from that image leads to, can lead to another. And I search for that lead that will be of maximum intensity; i.e. not along the line of likeness; because I do believe, as Charles Olson traced the word, that "like" does finally root back in the word "dead." And I have always sensed that to like something was ok (I like to like things), but it was a weak reference.

So I make my moves along the lines of maximum intensity, but then somewhere very quickly along that line some senses of overall shape begin to emerge. But then also in the beginning of any working certain levels I understand. By levels I don't mean in the sense of a hierarchy where one thing is above another, but levels as you might see them in space where there is no room at the top but a series of related planes. And each has a narrative line. All these narrative lines can touch and reach each other at various times. So the editing is along the lines of these possibilities. I must say too that many people have seen masks, demons, creatures of all kinds moving through *The Text of Light*, and I never have. Even though some of them have drawn pictures of what they have seen so I could locate the place where they got the image, I still don't really see it as I'm watching the film. And this is the other thing, is that the work grows very much beyond the maker. Does that entertain the question? Oh, you asked about length. Length again: in my case I'm more involved in *The Text of Light* in the fragile movements and flickers and shakes at the corners and edges (which are most visible at the edges of the frame) and all those fragile movements of the light within the frame. And the rhythms that they set up. So most decisions to cut are along the line of the integrity to these rhythms.

Q: I know that your 8mm works, your *Songs* were edited in the camera, and later you were very concerned with the energy you received from . . .

Br: Well no, some were, most weren't. It's always an ideal to edit in the camera, for obvious reasons . . . I think. The more obvious reasons are to me that there is an energy in the moment of shooting which editing again can leak out for you. What's interesting to me is the energy of immediacy. That comes out of my involvement with Charles Olson. The actual breath and physiology of the living person being present at its most, uninterrupted by afterthought. Editing is always afterthought. Though the way to beat that is to get that excited at the editing table. And that's very hard.

But in the case of this film it is very highly edited. And I prefer the word "arranged." And again I think we need a better word. "Arranged" is gentler and reminds me of the composer. "Compose" would be another word. We're talking about a composition in time. To make a construct that will fill completely the length of time it runs. I trust more myself what happens in the immediacy of shooting rather than in this afterthought process.

—

FROM *CANYON CINEMANEWS*, 75.3

Bruce Baillie

LETTER, MARCH 1975

Canyon Cinema began with a light bulb over the driveway and a sign that looked old the moment I completed it, 1961, I believe. Up the wooden walk to the back-yard, we had a big surplus screen stretched across a board framework on the hill above our Canyon house. It really belonged to Mr. Anderson . . . Johnson it was, who reminded me in the spring we'd have to cut all the beautiful tall, thick green grass, "or I'll have someone up here to do it and take it off your rent."

Canyon residents and their kids came every once a week night, the kids on the roof, adults below under our tree with low branches — don't care to know names humans give to trees, birds, places. Suzy and Johno Canon would collect the scattered benches from around Canyon the afternoon before the show. Kikuko made popcorn — we had free wine — sent out cards afterwhile, to a few regular patrons in Berkeley, San Francisco and Oakland. We showed whatever came through — only a few films around then, also the best foreign embassy short films — couldn't pay rentals. Any donations went to the filmmakers whose work we showed. I lived at the time on unemployment and had established my first work space — correspondence always self-addressed "Canyon Cinema."

Of course Johnny Melcher and his little brother were not allowed to sit among the other Canyon kids, there might be a film with naked bodies in it, so his mom and dad wanted to be close at hand to scurry off next door. He was finally the instrument behind Kikuko leaving, since I'd spent a week with my friend's girl, waking every morning on the roof with the sun coming up over the eastern hills and Mr. Peterson driving by above us in his pickup for work (another Christian).

Anyway, the purpose for all this was the fact that there was no place to show one's work in all of wealthy America. We did not know at the time of Jones Mekas' work out east, nor of the Stauffacher movement of the late 40's in San Francisco [Frank Stauffacher's Art in Cinema film society]. We had heard of Stan Brakhage and knew that Larry Jordan lived somewhere across the Bay.

After awhile we were down in Berkeley, a few people had joined in to help — 2 shows a week. Chicky Strand my partner, Paul Strand kept the gear and the VW bus running. We all had fulltime jobs then, families (the Strands), and were doing 2 shows a week, all the programming, ordering, mailing, poster-making and support-ing when the take was too small. At the same time, perhaps most importantly, we were learning how to make films.

Lyle Pearson
WAITING FOR GODARD AT THE FRONT: THE PALESTINIAN CINEMA INSTITUTION

It is well known that Godard and Gorin went to Lebanon and Jordan in the spring of 1970 to work on a Dziga Vertov Group film supporting the position of AL-FATEH with the help of PALESTINE FILMS, a cinema group created by AL-FATEH based in Beirut — a film which James Roy MacBean (*Film Quarterly*, Fall 1972, p. 30) claims "would have been their (the Vertov Group's) most ambitious film to date." Tentatively called TILL VICTORY, five years later this film has still not seen the day for one of several reasons, if not more than one: MacBean states that at least Gorin was disheartened by King Hussein's successful routing of AL-FATEH in Jordan in 1972 and AL-FATEH'S subsequent decline in power (but I can't imagine Gorin or Godard staying on the side of a winner for very long); a Frenchman who made a Super-8 reportage on Godard in mid-1974 tells me Godard has gotten into a critical bind and fears to release *anything* anymore, because almost everyone places so much importance on everything he does (even when he tries to work semi-anonymously, as in the Vertov Group; it is true that the Group has released nothing since TOUT VA BIEN in 1972). And a Tunisian, who is going to have his particular interest in this matter, tells me that Godard has not released the AL-FATEH footage because of threats on his life if he does, although it may form part of a coming feature-length film on revolutionary movements all over the world.

All three of these theories are equally probable: there is lack of cohesion within the PLO, although less so since its recognition by the United Nations and the consequent movement of its sub-groups, including AL-FATEH, toward a common platform; Godard is a victim of his own *auteur*-myth, even when he tries to work in the Vertov Group; violence over Palestine is threatened in all possible directions, even between separate Arab governments. And the black representative of TRICONTINENTAL at Carthage in 1974 told the newly formed PALESTINE-FILMS-PALESTINIAN CINEMA INSTITUTION* that the United States just "wasn't ready" for its films yet.

I myself, having stumbled into a refugee camp in Beirut in December 1974, was held captive as a spy for five hours until I was released and driven to the PF-PCI semi-secret studio, which I was trying to find from telephone instructions. And the PCI hesitates to send any of its films to any festival west of North Africa, sure of

---

*The PCI was created in 1974 under the umbrella-support of the PLO, with PF as its nucleus; another institution, THE ASSOCATION OF PALESTINIAN CINEMA, existed in early 1974 between PF and the PCI, but it is only the PCI which has received the support of the entire PLO.

having them rejected on political grounds, although they have been consistent prize winners at the Baghdad, Damascus, Leipzig, Karlovy Vary and Carthage festivals. Such films were rejected at Teheran in 1974 (Iran at least then did not accept the PLO as a National entity, and Teheran showed a pro-Israeli instead) and they are unknown in India. Needless to say, the PCI films are not distributed in France.

I have been following PF and now PCI's work since 1970,** seeing it at Carthage on three occasions, talking to the filmmakers, so that when I finally reached Beirut I had seen probably all but one of their 15 films — and that one is not about Palestine, but on the parallel struggle for the liberation of Dhofar from its parent government of Oman, on the south-east tip of the Arabian peninsula, 1200 miles from Israel. This film is called RIAH-AL-TAHRER (WINGED VICTORY) and I saw it in Beirut.

Now, whether the Dziga Vertov Group will ever release its AL-FATEH footage or not, it did work with PF in Beirut, and, although the members of the PCI would rather talk about Manfred Faws, a German who also worked with them, I cannot deny that these films appear to have a heavy dose of Dziga Vertov, or Godard and Gorin, or Godard, in them. Except for the 1972–3 collective realization A ZIONIST AGGRESSION, a reportage on the destruction of refugee camps in Beirut by Israelis following the Olympic massacre in 1972, these are not straight documentaries, as Egypt and Syria often supply to the same list of festivals. Nor, with the exception of Ismail Chammaut's 1974 ON THE ROAD FROM PALESTINE, on refugee children living semi-happily but uprooted in Kuwait, do they speak of any reactionary government in unpleasantly flattering terms — indeed, RIAH-AL-TAHRER is *against* such a government, supported by the late King Faisal and the Shah of Iran, and was banned at Carthage! (That's why I had to see it in Beirut; it is still about the necessity of revolution.) Nor are they simple renderings of historical events with statistics thrown at you, as Solanas would have Third World directors make; although Solanas does have his following at least in the Maghrib, from a manifesto and discussions prominent at Carthage in 1974*** — in fact, the PCI's

---

**Guy Hennebelle's "le camera et le combat," in *Contact* No. 11, June 1974 (Tunis) is the most complete list of films on the Palestinian Revolution I know, and *Cahiers du Cinéma* No. 248 includes his interview with several of these filmmakers (his regular publisher "n'en voulait pas"). I am informed that PF-PCI'S REVOLUTION UNTIL VICTORY has been shown on some UC campuses but this is not the same thing as having a film distributed by TRI-CONTINENTAL or a similar firm.

***Called *La critique maghrébine face à la critique occidentale*, this manifesto is based on the June, 1974 *Manifest de Montréal* written in part of Solanas and Getino. It is available from the Federation Maghrebine des Cine-Clubs, Mohammedia, Morocco.

only Solanas-like film, MAY . . . THE PALESTINIANS, won the Carthage 1974 short film first prize for its "scientific analysis . . . of the Palestinian Liberation Movement . . . replacing it in its historical context." Nor are they historical reconstructions, in the manner of Pontecorvo; they are rather a re-working of older documents with new footage some of it documentary and some of it made to convince ideologically, rather than to overwhelm or to train in militancy: these films do not advocate bomb throwing.

No, these are basically imaginative, aesthetically pleasing works, attempting to provoke thought rather than present answers; although Rafik Hajjar, who made MAY . . . THE PALESTINIANS stated in the Carthage press that "our role is to inform, the aesthetic considerations coming on the second plan," he claimed later in the same interview "we try to take account of the attractive element, in a way to envelop the dryness of the subject, that is pleasure by political reflection." And there is one filmmaker in this group, Mustafa About Ali, who makes such complicated thought pieces — like Haydn on the sound track while we watch a fighter plane swooping in the sky, as Godard used Haydn while his hero in LE PETIT SOLDAT clicked pictures of Veronica — that he feels his films are too highly mental for a jury, at least the all African-Arab one at Carthage, to understand. Most of the footage in Ali's SCENES IN OCCUPIED GAZA, which is the only PCI film in 35mm, was shot under Israeli supervision by an unknown TV crew and ended up in the then APC studio by "ways," Ali tells me. Ali is the most Godard-like filmmaker in this group, and his 1972 (or earlier — I saw it in 1972) ONE FOREWARD, TWO FOREWARD, with narration in French, a balletic and symbolic pantomime on a rooftop in long shots like the strike in the two-story factory in TOUT VA BIEN, and intercut shots of bomb destruction, is his most Godard-like film.

In fact, whether or not Godard ever will (or did) release any of his AL-FATEH footage, ONE FOREWARD, TWO FOREWARD appears such like an image "unmonté" from a Dziga Vertov film on the cover of *Cahiers du Cinéma* No. 240 — a fedeyine kneeling on a rooftop next to his rifle, wearing the checkered fedeyine scarf. (Sadly, *Cahiers du Cinéma* does not mention the name of the Vertov film, but it is almost without doubt TILL VICTORY.) I will not say that ONE FOREWARD is TILL VICTORY**** — but Ali does tell us there are "ways" of getting TV footage, and Godard *has* said he fears releasing anything about himself, and possibly that he fears Zionist recrimination if he releases anything, at least separately, on the Palestinian Revolution. While Ali's compatriot Hajjar in MAY . . . does use

****Royal S. Brown's Filmography in *Focus on Godard* (1972) says, p. 180, TILL VICTORY is in 16mm Eastmancolor, while the copy of ONE FOREWARD which I saw is 16mm Black and white. But this could be workprint, or an alternate camera, etc.

footage of Lenin in Moscow from the Russian Cultural Center in Beirut to analyze the Palestinian Cause, Ali does use irony more consciously not only in making use of Israeli-supervised TV footage, but turning the words of Golda Mier [Meir] against herself in a third title THEY DO NOT EXIST, to show that the Palestinians do exist.

Wouldn't it be interesting if, in the not only probable but sure influence of the Dziga Vertov Group in the PCI — Ali didn't learn all this irony while a student at USC — there really was a lost film by Godard? I don't mean that Ali is just using Godard's footage — the editing is tight enough, the choreography specific enough that ONE FOREWARD, TWO FOREWARD must be following some sort of pre-conception, if not the complete plan that was originally set out for it. I don't mean to state that this *is* a Vertov Group film, I only mean to ask — and as Bruno says in LE PETIT SOLDAT, "Perhaps after all, asking questions is more important than finding answers." The influence is there, why not the footage or at least the plan? You don't have to believe the content of a film to see it, and in this article I mean to take no political position whatsoever — this is a struggle on one front.

I have already been to Beirut and asked this question once. But is TRICONTI-NENTAL right? Is no-one in the U.S. "ready" for a possible Godard film on one of the greatest political obscenities of today, from whatever viewpoint you look at it? Instead of waiting for Godard, write to THE PALESTINIAN CINEMA INSTITU-TION, BP 8984 in Beirut and ask to see ONE FOREWARD, TWO FOREWARD for preview purposes.

Just don't send any letter bombs — if you do, then the officer in that refugee camp is right and I *am* a spy.

4/4/75: What becomes clear with King Faisal's death is his divided loyalty — he supported both the PLO, which in turn supports the Palestinian Cinema Institution, and the government of Oman in its fight against the independence of the state of Dhofar, about which the PCI made the film RIAH-AL-TAHRER (WINGED VICTORY). The divided loyalty of the Shah of Iran will perhaps become as evident as that of the late King Faisal at a future date.

—

FROM *CANYON CINEMANEWS*, 75.4

James Broughton

HOW TO COPE WITH THE QUESTION PERIOD

From *The Filmmaker's Guidebook*

Q: What were you trying to do in this film?
A: Get people to ask questions.

Q: How much did your film cost?
A: A pretty penny.

Q: How do you get money to make your films?
A: Knavery, deceit, prostitution, and robbery.

Q: What camera did you use?
A: The one I stole.

Q: What stock did you use?
A: Mostly livestock.

Q: What is your shooting ratio?
A: Whatever I get the best odds on.

Q: Do your films earn anything?
A: A great deal of neglect.

Q: What does your film mean?
A: What do you mean?

Q: Do you stick to a script?
A: I hate to get stuck with anything.

Q: How do you distribute your films?
A: Special 4th class parcel post.

Q: Why do you make films like this?
A: To keep myself in debt.

Q: Who is the strongest influence on your work?
A: Whoever I'm in love with at the time.

Q: What are you working on now?
A: A new answer print.

Q: What is an answer print?
A: A big question mark.

—

FROM *CANYON CINEMANEWS*, 75.5

Albie Thoms

AUSTRALIAN COOP NEWS

Next February the Sydney Filmmakers Cooperative celebrates its tenth anniversary. What began a decade ago as a loose association of independent Australian film-makers has now matured into a substantial business turning over some $100,000 annually that has assumed a role in Australia's developing film culture that falls somewhere between a political lobby for Australia's independent filmmakers and an alternative film information terminal.

Australia's film culture is still dominated by foreign corporations which monopolize distribution and exhibition outlets and take some $50 million a year out of the country in profits. In contrast the Coop now returns some $20,000 a year to its member filmmakers (representing 75% of gross income from the distribution of their films and 60% from the exhibition of their films in the Coop cinema). The Australian government has proven reluctant to act against the foreign control of the Australian film industry, but has spent some $10 million in the last six years assisting Australian film production. Approximately $1 million of this has gone to assist independent filmmakers (i.e. filmmakers working independently of the foreign corporations that dominate in Australia), with about $80,000 going to the Sydney Filmmakers Coop in subsidies to assist its distribution and exhibition activities. This obvious disparity between production and distribution subsidies has severely overtaxed the capacity of the Sydney Coop to effectively serve its 300 members (currently it is attempting to distribute about 500 films, including about 80 films from 40 foreign members).

At its inception the Coop was managed by members of the avant-garde Ubu group, but since Ubu's demise in 1970 it has had its own existence, registered under state law as a non-profit community benefit society. This structure has enabled it to receive grants from the government's Council for the Arts and the Australian Film & Television School, and these grants in turn have enabled the Coop to employ some of its members as paid workers for the Coop (currently six fulltime workers on $125 week — slightly above the minimum legal wage here — plus several parttime workers). There has been much recent criticism of the high cost of running the Coop in its present structure, its development of bureaucratic tendencies and its dependence on government subsidy. But its operations are clearly democratic with policy decided at monthly members meetings, elections for staff positions, and continuous discussion on how best to serve members' needs. It is a reflection of the state of the Australian film economy and the prejudice against independent filmmakers that the Coop has to spend $5 to make a dollar for filmmakers.

A large part of the effort of the Coop staff goes into operating the 100-seat Filmmakers' Cinema, situated underneath the Coop offices and meeting room. This cinema screens four programs each week — a feature program (usually new independent work or a subject-matter survey) nightly Tuesday to Sunday; late night shows (usually popular Hollywood-type fare) on Friday, Saturday and Sunday; children's matinees on Saturday and Sunday; and classics and filmstudy programs (at intermediate sessions on Saturday and Sunday). Films from the Coop's distribution library are screened as supports on all these programs, ensuring continuous showcasing of Coop films, giving particular opportunity for lesser-known films to be seen by the public. This Coop screening policy was arrived at after previous length-of-the-run and cinematheque programming failed to meet both members' and audiences' demands. About 50 different films, including features, are screened each month, with popular programs being recycled at later dates, and all films in the Coop library being screened at least once in a year.

Distribution of Coop films suffers from the absence of a real alternative market in Australia, with relatively few educational institutions offering film courses and most film societies concentrating on mainstream cinema. However, there has been a 1000% increase in film rentals over the last ten years, and the market is expanding rapidly, largely due to government film education programs and increased interest in the film medium. Initially, under the Ubu group, the Coop built a reputation as the major source of avant-garde film in Australia. Now it is equally known as a distributor of radical political films (including films from USA, Cuba and Africa), feminist films, and low-budget dramatic films (particularly those produced on Australian government grants). Since the demise of the Ubu group, Australian avant-garde film has been passive and diversified and now represents the smallest area of independent film production.

Recently the Sydney Coop combined with the smaller Coops in the other five Australian state capitals to produce a combined catalogue listing over 600 films (118 pages with 150 photos and alphabetical, filmmaker and subject matter indexes — available for $2 plus postage from the Sydney Filmmakers Coop Ltd., Box 217, P.O. Kings Cross, Sydney 2017). The Coop also publishes a monthly newspaper *Filmnews* (free to members, others $5 per year). This lists the Filmmakers' Cinema program, news of new productions, minutes of the Coop's monthly meetings, and arguments viz a viz [vis-à-vis] the politics of the Australian film situation.

A new development at the Coop is the establishment of a video room where for a small fee visitors can view some of the films from the Coop library on Sony video-cassettes, as well as tapes from the expanding number of videotape makers. Eventually it is hoped to transfer all films from the Coop library onto cassettes (filmmakers willing) and to also undertake cassette distribution.

It has long been the Coop's aim to provide production facilities for members, particularly in terms of editing, processing, printing and sound mixing. However, such capitalization has been deferred in favor of improving distribution and exhibition capacities. Instead, workshops have been organized by members that have provided elementary tuition to filmmakers working with government grants, emphasizing alternative filmmaking techniques. The most successful of these has been that organized by Coop women along feminist lines.

After ten years the Coop finds itself in a significant position in the Australian film community. For about 50% of Australian film production, the Coop is the only distribution and exhibition outlet, and is the only means for its members to exert themselves in both the internal politicking of the industry and the external struggle of independent filmmakers to communicate with the vast audience presently conditioned to mass-market mainstream film. Because of the latter it remains the main avenue for foreign independents wishing to have their work screened in Australia. In keeping with its pluralist attitudes, the Coop welcomes foreign members and their films and seeks wider international dialogue between filmmakers. Any filmmakers wishing to join the Coop or find out more about its activities are invited to write to Box 217, P.O. Kings Cross, Sydney 2017, Australia.

—

FROM *CANYON CINEMANEWS*, 75.6

Lyle Pearson

PRAYAG IN 35MM: THE FILM AND TELEVISION INSTITUTE OF INDIA

Mani Kaul, a leader among India's New Wave or Parallel directors, finds that Damle and Fatehlal's 1936 Marathi feature *Sant Tukaram* "combined the two incompatible forms of Lumière and Méliès — the real and the magic." *Sant Tukaram* "does not give out concepts but . . . demonstrates their function in actual life"; in contrasting the miracles of Tukaram with the daily work of his wife it blends "asymmetry and symmetry," "non-analysis and analysis," "non-linear and linear" material, that is a realistic story with songs and magic — in part, "realism is opposed by the magic of effect-photography." The balance between the two ends of a duality, of opposing forces, is named in Hindu philosophy "prayag."

Marathi, one of India's more than 15 regional languages, is spoken by the 30 million people in the state of Maharashtra, where one finds the 6 million people of Bombay and the 1 million of Poona. *Sant Tukaram,* based on the life of a real-life saint who at the end ascends to heaven on a giant bird while his wife washes the family cow, was filmed in the old Prabhat (Prabhat means *dawn*) Studios in Poona, which went broke in 1950. It is surely the noisy commercialism of Bombay films (more than 200 a year) that killed Prabhat, a commercialism based on a half-understanding and imitation of Hollywood, or Anglo-Saxon films, "a perverse gesture," to Kaul, rather than a complete misunderstanding of Hollywood's idioms. The Indian national government bought the dead studio and in 1960 re-named it the "Film and Television Institute of India." It is India's first real film institute.

It is primarily the students for the Institute and members of film societies, rather than the film industry, who are trying to make a new cinema in India. But outside of the state-supported Film Finance Corporation it is difficult to finance a New Wave, Parallel or, for India, experimental film, and even more difficult to distribute it. This has led Kaul to the happiness of alienation for he defends the fact that none of his films have been released except on Sunday mornings for one week to three. *Duvidha* (Two Ways), his third film, has not been distributed at all, although it won a critics' prize and the National Best Direction Award in 1973, and this year goes to festivals in Berlin, Moscow, New York and Chicago.

There is probably no real "prayag" filmmaker in the New Wave yet, for even Kaul is too depressing, not for my own tastes, but to successfully re-combine magic and realism. His first feature, *Uski Roti* (His Bread), about a woman waiting at a bus-stop to deliver supper to her bus-driver husband, is more obscure than magical and Kaul talks mostly of Bresson rather than Lumière-Méliès outside of the article I am quoting him from here.*

Another New Wave Director, Kumar Shahani, whose *Maya Darpan* (Mirror of Illusion) is about a young woman lost and bored in an enormous house, was actually the assistant of Bresson on *Une Femme Douce*. Both of these films seem far too boring for what they are trying to do in this, the International Woman's Year.

After 15 years of existence the Film Institute of India is drastically revising its curriculum. The specialized courses in direction, screenplay-writing, motion picture photography, sound and editing were not turning out composite filmmakers — that is, rounded technicians who could make a new cinema (because they weren't in a sense recipients of a terminal course in prayag) and also because the students in the sixth discipline, acting, who were more quickly absorbed into the industry as stars than the others, went on strike at regular three-year intervals protesting the lack of roles the directing students gave them.

The adoption of a new composite curriculum does not mean that Lenny Lipton's *Independent Film-making* is going to become the standard Institute textbook, although it is known here in its British edition. The institute has some silent

---

*Kaul, Mani, "New Perspectives," from *Filmfare* (a Bombay bi-weekly film magazine), reprinted in *A Selection of Writings on the Problems of Contemporary Cinema in India* (mimeographed). Available from the National Film Archives of India, Poona 4, India.

16mm equipment as well as much 35mm but there is not distribution set-up for 16mm, neither in schools nor in most film societies and the 16mm cameras are used primarily by new TV students for their first one- or two-minute films. Ironically, it is the Film Archives and not the Institute which is about to invest in a dual 8/Super-8 projector. Still, there is a slight movement toward 16mm in India: Kaul's *Duvidha* was shot in 16mm and then blown-up to 35mm, but few Indians will probably see it either way. And Indian TV recently shot its first feature film, quite naturally in 16mm. If 16mm projectors were bought some of these films, after their initial runs, could be distributed to film societies and schools over at least a brief space of Indian terrain. (Whereas in Africa filmmaking in 16mm is already quite advanced.)

Perhaps there will be no standard text next semester at the Institute just as there is no one Indian philosophic text (it could be the Bhagavad-gita, the Koran, or the Bible). One knows only that all students will get identical training for two years and specialize only in the third year, and that most prospective acting students will enroll in the National School of Drama in New Delhi. The director of the Institute, Girish Karnad, the oldest of the New Wave directors (although he is primarily a writer and an actor), may stay on for only one more semester. In any case it is an Adventure, an attempt to achieve a technical prayag in 35mm: to make in something like Lenny Lipton's terms "filmmakers" rather than "directors."

I dislike that inaccurate French encroachment into English, *auteur* — and if India continues to follow Bresson or the French Old Wave it is going to drown in French jargon as surely as did Brazil's *cinema novo*. With not only British documentary and Indian mythological traditions to choose from but the rest of international cinema besides it is time that Bresson and the French Old Wave drowned in another New Wave of Indian origin.

A few scholarships for African and Asian students at the Institute are available through the Colombo Plan. For further information on admissions, write to Mr. V. C. Shukla, Minister of Information and Broadcasting, New Delhi 1, India. Maybe there'll be more 16mm next year.

Poona, 1975

CORRECTION to 'The Palestinian Cinema Situation' Issue #75–3

Two or three errors crept into my report on the Palestinian Institution — the PCI was located in Jordan and not in Lebanon when Godard and Gorin worked with it in 1970 and REVOLUTION UNTIL VICTORY is not a PCI but a Newsreel film. REVOLUTION is in fact the first short film on the Palestinian problem to be noticed by the French popular film press, in *Ecran '75* No. 34, March 1975, p. 88, a review by Guy Hennebelle. This would mean that the Palestinian problem has passed through American cinema without touching American film criticism and that it has now made the jump from militant French film journals to popular

French criticism. Also, it is of course Mozart and not Haydn that the pianist plays in the barnyard in Godard's WEEKEND.

I regret these errors but I will give one Lebanese pound to anyone else who has written on the PCI films in the American press (other than translating Hennebelle). There being no Palestinian tender at the present time.

—

FROM *CANYON CINEMANEWS*, 76.2

Diane Kitchen and Gunvor Nelson

CHICK STRAND'S RECOLLECTIONS OF CANYON CINEMA'S EARLY BEGINNINGS
WITH ADDED COMMENTARY FROM CHICK CALLENBACH

[Editor's note: In this piece, "[laughter]" is always an interpolation by the original Cinemanews staff; other bracketed materials here, as in all other instances in this volume, are my editorial interpolations.]

Question: How did it happen with you . . . were you making movies and then you became involved with Canyon Cinema?

Chick Strand: Oh no, I was getting my degree in anthropology at U.C. and I had been friends with Bruce (Baillie) for a long time. He was my boyfriend for awhile. So when I married my second husband, we were still friends. And he was always involved in theater . . . I'm not sure about this part. But when we used to talk about what we were doing, it was all . . . his ideas were all visual in terms of theater. Somehow he got a grant. I think one of his old professors saw to it that he got a Fellowship at the London School of Cinematography, I think that's what it was. So he went there for a while. I'm not sure how he thought of getting involved in film. But he came back hating it over there. He didn't complete the course, he went to Spain to get warm. But he wrote letters about how damp the fog was. I guess it's different than our fog. He came back and got a job at the Chevy Assembly Plant. And started making money to get equipment to make a film. And he made ON SUNDAYS . . . none of us had really known anything about independent films. This was somewhere around '59 or '60. I guess I got involved in Canyon Cinema in '61, a few months after it started. But there was no place to show these films. There was an audience and Bruce felt there should be a place to show them. He would show films in Canyon (California) on a sheet in his back yard.

At first, my husband and I weren't really involved, except to come and see the shows. And we got enthusiastic about it, cause there were these really crazy guys all over the United States, who no one had ever heard of, making films.

. . .

Chick Callenbach: See that's really curious, what she says about not knowing any other filmmakers. Because here Broughton and Peterson and Stauffacher and all those folks had been doing Art in Cinema up until just a few years before that. The San Francisco Bay Area was one of the leading hot-beds of underground film. And yet it was another world. Nobody had ever heard of that stuff. So when Canyon came along . . .

Diane [Kitchen]: Which was when?

Chick Callenbach: When Canyon started? Well my first memory of Bruce was, I was living at this little house on the creek, where this photo comes from (see cover), and I got a call from Bruce saying, "I'm trying to set up some showings of underground films and I wondered whether you could help us." And I didn't have any idea how I could help them, but he sounded nice so I said, "Well why don't you come down to my house on the weekend and we'll have some tea or something and talk about it." So I'm sitting there in the sun by my creek and Bruce came in, I think wearing a T-shirt or something, and we just really liked each other. And he wasn't the sort of person I usually associate with. Cause he's not very verbal and he's not, ah, some sort of critical intellectual, or something like that. But we really got on, and he began telling me about how they had such troubles finding places where they could run because the fire marshalls were always after them. You know, you rent some hall and then it would turn out it didn't have enough exits. And it wouldn't have toilets. And so they'd close you down. You'd put up publicity and they'd come around and say, "You can't run here." Just when everybody shows up. They had tried schools, and they had done a lot of things, and none of them had really worked. So they were really desperate for a place to show. This would have been '61 probably; the summer we did it in my back yard was '61, or maybe '62.

Of course along about that time, Broughton had gone to England to work on THE PLEASURE GARDEN and then had stayed there. So he wasn't around. Frank Stauffacher had died. Sidney Peterson had I think gone to Los Angeles. So it had all just kind of dissolved. Pauline had dropped out of the thing . . .

Gunvor Nelson: Was Pauline Kael interested in this that early?

Callenbach: Well she lived with Broughton, you know. Had a child by him, and helped on MOTHER'S DAY and THE ADVENTURES OF JIMMY. According to interviews with people, Kermit Sheets I guess mainly, she did a lot of looking for locations and costuming . . . Pauline was very ingenious at living poor with style long before it was fashionable.

Gunvor: . . . Because the first interview, as far as I know, with Brakhage on KQED, she seemed very . . . like she didn't understand the type of things that Brakhage was doing.

Callenbach: Well, she probably wouldn't because they're very different from what Jimmy was doing. Everything in Jimmy's films is in focus, and [a] recognizable object, and it has a dramatic story, although perhaps of a somewhat poeticized form, and they're funny, and just an altogether different dish of tea from what Brakhage was doing I think, already by that time. Although a couple of Brakhage's early films were stories about anguished young men worried about masturbation and what not.

. . .

Strand: . . . And then for some reason it moved to Berkeley, and they were showing at the Bistro San Martin, which was an anarchist restaurant. A strange restaurant run by anarchists. But really great food. You'd go and sit . . . sometimes they had no money so the previous guys had to pay their bill before they could go out and buy the food. [laughter] Well at that time there was sort of a renaissance of the Wobblies (International Workers of the World) and a lot of people joined . . . it was an anarchist group but there was so much anarchy going on that there were never any meetings, nothing was organized. So we showed there and that's when I became involved in it.

Diane: Can you remember any of what you showed?

Strand: We got things like A WHITE MANE, THE DREAM OF WILD HORSES . . . And we had another person, Paul Tulley, very important man, who was a real film buff; he had gone to downtown theaters where sometimes he would see really weird things. Yeah we got things from the Consulates in San Francisco, French Consulate and Canadian Consulate. And then people started hearing about us. And it got to be a thing where weekly programs were planned and people had to be written to and things had to be taken to the post office and programs had to be written up.

Diane: It seems to have grown very fast from the beginnings.

Strand: It wasn't really . . . at first it was very sporadic in Canyon, when films were heard of and gotten hold of and Bruce would show them. But then it got to be a thing where people started coming and there was a mailing list and needed somebody to collect the donations. We went with a donation of a dollar. Sometimes we'd get an IOU, somebody'd have no money, and we always felt that people could come if they had no money.

Gunvor: I was in Canyon one time and it was a film festival.

Strand: That's right, the Canyon Film Festival. And that's where my very first film was shown. It was called ERIC AND THE MONSTERS. [laughter] It was really a stupid little film . . . Let's see, I know I'm leaving out so darned much. The cops would come or the health department would come and tell us we couldn't show at the Bistro San Martin, because the screen was blocking the exit and blah blah blah, and there was no permit. So we showed on a certain night, and we'd advertise it, and had a little mailing list, and people would phone. It was a very small organization, except the work that went out looked like it was done by 20 people. And then a lot of interested people started coming around. At one time there was maybe 7 or 8 really nuclear people that helped a lot. Ernest Callenbach was one that was very very helpful. It was his idea to start the *Canyon Cinemanews*. He thought there should be a newsletter. And Bruce's mother mimeographed it at her church. [laughter] Some of the stuff was mimeographed at the Anarchist Press, which was a mimeograph machine in somebody's garage. It would take Bruce and I days and days to figure out exactly how to paste up the program or what we could show, because we never had any money so we'd have to show a serial every week, CAPTAIN AMERICA or something . . . THE SPIDER, THE REVENGE OF THE SPIDER, and THE CISCO KID. We had to rent those. But Willard Morrison, it was Audio Film Center then, he was really good and got things for us cheaper. And not only that, he distributed films, underground films, and nobody else did. He helped with the lab, and introduced us to other people who were making films.

Diane: What was Bruce doing at this point in filmmaking?

Strand: Well he as producing right along. There was ON SUNDAYS, with Miss Wong. I can't remember the order, but right around then was HAVE YOU THOUGHT OF TALKING TO THE DIRECTOR.

Gunvor: At that film festival, I saw MASS for the first time. It was just finished I think. That really made me . . . that was the turning point in my life in terms of films. It was in the back yard, I don't know who lived there, and we had not heard of Bruce [Baillie] or anything. But they asked Bob Nelson to put in PLASTIC HAIRCUT. And Larry Jordan was one of the judges. There was about thirty people watching outdoors in the very cold.

Strand: The first time I had met Bob Nelson was in the San Francisco Museum. And he and Ron Davis with their little suits came, and showed PLASTIC HAIRCUT to a lot of those Museum ladies [laughter] . . . it was hilarious. And then they'd ask really straight questions, then they'd do a little theater answering the questions. [laughter] That's how the San Francisco contingent and the Berkeley contingent got together I think. We showed Sidney Peterson's films, Larry Jordan . . .

. . .

Callenbach: And there were about a half dozen of the newsreels that came out. I think Bruce did them all. And the idea was, like Chicky was saying, there was going to be this miscellaneous program, sort of like a regular theater program. And after all, a proper theater program in those days had a newsreel, so Canyon ought to produce a newsreel. There may have been a logo that came on at the beginning, like, "The Eyes and Ears of the World" . . . but there were funny little things. Like Bruce would go on some expedition to some place. I think there was one about Mt. Diablo. I think also . . . you remember the end of HAVE YOU THOUGHT OF SPEAKING TO THE DIRECTOR, has this thing down at the Bayshore; it's sort of a militaristic thing where his father claps his hands and there are people shooting each other or something like that. And I think that actually came out of a newsreel too. And what else? . . . I don't really remember. But the effort was to make a nice grab-bag of things for people to come and see. And there was a serial she doesn't mention, called THE DESERT HAWK, which I have since tried to track down. It was very well done by the standards of the Hollywood serial. It had Gilbert Roland, or Roland Gilbert, I can't remember what his name was, playing two roles: The Good Sheik and The Bad Sheik, his brother. And they would fight it out over some damsel in distress; with lots of riding to the rescue over the desert sands, and so on. [laughter] They were charmingly campy. They haven't been described in any of these summaries of the old serials. And I don't know why not. Whether it was so obscure that Willard (Morrison) had a print of it down there at Audio which he used to let them have for nothing or something, or what, I don't know. Willard is really one of the unsung heroes of the film scene. We were thinking of doing an interview with him for *Film Quarterly* because he has been in the thick of a lot of things. He's an old friend of mine from Chicago. We ran the Documentary Film Group, Film Society, he and I and another guy, at the University of Chicago. He's running the West Coast Audio Brandon office now. And he worked at the (Pacific Film) Archive for a little while . . . and is just a super guy and really loves film, he's not just a businessman. He really cares.

Diane: You came from Chicago?

Callenbach: I went to school there, I came from Pennsylvania. But I was there for a long time. Willard wasn't very interested in studying, but he was very interested in films. And I was studying to some extent, enough to get by at any rate, and this third guy, Rich Sawyer, who later became a hospital administrator [laughter] he went straight, ah, he was the third person. We ran the standard repertoire of documentaries and theatrical films and so on, and learned a lot . . . He's a good friend of Pauline's also. They each know that the other is incorruptible [laughter] in his or her fashion.

. . .

Strand: So when we closed down at Bistro San Martin we moved the operation, I think to another restaurant up on the north side, in Berkeley. And MR. HAYASHI was made there. They closed us down there the very day we were going to show. So we rented a hall and carted people down to the Finnish Hall. And *then* we realized we were in it deep, [laughter] really involved in it, it was going to go on regardless, it had an audience that was interested, and we were really committed. We just tried a lot of places, a private girls' school in Berkeley. And they wouldn't let us show because they weren't sure what underground meant. Gosh, what goofy things. The College of Arts and Crafts, in Oakland, decided they'd let us show there. About the same time we got showings at the Coffee Gallery, in San Francisco; that one went on for a long time. And there was a Berkeley show.

Diane: Bruce once referred to it as going in and setting up with projector and screen, and it was sort of everywhere; hit and run missions.

Strand: Everywhere. Three nights a week.

Diane: Incredible.

Strand: One in San Francisco, one in Oakland, and one in Berkeley which for a long time was in our front room. Sometimes we'd have 75 or 80 people in there. We'd have wine and popcorn. We'd sell wine for a dime a glass. It was just a real friendly thing because people came back and came back. We had a grand audience, they phoned us, "Where's it going to be tonight?" [laughter] Every week, when we had the 3 shows, we would go up and down Grant Street (San Francisco) with masking tape and our program, up and down Telegraph Avenue (Berkeley), and on every edifice we'd put something. I know the texture of every edifice. [laughter] For a while we showed in Chick Callenbach's backyard.

He lived in a house right over Strawberry Creek. Sometimes it would rain real hard, and the creek would be swollen, you could hardly hear the soundtrack. I don't think we got kicked out of his house. It became winter and we moved to Stiles Hall at U.C. It cost us $15 to rent the hall and we used Bruce's projector, as always. And every week we'd have a drawing. A door prize.

Diane: How did that work?

Strand: Well, when they paid their donation of a dollar, or even if they didn't, they got a ticket with a number on it. At intermission time, we'd have a little show, we entertained them, although we were both pretty shy. You know, Bruce he rubs his feet around, ducks his head . . . But we'd end up giving a prize. Well I remember a few times . . . Bruce is a great pie-maker. He makes pies. He makes pies out of whole wheat flour and wine to moisten it up . . . and grapes . . .

Diane: A grape pie?

Strand: A grape pie [laughter] . . . and geranium flowers in it . . . and pineapple was a thing we liked to put in it. Anyway, we'd raffle off a pie. One time we raffled off two tickets to the steam baths. It was our get-acquainted-week. [laughter] One ticket off to a man and one off to a woman. And we raffled off a lady's purse that we had filled with funny things. But kids would come, it was a real family kind of thing. People would bring food. And if it was too crowded they'd be lying under the screen, they'd bring their own pillows, but sometimes we'd have to go to Truman's Mortuary and borrow chairs [laughter] . . . We had a micro bus for awhile, somebody had a pickup. We lost a screen out of the pickup one night going across the bridge to Canyon Cinema at the Coffee Gallery.

Diane: What types of people did you get there?

Strand: Oh, that was a whole different bunch! There was a lot of people that hung out in North Beach, the old beatniks that were still there, San Franciscans that didn't want to go to Berkeley. But we really never pulled in hardly any money, and a lot of times the money to pay for the films came out of our food money.

Diane: You were the one to take money at the door?

Strand: Uh huh, yeah, in a little sewing basket . . . with a little lid, I'd clamp it down. And costumes. I'd wear a costume, be crazy every week, different. It went on, it really was a part of my life for 3 or 4 years.

Gunvor: Did you personally go around to the different places you showed films?

Strand: Oh yeah. We all did. It was a little travelling show.

Diane: Who was "all"?

Strand: Bruce and I. Chick Callenbach didn't always come, but a guy named Dave Cleveland came a lot and really helped, just physically and good will, and a lot of dumb work he did, a lot of dumb work.

Diane: Where did your filmmaking career go from there?

Strand: One day Bruce took me and another guy out, with his Bolex and taught me how to shoot. That's the picture that was on *Film Culture* years ago, Bruce and me and Mama Dog. It was a real sweet day, and I know how Bruce feels about his equipment, and how hard it is for him to get it. I was very pleased that he did that. And my husband's grandfather had a camera, and he died and left it to my husband. It was a 16mm Bell & Howell. I hadn't the least idea of how to make movies. Though Canyon Cinema had a little work shop in the basement of Chick Callenbach's house. Our plan was, if we made any money at all from the films, we'd buy equipment for the work shop. I think we bought a splicer, that was all. And then to start the *News*. Chick Callenbach suggested that because by then *Film Quarterly* was getting in a whole bunch of information about festivals and things. And he thought it was a good idea to have a newsletter about independent films. He felt that people wanted to hear about it. And by golly they did.

. . .

Callenbach: It occurred to me that what we needed to do was to put together some kind of quick and dirty publication that could be done very cheap and without too much work and without a big structure. In short, carrying out the kind of anarchist . . . I mean as I listen to this, I'm very impressed with the fact that Canyon has always been an anarchist organization. I mean, it never had any officers, or any dues, or any by-laws, and it never had a constitution. It was just a bunch of people that thought that something ought to be done, and who were doing it. Which was really the beautiful part of it. And the *News* was like that. I got this idea that it ought to be done, and I talked to Bruce I guess about it, and to Chicky (Strand) . . . Dave Cleveland was an important person in the money side in those days. He had a head for accounting and he used to keep the books, and he always was there selling tickets and keeping the show on the road. And I had a friend at that time named Sandra Ossipoff, whose name appears on Volume I, No. 1 as the Editor, and the story behind that is that Sandra was a beautiful blond of Russian extraction from Hawaii. And I had met her at the film festival and really dug her, but she didn't want to really go out with me because she had another boyfriend who was an artist named Wayne. But on the other hand she didn't want to forego my company entirely either. So we invented this relationship where she would be my Goddaughter. [laughter] And that way we would be able to be together without anything getting out of hand. [laughter] And this relationship does in fact continue to this present day. She is now a matron in suburban Washington D.C. [laughter]

Diane: She's not with Wayne the artist then . . .

Callenbach: No no. She married somebody with money and retired to the country. [laughter] But at any rate, Sandra was looking around for something to do with herself, so I said well why don't you be the editor of the *Canyon Cinemanews*. I would keep stencils down at my office. And every time a bunch of stuff would come in, I'd sit down and type out a summary of it, in a sort of telegraphic style. And after a month had gone by, we'd have three or four stencils, and I would give them to Bruce, who would give them to his mother, who would run them off on the church mimeograph, like Chicky says. And then we would get them back, a stack of paper, I think about 200 copies of each issue were done in the beginning. And we would sit, usually on my floor and drink beer and staple all evening. In one evening we could get it done. We went on doing it, and the subscriptions rose, I don't know, to probably double that . . . You need to get Bruce to give you some more recipes. In the old days that was the life's blood of the *News*.

Gunvor: Well I never did like recipes.

Diane: You don't cook.

Callenbach: I'm not sure anybody ever cooked any of these recipes. [laughter] They were things like strawberry tarts, and ah . . .

Gunvor: Seaweed . . .

Callenbach: Then there were things about kite flying. The other thing that needs to be revived is the Non Achievement Awards, which was largely Bruce's doing, but we all got into it. This was a means of being nasty to people who were doing things wrong. I gave one to the Bell & Howell Company. I had gone up to Bellevue to be the judge of the 2nd Bellevue Film Festival. And they had attempted to run the films on a Bell & Howell Auto-load, which kept eating the films . . . and it was impossible. Once the film starts through, you can't get it out again, you have to run it all the way through to the end. Finally we located an old Bell & Howell and managed to get through the rest of the films. And I therefore gave the Bell & Howell Company a Non Achievement Award, which they heard about somehow. And I got a call from Chicago saying, we understand we have won an award. [laughter] I said, "Well, it's not exactly an award, it's a Non Achievement Award." And he said, "Oh well, is there a plaque or something?" [laughter] "We'd like to get it." I said, "No, there no plaque, there's just a sort of Citation of Non-Competence." And then he began to get the idea that it wasn't a desirable thing.

Gunvor: How did Emory Menefee come in?

Callenbach: He was one of the people Chicky was talking about as a good-hearted, hard-working person, who . . . you know it's odd how groups attract people who are willing to do work like that. I was a film critic already and running *Film Quarterly* so it was part of my business almost, to look at films and associate with filmmakers. Chicky aspired to be a filmmaker by that time, and Bruce already was a filmmaker, so the three of us, there was a real rationale to be there. But Dave Cleveland, although he liked the films well enough, was not really a film person. And Emory Menefee is a chemist up at the Department of Agriculture in Albany . . . and ah, Emory was the editor of the *News* for years, and helped also put on showings. And Wes Paterson was a filmmaker sometimes, but also came around and helped put on showings. Well, people don't have that much to do in their ordinary lives that means much. Most of us just work at some crappy job or other. And so in evening and spare time activities, there were people around who were willing to put their shoulder to the wheel.

Gunvor: I wish we had a few more of those people around now.

—

FROM *CANYON CINEMANEWS*, 76.3

canyon cinemanews
#76-3

The winners of the Canyon Cinemanews Malaprop Contest are:
First Place: Kenya Cinnamon Ooze submitted by Tony Reveaux
Second Place: Can yon Cinema lose? submitted by Richard Lerman.
1st Prize is a 'Filmmaker's Emergency Kit'; 2nd Prize is a hand crafted bumper sticker of his choice. Thanks to the panel of judges: James Broughton, Carmen and Susan Vigil.

All the entries for the Canyon Cinemanews Malaprop Contest are:

Can-you sit-on-my-shoes	Freude
Canyon cinemamuse	Darrell Forney
K-onion S-enema N-ooze	Leonard Ellis
Can yon Cinema lose?	Richard Lerman
Cat yawn Cinema me(o)ws (pronounced muse) "	
Can you see my blues?	Diane Kitchen
Can you sin, eh Ma Goose?	"
C-opinions seem-in-a-noose	Jacqueline McCarthy
Ten yen seen on the loose.	"
Can you see a man's use?	Ann Sluzki
Kan John se Emmas snus? (pronounced snoos)	Gunvor Nelson
Ten yawns in a mass snooze	Gunvor Nelson and Diane Kitchen
Ken, your semen is in use.	Anonymoóse
Kenyan Urethra Snafus	Tim Shepard
Kenya Cinnamon Ooze	Tony Reveaux
Kane (yawn) cinnamon (nooze)	Darrell Forney
Kin-yarn sentiment-moose	"
Cajun Zimmerman Vues	"
Can yawn sin o'my Youth	"
Cañon Sand Déjà Vu's	"
Ben, you've been in my booze	Diane Levine and Shelley Diekman
Cannon Center and Noose	Rodger Darbonne
Can John send 'er a moose?	"
Ken, it's sin on the loose.	David White
Can you sin in a pew?	"
Candice, sit on my goose.	"
Can you send him the news?	"
Can yon sin be good news?	"
Phantom sin I am you.	

Cover of *Cinemanews*, 76.3, announcement of winners of the Canyon malaprop contest.

—

FROM *CANYON CINEMANEWS*, 76.4

Will Hindle

LETTER FROM LOWER APPALACHIANS, LATE JUNE 1976

— Some days I get an awful lot of mail and other days, like this week or so, it thins out to not even a bill. But a magazine came (people keep subscribing to film publications for me and I don't care to *read* about film) and in it was an article reviewing Lipton's new book on 8mm. I liked the part where the reviewer said Lipton isn't much in favor of wearing gloves when handling film. I like and understood that. It's a little like becoming so on-trusting-terms with this wild animal that you can come to handle it and you won't hurt it and it won't bite you.

— Want to right out in the open thank filmer/friend Paul Lawrence for flying to Alabama to help me right after the auto accident last fall. Isn't the first time he's come to my aid. When I was making WATERSMITH he'd come by my S.F. place and make sure I was eating properly during the year-long work.

— And for a long time I've wanted to mention Marvin Becker and all that he did to help me in my work. He helped Baillie and Ron Rice and a number of others with his patient attention to our starting-out clumsy questions. He's still in S.F. and I hope doing well and is comfortable. I met Baillie at his place in the late fifties. I can't speak totally for Bruce here, but as for me just being around Marvin was to learn. He exudes a certain kindness and great hunks of illumination.

— The new film (I think I'll call it PASTEUR THREE) moves along in great fits and starts. All other works were done like long un-stopped sentences or paragraphs right through editing. The new film has been done in chunks and occasional threads and isolated eddies of deep deep work . . . not to mention mixed metaphors . . . separated by auto accidents, meeting nice people like Lori Altmer in St. Petersburg, Dorn Hetzel at Penn State, Kathy Kline in Washington, D.C.; and lots of peaceful and/or thoughtless beings at the lodge/acres here. That last accident was a doozie.

— The place is still kind of always fresh to my mind. These isolated acres just go on giving and loving and ask for little in return . . . maybe just some protection. It's so green and lush and handsome and beautiful. California was majestic to me. When there was no housing development near and no smog, it roared subliminally with a great power . . . stark mountains and irrigated valleys. A great god ocean just beyond S.F. and huge fogs I really loved. But these lower Appalachians are violent with green life and foods and animals and waters.

— Health and happiness to all.

Love,

—

FROM *CINEMANEWS*, 76.5

·1970-2:

```
Last breath
let me speak:

Are you more than
there
roaring
up there
Stars
of my last vision

      --for a gull
       (in exchange
        for his gray
        feather.)
                      Bruce Baillie
```

★★★

ROBERT NELSON
Mixed feelings

1970-4:   STUDY FILMS CENSORED by Barry Wain   Two overseas experimental films bought by the National Library have been
cut by Australian censors. The films, which are regarded as major works, had their Australian premiere
at the weekwnd and are part of the library's film study collection. One shot, of about 2 feet has been cut from a 45
minute film, THE GREAT BLONDINO, by the highly regarded
American filmmaker Robert Nelson. The shot shows a girl turning towards the camera and using a 4-letter word. A brief
single shot has also been cut from the 9-minute film, BILLABONG,
by another American, Will Hindle. A petition, signed by about
60 people from 4 States who attended the school, will be delivered to Mr. Chipp at Parliament House. The two films that
were cut were among the first five to arrive from abroad.

★★★★★
1971-2 From the March 10th Board of Directors meeting minutes:

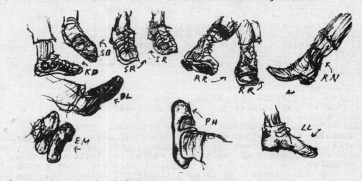

For the answers to the initials, see bottom of page 15.

4

Poem by Bruce Baillie, article about Australian censorship of *The Great Blondino*, and a drawing of a Canyon board of directors' meeting by Peter Hutton (the feet can be identified by initials; clockwise from lower left: Emory Menefee, Don Lloyd, Ken DeRoux, Scott Bartlett, Sheldon Renan, Roy Ramsing, Robert Nelson, Lenny Lipton, Peter Hutton). This is page 4 of an issue of the *Cinemanews* (76.5), celebrating its tenth year, in which various items from earlier issues were assembled in a collage.

—

FROM *CINEMANEWS*, 77.1

Willie Varela

LETTER

Dear Friends at the Cinemanews,

I just thought I'd drop you a line and let you know how much I've enjoyed reading the News the last couple of issues. This is the first time I have subscribed to your publication and I have to tell you I'm really diggin' it.

I also thought you might perhaps be interested in the couple of contributions I have for your magazine. First, I have a transcription of a taped interview I did with Stan Brakhage when he was here at the University of Texas at El Paso to talk and show THE TEXT OF LIGHT. I have also enclosed some photos I took of Stan when he was here. I thought maybe you could use them for your series of filmmakers' portraits you've been running.

I think that's all for now. Looking forward to hearing from all of you in the Bay area. Good-bye from the land of sun, dust, and cactus.

Best wishes,

EXCERPTS FROM A CONVERSATION WITH STAN BRAKHAGE

. . .

On Death and THE ACT OF SEEING WITH ONE'S OWN EYES — March 10, 1976

WV: I think if there's anything we all fear for sure that's death. I was wondering what caused you to make AUTOPSY, what happened to you while you were making that film, and what do you think will be the fate of that film?

SB: Well, you know, first of all, a lot of people don't fear death. In fact, I think the overwhelming majority of this world society we're living in wishes for death, and that's part of what's wrong with it. We have some proofs of people not fearing death 'cause you mentioned Mishima. He made a film of his death before he killed himself, showing disembowelment. He enacted his own death. I don't know if you've seen it yet. It's just a gruesome film and it's made additionally gruesome by the fact that the kind of music that accompanies it is something like Tchaikovsky. It's either literally Tchaikovsky or it's a close imitation, some Japanese imitation of Tchaikovsky, it sounds like. This was the "Swan Lake" to him, and it reminds one that "Swan Lake" is the love of death. In fact, the whole history of romanticism is a love of death. And that we get it from Rome. Roman, uh, roman-ti-cizing. That long bomb that's a great love of death. And it isn't only Christian, of course, as again, Yukio would show us. That was an absolutely Oriental death-wish going there. I had a doctor tell me about people who are dying, that he's never, in all his watching many, many deaths, he's never seen anyone afraid of death who was actually dying. Their embarrassment is usually for the living, that is, that they're gonna get better and so on and so forth, which they have to sort of sustain. Really what they want is, to say good-bye to people and then be left alone to die. Now that seems certainly reasonable. An old person who's worn out with life wishing to die and dying in bed, hopefully, somewhere, seems perfectly happy. What's unhappy is when they got the majority of the population, starting with little children, being fascinated with death. Really wishing to die. And that's really because we're not permitted to live in our skins in this time of our living. There's almost no one that's arranged a surroundings for him or herself that's at all reasonable to animal. And as we are animals, I mean we're constantly herding from the social limitations put on our life, and I don't mean just limitations like laws, I mean the whole assumption of human living is so rotten in our time and maybe has been for the whole recorded history of man. Maybe that's why it's recorded, and maybe that's why there is art. Certainly the poets were singing of it very anciently, how we suffer. You find people at the same time that they wish death they also fear it. And part of romanticism is to imagine what others will say about you after you're dead, I mean that's Huckleberry Finn going to his own funeral, which Mark Twain sets in beautiful perspective. That's also the fact that all the traditional lovers in the history of romanticism, they make love, they have one night, and then they die! That's Romeo and Juliet, Tristan and Isolde, Heloise and Abelard, and on and on and on. When I say Heloise and Abelard, I've got it back to what — the 9th century? That's another form, in the 20th century version of it, that's Didi and Gogo in Beckett's *Waiting for Godot,* which is maybe the bitterest pill of all in this long tradition. So until there's some shift of human consciousness that ends this great death wish, it'll be a crisis. For myself, I went into the morgue in the greatest fear and trembling. Fortunately, they were very gentle with me and they showed me things gradually, and I photographed them in the order in which they showed them to me so that grace is sort of passed on to the viewer in THE ACT OF SEEING WITH ONE'S OWN EYES. I call the film that because that's what autopsy means. And you can sense that the person that hatched, out of Latin, that term that we now use for dissecting the dead, blurted that out in the face of his first sight of a corpse — or hers, perhaps. It might've been a woman, that said "autopsis!" — the act of seeing with one's own eyes. And there's nothing very romantic about that. Suddenly all these bodies that were around me in the morgue were like so many hunks of flesh where once there had been the most marvelous anima, motion and possibility, and the most mysterious and incomprehensible innards, of which the brain is only one example. I mean I don't even like to separate out organs in this sense. It's one whole body filled with infinite possibilities — suddenly decaying meat. It's NOT very romantic. So I never could never again be tempted by that aspect of suicide, you know. To turn my body into something like a piece of furniture! What's interesting about that?

WV: I think this is the most horrible, the most primal thing that I was thinking about when I was seeing parts of it, what little I could see, was that, uh, what about this juice, what about this force, this intangibility, this mystery, like a light bulb or something, about our life. And all of a sudden you're just reduced to this kind of cold, impersonal dissection.

SB: Well, the body is anyway. What happens to the soul we don't know. Though I am convinced there is one, I'm not convinced that we know what happens to it. I'm not convinced by anyone's religious convictions as to what happens after death. I am certainly aware of the infinite possibilities of the living creature, and there it is, just a hunk of meat. Even more bizarre would be to make a film on morticians, where I study that whole beautification of the corpse in the attempt to make it look like it was when it was living so that the people can come and pay their last respects and have a last look on the body form of this creature that's passed on. I mean that's a whole, to me, extremely ugly, desperately ugly, twist. I'll never get the chance because morticians are very careful to conceal their labors. There's no possibility of permitting the photographing of the rites of the mortuary.

WV: Did you have nightmares during the filming of AUTOPSY?

SB: Terrible nightmares! Terrible nightmares! One of the worst of which was that I dreamed I was in the morgue and that all these dissectors were dancing around the corpse and they were teasing me as at an initiation rite or as I remember being teased as a freshman in college. And they said, "Come on! Why don't you try it?" And they were cleaning the tables of bodies that were on there and they said, "Lie down! Lie down! After all, you'll have to try it eventually." Which was a great truth that the dream gave me. They said, "You lie down. You try it." And then I realized that while they were doing this in a jolly fashion, that if I didn't lie down they would have to grab me and forcibly force me to be dissected.

. . .

SB: Anyone who mixes alcohol and sleeping pills or cold remedies or anything like that is risking death. In fact one of the corpses that was brought in was a beautiful young girl who had had two, no more than two martinis, and one or possibly two, they thought really one, sleeping tablet. And it just happened it killed her! It can, it always has that potentiality if the chemistry is just right in the body, the mix of some of these things can kill you outright. And she was a 22, 23-year-old girl, she was leaving two children. She was very beautiful. I don't know if you saw that section. That's where I almost passed out during the photography. I saw, out of the corner of my eye, the beautiful breast, jiggling, as in a dance, and I turned and they were ripping open her chest.

WV: Yes! I read about that shot. You started panning at her toes or something like that.

SB: No, I start right with this breast and then, because it's seductive! She's extremely beautiful and then suddenly you see that what's causing the jiggling is the knife ripping open her chest. I almost passed out at that moment. Many times I almost passed out in there. If I hadn't had a camera I probably would've. Though later, after making the film, I went back to show it to them for their approval. And they did approve of it and liked it very much. And then they invited me to come down to the room; so I tested myself to see what my attitude was now: and I found I was not bothered at all. In fact, there's an extraordinary aura of holiness in this room because there is respect among these autopsists for the human body and the preciousness of life. They know only too well!

WV: Could you say then, for yourself, do you think you conquered death, so to speak?

SB: No, but I conquered certain illusions of romanticism about death, and I restored to myself some admiration for the human body. And I think that's finally the effect that the film has. It shows that. It did that for me.

Herman Berlandt, Director, Poetry Film Workshop
WHAT IS A POETRY FILM?

For practical purposes the Second Poetry Film Festival is confining the entries to utilizing explicit poetry in narrated or printed form. A hundred filmmakers will consider the definition narrow and unfair. So many beautiful poetic concepts have been screened beyond the limitations of captions or poetic commentaries. This festival will not deal with these. Foothill, Ann Arbor and Bellevue will show them. This event will show only the result of collaboration between poet and filmmaker, often a single producer — a poet creating a film or a filmmaker transcribing his poem

The poetry-film uses visual interludes which enhance the suspense and anticipation of the subsequent line. The poetry-film seeks a symbiotic relationship of image, music and work; uses filmic rhythms as well as the tempo of music and meter to maintain mood and continuity. Voice-over interludes on black leader might bring out a significant line; well-timed pauses in speech will permit the viewer to digest a phrase while his eyes absorb a visual counterpart. Stills, animation, documentary, abstract design movement and narrative content can be harnessed to words and music to achieve an integrated poetry-film. So while the requirements are somewhat specialized, the variety of treatments are legion.

I've been peculiarly obsessed with the concept of the poetry-film for a long time. I feel that its magic has hardly been made use of technically, aesthetically or conceptually. For more than twenty years I responded to my environment and inner troubles by reaching for a pencil to transform my vision into words. For a lazy, inept, borderline schizophrenic like myself, written poetry was the next best thing to dreaming. But, when [I] started attending readings and began listening to my colleagues, I became aware of the incredible isolation that printed and narrated poetry had suffered. Too many poets mumbled and bungled a good poem through a poor reading. Those who remained active poets tended to become self-centered, morose and bitter, not simply in reaction to the karma of human existence, but because of their failure to communicate their feelings and thoughts to their fellow mortals. Those who were published were often infected with delusions of self-importance through incestuous bonds with other "recognized" poets and a small snobbish public. It occurred to me that it was too easy to abide with and re-enforce the sick and very romantic tradition of the poor struggling and troubled poet. The popular image of the poet had become far more masochist than that of the composer, the painter or the filmmaker.

I made a very personal decision to change that state of affairs. The medium itself must become better "show business," more interesting "theatrically." New forms of presentation must be found for talented poets. Why not publish in film form rather than in esoteric quarterlies?

Though I had not done any filming myself before I organized the original poetry-film festival in Bolinas, I felt confident that merging film and poetry would turn out a fertile experimental mixed-media through which the poem could be communicated more perceptively and dramatically.

The First Poetry Film Festival in September, 1975, confirmed my hopes. For me it was a perfectly practical way of reviewing what was happening in this mixed-media format. Ninety-one films were submitted and forty-eight films were shown during three marathon evenings. Every film that contained written or lettered poetry was projected. Totally inane and chaotic footage shared the evening with lucid, lovely and perfectly fused works. The matter of judgment was passed on to the audience through balloting. Six prizes, each an equal amount of the entrance fees, were awarded. One of the winning poetry-films was a black and white supereight-silent with captions, which had cost only twenty dollars to make.

The Festival received a lot of appreciation, as well as a lot of flak. *Variety* (Los Angeles edition) was very generous. Some reviewers considered the poetry-film format a contradictory amalgam; others found the concept inspiring. I was so sufficiently enthused that I withdrew all my savings and bought a Nizo-Braun Supereight and editing equipment and apprenticed myself to Larry Huston for ten private lessons.

This Second Poetry Film Festival, which will be held on May 12 and 13 at the McKenna Theatre on the campus of San Francisco State University, will have more ample theatre facilities and be under the supervision of a committee of four intensely creative and experienced people in both film and poetry. In addition the University location is much more accessible than Bolinas and, consequently, will permit a greater participation. Therefore, I expect our second event will more strikingly illuminate the potential of this new exciting art form than did the first. Hopefully it will get poets and filmmakers to collaborate more effectively, teach each other to see and hear more sensitively and reveal to an expectant audience a few interesting feats of alchemy.

—

FROM *CINEMANEWS*, 77.2

Commodore Sloat

A bit of scuttlebutt for your readers:

Couple of years ago, Stan Brakhage and I were having a couple drinks together at the Polo Lounge in Beverly Hills. Stan was in the midst of his epic project *The Nature of the Universe* (now retitled *The History of Civilization and the Meaning of Art*). Somehow the talk turned to linoleum. Stan was building a rec room and was looking for flooring. "Something that hides the dirt," he said, "and looks good on camera." So we headed over to Linoleum City in Hollywood. Stan walked in with his camera up and ready. The Flintkote and Congoleum looked promising to me, as did the old favorites Ruberoid and Azrock. Stan panned them all. Flintkote was too flat. The Congoleum looked good through the viewfinder but didn't pass the closed eye vision test. Ruberoid had a human skin quality with great possibilities — goose bumps. The Azrock was too expensive. We were about to leave when Stan noticed a new pile. "Hmmm, Text-o-Lite. Now that's got class. For that price I could even do the laundry room. Name's got a nice ring to it, don't you think?" Course what could I do but agree with the Great Man.

The rest is history. Stan headed back to Colorado with a load of Text-o-Lite. The family *loved* it, he *did* have enough for a laundry room. Not only that, but he got a film out of it (what did you think those gorgeous rubies of Pure Light came from). And a film title. And he's done so well that's he's been able to buy a new Maytag to go on top of that Text-o-Lite in the laundry room. Now goddam, THAT is Poetic Justice.

Maybe more bits of film history next letter: Hollis Frampton and my junior high astronomy book (which he won't admit he has and has refused to return).

Yours truly,

P.S. My new film *That Wasn't It* or *Annette Michelson Reads Broughton* will be coming your way soon — now in for timing at Deluze. Any chance of a show up there in May?

James Broughton
THREE POEMS

A Rune for Jerome Hill
in Praise of His Film Portrait

1
is the marker
1
is the maker
1
is the masker
who strengthens the wall
2
is the metric
2
is the magic
2
is the measure
of how the years roll
3
is the adder

3
is the antic
3
is the answer
that questions the toll
4
is the aspect
4
is the actor
4
is the alpha
that reassures all
But 5
is the wizard
5
is the weasel
5
is the wisdom
that dumps the whole haul
once and for all.

Tomfool for President
A Campaign Song For Bruce Conner

   Tomfool, Tomfool
     come forth with fresh foolery
Our moles have been making too many mountains
     Come bang up, come blow up
     their grim kaboodles.
We need champagne in the government fountains.

   Tomfool, come tickle us
     with authentic tomfoolery
Our motes have got too many beams in their eyes.
     Turn topsy these turtles
     on their lopsided noodles.
Clean sweep the whole country with indecent surprise!

A Prelude for Brakhage
On First Seeing Prelude: Dog Star Man

I saw in the frame
the cosmic game
of all that begins and ends,
I saw the whole screen
of turbulent dream
from which the world descends.

I saw on the sky
a human eye
in search of angelic friends,
I saw in the frame
a man's heart aflame
with all that begins and ends.

Steve Ellman
DISCUSSION WITH GEORGE LANDOW

George Landow has been making films since 1960. He taught at the Art Institute of Chicago for five years and is spending the current academic year on the faculty of the San Francisco Art Institute. What follows are edited excerpts of a conversation that followed a viewing of one of his most recent films, WIDE ANGLE SAXON. — Steve Ellman

SE: . . . So it may be that you're playing little tricks with the viewer?

GL: The way that you generally perceive things in film, that is, via a combination of visual pictures and words, is manipulatory. I think that I was playing with the idea of information, a film giving you certain kinds of information, in this case a story, and how you are told that story. Usually you're told through dialog and/or voice-over narration, or sometimes, at the beginning of the film, titles that give you some background. I wanted to see what could be done with a narrative or pseudo-narrative film in which this narrative doesn't really occur, and only certain hints or clues or fragments of it appear. So there's certain information that's given, but it's not given in the usual way. You have to put it together like pieces of a puzzle . . . When you get all the pieces it forms a story, but it's a story in which there's no resolution, no beginning and no end . . . It's an attempt to get into the area that narrative film's usually in without taking all the steps that a narrative takes to give you the usual story experience . . .

SE: Does every shot in the film relate to the narrative?

GL: It depends how you mean that. For instance, there are some things in the film that are a commentary on the process of making the film itself or upon the existence of the film itself or the filmmaker behind it. So this doesn't directly relate to the narrative but more indirectly. The narrative itself involves seeing a so-called experimental film so that ties it in. That is, since the narrative has to do with seeing an experimental film of the kind that you are seeing when you see WIDE ANGLE SAXON, commentary on that kind of film relates to the narrative.

SE: So you feel that you can address the audience directly and that's also a reflection of the narrative?

GL: I hope it would bring into question the whole idea of narrative so that the audience can begin to question the validity of a story in a film since it's never really happening anyway. That is, it's a highly artificial, contrived, and highly conventionalized thing that we call the narrative . . . I'm interested in stories but I dislike the way they're usually told in films. It seems like we've taken on these conventions so that every story has to begin, progress, and end in a certain way . . . You always know a certain kind of thing is going to happen. There's a small amount of variation. The hero might succeed or he might fail but he's still the hero and he still has that thing to perform . . . but I don't think the narrative is a hopeless thing either. I mean, storytelling is as old as people, probably. I think it's a valid thing to use.

SE: . . . I feel there's a skepticism, for instance there's a kind of poking fun at the notion of sin.

GL: In one sense a concept like that is always going to appear ridiculous . . . There's a man on the corner of Market and Powell telling people that if they don't stop sinning they're going to go to Hell and people just laugh at him . . . If you disagree with the information you're going to find it laughable and ridiculous no matter how it's presented . . . The response of the audience is something else, that's something that, to a great extent, I have no control over and I think . . . most of the people who see the film can see God as all these things, as the benign intelligence up there who doesn't really effect our lives very much or the prime moving force behind everything but very depersonalized; but as soon as we talk about the traditional Judaeo-Christian Biblical concept of a God who has a personality, definite attributes, and a definite will, and especially, a will that involves us in a very personal way, that's something that most of us can't accept . . . It seems to me a peculiar twist, not of fate, but of history, that we're living in a time when those things aren't believed anymore and when someone comes out on the street in San Francisco and says them point blank he's laughed at as some kind of a nut . . .

For me, being on the earth is only part of a much bigger thing. I see this as a very temporary part of life in the sense of illusory, although that's really a tricky word to use, but an illusion can be more real than anything else and this is a very real illusion. It's real enough so that we can place all our trust in it as being the ultimate reality. At times, we get to see beyond that. To me, eternity is much more important than the few years, comparatively, that we spend on the earth.

—

FROM *CINEMANEWS*, 77.3

Commodore Sloat
LETTER, APRIL 22, 1977

Dear Cinemanews —

A brief comment on Mr. Roy Lechtreck's letter in your last issue of the Cinemanews on the pervasive habit of filmmakers to use background noise to "create a mood" and make a film "more realistic" — Yes, Mr. Lechtreck, there is hope! The Los Angeles County Center for Audio-Visual Services to the Handicapped (or LACCAVISH) provides special prints of films to people such as yourself. These prints have had all background noise filtered out and have soundtracks suitable for playing on special high-volume, high-power (250 watts amplification) projector sound readers. For the visually impaired, two steps have been taken: 1) all projectors come with a 3000 xenon lamphouse, and 3) the prints themselves have all been stretch printed to 3X normal length. I personally have seen a print of Bruce Conner's *Report* modified in this fashion. Its new version is now 39 minutes and the soundtrack has been replaced by Beethoven's 7th//Pete Kubelka was just in town for Filmex's 36 hour Movie Musical Marathon. He spent a day at Universal showing the bigwigs there *Paws* (briefly — the story: a pack of wild animals terrorizes a southern town, stars Ben Johnson, Eli Wallach, Gloria DeHaven). Pete managed to swing a sweet three picture deal with him directing, acting, and writing. The first movie will be a feature length version of *Our Trip to Africa* with a release date around Christmas.

Hollywood *HAS* discovered the independent film scene. As I write, Mike Snow and George Kuchar are holed up in the Beverly Hills Hotel banging out a script for *Ramona's Nephew*, being produced through American International Pictures. Jonas

Mekas is shooting *Lithuanian Beach Party '77* and Hollis Frampton is cutting a 7-part series of educational films *Coping with Todays Dilemmas.* So all you Canyon readers who gripe about no public support, no money, etc. — check out an issue of Variety and see who is working in town.

P.S. I have a couple thousand 8mm film cores, which can be epoxied together to make serviceable 16mm cores. Free to anyone who will cart them away.

James Broughton
WINDOWMOBILE

They were living there
They were living there then
He was living there
He was living there
They were living there at that time

They were living there
They were living there inside
They were living there surrounded by out
They were living in
They were living out
They were living inside the outside
They were living out the inside

They were looking there
They were living there and looking
He was looking in
He was looking out
They were looking in and out
They were looking in to seeing out
They were looking into it at that time

They were looking and they were seeing
They were looking into seeing at that time
They were seeing what they looked at
They were seeing what they looked like
They were seeing eye to eye
They were liking what they saw

They were seeing the light in the wind
They were seeing the wind in the window
They were seeing the window inside and out
They were seeing the outside in the wind
They were seeing the light in the window

They were seeing the light there
They were seeing the light every day then
He was seeing the light
He was seeing the light
They were seeing the day and the night every day there
They were looking and they were seeing
They were living there in the light at that time.

8 March 1977
From the soundtrack of WINDOWMOBILE (1977)
by James Broughton and Joel Singer.

—

FROM *CINEMANEWS, 77.4*

The CINEMANEWS #77-4

photo by Wayne Cozzolino

dear folks,

here's a good pitcher for your cover if News still coming out. <u>News</u> has been good, amazing to see it survive thru the years.

Well, its the end of a long visit here. <u>Intro</u>. I & II (Roslyn Romance) just came back·from Palmers; looks good enough to show, so will do program here late May, then maybe visit up north – Ray and Tracy being married, then maybe up to Montreal for show and back again to load up for trip west, if that's the way we're going.

<u>Intro</u>. runs 18 min. Soon as I have time to make corrections, will have <u>print</u> for 2 co-ops – prob. be there by July or so. Rest of work is still in roll form, which goes pretty well as a presentation, talking some during projection, after showing the Intro. I don't know when/where, etc. I'll get to the rest of it – at least I'll be recording more Romance as I go. Meantime, I can show it myself in its present form, filling in the context by my own presentation. In the long run, there should be a video tape version as well. I've been looking around for a grant and some assistance to set up somewhere once again and catch up with it, editing, putting in sound, shooting notes and including with picture. 6 years this coming Sept. Prob. few more yrs.

Best regards to everyone. Hope to see you this summer.

                                         -- Bruce Baillie

Bruce Baillie on cover of *Cinemanews*, 77.4.

4 : Intellectualization

By the mid-1970s, Canyon Cinema's rental income leveled off, not at a particularly high level, but high enough to allow those working for Canyon and using Canyon to feel that the small business would continue to function and that those running the organization were doing a reasonably good job at providing a much needed service. Of course, now that the San Francisco Cinematheque was an entirely separate operation from Canyon distribution, the excitement that the original Canyon Cinematheque screenings had created during the late 1970s (several of those who worked with Canyon early on have mentioned that the screenings attracted many of the volunteers who helped Canyon establish itself as a distributor) was now directed elsewhere, much of it to the Cinematheque. The *Cinemanews* was maintaining a national readership, overlapping with, but probably not identical to, the filmmakers and renters who used Canyon Cinema distribution. By the late 1970s, there were two Canyon communities. There was the small circle of men and women who served on the board of directors and/or worked for Canyon. Judging from the *Cinemanews* and from minutes of the board, this ever-changing group remained, generally speaking, very close in spirit to the original Canyon, though this Canyon community was now visible only on relatively rare occasions when a controversy developed and erupted into the *Cinemanews*. There was also a "community" made up of *Cinemanews* readers, a community of intellectuals (including intellectual filmmakers) spread across the country.

Mark McGowan edited the first issues of the *Cinemanews* after Diane Kitchen left Canyon, but by the November–December issue of 1977, Henry Hills had taken charge (McGowan continued to do layout) and was soon collaborating with Abigail Child. Hills and Child built on Kitchen's work and helped to instigate a new stage in the history of the *Cinemanews*. At the very beginning the *Cinemanews* was little more than a bulletin-board listing of information useful for independent filmmakers. Under the leadership of Baillie, Menefee, and later Kitchen, it became the mouthpiece of Bay Area independent cinema, and a national nexus for informal commentary about avant-garde film. Kitchen had recognized that what filmmakers had to say could be not just interesting but significant in a historical or aesthetic sense. Hills and Child went one step further: for them certain filmmakers had become canonical figures, important enough in a cultural sense to be celebrated. This attitude was often reflected on the covers

241

of the issues of the *Cinemanews* Hills and Child edited. The cover of the 1979.1/2/3 triple issue, for example, includes a band of names across the top: "Snow, Jacobs, Lye, Lipton, Sharits, Jordan." Clearly, the implication was that anyone with a serious interest in cinema would, or should, know these names.

In a sense, this change represents a further, and perhaps final, influence on Canyon coming from New York, and from the Film-Makers' Cooperative in particular. During the early 1970s, Anthology Film Archives had grown out of the New York Cooperative and the Film-Makers' Cinematheque (the New York screening room established by Jonas Mekas that had been an inspiration for the Canyon Cinematheque), as an institutionalization of what P. Adams Sitney, Jonas Mekas, Peter Kubelka, James Broughton, and Ken Kelman called the "essential cinema": the canon of filmmakers of many kinds who were essential for anyone with a serious interest in cinema and especially in cinema as a visual art. The Anthology selection committee chose a set of films they could agree were "essential," in two senses: these films were essential for an understanding of film and cultural history, and these were the films that most clearly revealed/created the fundamental components of the art form, its "essential" nature. Of course, the "essential cinema" created no end of consternation, not so much because of who *was* included in the Anthology repertory (the set of films the committee had chosen were run, and continue to be run, at regular intervals throughout the year at Anthology Film Archives), but because of who was *not* included. In addition, a good many younger filmmakers and film enthusiasts coming out of the Vietnam/civil rights/women's liberation era were suspicious of any group of European American men deciding what was "essential" for everyone. I expect that Child and Hills and their colleagues on the *Cinemanews* must have had considerable problems with the "essential cinema," but their project had something of the same mission: to create a more thorough, more expansive discourse about and within avant-garde film, by recognizing particular filmmakers and filmmaking accomplishments as formative and crucial.

Hills and Child were, like their predecessors at Canyon and at the *Cinemanews,* resolutely anticommercial, but judging from the issues of the *Cinemanews* they edited, their enemy was not simply "business" or commercialism in general but, rather, what they saw as a lack of intellectual sophistication and exploration within the community the *Cinemanews* served. Indeed, for Hills and Child, the limitation of the *Cinemanews* they inherited seems to have been the very unpretentiousness that had, earlier on, allowed the periodical to function as a kind of literary common ground for independents. For the new editors, the excitement of breakthrough and progressive work had to do with its intellectual challenges, whether this work was in film, in poetry, in film theory, in music, or even in film reviewing. And not surprisingly, under their editorship, the *Cinema-news* frequently published various kinds of work that challenged not just those whose cinematic horizons were limited to commercial movie houses and television but the very audience that had formed for the *Cinemanews* during the previous fifteen years.

Hills and Child and their collaborators made the pages of the *Cinemanews* available to a range of direct and indirect polemic and debate, some of it accessible to most readers, some of it obscure to most readers. On the cover of the first issue he edited (the sixth issue of 1977), Hills included a photograph of the legendarily brilliant Hollis Frampton, who could talk cultural history and theory as well as anyone, along with a coupon that readers could cut out and send to Peter Feinstein Associates, Frampton's agent, in Cambridge Massachusetts, if they wanted to "Consider an Avant-Garde Filmmaker For Your Lecture Series." The gesture was both tongue-in-cheek (the small photograph of Frampton standing in front of split reels and other filmmaking equipment has the caption "an avant-garde filmmaker") *and* an announcement that intellectuality would now be front and center in the *Cinemanews.* The second half of the transcription of Frampton's talks in the Bay Area is entitled "St. Hollis (part 2)"; the "Saint" was also, no doubt, partly tongue-in-cheek—but only partly. In the second issue of 1978 the entire text of an extensive public debate between Stan Brakhage and Malcolm LeGrice, on "Structural versus Personal Filmmaking," that had taken place in Boulder, Colorado, was reprinted. LeGrice was an important figure in San Francisco at this point; he was bringing a new awareness of Continental high theory to the Bay Area. According to Child, "He was very interested in ideas. He influenced all of us" (Child, in Scott MacDonald, *A Critical Cinema 4* [Berkeley: University of California Press, 2004], 211).

The *Cinemanews* had not completely changed: new films available from Canyon distribution were listed at the end of issues, and the *Cinemanews* did continue to create a sense of intimacy within the community of independent filmmakers and those who were interested in their work by including "a certain amount of gossip, informal notes, jokes, and other miscellaneous materials." Increasingly, however, the letters that came in from filmmakers around the country were brief, and there were fewer personal items: the 1978.3–4 issue found a tiny corner of a page for the announcement that "James Broughton & Joel Singer were 're'-married in a quiet ceremony, Sun. evening, July 23, 1978. Janis Crystal Lipzin served as Best Man." A different sense of intimacy was evident in the follow-up to a piece of experimental prose on contemporary filmmaking,

"Catholic Filmmaking in America" (79.5/6), in which Henry Hills had called his era "a period of exaggerated mediocrity, of both auditor & arbiter & arbeiter (the George Griffin Era)." Three issues later (80.6/81.1), Hills offered an extended, embarrassed apology to Griffin and to *Cinemanews* readers for his reference to Griffin, whose films he admitted he did not know: "For this I feel ashamed. It was not only 'mean-spirited' but also politically abominable."

The *Cinemanews* continued to privilege the voice of the independent film-maker, a vestige of Canyon as a filmmaker-run organization, sometimes including extensive essays, as well as interviews with filmmakers and transcriptions of filmmakers' lectures and discussions—though there was less and less reliance on the San Francisco Cinematheque for these interviews and transcriptions and more contributions from other parts of the country. In fact, even the editing of the *Cinemanews* was no longer fully based in San Francisco. In the last issue of 1978 and the first of 1979, Child is listed as West Coast editor and Hills as East Coast editor; in the second 1979 issue, Hills and Child are listed as East Coast editors, and Carmen Vigil and Mark McGowan are listed as West Coast editors; and in the final issue of 1979, Hills is editor, and Child is East Coast editor (Vigil and McGowan are credited with layout). Even the fact that from the end of 1978, individual issues of the *Cinemanews* were becoming substantially larger—in part because each new issue included multiple numbers of the publication—suggests at least an implicit desire for the *Cinemanews* to be less a newsletter and more a substantial creative and theoretical journal.

The various changes in the *Cinemanews* seem to have pleased some. For instance, Brakhage read Henry Hills's experimental review of a Brakhage show in San Francisco, "Hyper kinetic Stan/dards," and wrote to say that it was the best review of his work he had ever seen. But others were increasingly unhappy with the new intellectual turn of the *Cinemanews* and with the now-frequently implied assumption that certain filmmakers were of particular significance. Soon after the November/December 1977 issue, with the cover image of Frampton and the coupon, David White wrote to ask, "Who let the boorish snobs in the door?" and to express his concern that receiving the *Cinemanews* for free as a member of Canyon might become "too high a price to pay." In a 1980 letter Ben Van Meter, who had been part of Canyon from its earliest days as a distributor, and whose films had seemed to be as quintessentially "Canyon" as anyone's, encapsulated what any number of Canyon people may have been feeling. Van Meter suggests that the *Cinemanews* needs only one thing "to make it a perfect comment on the Olfactory Essense of Current Elitist Cinema. It could even be a monthly feature. A scratch-n-sniff fold-out of Brakhage's or Snow's or Kubelka's ass-hole."

The final issue of the *Cinemanews* that was edited by Hills and Child included a cover story entitled "New York Cut the Crap," by Gary Doberman, a Super-8mm filmmaker from Albuquerque who was at one point a Brakhage protégé. Doberman's long tirade about the domination of American avant-garde film by an elite clique of filmmakers and scholars in New York City was an attack on the world that had grown up around avant-garde film, and Canyon Cinema, during the previous decade and a half. Doberman's essay had been written for *Millennium Film Journal,* but when Vikki Peterson, one of several early editors of *Millennium,* wrote to tell Doberman that his piece had been rejected (after it had originally been solicited), Doberman turned his considerable wrath on Peterson, assuming that it was his point of view (rather than, say, the flabby nature of his rant) that had kept the piece out of print. Canyon had had a minor tradition of nasty polemic (beginning with Nelson's attack on Robert Pike and Jon Jost's on Stan Vanderbeek), and so there was nothing unusual about such a piece being published in the *Cinemanews,* but when "New York Cut the Crap" appeared in unusually small print, Doberman was frustrated still once more, assuming that the tiny print was an editorial comment on the part of Hills and Child. Indeed, when longtime Canyon stalwarts Diane Kitchen and Gunvor Nelson agreed to guest edit an issue of the *Cinemanews* later in 1980, they reprinted the Doberman piece in even smaller print, so small that it could not be read without a magnifying glass—*their* way of satirizing not only Doberman but also Hills, Child, and the new, "more intellectual" *Cinemanews.*

During the late 1970s, issues of the *Cinemanews* were appearing less regularly—by 1979, double issues had become the rule, and in two instances there were triple issues: 79.2/3/4 and 80.3/4/5—though in general, these issues were unusually substantial. If the original Canyon spirit was a good bit less evident, it was/is difficult not to appreciate issues with so much interesting commentary by accomplished film artists. The 78.3/4 double issue, for example, includes not only the entire Brakhage-LeGrice debate but also an interview with Robert Nelson by Henry Hills (during which the changes in Canyon and the *Cinemanews* seem to hover in the air between the two men); a transcription of George Landow's introduction of his films at the Cinematheque, May 18, 1978; the text of a discussion with Hollis Frampton about his *Magellan* project; and a transcription of the discussion with Yvonne Rainer at the Cinematheque (April 6, 1978) after a screening of *Kristina Talking Pictures* (1976).

By 1981 this final major phase of the *Cinemanews* was over. David Gerstein edited one issue (80.1/2); Kitchen and Gunvor Nelson collaborated on 80.3/4/5; and the *Cinemanews* ceased publication after a special "Super-8 Edition" in 1981 (81.2/6), edited by Terry Cannon and Willie Varela, which seemed more like a

Bruce Conner's cover for the 1985 *Canyon Update 1985/Index.*

monograph than an issue of a periodical (Cannon went on to publish his own magazine, *Spiral,* which attempted to revive some of the unpretentious, light-hearted seriousness about alternative film evident in the early years of the *Cinemanews*).

Of course, even before the demise of the *Cinemanews* (it was revived briefly in 1995 by Timoleon Wilkins), Canyon had legally become an organization with a single function—though the listing of new films acquired by Canyon continued to be a regular feature of the *Cinemanews* up through the second-to-last issue (80.6/81.1). But as of 1981, Canyon no longer had a public presence, outside of its publication of regular catalogs.

Conversation with Bruce Conner, July 2001

Conner: You mentioned how dependable Canyon is as a distributor—on the receiving end; and I think it's also been dependable in the way that it represents the filmmakers, and how it represents what we might call a code of ethics in film distribution and in independent film.

Of course, the name, "Canyon Cinema Cooperative," as Canyon was called early on, was a misnomer. "Cooperative" was just a word that people used a lot in those days—they felt it meant "being cooperative"—but Canyon (and the same is true of the Film-Makers' Cooperative in New York) has never been organized, legally, the way a farmers' co-op is. One of the general problems of running the organization is that many times the people who are involved have no understanding of what the legal requirements and limits are. That's been a stumbling block for Canyon over the years.

Generally, though, Canyon has been run ethically. It's not just that it's dependable, but that it's run *by filmmakers,* and you have to remember that organizations run by filmmakers handling their own work were not common then and are not common today. The fact that independent filmmakers many times had to find their own venues, put on their own showings, publicize their own films, carry them around, and sometimes the projectors too—like itinerant show people—was the motivation for establishing Canyon Cinema distribution. It allowed us to come together in a group and share the costs of the organization.

In the 1960s when the first discussions of Canyon Cinema, as a *distribution* organization, started, these discussions were part of the general communal attitude and the idea of sharing and participating without concern for competition or personal gain. Right from the beginning, there were certain limitations in how we believed things should be. First of all, *no* filmmakers should be promoted above other filmmakers, and that aspect of Canyon is almost unique. Of course, it also hamstrings the organization over a period of time because Canyon can't promote what's hot; and they can't say, "This is better than something else." This keeps them from competing with other organizations that do promote what and who is hot.

MacDonald: And as the collection grows bigger and bigger, it's harder and harder for people who don't know the field to find their way into it.

Conner: Yes, you have to do your homework *before* you can begin to rent the films. You have to figure out who the filmmakers are, so you rely mostly on whatever personal experience you have and on whatever information you can find within the literature of the field.

It's amazing that Canyon has survived as long as it has. The general social and economic milieu of the sixties, as I saw it, was structured basically on the idea of the small, independent, self-employed businessman. We were filmmakers (and poets, writers, dancers, painters, sculptors, et cetera), and because there was a lack of places for our work to be shown, we had to create places ourselves, and we became involved in developing our own economic structure, wherein the rewards from whatever attention we did receive through this process would go to the artists themselves, and not to *anybody* else.

This process was beginning to come into a very strong form until the early seventies, when people who were not artists chose to take the role of "making it possible for the artists to have their work seen." The entire thing got taken over by nonprofit and profit-oriented organizations that basically were not run by artists, or were run by artists who did not have the Canyon philosophy. This totally changed the aesthetics and the value system, and the resulting economic situation turned out not to be to the advantage of the filmmakers.

The founding filmmakers in Canyon Cinema were inventing their own history as it was going along. If something didn't get an audience, either the artist or somebody else had to help push the stuff, or it disappeared. Developing audience was a firsthand experience, not the second- and thirdhand experience that we get when academic viewpoints decide how we must communicate and what we should communicate about.

At the beginning, we could expect that the majority of films at Canyon would be rented at least once. Now, Canyon may have two thousand films, and some of them have been there for ages. It's been a difficulty that there's a lot of dead wood—films nobody has ever rented. And there are members who haven't paid their dues, but still receive all the benefits of Canyon Cinema: the films are still in the catalogue; they're looked after, kept safe. Just a couple-three years ago there were people that hadn't paid any dues for eight or nine years. It takes a lot of time to deal with all this stuff, but these filmmakers will still call up and complain and make all sorts of trouble.

MacDonald: How did your involvement with Canyon begin?

Conner: At the very beginning, I thought Canyon was not going to last very long as a distribution organization. And from now on, when I talk about "Canyon," I'm not talking about the early Canyon in Canyon, California, and those screenings prior to the beginning of Canyon as a distribution organization. I'm talking about Canyon-as-distributor.

I got a letter or was told that some people were planning to meet over at the Straight Theater on Haight Street, a movie theater—they called it "the Straight," even though its name was "the Haight." They were going to talk about starting this film cooperative. I think a dozen or so people were involved.

MacDonald: Do you remember who?

Conner: I think that Ben Van Meter was there. And Robert Nelson. I probably heard about the meeting from Larry Jordan. [According to Emory Menefee, who was also at this meeting, it took place on August 16, 1966 (unpublished interview with Menefee conducted by Steve Anker and Kathy Geritz, February 22, 2001), though the November 1966 *Cinemanews* announcement of the formation of Canyon indicates that Canyon began on August *14*).]

When I got the announcement, I thought, "I'm working at four jobs"—I was teaching at the Art Institute, working as assistant manager in an import store on Haight Street, working on a light show, and working as a graphic artist and a filmmaker—"and, if this is going to run, I want to hear about it after they've had a couple-three meetings; I don't have time to waste."

I do remember going to a meeting at Emory Menefee's place and talking about it all. Emory had dedicated his own home and his free time to working on this process.

I'm not sure exactly when I put my films in Canyon, but at a certain point we had a short list of filmmakers and films. At that time, there was a lot of interest in independent film; there were a lot of screenings, generally at film societies and in museums and sometimes art galleries, schools, and wherever.

My film *A Movie* (1959) was picked up by Cinema 16 right after I made it, and when I went to New York a year later, I remember going to a Cinema 16 program and seeing a couple of films where it was clear that someone had already seen *A Movie.* They had used the same shot of the underwater bomb test at Bikini. Because of *A Movie* and *Cosmic Ray*—just about fifteen minutes of film—by 1968 I had my films at five or six distributors: Canyon, and the New York Film-Makers' Coop, the Museum of Modern Art, Cinema 16, the Creative Film Society, and maybe somewhere else. As Canyon was beginning, there were certain films that were already recognizable, and so it was helpful for *my* films to be at Canyon, along with the work of other people whose work had gotten noticed—because then *Canyon* would get more notice and attract more filmmakers.

But it was individuals like Emory who were able to keep Canyon running—until it got too difficult, until there was too much to do. Emory was not living at a high economic level at all. Many of us weren't. Jean and I would eat out once a month at the cheapest Chinese restaurant we could find. The rest of the time we'd eat hot dogs and peanut butter sandwiches. And we didn't have a television or a car and all that other stuff. A lot of the people involved with Canyon were living at a level that people working in film today would see as poverty. But many of us had decided that this was the life we *had* to live if we were going to be artists or filmmakers. It was almost like taking a vow of poverty in a religious order, and we had a faith that this was one of the more important things in life. We did not consider what we were doing as a career—unlike people who go to school today and take film classes or video or art classes and consider this preparation for a career. That idea didn't exist then, at least not among us. We were people who were willing to suffer a lot of indignity and deprivation, and to withstand things that might damage our health or well-being or standing in society, to do this type of work—we dedicated ourselves to art. There were people going to jail because of what they were doing as artists and filmmakers. It was a social environment that's very hard to convey to people now.

So this organization did get started, and it became better known because Canyon had the Cinematheque, a film *presentation* venue, and the *Cinemanews,* which relayed information about places where films were being shown, and listed new films from Canyon Cinema—it was comparable to tapping into the Internet today and getting information. At that time, there was very little information, and the *Cinemanews* was one of the main sources.

I know there were certain difficulties along the way. One of the very first difficulties and one that continued was the idea the Canyon was, or could be, a nonprofit organization. Since the sixties, when Canyon first applied for nonprofit status, and didn't get it from the IRS, people have been confused about this. They think that because the organization was not designed to make a profit, or because it *didn't* make a profit, that it was "nonprofit." And also, in some instances, some members seemed to think that whatever they wanted Canyon to be was the way it *would be.* If I told them, "I'm sorry, but federal law doesn't allow this, California law doesn't allow it; it's illegal and improper," I was seen as a negative person, just being difficult, and creating a situation that was totally unnecessary to the cooperative environment.

So between the beginning of Canyon and about five years ago, time after time, different people on the board of directors or on the Canyon staff would hire a lawyer to make sure they got a nonprofit, tax-free designation, and *every time* the end result was that they'd find out they couldn't do this: "You are an organization run by people who profit from the organization's renting the films; you are not a 'nonprofit organization.'" It was actually a very simple premise, but amazingly difficult for some people to understand. The wishful thinking of people and their confusion of a "nonprofit organization" with an organization that doesn't make a profit would cost the organization lawyers' fees and wasted time, over and over.

I've always found that both the Canyon membership and the board have a tendency to function as though no rules apply to them. One of my issues has always been that we can't have proper meetings or anything else unless we follow the bylaws. They may be flawed, but we have to work with the bylaws we have *so far*. We can't just dump them on a whim because we don't like them. If we want them changed, we need to go through proper procedures.

For two years I was part of a committee that was working on a revision of the bylaws and submitting and discussing them with the board and members—and finally there was change. I paid for most of the legal fees involved in those changes. At the beginning, I got Peter Buchanan to donate his time to Canyon Cinema, by trading my artwork for his time; and then when that stopped, he still worked a while for free, but in the long run, I think I financed the legal aspect of the revision of the bylaws up to about $7,000 or $8,000.

I may make more money from Canyon rentals than many people, but I've always spent more money on Canyon Cinema than I've made. Even back when I was working on the Cinematheque programs at Intersection in North Beach, I would come in with door prizes, just to make the screenings more of an event for the people who were there, and I would leave my rental money in the Canyon bank account for long periods because the interest would go to Canyon—I wouldn't collect rentals for seven or eight years.

MacDonald: How early on were you involved with the board?

Conner: I think I was first on the board in 1968 or so. Maybe even earlier. I know I was on the board a couple of times in the sixties, and again in the seventies, and that I wasn't on the board in the eighties or nineties. I was pretty sick much of that time.

In those early days, Edith Kramer suffered, running things. If Edith hadn't been there, Canyon wouldn't have worked. She devoted her whole life to it, and she took a lot of guff from all the people who considered themselves her boss; they'd come in and make life miserable for her, demanding all sorts of stuff.

I can't remember who took over when she left, but I do remember that at one point Don Lloyd was running the office—this must have been about 1969 or 1970. Canyon Cinema was in a big converted warehouse building in Sausalito out by the docks; most of the area had been converted into artists' studios. I was on the board, and I was pointing out that when I called, I didn't get anybody on the phone until after eleven or twelve o'clock in the morning. If people from New York are going to rent films, they're ready to do business in the morning when there was nobody at Canyon, even at normal West Coast business hours. Lloyd was not cooperative. He said he wasn't paid enough to drive to Sausalito and do all this work: "It's not worth my time." This didn't sit well with me, because I was making ten cents less an hour than *he* was, and I was working in Sausalito and driving over there, and damned happy to have a job. And later, when we said, "We want to look over the books," he said, "I'm not going to show them to you." "We need to have an explanation of what's happening." "No. You can find out for yourself."

I remember one reason why Canyon had to leave Sausalito. The board decided that they wanted to insure everything at Canyon Cinema. I wasn't part of the discussion, but I did talk to somebody on the board and said, "We don't have the money to insure all this stuff, and besides, all this stuff is already defined as being the property of the filmmakers. We're just acting as an intermediary." Well, they decided to go ahead and contact an insurance agent in Sausalito, and they started discussions about the value of everything at Canyon, and within a week a tax assessor was coming in, telling them that they had to pay property tax on all this stuff at the valuation that they claimed. So not only couldn't they do the insurance, they couldn't possibly pay the property tax! That's why they left Sausalito. They had to get out.

MacDonald: I know you've been in the middle of more than one Canyon controversy. Could you talk about these experiences?

Conner: One of the big, early conflicts was the separation of the distribution organization from the Cinematheque and the *Cinemanews.* Early on, the Cinematheque and the *Cinemanews* made money for Canyon Cinema. But after they became nonprofit, they not only didn't make money for Canyon Cinema, they didn't make money, period. And yet, the members were expected to support both of these activities. Members were required to have a subscription to the *Cinemanews,* whether they wanted it or not, which hadn't been the case before. And Canyon Cinema was letting the Cinematheque show films in the catalogue free of charge.

I remember the discussions and the arguments. People were saying, "Oh, this will be great; we'll start these nonprofit organizations that can publicize Canyon Cinema films and it will help Canyon's distribution." I kept saying, "No, once they're nonprofit, they *can't* promote a moneymaking organization." So the change happened, and within two months it became clear that, in fact, the Cinematheque couldn't turn money over to Canyon Cinema. Also, the *Cinemanews* wasn't just for the members; it was sold at City Lights—to a lot of people, film instructors and everybody else. So these were the two main communication vessels for Canyon Cinema, and both were lost to Canyon distribution.

I see the separation of Canyon as distributor and as exhibitor as something that really hurt the organization over the years. As long as Canyon had a screening venue that could be identified with the films, people who came to the city and attended the screenings would see the films and know where they came from, and that increased your rental clientele and your new memberships as well.

Of course, in time the *Cinemanews* became completely separated from Canyon and from Canyon's mission. After a while you could read the magazine, and it no longer had anything to do with the practical interests of the filmmakers—like where to get film developed and that sort of stuff; it became academic and began to use language that put you on the outside. All the earlier issues of the *Cinemanews* were in plain English. But later issues were designed for that exclusive environment that closed groups establish to prevent people from entering, to make some people "experts" because they use language other people can't understand.

The reason Ben Van Meter quit the organization was that he was disgusted with a *Cinemanews* that had been sent to him; he wrote and said he didn't want anything to do with this academic bullshit. Ben and I had worked on the *Cinemanews,* and we felt this was a betrayal of its values. Ben has never been back; I don't think I ever saw him after that.

There was a conflict in the 1980s about the distribution of early experimental and independent films. Someone was able to convince the board that they should put *An Andalusian Dog,* and Man Ray's films, all of the early silent, experimental films and early sound films, into *our* catalogue, with whatever rental money accrued being divided between Canyon and this particular person. I objected, first of all, because these were films that were not made by members of Canyon; and second, because we would be exploiting other independent, experimental filmmakers and not giving *them* any money.

Of course, the defense for this was, "Well, they're all public domain films, and we don't owe anybody anything." But I said, "You owe it to Canyon to uphold the values of Canyon; you have no evidence that these films would be seen the way the filmmakers wanted them to be seen, or even that these are good prints, complete prints. You're insulting what Canyon Cinema is supposed to be about: *we ourselves* don't have copyright on the films that we distribute. Would you want someone else to distribute *your* films and pocket the rentals, just because they can legally get away with it?" What this person had of the early filmmakers were *copies* that someone had made from Museum of Modern Art prints, versions that were certainly not close to the originals.

I objected to this proposal enormously, and we had another big battle. I was extremely sick at the time with the liver ailment I still have, which is progressive;

very few people live more than a few years with it. At that time, the doctors didn't expect me to live for two years. I was jaundiced, and could hardly get out of the house. I couldn't go to the Canyon meetings, and I couldn't talk to people.

Even when they sent out mailings, I didn't respond, because it was dangerous for me to put into words what this situation was: if we put into words that none of the films in Canyon are copyrighted and that anybody can exploit them in exactly the way Canyon was going to exploit these other films, we'd be announcing that anybody could come into Canyon and rip off all the filmmakers. I ended up in a communications problem where nobody understood what I was doing, and many figured it was just my ego challenging the board, and that I was trying to run Canyon.

MacDonald: Of course, you would know something about this copyright issue, since your films have so often . . .

Conner: My films are always going to be underground, because the only time I'll have any problems is when they start making money. There's a problem having them on television, there's a problem putting them in commercial theaters, there's a problem putting them out on DVD. Particularly nowadays there are so many people doing music videos and other films that are secondary and tertiary imitations of my films—using footage from other people's films and other people's music—that there's a new international industry that does nothing but review this stuff to find out if the copyrights are there. Back in the eighties I had five or six places that wanted to put my films out on videotape, but more recently, when I took the films out of distribution at FACETS, I couldn't find anyone who would touch them.

Of course, all they would have to do is go to one person and say, "I want this music" or "I want this picture," and have them say no, and *I* don't have a *movie*—forever. And then they know what I've got, and it's off the market. Early on, I was naive enough to think that whatever I was using was public domain if it didn't have a copyright mark on it.

But also, I didn't think about the music particularly. I thought you didn't have to worry about old music, stuff that was written in 1915 or so; and if it was contemporary music, I would send a print of the film to the people that made the music—Bob Dylan, the Beatles, and so on—and say, "Here's the film; I've used your music; if you don't like it, tell me and I'll take it off, and you'll never hear about this again." Well, I never heard from Bob Dylan about *Permian Strata*. I did hear from the Beatles, and they thought what I had done was absolutely terrific; they loved the movie and blah blah blah. But today, the Beatles sound track I used with *Looking for Mushrooms* is not owned by the Beatles, and whatever they said to me has nothing to do with Capitol Records or whoever, and I can't show it. The rights might cost $30,000 or $40,000—an enormous price for someone like me.

In the end, I think the board felt that this was causing too much dissension, and decided to drop the whole thing.

MacDonald: Canyon has a reputation for distributing good prints.

Probably the conflict I heard the most about was the one a few years ago about whether Canyon would distribute video.

Conner: Yes, there was a big push to have this free and open environment, which does work with film, but now was supposed to be extended to all these wonderful video people who *needed* Canyon Cinema. I was arguing that these people *don't* need Canyon Cinema; they've got their own video distribution organizations; and *those* organizations are not inviting *filmmakers* in.

Also, the economics of video are totally different from the economics of film, and the clientele is different. Video functions on large volume and low price; Canyon works in an environment where we have to charge high prices to keep the organization running. In fact, without eight or nine filmmakers in the organization whose films rent often, the organization would collapse! Another three hundred filmmakers are part of Canyon, and pay a fee. But all the members can voice their opinions equally.

When I argued against Canyon distributing video, I was "wrong"; I was "disruptive"; I was "an egomaniac trying to take over the organization"; I was "totally opposed to *new* experimental media." They saw the issue as video versus film.

MacDonald: That *is* how the word got out about the controversy—or at least what I heard about it.

Conner: I'm the first person that I know of, at least the first who had anything to do with Canyon, who had *ever* done a videotape production. The *very first.* In 1968 I was invited to direct a video segment at KQED, the first time they'd ever invited anybody outside of their staff to direct something. The invitation was part of a larger program that included representation from the different arts in the Bay Area.

I worked out a shooting plan for a poem by Michael McClure, which would be recited by Michael McClure. I had it broken down into about four or five segments, each of which was shot live. I worked with Michael, told him what I wanted him to do in the scenes, trained him. He'd memorized most of the poem. I set it up in a bare, black room, with monitors in the room and three cameras. The three cameras would see each other; they would see the monitors; they would get feedback effects, and we also created other effects by changing from positive to negative, and using soft focus. The only thing that remains of that project is a five-minute section, called "Liberty Crown"; it's in the collection of the Pacific Film Archive. I did have a kinescope of the whole piece, but it had distortion in the sound—it gave a sibilance to Michael's recital; after Michael let me put the kinescope out for a while, I think he got embarrassed because people would say, "Does Michael have a speech defect?" So I cut out everything except this one five-minute segment, destroyed the negatives and all the prints—and just left this one piece at PFA.

But here they're talking in the 1990s about me not being in sympathy with new, experimental video! There was this pretense of doing this openhanded, generous thing—which in fact was totally foolish. They were going to expend all Canyon's resources and end up with the organization being totally taken over by videomakers.

Actually, none of my items on the agenda had *anything* to do with video versus film. Those at the meeting were finding one justification after another to discount the bylaws, to discount the legal requirements of the organization, the correct representation of the members, the annual meeting requirements, and everything else.

By the way, I made absolutely none of my arguments in my presentations to the proxies whose votes I presented at the meeting.

The most recent controversy had to do with the question of whether Dominic and David Sherman should get raises. The board didn't want to give them an increase in their salaries, even though the board would keep giving them more and more work to do, work not in their job descriptions. They couldn't even get the board to write out their job description! The board was saying, "What we *tell* you to do *is* your job description."

Well, Dominic runs the office all day, but he's also asked to write grants and deal with all sorts of other stuff. Sometimes I ask him, "Are you still going to be around in another year? What are we going to do?" And he'll say, "Well, you know, if the whole thing folds, I could try to run a personal for-profit distribution company with the Canyon people who get the bulk of the rentals." He'd cut out all the chaff and publicize the films that would rent, and do all the selling he needed to do. Of course, that would be a *lot* easier job for him than what he does now. Canyon has come to be seen as a public service organization, and the board and the members expect Canyon to act like a nonprofit.

Canyon is still hamstrung by the fact that they're not supposed to promote particular films or filmmakers; but the board *has* given the staff leeway to give their personal opinions, which is not the same as putting together a mailer and promoting certain films. When Canyon was just a Bay Area organization, there was no problem; but now there are members across the country and in Europe. Of course, the Europeans can't understand why they have to pay a membership fee, because they have all this state-supported distribution over there.

Keeping good people at Canyon to keep the distribution afloat is a constant challenge. We were able to keep Dominic, but in the end we lost David Sherman.

One other issue that's come up in the last two years is that Canyon Cinema was brought up at a congressional hearing. It had to do with a lesbian film—the people at the hearing hadn't seen the film; they'd only seen the catalog and the description. And as a result of the hearing, the grant that we'd gotten through NEA for the production of our new catalog was rescinded—after they'd already given us the grant! We made complaints, and they said, "Sue us!" So right now the only funding that we can get has to go through the Film Arts Foundation and it has to be very precisely structured for certain activities: the book you're doing is part of that.

The board was talking about putting our discussions on the Internet. They're so enamored with this glorious new technology, without understanding that it can have repercussions. "Oh, I don't care what anybody knows about me!" they say. But they're only judging the situation by what has happened in the past. They don't realize that there are individuals who can cause us all kinds of problems. And when the board starts talking about putting the *catalog* on the Internet, I have to keep telling them, "This means millions of people are going to read this stuff; and it's not going to be just one politician in Washington, D.C., who gets upset. We don't need to tell our enemies everything. If you want to put the catalog on the Internet, you have to consult the filmmakers as to whether they want their current descriptions of their films to go out to millions of people, including their own relatives who may not know what they're doing."

If somebody says in a catalog description, "This film uses pornographic images," you're potentially in trouble, because pornography is still illegal. To go around *telling* people it's pornography is putting your head in a noose! In court, they'll ask, "Why are you saying it's *not* pornography, now that you're in court?"

At the last meeting I went to, the annual meeting, Elizabeth Sher and some other people were talking about the content of films and pornography, and Elizabeth said something like, "I can't believe that there's any film at Canyon Cinema designed to excite prurient interest." I said, "I disagree! I've made at least two of them!" [laughter]

Another problem is that if somebody disagrees with the content of some of the films, that person can create a nuisance legal action, and then it's not a matter of whether you'd win the court case or not. Just by having to respond to it, Canyon could be out of business in six months.

This one representative who got our grant rescinded wasn't the only one who wants to do this sort of thing. Canyon is a very vulnerable organization. And of course, from the very beginning, it was designed in a way that makes it particularly vulnerable: *any* film that you wanted to have in Canyon could be in Canyon; you just submit it. We left it to the filmmakers.

Finally, I convinced them that they had to have a review committee, because nobody knew what films Canyon actually had. They hadn't even looked at some of them. I said, "What if somebody wants to set us up? They get a membership application, and they send you three films, and you accept them and put them into the catalog and rent them to somebody who's a shill of this person who put the films in, and the film turns out to be child porn, and they've got a perfect reason to put Canyon out of business."

There are a lot of pitfalls. I guess the sad part of it is that all of the vision and structure of a *truly* alternate society that was happening in the sixties has been totally co-opted and reversed. One of the things that made a difference during the sixties was the amount of communication that was happening through this system, through the films that were being shown outside of the movie theaters, through books and poetry being published outside of the main publishers, through performances, theater, speeches, lectures—all sorts of stuff. These activities had a tremendous impact. One poem by Allen Ginsberg could change things.

Of course, you couldn't have this impact unless you had more or less taken a vow that this is what you value. I decided I valued freedom, and whether it was good judgment or not, I assumed that, sooner or later, the junk would go away and the best work would rise to the surface—not an assumption I would make now.

During the seventies, the films started being taken over by nonprofits and everything was getting funded. When I saw what was happening, I realized how clever Nixon was to put so much money into funding the arts through the NEA: they threw lots of money into publications of poetry, lots of money for all kinds of stuff, so that instead of having a few people absolutely dedicated to what they were doing, people who would be noticed, who would spend their *own* money publishing a hundred copies of something that would influence thousands and thousands of people, you had thousands of people making money by being part of a big system that was part and parcel of academia. At the San Francisco Art Institute, there was suddenly a whole course in how to apply for grants—getting grants was going to be your livelihood. I remember talking to a filmmaker who said, "Well, if they don't pay me to make any movies, I won't make any movies"—this was somebody who made nice movies—and when they stopped giving grants, the filmmaker stopped making films.

This has soured me completely on government funding of the arts. I don't see the point of it. It's *always* political, and people's objections to attempts to disband the National Endowment for the Arts have always been couched in talk about freedom of speech and freedom of this or that. People take it for granted that their views of art or poetry or film are objective and permanent. But there's no reason why in another three years we might not see the NEA funding dissertations promoting NRA policies, the opposite of what is so "politically correct" now.

I live in the middle of Politically Correct, USA—San Francisco. I talk to friends of mine in Kansas and other places and they say, "Oh, we've got all this right-wing bullshit going on here, blah blah blah." And I say, "Well, we don't have freedom of speech here either!" When I told one friend about some of the things that happen here, he says, "I can't believe it—that sounds like right-wing conservative talk." "Well, that may be," I tell him. "What's going on here is the same political control and intolerant attitude that you see in conservatives from other places." In San Francisco it's open season for impugning the character of white males in general: we're responsible for everything that's wrong, and little that's right.

What I'm saying is that the sense of freedom that was happening in the sixties, and that resulted in the formation of Canyon Cinema, has been so distorted that it's affected my enthusiasm. I am still involved in Canyon; it's an old dinosaur but it has a history that can be valuable for people to know about today, and it still provides a valuable service.

MacDonald: Do you still go to Canyon membership meetings?

Conner: Oh, yeah. In fact, for years I was carrying proxies to all the meetings, until the last meeting in April. I just couldn't deal with that anymore. Dominic took over most of the proxies.

MacDonald: Is Canyon your primary distributor?

Conner: Absolutely. Canyon is my *only* distributor.

I found that the other distributors didn't pay me. I had an agreement with MoMA that they were supposed to send me an accounting every six months. They wouldn't pay me for two or three years, and I couldn't get them to respond, so I finally pulled my films out. I mean if Canyon Cinema can pay the filmmakers, moneybags MoMA ought to be able to do it, too. I don't have my films in the New York Film-Makers' Coop for the same reason. They would rent the films, but they wouldn't pay me, and they wouldn't return the films for some time. Finally, in the eighties, I sent them a copy of my medical prognosis, and said, "I'd like to have the films back here with me." They felt sorry for me and sent the films and actually paid me. But you know, they owed Stan Brakhage tens of thousands of dollars, mainly, I suspect, because back in the sixties they started financing and distributing 35mm films by Jonas Mekas and a few other people and ate up the money.

MacDonald: Has there ever been a time when Canyon hasn't paid you your rentals?

Conner: Never. Never. I could ask them for the rentals every month if I wanted to: they wouldn't have any problem with that. And if I want to take the films out, that's no problem either. Canyon is it—I wouldn't know where to go otherwise.

PORTFOLIO

FROM *CINEMANEWS*, 77.6

FOUNDATION FOR ART IN CINEMA

CINEMANEWS

NOVEMBER/DECEMBER · 1977   VOL. 77-6 $.50

Consider An Avant-Garde
Filmmaker For Your
Lecture Series

an avant-garde filmmaker

Peter Feinstein Associates   36 Shepard Street, Cambridge, MA 02138 617/547-0359

Please help us. We want to know who is interested in avant-garde film. If you complete this form, whether or not you
intend to arrange for a lecture, it would be greatly appreciated.

Telephone

Name
Title
Organization
Address
City   State   Zip
☐ I wish to book Hollis Frampton. Dates: 1st Choice   2nd Choice   3rd Choice
☐ I am interested in booking Hollis Frampton at a future date: ☐ 6 months ☐ 1 year.
☐ Please send additional information about ☐ Hollis Frampton ☐ Other filmmakers: Names
☐ We are interested in film as an art form. Please keep us informed.
☐ We have no interest in avant-garde film. Please take us off your mailing list.
Additional comments:

Hollis Frampton and form for booking "An Avant-Garde Filmmaker For Your Lecture Series"
on cover of *Cinemanews*, 77.6 (November/December 1977).

Joe Gibbons

AN ART LIBERATION FRONT DIS'COURSE ON AVANT-GARDE FILM

(A polemical response by the ALF to a question posed
by radical news-monger Spencer R. Rumsey)

SPR: What time is it?

ALF: That's a particularly pertinent question at this moment since it's getting quite late. Though if one makes art for eternity, one doesn't need a watch, just a mirror. 30 years ago one could've answered "time for a change" but now change itself has been appropriated and trivialized by the "modernist" sensibility, the front lines of which, presumably, are occupied by the "avant-garde." Avant-garde film should be exposed for the dung-heap that it is, notwithstanding the increasing numbers of flies buzzing around like art-historians. Actually, maybe that dung-heap metaphor would be better reserved for "art history." Dung-heap? Avant-garde film should be exposed for the elaborate masturbation technique that it is, a metaphor all the more appropriate in view of its prematurely menopausal state (and there are no virgin births in modern art, its patent religiosity notwithstanding). Avant-garde film should be exposed for the tired body of pre-masticated aesthetic dead (t)issues left over from the more moribund, more venerable art-making traditions that it recapitulates. The social significance of avant-garde film-making lies precisely in its inconsequentiality, its triviality, its marginality. Enough, it seems, is never enough. Underneath the work-shirt of the visionary artist lies (difficult as it is to imagine) the robes of the hierophant. Remove the pseudo-scientific goggles of the "problematic investigators": in spite of their expensive tastes they have no idea what time it is. In the academies clocks tell a different time from those in the outside world.

Not so much that it's getting late as that it's getting (us) nowhere. Time and other such specifics needn't be considered when one makes art for an indefinite future, or for an eternity which goes in the same direction as a self-validating "art-history."

The creative myth, examined closely, reveals itself to be composed of subtly-concealed compartments where artists may hide their dirty linen: a rather expensive laundry bag.

We attend wave after new wave of avant-garde insipidity, each breaking more stridently than the previous, but it's still the same old ocean. It's tiring: every year manufacturers are compelled to come out with a new line of consumer products; the avant-garde is the apotheosis of this enervating ideology. In the long run, in the by and large, such has generally been the sad situation of art. It's time for a breather.

Jose ph Gibbons-Gibbons
ALF Minister of Information

Henry Hills

HYPER KINETIC STAN/DARDS

We look at film we who look at film look at film for one reason. To enter an exalted state. THE TRANCE FILM. Definitely not the exaggerated re-enactment of obscure agonies: the stench of that corpse still hovers, alas, viz. the Dartmouth sign in *Sincerity Reel 1.* I mean, I'm certainly not out to purge personal, emotional content. Impossible! Our films grow out of our lives. But what makes repeated viewings is what is there, not anything it points to. Film is very much like jazz. Athanasius Kirke/ Marie Lavaux. You sit through a lot of crap, but the charged moments are addictive.

"Kubelka is just what he says . . . His work is ideal (??) and his life is ideal (????) . . . But Brakhage's work goes one way, his life, his words another." — Jonas Mekas's diary. I mean, his bullshit may often be ridiculous, but I thought Brakhage's films were about his life, *are* (except making babies) — such prolificity — his life. It's interesting to look at the chronology and imagine the production rhythm. Somebody raves about John Coltrane and so you go out to the store and are faced with stacks and stacks of records. Where to begin? How many people pick up a couple at random, say an early Prestige and a posthumous Impulse, listen once and feel perfect justification in writing off the fanatical following to a perversity of the modern spirit, whereas if they had gotten *Olé,* say. . . . Last year when Brakhage was in San Francisco he showed *Desistfilm/Way to Shadow Garden/Flesh of Morning* along with reel one of *Sincerity:* endless pimples! Even the most devoted fan could not help but feel that perhaps this time he was really over the hill (so said after *Dog Star Man,* then came *act of seeing, Riddle of Lumen*). A year and a half earlier he had been around with *Text of Light* and the 74 short films and he was *so* HOT, the audience was *so* hungry, I mean, even his lecture was fantastic (see *Cinemanews #75–* 2). Well, he didn't die as expected and the package of new works he has been releasing over the past few months makes a strong argument that he's still the Big Daddy.

Sometimes you wait not so eagerly for the promised sequel to a juvenile bit of *Tom Sawyer* and what you're given is a *Huckleberry Finn* where the same sort of material takes off and assumes universal significance. My expectations, may be inferred, upon sitting down to view *Sincerity Reel 2* were none. Admittedly, I saw it in a living room which is a much better setting for such a work than a theater. But what a jewel! Since seeing PFA's recently acquired print of Esther Shub's *Fall of the Romanoff Dynasty* the manifold possibilities of the compilation film had been rattling around in my head. And here Brakhage creates incredible visual treats in the interplay of a wide palette of B&W and color stocks — 20,000 ft. of home-movies, out-takes, etc. — accumulated over the years and, unlike reel one, very tightly edited. Passage of time: adjoining old B&W footage to new color shots of same locales. The beautiful young Jane weaving through the crowds (since *Hymn to Her* Brakhage has apparently ceased to exploit her image and here you have a person, God such a beauty). The funky marriage. Each lovemaking followed by a birth. All the silly charm of the three infant daughters. You walk away feeling the radiation of the love he has brought to this assemblage.

Dichten/Condensare. Me here as much as him there, I mean, this is getting too reviewy — I can't do it — I'll just say it: *Short Films 1975* is among *the best work* Brakhage has done, near ideal Hypnokinetic phenomena, clean, controlled, concise, the work of a master, of one who has dealt openly with the medium for 2½ decades. Gems. What an editor! And *Short Films 1976* likewise, mostly. Like Vertov, his genius is lyric (I haven't been able to see *Art of Vision* yet, but it seems) rather than epic, certainly not dramatic. Beginners: this is the point of entry. Devotees: a culmination. These are difficult works to talk about. (Has anything worth reading *ever* been written about film? Even *Film Form* could be condensed to a page. What is worth seeing cannot be translated to verbiage.) 75: there are 10. Quite a bit of variety — still photos/strips of color; horrific portrait of nouveau-riche mansion as vast empty whorehouse ending with flash of the artist as fat man with small penis; scratched leader/paint-on-film/dot screen (to Bill Brand's shaman film as *The Process, Born, Suffered, Died* and *#1*, "Jane's Memory," are to Sharits's, only better); various light explorations in the post–*Riddle of Lumen* mode; a couple of light weights: Frampton as pigeon (?), a fuck scene with an almost non-existent female where he pulls back when he puts it in; repeated familiar themes: family and animals, windows, candles, snowscapes, hotel rooms, small town streets, plane trips; generally a summation (as seemingly seemly accompaniment to the course he is currently teaching on himself), generally magic. Ibid 3 (the snowplow scene, unf., not as entrancing) of the 4 from 76 (which includes his first *western*: Doc Holliday endlessly strapping on his holster, a quick incomprehensible shady scene with a woman, then endlessly unstrapping his holster). The less demanding bits allow you to touch down a moment, keep from totally losing it in ecstatic vision. Programmers: rent these films! If you got bucks (75: 52, 128, 33, 22, 48, 112*, 53, 46, 97, 108 or 668 and 76: 335): buy them! (so maybe someday us poor filmmakers can pick up a copy cheap at the used-movie store)

Tragoedia (from the probable Gk. origin of "tragedy" as goat-ode): if you like goats (I do), you'll probably enjoy this film. An informal reply to Hollis's formal cow movie (*Summer Solstice*), in sharp focus even. As with Frampton's, could only be made by one who lived in proximity to and in sympathy with these animals. They graze away, make funny faces, and you nervously await the moment of calamity, the conversion of pet to meat, but . . . it never comes, it ends as it begins. Kind of wonderful, or kind of nothing, but kind of wonderful anyway.

The Governor is another matter. Here we evidently have a commissioned work (I mean, would he waste so much footage?), apparently made for television (60 min., 2 one-minute breaks for commercials included). Perhaps it'll be the best thing to hit the tube since the Chicago convention, but as a film, well . . . the first third is tight and more or less coherent (and includes amazing scene from inside official limousine on July 4, 1976 small town parade of secret service men walking alongside suspiciously eyeing the sparse crowd, as well as some interesting dissolves to reticulated workprint), though, despite shots of the politician picking his nose, Brakhage seems to exhibit an ambiguous attitude toward his material, a kind of nauseating spectacle of ambitious mediocrity, I mean I'm sure Lamm is a nice guy and all that and has a lovely family although they appear to be Zombies. After the first break, however, he becomes obviously bored and, except for the freak-out in the television studio, it is Brakhage at his worst — flaccid, abounding in arbitrary opticals attempting to jazz-up enough dull footage to give the product proper length (maybe if it were a ½-hour show?). I kept looking back to see how much was left on the reel. If this is all he showed the last time he was in New York, no wonder he got a bad reception. I mean, how many films can you crank out in 2 years? It's just a case of one too many, not an uncommon malady for those of us who love to stay intoxicated on the medium. Whatever, through the years he continues to give us plenty to keep us reeling.

Hollis Frampton in San Francisco

[Editor's note: In the Cinemanews *the date of this event is listed as April 21, 1976, but it seems quite unlikely that the editors would wait an entire year to publish Frampton's talk, especially since his visit to Mills College (part of the same piece) is dated April 29, 1977. I must assume the correct date is April 21, 1977.]*

San Francisco Art Institute, April 21, 1977

JAMES BROUGHTON: You were speaking at the beginning upstairs about — it's not the filmmaker who's in there, but the language. Would you say that's a better way of talking about it than labels like *Structural Cinema?*

HOLLIS FRAMPTON: Yeah, I think it's a whole lot better way. I always somehow hope that I would never myself get into one of those situations where I had to have a burr under my saddle of that kind. In an essay about translations of Greek in the early 1920s, T. S. Eliot has a remark about Gilbert Murray's translations of the plays: that they erect a barrier between the text and the reader more impassable than the Greek language. That incorrigible tendency to label, to make movements, always has the same effect, and that effect is to render the work invisible. It effectively gets rid of it. And of course, God knows it's been going on for a long time. The problem is not only in the labeling itself, which, if done in good faith (and it has not always been done in good faith), proposes to be helpful. It's some benighted attempt to try to present the work, were it sincere. But the problem is that almost invariably it is erroneous. The great example, of course (and I don't know who it was, but I would gladly go piss on his or her grave if I did), was the person who labeled Cubism. Now that's a real peach. It came about because of course there were a small number of painters who felt a certain sympathy for each other's work who were trying to renew painting; and they had a little show. Picasso and Braque were both in it and, as it happened, Juan Gris was as well. And there was one painting, I've seen the painting — one little landscape which was very much kind of schematized and flat, and then there was a sky with clouds, and Gris had rendered clouds sort of geometrically, as if they were solid and heavy — very frontal, graphic rendering. And to this ding dong, whoever he was, they somehow looked like cubes. The cubes of Cubism came from an attempt to name something about the white clouds in one small landscape painting by one painter.

JB: It wasn't attached to Cézanne?

HF: No. What that did, of course, was to erect a barrier between the viewer and those paintings that lasted for decades, absolutely for decades. Because, of course, there you were: It's like when you're a little kid and you go to the barber, the barber turns your head — it grabs you and it turns your head, and you're looking for cubes, cubes, cubes . . . I mean, cubes are of no particular interest anyway, or they're very interesting, or something like that. But the kind of thought about the space of paintings that was actively going on in painting at that time just got totally submerged. Nothing, I think, mitigated more against the understanding of Joyce's writing than the term "stream-of-consciousness." When we come to structuralism, and of course there are two of them: there is the French intellectual commodity, which has rescued more failing and undistinguished careers in American universities than almost anything else since the theory of relativity; and structuralism, of course — in France, even — the real thing, does at least have a paramount feature that can be named. That is to say that among themselves — taking off very largely from linguistics and from the linguistics theories in particular of Saussure in France and then of course of the Moscow and Prague linguistics circles — certain people, most notably Oesterhaus and Jean Piaget, were able to make some interesting discoveries by pretending or behaving as if everything could be examined as if it were language. Now that's a critical device that's called superimposition. You put an artificial grid over the thing that you're looking at and you watch where the points intersect and it's possible to discover quite interesting things that way. But gradually that situation even became so confused that Piaget (who is, of course, I think — of all those people — a great man, a person who is attempting to discover something about the origins of consciousness by playing with children, which he does very well, in a most enlightened fashion) felt it incumbent upon him to write a little book called *What Is Structuralism?* in which book, by the way, Piaget, a real French structuralist, comes to the conclusion that, roughly speaking, there ain't no such animal.

We move now, we take you now to the year 1969, and to lower Manhattan, and the confluence of a set of circumstances. One, of course, was that at that time and in that place film was still (and still is, but one felt it very acutely there) — film was absolutely embattled. To make films, to attempt to make films, at that time was to be certainly an outcast, and in those circumstances a pariah. Art was painting and sculpture — that was it. Yes, there was a dance, yes indeed, because it was undeniable there was music, and very strong and adventurous work was going on. Nevertheless there were a few pariahs, a few benighted and degenerate scumbags, who persisted in making films. And Warhol of course had become fashionable long before he ever made films anyway, but the rest of us mostly were, as it were, huddled together for protection against the icy blast from Castelli, the sort of boyars of the New York art world; and there were certain things probably that we could agree upon, one of the very few things I think was that it was important to retrieve (and particularly the discoveries and accomplishments of abstract expressionism) — retrieve them out of the general mess of speculation and the personal myths of the painter that had come to encapsulate that painting. That is to say, I do believe that one of the important axes of endeavor at that time was to rationalize action painting and its consequences. There's only one reason I think ever to rationalize anything, that is to solidify it so you can put a foot on it and push off and take a new jump. There were certain shared views and aside from that there was the utmost disagreement, even among the principals there. This was good, you see. It has been my own observation that — and I have seen it at least three times and I have seen the opposite oftener — when an art is alive, when it's in an energetic phase, when something's really happening, people of absolutely opposing views can embrace and kiss. When it's dead, the first sign is that people whose work is so similar that you can't tell them apart detest and hate each other and are constantly at loggerheads, and tend to hang around to produce, finally, work that cannot sustain itself but must be sustained by what Samuel Beckett once referred to as "incessant critical salivation." Which is '60s painting in a nutshell, in New York, or a great deal of '60s painting. My experience at openings at Sidney Janis, at Castelli, at Andre Emmerich, at John Weber and a lot of other places was that if you went to an opening the whole room would be full of beautiful people. It would be full of the Velvet Underground, it would be full of the entire staff of *Harper's Bazaar* (I'm not kidding you), it would be full of the more vicious critical faculty — I mean, Barbara Rose would be very much in evidence, for instance — and there would be three or four poor sad artists (going around the room, saying "over here, . . . "), furtively eyeing each other to see whether anybody was catching more flack than they were. And all you had to do at that time was to clear out and go down to Avenue B where the price of admission was either a buck or a tin can, and it was an absolute free-for-all; I mean the price of admission was either a dollar or a can of film under your arm. And God knows it was messy, and God knows a lot of the work was catastrophic, but it was alive, you see, and it did not have the stink of Lysol and formaldehyde about it at all. With that kind of very sudden resurgence of sculpture early in the '60s the élan among the sculptors was extraordinary. It got gobbled up very fast. It tends I think still, in dance and performance, to be the case that people who one would expect to be very much at odds with each other in fact are entirely in sympathy with each other and mutually supportive.

Okay, well, enter into that situation then another factor, that of P. Adams Sitney. P. Adams had, at the tender age of something like 19, been sent to Europe with a truckload of movies and his young bride and he stayed over there for something like two and a half years, and sort of did every town from Zagreb to Stockholm, or something like that [Sitney made three separate trips to promote the New American Cinema: the first, to Europe from December 1963 to August 1964; the second, to Buenos Aires from July to August 1965; the third, to Europe from June 1967 to August 1968; Sitney's first wife, Julia, accompanied him on the third trip] and points in between; and came back to find, as one always does to anyplace, to find a situation that was utterly changed. Among other things, six or eight or a dozen filmmakers had kind of appeared on the horizon and had in fact appeared with considerable bodies of work.

At the same time, of course, he had set off with a certain kind of intellectual equipment, and that equipment, as one can very readily see from the book, *Visionary Film*, derived largely from an undergraduate seminar in romantic poetry with Harold Bloom at Yale. That makes something of a Procrustean bed. Brakhage gets to be Wordsworth, by an extraordinary piece of prestidigitation. And Stan professes at least not to be totally uncomfortable with that; I mean, how one squares the Stan Brakhage one knows and loves up with the notion of emotion recollected in tranquility I'll be god-damned if I understand. And it's mercifully not cartooned out too heavily. I mean, we don't have Harry Smith as Robert Browning and Lord, isn't it wonderful? Peterson as Keats, and who the devil are you, James? But that was the extent of the intellectual tool kit that he had to tinker and unlock this strange device. It worked a little — you can sort of pile a little Freud on top of that, and so forth. Freud according to the American gospel only and the Freud of course of *The Interpretation of Dreams*; not, for instance, of *Civilization and Its Discontents*, but that's it. He then comes back, and here *is* all this work which is, as it were, baying outside the door. What to do about it? Well, you can ignore it. P. Adams was much more honest than that. He wanted to do something, in a universe dominated by language — nothing exists until an essay has been written about it. He wanted to sort of try to square it away and bring it up into the light, and so forth; and so he wrote this text, which began, "Suddenly, a cinema of structure has emerged." (Sigh) And ended with me. That essay, of course, has been twice rewritten, and there were a set of descriptive prescriptions and proscriptions: the exact repeat, or the loop, the one-take movie, and so forth and so forth, and of course he made one of those wonderful valiant efforts to tie it all into the tradition so that the grandpappy of us all became that kindly and fatherly figure, Andy Warhol . . . , and poor Stan — hog-tied, lassoed and branded, clothes-lined and sandbagged — got MY MOUNTAIN made into a structural film.

Mills College, April 29, 1977

There is a problem, I think. Filmmakers are illusionists, are magicians. The history of magic is a history which goes back to a time before there was history of changing the world by manipulation of images. I do not think of myself as a changer of the world but I certainly am a manipulator of images. I indulge myself . . . A manipulator who changes space, time and matter and usually not for the better, just for the different. Film depends, however it challenges illusion upon illusion, on your cultural reflexes not mine to believe what you see. It is never true, it is always false, it is an artifact. Reality, could we but see it, clearly would not look like this . . . but it might look like some of our imaginations of it and that is the reason we are able to talk with each other . . .

(shows *Otherwise Unexplained Fires*, etc.)

Film is a young art. It is extraordinary that it is as complex as it is. When we talk about language we are prompted to recall that the natural languages that we know have not become more complex as they have matured, they have become simpler. Language is very old. Film is very complex. It suggests that film, however fascinating it is, however much we may be deeply involved, implicated — I am implicated with film at this time — may as it gets older, as it matures, become simpler. It may of course also turn into something else and we should perhaps be prepared as I am trying to get prepared for that idea. It's a machine and obviously machines have got to go and they *will* go . . .

Film is an art like music and like dance that is extended, is experienced in time. So, if it has a form that form exists only in the mind of the spectator. It is invented as it goes along. What that tends to mean is that music and dance and film — you'd be tempted to say poetry except that's mostly read rather than being experienced as an oral thing, as a recited thing that takes time — tend to be about time and the experience of the passage of time in one way or another and then after that they tend to be about how the passage of time is inflected, about how it is modulated in the light of change. So that it seems to me that the notion that film should be very involved in rhythm, that filmmakers should be involved in complex rhythmic structures in their making process, is one of the starkest pieces of realism imaginable. . . . But you understand that it's a complex subject. We're not talking about, say, the absolute length . . . an image is perceived . . . The momentary set of the perceiver is elastic and that elasticity is of enormous interest to me. There are some minutes that are longer than others . . .

The interesting thing about color is that it stands in a special relation to meaning. Think about this: there is something called drawing. Now drawing brackets a whole bunch of things. It can go from the most chaste sort of rapture, I'm thinking about the drawings of Ingres, I mean Ingres's nudes are drawn with the very end of a sharp pointed pencil as if with the tip of his tongue, so to speak. There is no surface, in a sense it is absolute edge, it is virtually featureless and yet manages somehow to imply a volume, to imply even a surface. There is drawing that is more replete, that implies and often idealizes surface and volume. But drawing is a whole art that is obtained for a long, long time essentially without color . . . Drawing seems to be about space mostly and what is in space and drawing goes fine with more than suggesting, with implying, depicting space and everything that's in it without using color. So it seems that color is not an attribute of space. Which is to say that it is not an inseparable attribute of space. Which is to say that it is not an inseparable attribute of the recognizability of things on the one hand or the way they pass through the world on the other, the way they relate to each other in habit and code of habit, and intellectual space of what is known and understood and recognized. Nevertheless, we perceive it. Well okay we are animals and to perceive color, presumably, since many animals do not, is adaptive, it must serve some function. Carnivores typically do not see color but they perceive movement because what moves is edible. Herbivores are not very sensitive to movement, in fact they tend not to see well at all, I mean I perpetually have confrontations with deer and as long as I am downwind of them . . . But on the other hand if they are to live they had better see color because they have to be able to tell what is edible, that is, green chlorophyll things, from all the other things that are not edible, like rocks. We are half carnivore and half herbivore, so we have a double heritage of seeing from the point of view of survival. We can see things that move because we eat meat and we can see things that are green because we eat vegetables. Chlorophyll green is right in the middle of our color spectrum . . . I would like to start thinking about color, and even about movement, from levels that materialistic, that physiological . . . So it turns out to be a very complex subject that doesn't have to do with *things* as far as recognizing them, separating them from each other. It seems to have a lot to do with our attitude towards them . . . It is a super-big subject, it is of such a size that it is like the *I Ching*. Confucius said if he had another life to live he would spend it studying the *I Ching*. I've already planned my next life. I want to be a woman and a musician. . . . It's very dear to my heart as a topic because it is one I plan to be completely confused about the rest of my life . . .

Barbara Hammer
BODY-CENTERED FILM

Structural film is usually thought of as film that explores the nature of the medium, the zoom ratio of the camera, the sprocket holes, the linear succession of static images, etc. Conceptual film can arise from another source than the mind, the body. From scientific understanding and intuitive feelings I experience wisdom in muscles, internal organs, skin. Body intelligence is sister to the mind. Letting the concept, the structure, the odor be body-determined is another way of making structural film.

Many early educators write of the need to exercise the body at the same time as the mind; other experiences often show that those with a strong and active body are more intelligent (this form of intelligence is limited to a verbal test score usually and so is quite biased), but again there is this strong link between body and mind. One psychologist broke the concept of intelligence itself into 110 different types from mechanical to spatial. Undoubtedly there are hundreds, perhaps much more, ways of identifying and differentiating intelligences.

With body intelligence leading and determining the form and content, the notion of conceptual or structural film is released, expanded into a more encompassing genre. More specifically, I will write here of my own experience. In *Available Space*, a film in progress, my body gave me images and sensations of being tied to my camera, of being yoked into the rectangle of the frame, of being confined. The longest cable release I could find was still an umbilical cord. I wanted a private art again (I worked as a studio painter before film) and would accept the limitations of a static camera, tripod, cable release to gain this privacy of experience in shooting. At the same time I had an interior sense of the limitations of the frame which I experience as a form of claustrophobia (not the right word but for the sake of a beginning explanation it will do). I want to fill and define and push that rectangular frame as fully and from as many ways that I can. My body tells me to do this and from this sense of filling up the frame, pushing (literally with my hands and feet against the edges as the film image) against the walls of illusion, the frame, as determined by the arbitrary nature of the camera, projector and film, I find, *experientially* the next step. The next possibility, the next link. Film in this case is not a priori, but is spontaneously considered, added, subtracted, linked in an ongoing process of dialogue and exchange between the body and mind of the filmmaker.

In *Available Space* after I traced the permutations of filling and pushing the frame and the limitations, I began to rotate the projector so that the frame although still static would move around the room, the space available at the showing. Mounted on a 360 degree turning table the film image is a woman pushing the frame. The projector moving at the same ratio as the image. Will this be enough? Satisfactory to complete the film with moving the projector? I'm not sure yet, but one thing I am sure is that my body will know.

George Kuchar

THUNDERCRACK

[Editor's note: This cartoon was made in conjunction with the shooting of Curt McDowell's Thundercrack *(1975), in which Kuchar starred.]*

—

FROM CINEMA NEWS, 77.7

Abigail Child

MATINEE

MATINEE   Abigail Child

lights*   ORGAN---------full to open blackness   hand on the throttle
shadow   hennie-pennie
                              "the full size car which we are
about to create   ov/infantry shutter MERCURY SILVER PLASTIC
                                                           WITNESS::::::::
←————————— the distance————————————→ Rain that is fire
3 minutes up/3 minutes back
        grayish black, blue, bluish grey, purplish black   /▭▭▭▭/dark.
        slotshutshot.
        NOT BLIND, but black   inOperaScalarLUMBAR   /What is that
strange noise...

NEW ROLL: RED bird REDfox RED robbin RED hat (cardinal) RED shirt RED belly RED
          handed RED HERRING
          ///red RED regulations
))))))))terrific scenery for jokes
          while truly it is this situation of the entire bizarre and
controlledworldohhowhigharetheirchinstheSunfelldownandprosperedandgrew
eaten   /Geography has always been my favorite subject.
          (whispered)

NEXT SCENE: there is music, turning around. there is movement. turning around
            to watch at the mouth
                  STA* AK* AK*ACK*TO
            SOSSOSSOSSOSSOSSOSSOSOSOSOSOSOSOSOURCE
**TECHNOLOGICAL FACT: my stereo sputters police broadcast signals south of market;
1952 - I listen as child in suburbia to coast guard calls during storms across
Atlantic emitted from our 3 foot RCA(his masters voice)cabinet TV console.
            the RECEIVER becomes→
                        ←————TRANSMITTER
...no longer sleepers.   "What a surprise...

"If the load of the car---great lead weights---be dumped about in new positions,
the car adjusts itself to the new conditions with great quickness.... cloud
     rushing rifle////night coming double////galloping tigers double double
exposed....A startle....A sudden white///eye-sighted sound///waving grain
     n*O*T*H*I*N*G   ten pairs of turquoise
            cow/red/wipe/cow/red/cow/wipe/red
        ******LIGHTS   (again and again)

            filling in blackness
            2 4 33 22 8 23 48 54 *
            / / // // / // // //
*After a sequence when first one animal and then the other runs back into the room.

7

George Kuchar
THE DIETRICH DOSSIER

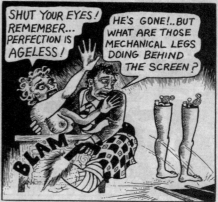

Joe Gibbons

ALF COMMUNIQUE

Re: The State of California vs. Joe Gibbons

The Art Liberation Front, acting in what would seem to be almost everyone's best interest, find themselves presently in dire straits. In this memo I shall briefly relate the events leading up to this current state of affairs, sketch out a bit of our philosophy and end with a plea.

One evening towards the middle of last October, it may or may or may not be recalled, I was possessed in the presence of a plethora of over-inflated art of the "modernist" sensibility, to remove one of the paintings (Scissors and Lemon, R. Diebenkorn, 1959 13"X10") and conceal it rather unconvincingly under my waist-length coat. Then, well-lubricated with opening nite champagne, I managed to slip past the 3 security guards and 20 museum officials and disappear into the criminal darkness. The painting was sent back to the museum a few days later, though in a circuitous fashion. Minus its frame, it was mailed to KQED in SF, accompanied by a list of demands whose fulfillment was required before the frame would be released. Unfortunately, the package was apprehended at the mailbox by tipped-off police, and shortly afterwards I myself fell into their hands.

Originally the Oakland Museum had announced that, were the painting returned there would be no questions asked, nor charges pressed. As soon as the publicity died down after the recovery, however (or perhaps because of the publicity), they, colluding with and hiding behind the D.A. filed charges and I was subsequently booked for grand theft. I am due for arraignment in Superior Court on February 21st, 1978.

It is this state of affairs which constitutes the ALF's aforementioned "dire straits." Neither Gibbons nor the ALF is in a position to afford defense funds, since they are not yet supported by the National Endowment for the Arts, and subsist substandardly. This, then, is where we extend a sincere plea for monetary assistance from you, kind reader, to help finance our defense. At stake is the right of free expression and irrational behavior; the hegemony of "official" culture vs. a form (and a content!) of expression (which the ALF is only trying to index themselves to) which strives to be a somehow meaningful, somehow more direct and more relevant to a Present which art museums and their attendant mythologies must perforce exclude, since their ideology consists in (and fostering the illusion of) their existing outside of Time, outside of Context, outside of Life as we know and experience it.

Why should we let pretentious and overbearing institutions dictate the form and content of expressivity and creativity of individuals? The history of "modernist" art can be read as a series of somehow evolving constraints, each new "movement" serving to further constrict, further channel personal expressivity and creativity into a conjuncture where, for artists (begging the question) practically nothing can be said of any immediacy or significance, and for those of us so hapless as to be excluded from the ranks of the select few, the Chosen, art becomes, in Terry Smith's words, "not something *we* do but something *they* do, putting us in that role we've become so accustomed to: that of the consumer, the passive "spectator."

So, don't delay, send in your dollar today! For every donation over $5.00, we will bestow honorary membership status in the ALF, with all the privileges accruing thereof. For every donation of $15. or more, the donor will receive, in addition to membership privileges, an official ALF t-shirt, handsomely emblazoned with the ALF insignia (scissors menacing lemon). Give a hoot! ALF Defense Fund c/o Treuhaft & Walker, 1440 Broadway, Oakland CA 94612

— Joseph Gibbons-Gibbons
ALF Minister of Information

Stan Brakhage
Box #170, Rollinsville, Colo. 80474
LETTER TO HENRY HILLS, JANUARY 13, 1978

Dear Henry Hills,
I want to thank you for one of the best reviews I've yet read. You presented your opinions just exactly as that — opinions — leaving the reader free to find out for him or her self; and yet you did give enough personal orientation (re: jazz, Coltrane, Mark Twain, earlier films of mine, "THE TRANCE FILM," etc.) that we know where you're coming from, have lines of perspective on yourself. It is clearly a human being writing (a rare clarity); and you do treat me most humanly. I, of course, don't always agree with you, but I ALWAYS respect your opinion and even wonder if perhaps you might be (might prove in the long run to be) correct. Which of any of us KNOWS the signification of new creative work?: only a fool would claim absolute surety . . . certainly not the maker. I think and very much feel that "The Governor" IS one of the greatest works ever given to me to do; and it more than fulfills (so far) every expectation I had of it while working on it: but only Time will tell, like they say . . . One clarity from me which you do deserve: "The Gov." was NOT commissioned. In fact, it was emphatically stated to Governor Lamm that there could be NO interference with my making. The deal, as is my usual in cases of portraiture or similarity of Doc., WAS that I would pay for the film myself (so there be no strings attached) and that I would complete it the same as any other film of my making AND that then he would be allowed to decide whether or not it could be released.

No changes were permitted him, nor were requested. If he hadn't accepted ALL of the film as is, then I would have stuck it away in the vault until one of us was dead . . . (preferably, had that been the case, him). The work could never have been made if he hadn't accepted these terms; and happily he does very much like it. Another point of fact: it was absolutely NOT made with T.V. in mind; and there are not, nor ever have been, any hopes of it being shown on television. Its length, and those 'blanks' you think were designed for "commercials," is/are integral parts of the form. It is important to me that those misapprehensions of yours be corrected because I think they may have biased your viewing, will certainly bias the viewing of some people, and DO suggest that I work under commission . . . something I've been at great pains to discourage other artists from doing . . . and something I've suffered a great deal to avoid doing myself: (for instance, during the making of "The Gov.," at a time I very much needed money, I turned down a commission to make a film on the President of Mexico). All this is NOT to suggest that your opinion of "The Governor" is wrong. It is the most generally dis-liked film I've made since "Anticipation of the Night"; and that also is NOT to suggest your opinion is wrong. We'll both have to wait and see . . . if we live so long. Another fact I'd like to correct: I do continue photographing Jane. Much of this footage will, if as usual, come to something in the future — most not (tho' I shouldn't really try to out-guess that, as I've been unable in the past to ever know what will finally turn up in a completed film): BUT it should at least be noted that the face of the sleeping woman in the first of "Short Films: 1976" is that of Jane, AND it is her childhood photos which start "Short Films: 1975," her vagina which touches off the 'trip' in the second film of that series . . . other parts of her anatomy weaving throughout that series, AND her face and figure which dominate much of the Super 8mm films. I hasten to correct this assumption of yours that "since 'Hymn to Her' Brakhage has apparently ceased to exploit her image" because it seems similar to that assumption YOU so carefully contradicted in your review — i.e. that I'm "over the hill" or somesuch . . . put in perspective by your witty "he didn't die as expected." Every couple years some reviewer suggests that I don't photograph Jane enough; and about once a year a number of our friends call to make sure we haven't separated or divorced, prompted by some recurring rumour. I can only guess at what prompts these rumours, this particularity of gossip; but I am naturally quick to correct it. I commiserate with Jane's fans wishing more image of her, and I bow to their (and her) criticism of her image in the films; but it is precisely beCAUSE I do NOT "exploit her image" that The Muse (or the subconscious, if you like) has the last viz-a-vis. in the matter. A couple other points, just 'for the record': it is not "a fuck scene," nor ever visibly such, which puzzled you (perhaps thus?) in "Short Films: 1975," but rather something more resistant to naming . . . but which, had it been named, might have been called

"Dalliance" — tho' I hadn't wished to be so Elizabethan as that either; AND it is "Doc Holliday's/Jimmy Ryan Morris's daughter who appears in that scene with him . . . Pagan Morris her name. Had you seen her as a little girl it might have made the scene less (or possibly more) "incomprehensible" for you: and I DO realize how difficult it IS to comprehend all these particularities of detail in one, or even several, viewings of these films — and do thank and praise you for the extent to which you HAVE been accurate in your review . . . this letter in homage of the worthiness of your review rather than any criticism of it.

I don't know if you are one of the editors of Cinemanews, but I did want to comment that I found this issue of it unusually interesting: the interview with/of Hollis Frampton was excellent . . . Hollis at his best, which is (in my opinion) the VERY best.

— *Blessings,*

P.S. Jane says I'm too "picky" about "a fuck scene" and Jimmy's daughter AND that you deserve MORE praise — it being the very BEST review we've seen in some time. And I think she's right, as usual. A film must survive its suggestions — i.e. if the suggestion is fucking, then the film's particularities OUGHT counter-balance that for some full measure of meaning which contains place for tangential interpretation or counteracts them altogether; and I don't think that film successfully does that . . . and the little girl DOES pun on woman (a shade of that scene I'd not thought of before). Okay, so, and PRAISE PRAISE PRAISE!

David White
7408 16th St., Rio Linda, Ca 95673
LETTER

To those responsible for the writing of the "CINEMANEWS,"
I just recently read the Nov.–Dec. issue of the Cinemanews. My God! What is happening there? And who is this Hollis Frampton that is stamped all over the issue and what looks like a subscription form on the cover? 'Yes, please send me 12 weeks of Hollis Frampton at the mere price of 8.95, a saving of $4.95 off the newstand price. And yes please send as a special offer for subscribing right away, the last three fingers off Hollis Frampton's left hand.' And that picture! I thought I was picking up a zoological survey on the North American 'Avant-Garde filmmaker,' a new species discovered, bearing a haggard and distrought face (similar to his cousin, the 'Artist') and commonly found in a habitat of split-reels and film cans after just having exhausted himself, as they commonly do, by a brutal examination of his soul, resulting in an hour-long film of garbage rotting away. And then on the inside! Incredible! All those words and that timeless quote; "We must recover the world. We live as if coated with

rubber." Surely the Greeks themselves would envy the clarity and wisdom of this statement as they would the endless and boring sophistry the issue was filled with. Who let the boorish snobs in the door? I wouldn't say that there weren't a few lines of substance and clear observation but I would have to say that there wasn't any more than that. What happened to the personal statements, and the sincere dedication that the old Canyon Cinema News gave? Are we to be flogged by intellectual bureaucrats whose understandings of things expire with their library reference cards? If people are paying you then they should stop. If they aren't paying you then they should start. But let me depart from sarcasm and describe a little more accurately my disappointment. As an 'Avant-garde' filmmaker and a self-appreciating intellectual, I am disgusted. Please rectify your attitude immediately. I am currently receiving the Cinemanews for free as a member of the co-op. Don't make me think this is too high a price to pay for reading it.

—

FROM *CINEMA NEWS*, 78.2

Henry Hills

GEORGE KUCHAR IN EUROPE

KUCHAR: . . . England, and they said, "Would you like to come to the T — , we'd like to have you at the Thames Film Festtival, plus you will also go to Rotterdam, as our sister group," you know? So I said fine, I would like to go, as I was going to make it my business this year to go someplace exciting, like if I was offered a trip of travel, I would accept. Because I t — , last year I turned down a trip to Newfoundland, just because I didn't feel at the time like I wanted to go to Newfoundland, because I was going to Hollywood for one day. And I turned down this free trip to Newfoundland to be on television. Isn't that riduculous? In Canadian Television. I'll never forgive myself for that, you know? I'll never forgive myself because I could have learned something, I could have been on television, and it might have been an interesting experience, you know? So I vowed I'd never do that again. And the thing came, I said yes — which meant I had to get a passport and everything. So I did all that stuff and I got it real fast. And then I went to New York City on my stopover to stay a time with my parents. I stayed three days with my parents, and I was supposed to leave on the fourth day. But on the third day I found out . . . the sky looked funny. And I said, oh-oh. Looks like we're gonna have bad weather comin'. And at six o'clock there was a storm warning that a blizzard would probably come. And so I made my decision to leave New York in a hurry a day early because I had a feeling that all the airports were gonna be shut down. So I did leave. I left that night. It was one hour — in one

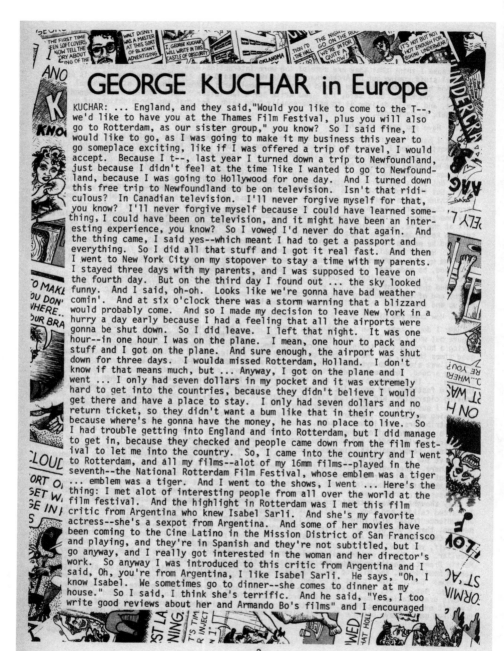

GEORGE KUCHAR in Europe

KUCHAR: ... England, and they said,"Would you like to come to the T--, we'd like to have you at the Thames Film Festival, plus you will also go to Rotterdam, as our sister group," you know? So I said fine, I would like to go, as I was going to make it my business this year to go someplace exciting, like if I was offered a trip of travel, I would accept. Because I t--, last year I turned down a trip to Newfoundland, just because I didn't feel at the time like I wanted to go to Newfoundland, because I was going to Hollywood for one day. And I turned down this free trip to Newfoundland to be on television. Isn't that ridiculous? In Canadian television. I'll never forgive myself for that, you know? I'll never forgive myself because I could have learned something, I could have been on television, and it might have been an interesting experience, you know? So I vowed I'd never do that again. And the thing came, I said yes--which meant I had to get a passport and everything. So I did all that stuff and I got it real fast. And then I went to New York City on my stopover to stay a time with my parents. I stayed three days with my parents, and I was supposed to leave on the fourth day. But on the third day I found out ... the sky looked funny. And I said, oh-oh. Looks like we're gonna have bad weather comin'. And at six o'clock there was a storm warning that a blizzard would probably come. And so I made my decision to leave New York in a hurry a day early because I had a feeling that all the airports were gonna be shut down. So I did leave. I left that night. It was one hour--in one hour I was on the plane. I mean, one hour to pack and stuff and I got on the plane. And sure enough, the airport was shut down for three days. I woulda missed Rotterdam, Holland. I don't know if that means much, but ... Anyway, I got on the plane and I went ... I only had seven dollars in my pocket and it was extremely hard to get into the countries, because they didn't believe I would get there and have a place to stay. I only had seven dollars and no return ticket, so they didn't want a bum like that in their country, because where's he gonna have the money, he has no place to live. So I had trouble getting into England and into Rotterdam, but I did manage to get in, because they checked and people came down from the film festival to let me into the country. So, I came into the country and I went to Rotterdam, and all my films--alot of my 16mm films--played in the seventh--the National Rotterdam Film Festival, whose emblem was a tiger ... emblem was a tiger. And I went to the shows, I went ... Here's the thing: I met alot of interesting people from all over the world at the film festival. And the highlight in Rotterdam was I met this film critic from Argentina who knew Isabel Sarli. And she's my favorite actress--she's a sexpot from Argentina. And some of her movies have been coming to the Cine Latino in the Mission District of San Francisco and playing, and they're in Spanish and they're not subtitled, but I go anyway, and I really got interested in the woman and her director's work. So anyway I was introduced to this critic from Argentina and I said, Oh, you're from Argentina, I like Isabel Sarli. He says, "Oh, I know Isabel. We sometimes go to dinner--she comes to dinner at my house." So I said, I think she's terrific. And he said, "Yes, I too write good reviews about her and Armando Bo's films" and I encouraged hour I was on the plane. I mean, one hour to pack and stuff and I got on the plane. And sure enough, the airport was shut down for three days. I woulda missed Rotterdam, Holland. I don't know if that means much, but . . . Anyway, I got on the plane and I went . . . I only had seven dollars in my pocket and it was extremely hard to get into the countries, because they didn't believe I would get there and have a place to stay. I only had seven dollars and no return ticket, so they didn't want a bum like that in their country, because where's he gonna have the money, he has no place to live. So I had trouble getting into England and into Rotterdam, but I did manage to get in, because they checked and people came down from the film festival to let me into the country. So, I came into the country and I went to Rotterdam, and all my films — a lot of my 16mm films — played in the seventh — the National Rotterdam Film Festerival, whose emblem was a tiger thing: I met a lot of interesting people from all over the world at the film festival. And the highlight in Rotterdam was I met this film critic from Argentina who knew Isabel Sarli. And she's my favorite actress — she's a sexpot from Argentina. And some of her movies have been coming to the Cine Latino in the Mission District of San Francisco and playing, and they're in Spanish and they're not subtitled, but I go anyway, and I really got interested in the woman and her director's work. So anyway I was introduced to this critic from Argentina and I said, Oh, you're from Argentina, I like Isabel Sarli. He says, "Oh, I know Isabel. We sometimes go to dinner — she comes to dinner at my house." So I said, I think she's terrific. And he said, "Yes, I too write good reviews about her and Armando Bo's films" and I encouraged him because I think that they are some of the more interesting — one of the more interesting personal stuff coming out of Argentina, he told me. He said the film scene in Argentina is pretty bad. And he felt that Armando Bo and his star, Isabel Sarli, were making real nice personal pictures, you know. So I said, I'm gonna write her a fan letter. And he said, "You go ahead and do that, and I will deliver it to her personally," he said. And that was the highlight of my trip, I thought, to Rotterdam.

HILLS: Have you heard from her?

KUCHAR: I haven't heard from her yet, because he's in New York I believe, and then he's on his way to Argentina. And I don't know if I will hear from her but I left him my address and phone number and that. I told him all about the situation, what I thought of her, and her work and stuff. And I go to movies — I recommend her movies to my students. Which is not an easy thing to do in today's . . . women's rights, and women's lib and stuff. Because Isabel Sarli's a big classic sexpot, you know? But she's the perfect example of an abused woman, abused by the men in her country, you know? But she fights — she goes through that abuse with dignity. She puts up a fight, you know? And I think it's a great thing for women to see because she truly plays strong people, you know? Strong characters. So anyway, I tell the graduates to go, but only one — I bring my friends — but only one student I know went up — went and checked on her for sure. But unfortunately her picture left at the time, so he didn't get a chance to see it. But anyway, that was the highlight of my trip to Rotterdam. Also I met this guy in Rotterdam who's down near Hollywood — lives in Hollywood now, and he made a very good 35mm black and white film called HOT TOMORROWS. His name was Martin Brest. He had trouble getting into the country too. And sure enough he was from the Bronx. He was from my old neighborhood, you know? And he's about my age, you know? And he was down in Hollywood, he made this big film. Well, he came to one of my screenings. I personally never went to one of my own screenings in Europe. I don't know why, I guess I was in chaos, you know? But he went, and then I went just at the end. I didn't go to any of my own showings except twice I went at the end of the picture to talk. No, once at the end of a picture, and once in the beginning. I got up and right away the audience started laughing.

HILLS: How come you didn't go?

KUCHAR: I don't know. Isn't it strange, Henry? But I hardly went to movies. I was trying to figure out why I was in Europe, most of the time. I was trying to understand where I am. And I was having a horrible time trying to understand. Because I . . . I was a wreck in my hotel room. I had good times though, and then I could go out and meet people. But I was a wreck in my hotel room. I guess I was alone with myself in the hotel room and I had a . . . in Europe, and I wasn't used to getting around, you know? I didn't know why I was there, and where's my homeland. And so it was strange . . . it was very bizarre, so I had difficulty personally, you know? But, then I'd go out to the film festival, and meet alot of people. And everybody was a nervous wreck. They were all smoking cigarettes, and they had like three bars in the place, and there were people milling around, and . . . I guess it's called a high-pressure festival, you know? Maybe that's how it seemed because everything was so high-pressure. And so many people converging on you and other filmmakers looking for distributors, and it was strange . . . but it had a very nice — it was a very nice festival because it had a wonderful coffee-shop atmosphere, like a old beatnik coffee house. You know what I mean? They were serving coffee all the time, they had three bars . . . and the people were nice, they looked like clean, happy beatniks — European version, you know what I mean? So, anyhow, I was saying, I did get up at the end of one of my pictures, UNSTRAP ME, it played, and I remember that the audience was still there. They were all sitting there, even after UNSTRAP ME, my big picture, which I personally like, but it's a little tough on audiences if they're nervous, you know? They don't relax. I got up and they started laughing right away, the audience. I didn't open my mouth. It was because my eyeglasses were broken, and I had a makeshift attachment to go around my ear to keep the eyeglass on. So they thought it was pathetic or something, the director coming up with broken eyeglasses. Anyway, I started talking and they were all talking among themselves too, while I was talking. It was not an audience frozen with interest. And I wondered, I asked them, "Are you bored, is this boring?" But, no, that's the way they reacted. They wondered, "Who is this person getting up? Why is he saying these things?" I asked for questions and nobody raised their hand, so I just started spouting out stuff, you know? What I would think that the audience would like to know. And it was sort of peculiar. And then I saw several people were really enjoying it, and one of them was that guy, Martin Brest. Really enjoying the presentation at the end, you know? And the rest of the audience seemed bewildered, and milling among themselves, and occasionally looking, giving me alien stares, you know? But I think it was in my own head, because I asked them if they were bored, they were all talking. But, he was really at the edge of his seat and enjoying every minute of it — every minute of this presentation I made. Then I heard clapping in the last couple of rows. And the clapping — I wasn't even finished talking, they started clapping. And it was meant to get me off, like . . . the guy asked me to leave because the next picture was coming on, you know? So, I did leave, and the guy, Martin, came over to me and said, . . . We got drunk that night. He hated — didn't like being in Holland, couldn't relate to the Dutch people. And he got drunk, and we had a good time. We were talking about, you know, movies in general, and he said that he so much enjoyed my talk I had, like. And that I was real good, and especially toward the people who were clapping to try to get me off, the way I handled it. Anyway, I didn't understand it. But I enjoyed meeting him, you know? And then I saw his film the next morning. I went — there was a screening of his picture the next morning, and it was a great picture, I thought . . .

HILLS: This is the guy from Brooklyn?

KUCHAR: Yeah, from the Bronx, my old neighborhood. And he made a 35mm film in Hollywood called HOT TOMORROWS. And thought it was a wonderful picture, and I cried — and I told him at the end I cried, you know? And that was the end I saw him, 'cause he went to Amsterdam afterward for a day. I told him to go to Amsterdam, you won't be depressed, I said. And he went to Amsterdam, he felt great — changed his mind about Holland, and the Dutch and everything. So . . . Amsterdam's terrific! Were you there?

HILLS: Yeah, yeah.

KUCHAR: Yeah, that's terrific, yeah. It looks very good. So I went there for a day. Then I went on to . . . that was my trip to Rotterdam. I had an interesting time — it was educational, you know? Then I went on to London. And the London thing was a bomb. Because it took place in this school that looked like a high school, you know, and the students were on strike. Am I still talkin'? Is it alright?

HILLS: Yeah, yeah.

KUCHAR: The students were on strike. And the building — the heat was shut off in the building, you know, it was kind of cold in England at that time of year. And the heat was shut off in the building, the students were on strike, and the festival was never advertised. And it was in this strange community somewhere near the Thames River, but not, what you would call in downtown London. It looked like some sub-urb like Queens, you know, would be to Manhattan. Anyway, so the audiences were few and far between. They were very little. And none of my films came out of cus-toms. They were stuck in customs for the whole week I was to be there, and they were to show. What a ridiculous thing, huh? And this I go to London for? What a stupidly . . . stupidly-concocted thing! But, you know, I didn't get . . . I realized, well, this was the way it was, and I was gonna do my best and take advantage of the situation. So I did make some interesting friends, some nice friends, and a student played me . . .

HILLS: You couldn't show your films?

KUCHAR: No. None of my films. He did manage to get two films of mine from my old distributor in London. He got two films, and those had been seen. And they were played all the time the other films were supposed to be playing. These two films, they just went on and on . . . HOLD ME WHILE I'M NAKED and COLOR ME SHAMELESS — two of my good films. But none of the other films ever showed. I had all of them — there must have been 15 16mm films — so many, you know? Never could get out of customs, because they had to check 'em, you know, and it took time. Anyway, that was a big . . .

HILLS: They looked at all of 'em?

KUCHAR: I think they must have looked at all of them. Because I heard they have a projector that goes at 90 frames a second. So they're checking on objectionable material. But . . . anyway, I made sure I went to London to see the sights, you know? Big Ben and stuff, and all stuff like that. And I took a boat down the Thames River to the London Tower, Tower of London. You know, I did all that stuff, and I met my ex-distributor, who everyone said turned out, was a bum, and was no good, and was washed up, and everything. And maybe it's true, but I had a great time with him, and he gave me $60, you know — he was the only one that I got money from. And he took a cab all the way from downtown London to this community, which was like $10 or $20. Ridiculous . . . $20, because it was 10 pounds, you know? To take a cab. Spent $20, you know, on a cab, to go pick me up and take me to his house so his girl-friend could cook dinner for me, and he can get on my good side. And he told me why his business fell down. He was trying to distribute DEEP THROAT and the Mafia was . . . and he ran into so much difficulties and it lost so much money; he also tried to finance a Kenneth Anger movie and lost about $40,000 on that. So he wrote a screenplay about his experiences and he's been writing for two years. And I saw it, and it's a big fat screenplay and he said, "This is why my business has fallen down." And I said, "Well I think it's worth it, because this seems like a real good screenplay." I read part of it, and it was sort of, he's a good writer. And so I had a wonderful time with this bum — washed-up man, that's supposed to be a washed-up man. You know, whether he is a bum or a crook, he was a nice guy — he treated me real good. The other people treated me good too, the festival director was very nice — I stayed in his house. But the festival was so badly run that, I mean, so unadvertised, so silly, that, I don't know, it was sort of like a joke, so I couldn't get mad. It was just sort of funny, you know? I thought it was funny and a waste of money to have me stay there, you know?

HILLS: But they paid you to go over there.

KUCHAR: They paid me to go over there and they paid plenty to send me back.

HILLS: So it didn't cost you anything.

KUCHAR: No, it didn't cost me a damn thing. The whole trip was paid for, which was very good, because I had no money at the time. Yeah, I had no money at the time, I was broke two days after I got paid on payday — I had so many bills. So it was all paid for, and I had a very nice time. But, I don't know. I'm glad I saw the other side of the country. I know in England the people I talked to took films very seriously. You know, very seriously, I don't know. They got me nervous sometimes when I had to talk with them, they were so serious, you know? And then one girl who was there, I don't know, I was introduced to her, she said she was a critic or something, she was a young girl, she was there with her boyfriend, you know? So she was talking about THUNDERCRACK, you know? And I said, I started to bring up some sex matters about the film, how the guys tried to get excited, and she didn't want to hear about it. She said, "Oh no, please don't tell me any more, I'm so embarrassed." And she tells me to stop it. She didn't want to hear any more, she was . . . she almost fell on the floor. She asked me to stop. She said, "Please, stop, I don't want to hear any more stories." They're so serious, some of them made me sick, you know. I didn't want to be around them. I get scared. I guess it was the school, they took the whole damn thing so seriously. Ecchh. It was just a few that were real interesting and nice, you know, and had a sense of humor. One of them was a girl who ran the London Co-op. She got a, she's — the London Filmmakers' Co-op? — there's a girl there running it, you know? named Felicia [Felicity] Sparrow or something like that. And she's really good — she had a sense of humor, you know? And I tried to pass out good information about this ex-distributor of mine, so she could pass it on to other filmmakers. 'Cause all she's been getting is bad, bad vibes, from this . . . you know, other people have been saying this guy's real bad; so I tried to add this little bit because he gave me $60, you know. And he was writing a screenplay, so . . . But she had a sense of humor, she was able to laugh, because she used to be a waitress and stuff.

HILLS: He still had your prints?

KUCHAR: He had my prints—he's got two of my prints. She wanted to know if I should ask for the prints back—if I should demand the prints back, because Ed Emshwiller was suing him and stuff, to get his prints back. But I said, "Naaaa, leave 'em with him," because I gave 'em to him eight years ago, or nine years ago, what do I want 'em back for? Let him have 'em. I made the deal—he gave me a couple of thousand—I got a thousand dollars or more out of him, you know, before the money stopped comin' in. But evidently the money stopped comin' in because he didn't dish out the pictures, you know? So, you know, I don't really care. It's alright, he's got the films. But then I came back to the United States, and I did go with my agent, Babeth, to Rotterdam and Amsterdam. She's a very good agent, you know? She's very pretty, and she's glamorous. And she's pushy, you know? Which is good. But, you know, she was very good and she was able to translate stuff. So, you know, I had a very good time. I thought I had a good time. I like to think I had a good time.

Jonas Mekas
AUNT KASTUNE

I remember her well, our aunt Kastune.
She used to come each summer,
appearing one day out of the woods
to join in raking, binding rye and carting hay.
Wearing the same blue dress, and that bright
flowered kerchief. And she'd bring the two of us, my brother and me,
and a handful of nuts.

We'd run out then, down to the thicket
for our pickings: ripe red raspberries,
and strawberries. And back on the run
set them down on the table, in front of our aunt.
Then climb on the bed, and dangling our feet off the edge
sort through our matchboxes, smoothing the new wrappers.
And from there watch mother, her back against the wall,
talking with aunt Kastune: the two of them
handling linen out of the chest
while they talk of bugs assaulting the crops,

of a new barn now building,
and uncle Povilas, due back from Switzerland next spring.

Then they're up, tying their kerchiefs under the chin
and heading for the barn. Where aunt Kastune
pulls up a pail to help milk the cows
and makes a point of saying, how much more
they give this summer. Then
it's out to the field, for a talk with our big brothers,
where they're digging the new ditch. And on
to check on the oats, and out to the fallow
where we're to sow the winter rye.
And on the way we strip a handful of peas off the vine
and split the full pods open, to give our aunt.

And with the herds back, in the evening,
and all the family together after work,
with aunt Kastune there we used to sit
out under the large, shading lindens
and listen to her; each with so much to ask her
before she's gone again. If not the next day
soon, maybe by Sunday. For then our aunt Kastune
goes off again and disappears
into the trees, until next summer.

(from *The Idylls of Semenishkiai*; translated from the Lithuanian by Vyt. Bakaitis)

Tony Conrad in San Francisco, February 28, 1978

San Francisco Art Institute, February 28, 1978
*(displays Kalvar films, boiled films, deep-fried film, etc., having performed a film
sukiyaki 2 nights earlier at Eye Music)*

GERSTEIN: I think . . . very much something that is for your benefit only, and it's
that which makes me question — I hate to use words like "artistic integrity" or
"relevance" . . .

CHILD: Can I ask a question before you answer that? Because somehow I think it
relates — I mean, it's interrupting . . .

CONRAD: You're getting me a whole hour, you know.

CHILD: . . . which is, you have just said you've moved away from this, which I think
also was said up when you talked about playing with a narrative. And I mean, in a

way, it's the movement, I mean — somehow relating to what David said I see, you know, even as you're talking sort of the *art-scene* and what was *current* and what was *in* vogue, and then you did something for another reason — it was "in" — and I'm asking it I suppose for myself and because I see it in . . . I see it in all art: writing, film, across the century, and from the beginning of the century on, and there seems to be this tearing apart, I mean, and you spoke last night of antidote, which somehow is there too . . .

CONRAD: Yeah.

CHILD: And then coming towards sense again, and so somewhere — between David's question and this throwing out, I'm asking, what do you see?

CONRAD: I pick up on the fact that these two questions are equally vicious, you know? One . . . well, I mean, you know, I'm happy about . . . the thing about it is I think there's a lot of reason to feel very bad, you know? And one of the reasons to feel bad is on principles, which sounds more like this one, and one of the reasons to feel bad is because of just personal reasons which is more like the way I'm reading what you're asking, and I felt . . . I feel bad for both reasons, you know. But I thought a lot about what I was doing, actually. Well, I've always wondered why, I didn't even *want* to make film, you see, actually, to begin with, but sort of felt like I was lured into it, and then when I started teaching I wondered even more what I was doing. And because of the fact that teaching had to have some kind of, first of all you have to have some kind of structure to relate to, if you're involved in an academic situation. Like, *here* is an academic situation. There's something, you know, like that supports it, I mean, even if we all got together and said, "OK," you know, like "secretly, we're just going to drink beer." In any case, no matter what we decide we would have to have some kind of a context or an agreement, in a sense, you know, that there is something that this is about. And the problem with film or with art or these subjects is, who knows what that is? you know. Who knows what it's about? I felt that there was a *role* for me, and that it was a legitimate role, and that it was one that I should play, and this was, like, to *be* a responsible film artist, you know. And, so, how do I do this? Number one, I want to play this game right now. In the game, you see, the rules are this: If I give you ten million dollars, right? Then you have to get a hundred million people to come to that movie, right? If I give you one million dollars, OK then, we'll settle for ten million people to come to the movie right? If I give you a hundred thousand dollars, OK you'd better get a million people to come and watch the movie, you see? Otherwise, no more money, no more goodies — *plunk,* you see, in a sense. Now, I am a person who doesn't want to have any responsibility except perhaps to a group that's as small as *ten* people, you see? And in short I want to, first of all, start by being able to make a movie for one dollar, you see? . . . And, OK, that sounds like really kind of slack-jawed kind of political strategy, and in fact, you know, I don't claim to be a, like a committed radical in a sense of really maintaining a coherent strategy, you know. But all I can tell you is it was important to me to make them cheap, you know. I didn't have any *money*, you know! So, it *was* important. And I think that that's very relevant to film*making*, you know. Now, another thing that's relevant to filmmaking that was relevant to *me* about filmmaking was the fact that *it just galled me* to see people making films in the way that they were supposed to make films. Like, I don't care if it's students, or people making them for television, or whatever, like, who in other words, like, I mean, here's the instructions, you know, like, you want a film teacher to tell you how to make films, go to the store, buy something in a yellow box, right? Put it in a camera, right? And then you get to push the button, you know. After you push the button, carefully, you know, send the film away, you know. The lab will do the rest, you know. When it comes back you can cut it up, put it back together, but, you know, like, basically all the interesting steps are removed from your control, you know? Now, like, making the film is removed from your control. Processing the film is removed from your control, you know. Designing the instruments that deal with the film is removed from your control. All of these stages I envied, you know. Also, "you see" it's even worse than that because you know how pedantic most of these steps are, you know, and so, like, well . . . My idea was, frankly, to try to make a message that would not be for the masses but would be for people who were committed as I was, to filmmaking, and who don't need to see films that are beautiful, pretty, because I, I mean, it's hard to make a film that's not beautiful, you know. I mean, you just *try not to*, you know. But, to make a film about the process seemed to me to be very relevant, you know. I mean, those are excellent questions. I mean, I'm not trying to say I answered them at all. But these were alternative aspirations, that seemed to me to be pretty dignified, you know, at the time . . . Well, it's OK, I mean, you know, I enjoy beauty — it's alright. In fact, to tell you the truth, sometimes if you're really successful in getting away from beauty, it can get to you, you know. And I've made some films that were so *bad*, you know, that I was really pleased until I realized that I wasn't, you know; and that I'd really like to make them actually look a little better. And it seems as though everything fits together.

QUESTION: I liked how that worked, the way you did it. And by the end, I mean, I really liked that last one (*Pickled Wind*) with the color and every scratch seemed to have some kind of meaning. Almost like a Brakhage film, almost like mocking that kind of manipulation.

CONRAD: It's not mocking . . . It mocks it in a way that's intimate with the material, intimate with everything about it, with working it in every way. And, that kind of loving attention to the material — I mean it's, I mean, I'm using the word "love" in a way that I mean I think is a good idea, even though it sounds corny, I think he really loves film material, like *everything*, sprocket holes and the cement, and the little pictures and everything about it. And so it's, that's a preparation for being able to in a sense transfer that love over to a kind of image like this, even though without that kind of precedent it might seem like just "brrrrrrrrrrr," you know. But I can easily share that kind of feeling, that attentiveness, you know, like to all the little things that are going on . . . I think that the medium is maybe not such a great resource as I thought it once was. I mean, just seeing how film and video sort of melt together into the same problems, you know, it's really interesting. Like, I'm not saying that they're identical media, or that they have identical problems, but it's weird the way, if you make a film, or you make a videotape, it turns out that there are analogous difficulties in each medium. . . .

GUNVOR NELSON: Because it seems like exploring this, these melting qualities or whatever you can do with this (undecipherable word) immediately remind me of records, or whatever, other thing. But then it's like you're calling yourselves film-*makers*, so . . .

CONRAD: That's a problem, you know. That is something I don't really understand myself . . . Like, say in a standard environment where I'm not just talking to film people, then that really becomes a question, you know, like, "So, it's film, and so what?" you know, in a sense. Why isn't this just *anything*, you know? And whether it's that interesting as just anything, you know, or whether it's just a specialized application of a more general process, like Boil Your Telephone.

ROHIT: I was coming up with how you started going "anti-medium," "anti-image." OK, having denied that, now you seem to have been going full-circle, and again denying the anti-image, anti-medium, again, and again denying the anti-image and saying that you didn't really care for either. And I know you wanted to ask, "What was it that fascinated you?" but then again you turned around and just now said that you weren't fascinated with the thing. So I really don't know what to ask next.

CONRAD: "So this is a film, so what?" That's in a sense what it boils down to, and I think that's a very valuable kind of thing to discover. I mean, I don't mind if I sink under the weight of this particular problem. Because if I sink, you see, what I sink under is a problem which is basically this kind of question: it is saying, "How specialized is your critical environment?" In other words, it's like saying, "Do we treat everything by the same rules, or do we have different rules for some things and different rules for others?" . . . Well, OK. If I want to just fly, you know that would be something a little different in the sense that I think you're maybe alluding to. And I've been interested in that problem and tried to do that too. But not so much with these kind of words. And the thing that's interesting to me about trying this is, you see, that if there's a chance of getting another kind of flight to happen, something completely different from what you expect, that's fantastic to me, you see, I mean, in other words, like, well, . . . My experience tended to be that the ability to *get there* was an internal ability, that depends on the person who is doing it, and not so much on the climate in which they are receiving material. I mean, *you* do it, and art isn't gonna necessarily do it for you, you know . . . Jeez, I mean, I don't know what I'm saying now, but, I mean, we have to start with a cultural context, you know. And if we don't have one then I can't even say another word.

Henry Hills

CHILD LABOR

Presumption? (re: A.T. on M.S./october, or Ezra Pound on Olga Rudge), so . . . BECAUSE a certain film was omitted from a certain show, BECAUSE those included had shown in EM's lst yr. for a little or no $, a grant since received, since spent; BECAUSE said show has received a certain notice: BECAUSE a new figure has since appeared. "Humanity under monasticism" ???

Abigail Child seems to be attempting things which no other artist of our generation on the west coast has chosen to direct serious attention towards, that is exploring the relations of language and film, of language and movement, of movement and movies. (Joel Singer, in his collaborations with James Broughton, combines poetry and film, but this segment of Singer's work is an extension/continuation of Broughton's previous achievements; Child's current films are silent).

Here: attempt to see a unity in a diverse output. Here: she comes mumbling muttering singing screaming ("a kind of purely vocal improvisation which sounds at first like jazz scatting used to translate contemporary philosophy" and goes on to mention David Antin, Baikida E. J. Carroll and Julius Hemphill, John Cage at Black Mountain College — Ron Silliman, "Art With No Name," *State of the Arts*, Nov. 77, v. I. #10) variations on:

diablo diabolic diabolique abolish abandon

a ban don bo lish lique di a
a ban bo lique a di a bolish
ban a don bo lish a di
ban a don bo lish di a
don a ban bo bo a
ban a don di a di a
ban a don di a di   a
ban a ban lish bo di
        da

("a song in Base 5"), down the street muttering mumbling singing SCREAM-
ING ("Come on, Abby."/"You fucker, you anti-life fucker!"). So reading is held —
last July, Terminal Concepts, S.F. — there, the standard yawning audience, there
some Mutants, and there is A. Child, swinging from a rope spouting questions as
tape recorders (bird songs one and her voice #2) accompany at either end of the
room. QUESTIONS. I go home and write.

"the birds that came with the loft she sublet and had to feed & water 4 genera-
tions removed (with added reality each layer) on the discount cassette to the west, to
the east the mass, herself once removed, the East Bay Terminal, Porter Springs,
India, south = 'pate' roast beef, Clos des Perrieres BEAUNE, a bath,,, north a blank
wall, prior the 19th century, an English accent . . . and the Center, the still point,
hanging: with unchanging expression the mass (an occasional glint or chuckle) . . .
herself as 'the propellor'; the bay, the Pacific, the map spinning on the axis like a
clock. The physical presence (not now, a little while ago) not an assault, duration,
mechanical with breaks of passion, system of repetition? your eyes darting around
like a single-frame movie. The secondary text = a chronological selection of veils
veiled by the primary questioning (system?), the sufficiently subjective secondary
subjected to ritual. The collective longing of the solitary. A gift of sweat. The hug-
ging after. The map. Where I am now (point A to point B — cyclical vs. progressive,
wave/particle, body/mind): the greatest hits of the last few notebooks, revised — spinning (while A to B), our generation moving toward reconciliation. The spinning primary, tho, & A to B in the gaps. But so it is! Never lacking in confidence, not as confident as could be. A self-portrait in glimpses." — July 24th, 77

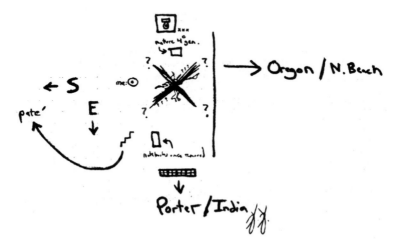

Then again in February 78 at Grand Piano Haight St, the programmer obviously expecting oddity double-billing her with a poet who read his work in sign language — her text on music paper music stand she brings the formerly veiled formerly secondary to fore — the notebook sentences: a classical poetry reading and what emerges verges on a novel. Tearing apart/coming towards sense again.

Child began her film   career making documentaries, what everyone calls documentaries: *The Game*, street gangs on NBC, PBS. ETC. AFI grant: attempts what everyone calls a narrative, *tar gArden*. Ends in terror & disgust. Never distributes. Two years wandering, filming & canning (accompaniment to her endless notebooks), contact improv., studies in physics, tearing apart. Tearing apart, then coming towards sense again: *Some Exterior Presence*, the first step, calling something finished. *S.E.P.*, what the soundman said, does with film what the Diablo poem does to language, hence it is the easiest to write about (see New Films, also Dackman review *Cinemanews* #77–5). Then a month of silence at Floras Creek, Oregon and the discovery of THE SUN. The opening shot straight shot more magical than most magical Pat O'Neill matte magic. Silence. No electricity. Ends as Beaulieu battery runs down. Then back again to the canned past, finishing, Finishing. *Daylight Test Section*, Confucius Tower, N.Y. In this fragment some of the most ENERGIZED montage to hit yr. eyeballs yet. Then back to San Francisco, a years view from Shooting Star Studio of the changing skyline in all its absurdity, *Pacific Far East Line*. Forthcoming *Ornamentals* (title from Blake, also seed catalogues), the details details of mundane life that give constant pleasure, Ed Dorn's delight in "the apparencies". All to be viewed over and over and over and

Trying to find the connections. Making the connections. Staring reality in the face. First tearing apart words, then building up sentences. First chopping, flipping, reprinting backwards, forwards, upside-down, then . . . always a return to the body. The body. I'm always surprised at her size. So large a grasp, a grasping. Our generation moving towards reconciliation. . . . if movies can save the world. save the world. The power of the imagination. Look at the skyline and you see how debased our imagination has become. Beauty is not enough, Tony Conrad says, meaning a superficial loveliness. There is another more enduring, born from intellectual honesty. This is transformative beauty. Laodicians gag at its ugliness. Such is the work of Abigail Child. Beauty is so difficult, Beardsley tell Yeats. So very difficult.

Commodore Sloat
LETTER, FEBRUARY 18, 1978

Dear Canyon Cinema:

The wave of the future is Here! Independent Cinema as showbiz! With Peter Feinstein as the Colonel Tom Parker and Hollis Frampton as Elvis, coming right at ya. The talking head act is about to hit the big time. Gives me the chills just thinking about all those Big Bucks waiting to be raked in. Imagine . . . you, are There. Just made the long drive to Vegas and goddamn if it doesn't say in letters six feet high Live! Mr. Excitement! (As shown on the Ed Sullivan Show but only from the waist up) Hollis! Guest slots on the Donnie and Marie Show. /Jus cuz P.F. (the Colonel) saw which way the wind was blowing first doesn't mean there isn't room for everyone. The world is *starved* for celebs: TV game shows, variety shows with "special guests," county fairs, and (a real gold mine) the Midwestern Dinner Theatre circuit./ High caliber celebs like Stan Brakhage, Mike Snow could (and probably ARE) get 50% off the TOP. (OK, figure 500 seats at 10 bucks a shot. That's 2500 to start. Add a percentage from liquor sales, two shows a night and you're grossing 10–15 grand for a lousy weekend.) And for the folks, that's Top Entertainment Value: artful fun, or funfull art — better than Sammy D. Jr. The co-op (since it can't get non profit anyway) could do a snappy William Morris number, and take a healthy percentage off the top for its pains. What does it take? Well, you artists out there have to admit to yourselves that the art hustle is, after all, just another hustle. Audience like to see a live body tap dancing up there on the stage. So, send me your films on metal reels *with the ends taped* (shows you're a real class act if it comes in a new Goldberg fiber case) plus an 8 X 10 glossy photo, plus name, address, phone number and bio information. I'll see what I can do. By the way, be sure to catch the Gregory Markopoulos Easter Special with special guest stars Sammy Davis Jr., Paul Lynde, Ruth Buzzi, and special special guests Johnny Cash and June Carter, extra specially nice guest Bob Hope, and extra added attraction Bruce Jenner.

Yours,

Bruce Conner

LETTER, SEPTEMBER 22, 1968

[Editor's note: This letter originally appeared in the Cinemanews *in 1968 (68.8) and seems to have been reprinted because of its relevance to the new focus on experimental writing.]*

September 22, 1968

(Please Prent)

Dear . . . .Cinema News:

Yuk rak tlitchleflu im ti plic. Yourgk t ut er thiyslet e
zyygre. Mougg ygg eggyug ousgug. Yummin yummin yummin
yummin yummin yummin yummin yummin yummin.
Exbliz: mummbhie 1/2 * kruhuhuhuhuhuhuh.
Merrifliger uppleligher nonmonplisser poppojitser.
yi yi yi yi yi yi yi yi yi yi yi yi yiyi ayesblunk.
Oh.
Robert J., Elbert S., Mary Y., Suesan M., Robert B.
    Y   LS   xX   . l p..

(aO) k 498 lwus

( ) o   o o vx"

((

).(
         "

Sincerely yours,

The Incredible Bruce Conner

MABUHAY
Gardens
443 Broadway San Francisco
956-3315

—

FROM *CINEMA NEWS*, 78.3/4

Henry Hills
ROBERT NELSON INTERVIEW

NELSON: OK, Miles, you gotta stay out.

MILES: Is that your tape recorder?

NELSON: Yeah, I'm gonna lock the door here.

HILLS: So, I was just thinking, I've always thought of you as, like, a California film-maker, I mean like you were born here, uh, almost more representative of my idea of a California filmmaker than anyone else around I can think of. I was wondering about your plan to change your base of operations entirely [Nelson had taken a job at the University of Wisconsin at Milwaukee], and, well, it seems like that will nec-essarily affect your filmmaking and I was wondering about how you saw what you're getting ready to be doing?

NELSON: The only plan that I have is to edit part three of SUITE CALIFORNIA, back in Wisconsin. Those are the only filmmaking plans that I've got besides taking that new job. I think it would be interesting to work on the editing of the piece on California there after doing the first two parts here.

HILLS: You're basically going just because it's a job, right?

NELSON: Yeah, I'm going because of the job. Right.

HILLS: You feel like it's a big change?

NELSON: Yeah, it's a big change, it came at a time when I was ready to experiment, look for something new, or to look outside and make that kind of leap, it just came right at that moment. I've spent some time out of California but I was still born and raised here, spent most of my life here and I'm looking forward to not working in my own home town.

HILLS: My impression is that there was kind of a film scene out here at one point, and you were very centrally involved, and then people kind of filtered off, and started getting into things more by themselves instead of as a "scene" and a lot of people quit making films. Then I found out that you were getting ready to come up with a new film and you were back in San Francisco, I thought you'd been in Mendocino and northern California somewhere, and other people are being seen around again, like Bruce Conner has been an obvious presence the last year or so . . . It seems a move like this is definitely a move toward self sufficiency in your work. I've noticed in early films, that is in the catalogue, there's almost always someone listed that you made them with, and then in this last one, you've gone off and made it by yourself. The move is choosing to continue that kind of work.

NELSON: By myself?

HILLS: Yeah . . . I mean maybe, I don't know.

NELSON: I don't look at it that way particularly. I just look at it as a move. I don't know what opportunities will come up, but I imagine getting into something back there and using that difference. Somebody was telling me the other day that Milwaukee was Gothic compared to out here, and that might be an interesting ground for something different to emerge.

HILLS: When I first got interested in film I had the illusion that there was this big film scene, and as I got more involved it looked very different from my imaginations of the scene before. The other day, you said something about the whole damn thing is absurd . . . the whole film movement . . .

NELSON: I don't know what context that was in . . . but go ahead.

HILLS: . . . then I started thinking of it as really absurd, and what in the world are people making films for.

NELSON: Yeah, well maybe it should be questioned every once in awhile, I don't know.

HILLS: Do you keep in contact with other filmmakers and see what they're doing?

NELSON: I keep in contact with friends, and some of them are filmmakers, most of them are doing something else besides and maybe they're not primarily filmmakers. I go to the Canyon shows once in awhile, I go to the meetings, the same thing you're in, the fake organization — that's all keeping in touch. Yeah, I don't know how else, just by those things. At one time it was all very small and it was like ten people could get together in San Francisco and they represented just about everybody that was making independent films in the whole town. And there also was a moment, in the 60s, when the public spotlight looked at independent films; there were articles in *Playboy* and *Time Magazine* and that generated a lot of excitement and enthusiasm. All the worms squirmed under that spotlight. There was some recognition, and that suggested that there *were* possibilities, other possibilities. There were a few people around that happened to be working in films at that time, and I had just gotten into it, and so it seemed natural to get together with those few others around who were making films. Bruce Baillie had the yearly Canyon Festival — I forget what he called it — it was literally in Canyon, California, behind Berkeley Hills, so everybody that was around in the Bay Area at that time, if they had a film they put it in that festival, which was one of the few places out here that you could even show those films. It was a tiny group of people. So they got together to try and form the co-op at one point, because all of a sudden they didn't want to be renting their own films out for instance, it was a small, politically it wasn't like trying to communicate with several hundred people, or thousands, or whatever. There was no place you could even study filmmaking at that point, except UCLA, but I understood that that had a Hollywood bias that was very formidable and unless that's what you wanted to do, which *was* what most people did want to do, but if you didn't there was no other place around to study filmmaking or to approach it as a personal kind of thing, or to study nonconventional filmmaking — there was no place to do it. I don't know if that was good or bad, but now there are a lot of places to do it and there are thousands of people around.

HILLS: You weren't interested in getting into Hollywood?

NELSON: I wasn't interested only because in my mind and in my situation anyway, that was never a possibility to tempt me. I got into films without ever having studied film, and strictly making homemade movies, and I could see very quickly, after the first couple of attempts, that the production value or veneer was a long way from any kind of "marketable product." So I never had any illusions about it. But I suppose before I ever made a film, when I used to dream of filmmaking, the only filmmaking I knew of to dream of was something like films I had seen. So when I was a young person, I didn't really think I could be a filmmaker — no — I did, because long before I made a film I dreamed up some money schemes to make a film, that was going to be some kind of theatrical piece. I wanted to make a theatrical piece. That's what I imagined filmmaking to be and what I would have liked to be doing. That was before I got into it. I still like to do theatrical pieces and there's some of that in the new film I made, SUITE CALIFORNIA, there's a ten-minute piece that's all done with actors, and then with Bill Allan a few years ago, I made WAR IS HELL, and that's all acted and directed, so I like that, I'm interested in that format, that way of generating images. I'm not terribly interested in conventional story development, but I'm interested in generating images with actors, I like that. So I might do some more of that sometime.

HILLS: Your new movie is only partially that.

NELSON: Just a little bit of that, right, ten minutes, the rest is just total indulgence. (Sound of liquid being poured in the background)

HILLS: Do you shoot a lot?

NELSON: Not lately, I haven't because I've been working for a couple years on editing, and I had so much footage that I had shot over the last eight or ten years, most of it in the last five years, I had a huge amount of film and I shot a lot of that when

I was teaching at Cal Arts because I had access to equipment there, and they had a system in which teachers could charge film, and they'd take it out of your check; so I shot a lot of film. As a matter of fact, the last year that I worked there I only got $65 a month because the rest was all taken out to pay off the film. I had to fly all the way down there for that once a week to pay off my film debt.

HILLS: So you knew Pat O'Neill real well.

NELSON: I knew him before, but I got to know him a lot better, because he was working there at the same time.

HILLS: What is your relation to Michael Snow's work? I know you were real sympathetic to Brakhage in the Brakhage/Grice debates ["Stan Brakhage and Malcolm LeGrice Debate," originally published in *Criss-Cross Art Communications*, was reprinted in this issue of the *Cinemanews*; the debate was held in Boulder, Colorado, in December 1977]; you know, but also it's like he's saying one thing and being interested in these other filmmakers is a whole different thing, I think. And in one of the Michael Snow write-ups somewhere, I saw you wrote something about WAVELENGTH . . .

NELSON: In the catalogue maybe . . . it was a long time ago . . .

HILLS: Yeah, in the catalogue.

NELSON: Well, I like Michael Snow's work very much and, you're asking what relationship . . . ?

HILLS: I was wondering if you saw his work and it really changed your work or if you thought you were working along the same kind of lines. As far as he deals with time, and you have the movie with the fishing rod, in almost all your movies you have these long, these unexpectedly long pieces of film.

NELSON: I see a similarity of pursuit, or correspondence of ideas and I am sympathetic to everything that he's done, all the movies that I've seen of his. Sympathetic to the impulse to do it. And I think that . . . I'm very glad that his movies are there. I think if they weren't there, it would be like a hole in the scene. I completely respect what he's doing, I think it's a lot different than me in that he is more formalistic and more focused on a particular direction than I am — my stuff is alot hairier, but with some occasional correspondence, I think, to what he's doing. I mean, I'm sympathetic to it and see what I think of as a similar kind of interest often emerge in me at some place or other in some film, but it's like I dabble with it and he is formalistically structuring a whole body of works around these principles that make a beautiful clean expression. I really like his stuff. I like LA REGION CENTRALE very much, especially lately. I'm a little tired of WAVELENGTH myself at this point, maybe, maybe not, but that too, even though it was obvious at the moment it was done, it seemed to me that still no one had done it. And to live through that experience, was . . . you know . . . all that time that's in that shot and really experience it as a film was a pretty exciting experience, I mean really.

HILLS: Did you see RAMEAU'S NEPHEW?

NELSON: No, I haven't seen it yet.

HILLS: Oh, you'll like it. You were saying yours were a little hairier, and it's pretty hairy too, ha, ha.

NELSON: But I don't think Michael Snow has been a particular influence on me, where I have felt that sensibility that's come from someone else, being something to really deal with in my own mind. The only person's works that I have felt that about were Bruce Conner's films. He was the only one that created a struggle within me to try and separate the enormous impression it made on me from my own things.

HILLS: When did you see his films?

NELSON: Those were the first ones that I saw that turned me on to independent filmmaking.

HILLS: Before you started making them?

NELSON: Yeah, before I started making them. I was interested in independent films, or whatever they were called, "underground" — they weren't even called — yeah — they were called underground then, I guess. Jonas Mekas was writing about them in *Village Voice*, this was about '63 and '64, and uh, I had been struggling with being a painter before that. In other words, I was into art and that's what I was trying to do. I was always interested in films and I started to hear about some, what were they called . . . not experimental, anyway, I guess they were underground at that point . . . I started hearing about some of the films and I can remember a couple of columns that Mekas wrote in the *Village Voice*, that talked about films that very likely one would never be able to see; you know, they were shown once in a loft somewhere, Harry Smith's films and stuff, and my interest to see them was enormous at that point. So whenever I heard about films being shown I made the effort and went, but there were none that I responded to. None of them tapped me. I didn't like the crude home-made-image look and I was, uh, there was nothing there at that point that made me want to surrender my critic as I sat looking at them, I just stayed in a negative judgement of just about everything I'd seen. I wanted to be won over if there was anything there, but I didn't see anything. Until I ran into COSMIC RAY. And that was the first one, that did it, and that was what really made me realize that somehow it was possible. Obviously it didn't cost any money, relatively speaking, compared to what movies are supposed to cost and it was the first one that really made me realize that some amazing power could generate from images that you put together at home.

HILLS: Well, you were both working in San Francisco at the same time later on, or was he still making films then?

NELSON: Well he was making films before me.

HILLS: Yeah, but he quit then . . .

NELSON: Well I never thought of him as quitting, maybe he might say something different about it, I don't know. He's an artist who works in a lot of media, he's got a good reputation as a painter and sculptor, I'm sure you know that. I think he just continues to make films. Maybe he quit for awhile, I don't know, or maybe he was just in-between films. But, incidentally, I just wanted to say, about COSMIC RAY CHARLES that of all the independent films since, I can't think of one, besides Bruce Conner's, where they have used some commercial music, and where it didn't look awful to me, because they've used it as a crutch. To me the brilliance of Conner's work was that it truly celebrated Ray Charles' piece, *What I Say*, and it was like the guy with the saxophone who walks out on stage from the audience before the guards can get him, walks up to the microphone and plays with, you know, with whoever, Dizzy Gillespie or somebody, it's the guy who walks out of the crowd and *does* it. Bruce Conner jumps up and plays with Ray Charles, and not only does he play with Ray Charles, but he brings the house down, he does it. He made pictures that looked as good, that worked with that music and was an illustration of that music that was as exciting as the music in its own way, and so it was a beautiful marriage of those two things. And I thought that was just . . . to come out and turn that trick I just think is beautiful. It just really blew me away and made me want to make movies immediately. Well, the two that do it for me still are A MOVIE and COSMIC RAY, number one. A MOVIE also number one. They're like a pair to me . . . I like all his movies actually, but those two . . . are really best. I think the new one is number one too — CROSSROADS. You see it?

HILLS: Yes. Did you see MONGOLOID?

NELSON: MONGOLOID? No, I didn't, is that a new one? Oh, no I haven't seen it.

HILLS: Yeah, it's got, uh, Devo on the soundtrack.

NELSON: A devo?? What's that?

HILLS: It's a punk rock band. I guess he's real heavily involved in punk rock, you know, and a really big fan, you know, and Devo, I guess, is what he thinks is the really "hot shit" one.

NELSON: Well, he's got really good taste in music for sure. I'll just about go for Devo, sound unseen. Have you heard that group? Are they any good?

HILLS: I never heard them.

NELSON: Anyway, he's the one that turned me on to filmmaking on the basement level. I mean, homegrown filmmaking.

HILLS: Did you get to know him?

NELSON: Well, I got to know him afterwards, yeah, I made a whole bunch of films first. I got interested in some other things besides, at that point, I started looking around, and I mean, once I got into it, as soon as I got making films, my sensibilities deepened, or broadened, or my appreciation broadened and I did surrender some of that critic. A lot of it wasn't necessary for one thing, and I was able to get a lot from a lot of other people besides Conner. I mean as far as feeling an exalted experience from the effort. But, like I said before, that was the only one that impressed me that much stylistically.

HILLS: What about all the films you worked on with collaborators? How was that? I mean, these were just friends and you decided to get together and make a film?

NELSON: Well, the collaborator I worked with mostly was Bill Wiley, I made a bunch of films with him. Mike Henderson; I made three or four with him. Steve Reich: I worked with on a film one time, and he did the soundtrack for OH DEM WATERMELONS. Bill Allan; I made AWFUL BACKLASH and WAR IS HELL with him. Those are the collaborators for the most part. It's possible that I'm leaving someone out, but I don't think so, I think that's it. There was a collaboration with Ron Davis of The Mime Troupe on OH DEM WATERMELONS, and PLASTIC HAIR CUT and okay, there was a bunch of collaborators. I also, during that time, I also made some films without collaborators.

HILLS: Well, Steve Reich has gotten pretty famous in the last couple of years, he's got records on Deutsche Grammophon.

NELSON: The first tape piece that he ever made is on PLASTIC HAIRCUT, which was the first movie . . . actually the first two movies I ever made, I made with Gunvor . . .

HILLS: Oh, she was making films before you were?

NELSON: No, we made those two. They were the very first two and we made them together. Made one called LAST WEEK AT OONA'S BATH and the other one was just a movie of us building a house near a beach. But the first film that I ever sent out in the mail to be shown somewhere was PLASTIC HAIRCUT. And that film, I made with Wiley and Ron Davis and Steve Reich and Bob Hudson, I ran the camera because I knew how to run the camera, not very well, but better than anyone else, and I did the editing because I ran the camera. I was the one who handled all that messy film and so if there was anything to be done with it I was the one to do it, so I did the editing. Ron Davis did the acting, Hudson and Wiley did the sets. We generally shared ideas on what to set up and stuff. 1965. Gunvor, shortly after, made a film with Dorothy Wiley called SCHMEERGUNTZ so we definitely started film-making at exactly the same time, since those first two films made together were the first films ever that either of us had made. And after that, we both went on making films, neither one of us has stopped yet.

HILLS: Well, like, OH DEM WATERMELONS was the first one that I ever saw of yours. When I first saw independent films, I saw a program with COSMIC RAY and OH DEM WATERMELONS and HOLD ME WHILE I'M NAKED, and — what else — Oh, Landow's film with the scratches and dirt particles, and you know, so like, like that film must have been very widely seen.

NELSON: It was and still is, as a matter of fact. Amazingly, it still gets a lot of rentals.

HILLS: So, it gets through to a lot of people?

NELSON: It gets through to what seems to me a great number of people. But it just depends on what market you're talking about. In terms of the number of people that see television shows, all the people that have ever seen OH DEM WATERMEL-ONS is very small. All of this is very tiny audiences everywhere.

HILLS: How do you feel about that?

NELSON: About the tininess of the audience? I think it's tiny only in relation to a huge one. It's huge in relation to, uh, you know, what I was ever used to. Well, I don't rail against that fact that there isn't greater acceptance of nonconventional films, I sort of accept where it's at. I don't know what to say about it.

HILLS: Then, you, um, I mean, the fact that your audience is a certain number of people, that's just who your audience . . .

NELSON: Well, I mean when I first made films, I was astounded by the fact that I could get them shown, that's a surprise from the beginning. After we did PLASTIC HAIRCUT we sent it back East to Filmmakers' Co-op and the Cinematheque, and there was a write-up about it in the *Village Voice*. That we could send it out through the mails and get it shown and get something done about it in the press, that was astounding to us. So, from the beginning I entered in without a lot of expectations about it. And so, from that point of view it always seemed plentiful and bountiful in a sense.

HILLS: Well, what you're working on — like SUITE CALIFORNIA, for instance, you must, I mean, well, I don't know, you must have some idea of what the audience of that film will be.

NELSON: I don't think that I do. At least not that I can name. Ummmm . . . the . . . uh . . . the thing about making the film is . . . oh . . . I don't know. I was going to say something about when you're working on it and you have the feeling that it's going well, or can sense some dimension forming in the material as you're working on it, and there's that great fulfillment or excitement about it — when that's happening — there's an urge to share that with somebody, so that you can get verification off another person, you can both share in that depth, or that space that seems to be created in there, of meaning or suggestiveness or whatever it is that reverberates and seems profound and stirring at that point and what is exciting about it. That happens, then that's hypothesizing, or wishing for an audience, it may even be a specific person. But I think that when you slip out of the focus of the practice of it and you start fantasizing about an audience it's a disconnectedness. When you're really connected with the work you don't need to do that. There's another ground that doesn't preclude audience, but it doesn't look at them either. After you've finished the film, then there's the co-ops and a few places that will rent these films, there is an audience and that's a whole other business, after you've finished working on it. For me it's sort of a scary situation because you're vulnerable suddenly and you realize it, to the same kind of resistance that you yourself can bring to things; and you're vulnerable to that from others who you want to surrender to the experience. And so, there's a certain amount of anxiety, that I feel, about presenting it to an audience. Although, I also get a lot of gratification, especially if anybody really seems to connect with it. "Audience" is like another step and it's related to all the rest of it but quite separate, and it's not one I devalue in any way. It's a whole other intense aspect of it.

HILLS: It seems like you've been reticent about showing it up to now, I mean, you showed *Part I* [of *Suite California*] at Canyon in a big weekend kind of group show, and you just showed it recently at the Whitney, and you're just showing it now here, at PFA, in kind of the middle of summer . . .

NELSON: I was working on *Part II* and I wanted to have a longer piece; I wanted to finish it. I showed it at the Whitney first because I had that opportunity. I think that the Whitney is a very nice museum and it's an honor to have a film there and all that, and after seeing *Part I* here in California, I was very anxious to see that with an audience that wasn't Californian, because I wondered . . . there was a . . . well there's a certain kind of nihilism, or negativity in *Part I*, about California, I don't know if it's about California, it's about Hollywood. I don't even know if that's true, it has that appearance, anyway. And some people reacted to that. Some people reacted to that as though that were the fact. Whether that's really true or not, those words are pretty loaded and I don't know if I'd really use them to describe that or not. I just wondered if some reaction to the film that some people seem to express to me, that didn't like it, if some of that was defensiveness about California. But I don't think it was, now that I showed it in New York.

HILLS: Do you have any particular reactions to showing it in New York?

NELSON: Well, I said earlier about films looking hairy, uh, I think New York, it reminded me of what I imagined Egypt to be like at the height of some majestic dynasty. Because, the artistic formalism, the formalism everywhere, in every expression, even on TV, was very exciting. And to come with a film . . . once I got there, the film looked to me in the context of that formalism in New York, it looked to me like something a gypsy brought in a blanket and rolled out on the sand, like a bunch of hairy handmade objects that were all sort of laying there. That was the reaction I had to the film, in New York. That it looked very hairy.

HILLS: Abby was just remarking that you seemed to really associate with real strong women in your life. And your wife now, Diane, is a psychotherapist, and Gunvor is a real active woman, independent, self-assertive type woman . . .

NELSON: My first wife . . . she was a strong one too.

HILLS: So you got one kid with each wife?

NELSON: Yeah, right. Yeah.

HILLS: I don't know how you can comment on something like that.

NELSON: I don't either.

George Landow at the Cinematheque, May 18, 1978

(fragments retrieved from a poorly miked tape, cinematheque, s.f., 5/18/78)

. . . things that I'm interested in at different times, so you sit through the whole program and you get a pretty good idea of a long development. I started making films really around 1961 and at the same time I was a painter and a sculptor . . . I went back & forth. I wasn't constantly making film all that time. So there are periods where I stopped for a while and then other things happened and then . . . so that probably accounts for the jumps stylistically & even perhaps in terms of subject matter, although I *think* they're all *about* the same kind of thing, even my very early films . . . I'm much more interested in talking about subject matter than formal concerns which I find not all that great to talk about. The first film you're going to see (1965) I made when I was studying painting and wanted to investigate the nature of the moving picture image as a flat rectangular thing and at the time it was very difficult to get that across, I mean people didn't respond too well, they really didn't want to sit there and look at a flat rectangular object, they wanted a movie image, there was drama or something like that, so my earliest work has a lot in common with dada or neo-dada work in that it's intentionally provocative. A lot of stuff I did involved performance where I would do things like attacking the film in the projector and destroying it so that the physical act of showing the film became highly problematic and created a certain type of dynamic which doesn't usually occur in normal film, but after a period of that kind of investigation I decided to package all that and do something that could be easily sent around cause I didn't want to have to *be* there all the time and depend on whether the film was going to burn in the right place or something like that, so I made this film which is called *Film in Which There Occur Edge-Lettering, Dirt Particles, Sprocket Holes, Etc.* and it kind of mocks the idea that we're sitting here watching it because it goes on but it doesn't change. There are slight variations but there's no development in the dramatic or musical sense. To me when I watch the film I feel very silly about sitting in the seat in a dark room staring at the wall and in fact when *I* watch the film I usually get up. Sometimes when I show the film I get up and I point to things on the screen just to get people's attention to them, in fact that's probably the best way to show this. It's really kind of an educational film when it comes right down to it. I usually show it first when I show other films because it focuses attention on certain areas, those little flecks and things that appear before your eyes, dirt and scratches which are usually neglected or more than just neglected, they're prejudiced against, I mean they're really, we try to pretend that they don't exist and almost everything in this film are things that *occur* in a normal commercial film that you never see, you're not supposed to see. That is, the main image itself which is a test, a color test image which usually occurs just one frame at the beginning of a film so unless your perceptions have been conditioned by watching a lot of single-frames you won't be able to see that and sprocket holes are something that you're not supposed to see, it's supposed to be out of the field of vision and scratches are something that aren't supposed to be there if the print's in good condition, dirt particles are supposed to be cleaned off, edge-lettering is supposed to be outside of the field of vision. So these are all things that you're not *supposed* to see being made the subject matter of the film. It seems like a perfectly logical idea, in fact you could cut the gate of this projector, any projector, and you could expose a lot more than what you normally get to see . . . which are probably more interesting visually than the part that you normally get to see, but then I'm interested in . . .

(No Sir, Orison): I wanted to have a person in an environment that was to me a symbol of oppression and have them do something to react to the oppression that was not the obvious thing that you would expect . . . Supermarkets as a symbol of manipulation: if someone can control what you EAT, they have a lot of power over you, if they can control what you BUY to eat even more so and on and on, if they can control how it looks when it's on the shelf, that's even better, if they can control how you think about it before you're even in the store — you *want* that product, even though it's not only maybe not good for you but even destructive. So somewhere behind this film is this vast power-structure which is causing people to do things that they don't really want to do, but they have no choice anymore . . .

I consider myself an *experimental filmmaker,* the term doesn't bother me as it does some people and a lot of these things are experiments for me, that is to see what the medium can do, how much it can carry with a kind of minimum of means, or what will happen if certain things that are ambiguous or contradictory are put together in a way that is not harmonious, say. I have, all my films have a tremendous amount of contradiction in images and sound which play against each other intentionally, so I try to set up a tension within the work that is ultimately destructive against itself. Now, I can't totally answer why I do that, I can talk about it a little bit. I read something by Jorge Luis Borges (preface, *A Universal History of Infamy*) who talked about his idea of the baroque in art and he said that the baroque work is one that tends towards self-ridicule and self-contradiction and self-destruction . . . and another thing which he talked about, in another one of his stories ("The Garden of Forking Paths," *Labyrinths*) he talked about a novel written by a Chinaman that no one could understand because the subject had been left out . . . and at the end of the story Borges concludes that the best way to really deal with anything is to not mention it . . .

My concerns were more visual in the beginning and then more elements of literature were added which makes it much more complicated to deal with because I always have to make a choice how literary the idea is and how visual the idea is and ideally they both should be fully operative, form and content, inseparable, but I don't think that happens, that's why my films seem unsatisfactory to me most of the time. It's a kind of synthesis that I have as an ideal and I've hardly ever seen it either in my films or in anybody else's and I think it has a lot to do with the nature of cinema as a medium being so dependent on photography and photography being such a literal recording device and my interest now dealing with the unconscious and making images that one could never see in the world, could only see in the imagination, in the mind, if "see" is the right word, that could only *exist* as mental images, imaginary, and up against photography you have a problem, photography makes recordings of light bounding off real objects.

Anyone who makes films is involved with repetition even if there's no obvious repetition in their films, because of the very nature of the medium, I mean, if nothing else the fact that you're going to have to repeat the same film over and over again and see it yourself many times so you start to . . . I think all filmmakers have a built-up kind of relationship with repetition, and musicians too, anyone who is involved in recording some kind of time-art and then having to play it back and then change it, so you start listening to or looking at the same thing again and again many many times and I think when you do that certain things happen, you experience totally new awarenesses that you might not have had by just the first experience, so . . . this can become a trap, I suppose, but repetition is a sort of technique that someone can use in their life, I mean I'm not talking about films now, to create a certain kind of awareness about reality, say a perceptual tune-up, that's pretty obvious, so a film might force an audience member to experience that with the idea that maybe he will learn something about what he is seeing by that constant repetition, but I don't really like that technique that much anymore because it seems, I suppose, too obviously manipulative, but I think my films should be seen many times by people who are interested in seeing them, so, the result is about the same . . . 20 times or something.

My awareness of what I'm doing is always something that's very subordinated to the making itself . . . Any viewer who has seen the films a lot says things that are just as valid as anything I say about it . . . Ideally one could make a work of art in a trance state or in sleep.

If this life is not everything, if there's something that precedes and that follows it and there are other forms that we take, it seems like that would be such an important fact that we'd have to deal with that every moment of our life . . . It seems to me it has to be always the subject of a work of art or at least it has to inform the work in some way, but that's so obvious, it's always there somehow. But then there are degrees of consciousness. No, it's not always there, it's not always . . . I don't see my work as an artist as having anything to do with philosophy or explaining anything or giving specific information about reality, because that's not my function, so again you see that's the same issue of the relation between form and subject-matter. The subject-matter is sort of bobbing its head up and the form is the making, the object, the work, and all I can say is I'm really not satisfied with the way that I've done it. I'm still not finished with somehow trying to do it again, deal with it. One problem is that it's not like say the Middle Ages where people had this world view that it is always officially agreed on so that they could make religious works of art and there's really no question (tape interruption). Now, since most people do not really recognize metaphysical realities, not in the same way, the work of art that deals with that is either seen as ironic, not seriously really saying that or else if it is that it's maybe viewed as naive art or somehow the artist is completely flipped out.

Most filmmakers answer these questions by saying it's none of your business. I can talk about it because I've seen the films a lot. But, you know, I don't know, I don't know all the answers. Well, I really know, but it's such a *drag* to get out and admit to yourself that you're not perfect . . . I think it's important to be able to function to not really know why you're doing it but just to know that it's *right* and just go ahead and do it. If you think about it too much you might very well decide not to do it. I probably, if I really thought about all of these films now I probably wouldn't make any of them.

((George Landow is currently working on a screen version of Sigmund Freud's *Wit and Its Relation to the Unconscious* with Morgan Fisher and an all oriental cast))

Hollis Frampton in San Francisco, part 2
[ST. HOLLIS]

[Editor's note: "Part 1" was "Hollis Frampton in San Francisco," in 7.7.6.]

FRAMPTON: I don't think I've made the heavily entropic parts of this film (MAG-ELLAN) yet. Unless it completely collapses. I don't know how to do that . . . This is one of the most difficult problems, formal problems, that I see on the horizon, as it were, I do not know how to make the parts of it yet that must be *truly* chaotic. You see? I remember a year and a half ago, having a conversation with Mike Snow who for the past two or three years has mostly been playing music with the people in Toronto. And I asked him, I mean, I had heard him a couple times and I thought it was quite interesting, but it's essentially, it's an extreme development of third stream jazz properly and so it's certainly not something that has a large audience at this time. But I am certainly part of its audience, and I asked him, kind of fidgety, about how was it going, and he said, "Oh, it's going very well," he said, "at least half a dozen times for a second or two, we have achieved real chaos." Which a few years ago, for instance, a few years before that, was something, say that Milford Graves could not claim, although he cut it real close a few times. Where has this wave asserted itself? You see, one of the easiest ways to appear orderly is to use a relatively small set of chance operations. That produces immediately extreme tidiness. One of the tidiest works in music I know, for instance, is Cage's *Music of Changes*. His immediate experience after the first time it was played, he and Tudor walked outside the theater and someone was whistling it. It actually horrified Cage. "What did I go do all this work for, I get a happy tune." And he told Morty Feldman what had happened and Feldman said, "Well, you know, John, you give it twenty years and *any-*

thing we do becomes a melody." Alright; it appears completely orderly, because of course what has happened is that the internal principle of order has been found. So that's very difficult; real entropy which, I don't know, unless a filmmaker immolates himself upon a pile of outtakes, or something like that; *that* doesn't even work . . .

HILLS: You call MAGELLAN an autobiographical work, and you've also said that the protagonist is the spectator, and this seems to me to be a paradox and I was wondering if you could unravel it.

FRAMPTON: Yes, I'd be delighted. First of all, it is an autobiographical work. It has to be. I am for better or worse, all I have. And embarrassing though it may be, that's what I've got to use. Furthermore, it's much worse than that, since now a good half of my biography consists primarily of making films and talking about them. Okay, so it's very easy to make an autobiographical film that's severely reflexive. However, I am also, and this really is growing more important to me all the time, the first spectator of my own work, you understand . . . I try to be a good one. Some of my knowledge is, yes, privileged. Most of that privileged knowledge is far too painful and also far too trivial for most other readers to be interested in, but . . . quoting Barthes . . . there is an essay called *The Death of the Author*, which is a predecessor to the book S/Z, which ends with the line, "The birth of the reader is the death of the author."

HILLS: This seems to contradict what you said about never being able to see your own work. Because everybody that sees it is going to have a different interpretation and so, as a viewer of your own work, your own interpretation is not going to be any [less] different from mine, than mine is from Carmen's, say.

FRAMPTON: I simply said I was the first spectator, I did not say I was its prime spectator. I make these things, by the way, because I want to see them. Believe it or not! That is my main propulsive force. I really am not sure I see a contradiction, you see. My work as the maker of the film is over when I have spliced in, on any given segment, the very first thing I hang up on the clothespin which is, by the way, the 4-frame theater cue-punch. When I put that in I know it's done. I hassle it through the lab, and then I will never be its maker again. Okay? That part is completely over for me. I will on the other hand always be its spectator. I happen to be its spectator first literally because I see it in here, before it physically exists.

GERSTEIN: In your films, particularly in MINDFALL, there is a great need for memory in order to understand the syntax you are attempting to build, in order to just understand grammar that you are attempting you have to be able to remember relationships that are 40 minutes apart, you have to remember that the car crash is followed by silence and the similar image and that is interesting, but what I'm aiming at is the idea that that is very difficult to do and most film viewers are not going to perceive that syntax based on the amount of viewings they are given and it gives me the question of . . . who's it for? What will you achieve in doing it?

FRAMPTON: The first thing you said is true, it requires a certain adeptness at memorizing, at REmembering, as distinct perhaps from dismembering, which is something that one must also do as one goes along to a degree in order to retrieve a system at all. The unlikelihood that you posit that this is going to happen is of course heartbreaking to me. The capacity to remember on the part of the spectator (I, after all, have my intricate planning systems and I practice more than any other spectator) . . . is, I fear, an irreduceible axiom of the work. How is one to live with this problem?

GERSTEIN: Not so much how one is to live with the problem, what my question was aiming at, though, was towards more political lines: which is, who your audience is intended to be?

FRAMPTON: And, indeed, what do I expect of that audience? That gets to be a real problem, you see . . . One is free to come and go and indeed there are other films in the world, however . . . whether the entirety of the work is remembered, indeed whether the entirety of the work is retrieved by anyone else and understand that I am implicated in this too because I can never have the spectator's view of the work, I am with regard to my own work in a tragic predicament because I can never see it, you understand, exactly this way. I see it in all the 800 ways in which it once was, will never be, including mistakes, moments when I was out to lunch, timing errors, the works. Speaking soliloquy, that probably should be a matter of indifference to me. Why should I insist that my work be understood, retained as a whole, or what have you . . . That possibility is contravened by the difficulty of seeing films. That problem is indeed a political one, because it is a problem of DISTRIBUTION which is certainly not under my control. If the video screen did not cut off so much of the film image, I would probably have no very serious objection even to MAGELLAN being on television, the MAGELLAN TELETHON, if that would make it more available. On the other hand, although it is bulky, I'm not, I think, making it for the same general reason that very large works in literature are typically made. The large work in literature usually is undertaken to perform a specific task within literature itself. It's possible to generalize, it has been done, and to say, for instance, what the enterprise of *Finnegan's Wake* is, its central enterprise, which has to do with a thesis about language which seems to divide subject and object from each other, to cleave them, *FW* tends to dissolve the boundary between subject and object. OK, *FW*, a bulky work, *assumes* the existence of literature. I cannot in the same sense assume the existence of film. Alright, film is not only infantile and subject to a certain kind of physical attrition that the book is not, and subject to a certain expense and rarity, but film has not thus far achieved levels of organization that are in any means comparable with literature and especially I think it has not constituted itself as a mode of production on the one hand or a field of cultural potentialities on the other such that it can contain the large work. This is a film outside of a film, for the most part. So that I'm not interested nearly so much in performing a specific task within film as I am of, not seeking but redefining the boundaries of filmic discourse. So that my worries aren't the same as they would be if I were, for instance, writing a 1000-page novel. I worry about other things, like for instance am I totally haywire? Seriously. Am I going to finish the goddamn thing? You see, that is a serious problem. If you don't finish an epic poem it is a more or less magnificent ruin. *The Canterbury Tales* . . . *The Cantos* . . . This I probably have got to finish or I have blown the whole thing, in my own mind, since it has the problem of establishing its own context . . . To borrow a term from the "dependent" cinema, I would like to *release* this work.

QUESTION: You said before, talking about MINDFALL, that the epileptic scene worked only because the protagonists win. Who do you see as a protagonist?

FRAMPTON: It's all in favor of the protagonist. The protagonist of an epileptic seizure is the sufferer, the victim.

QUESTION: Why does it resolve in favor of that protagonist?

FRAMPTON: Okay . . . epilepsy is not a functional disorder. It is not a disease, I'm sorry, it is not. But it is called a disease, it does not involve either gross or microscopic pathology in the central nervous system. It, to put it very briefly, represents a struggle, a violence, in this case, between the two largely separated hemispheres of the brain for control of the body. In right-handed persons, the left hemisphere which is the one that is chiefly concerned with linear, analytic, causal thinking, also is in charge of language at least in its ordinary power-wielding aspects, which are its most important ones in society, and it usually totally dominates and subjugates the right hemisphere. The right hemisphere in certain instances is imperfectly dominated and subjugated, gets a general idea unto itself that every brain deserves a body of its own to play with. And in certain moments, when the guard is down, the right hemisphere takes things over. This is a very crude cartoon of the situation. But a reasonably accurate one for epileptic seizure. Most of, indeed all of the people I've known who have been subject to seizure, who haven't actually hurt themselves physically, albeit the proceedings themselves are obviously very embarrassing to go through, generally, feel, after it is over, a kind of euphoria, they feel, in reports throughout the literature, that some very fundamental and very painful conflict has at least for a time been resolved. Alright. Nothing could possibly feel better than that.

That is certainly a resolution in favor of the protagonist and therefore of course for all of its embarrassment and absurdity in the exact formal sense, it must be a comfort. Obviously, if you fall off a cliff then it is not resolved in your favor and the outcome is not comfortable. But that doesn't happen very often. So that's exactly what I meant by that, on the other hand it's also in there you understand, because the person undergoing a seizure especially here is really out of control in public, in an entirely mental life, or from causes that are entirely mental, and on balance, with perfectly normal equipment in front of a whole lot of spectators, indeed there's a camera pointed at them, in this case, which is exactly the predicament in which I find myself every time I make and show a film. Whether my options are quite as comical or not I don't know, but I'm trying to make work in which your options as spectator, you are protagonist, will be comical because I hope to make finally a work resolved in your favor. That doesn't mean it has to be funny. That helps too. A lot of people left not wanting to see such an embarrassing sight, perhaps assuming that something much worse was going on than what actually was going on. It should be something, that if we weren't such creatures of our culture would happen to all of us all the time, indeed there are countries in which it happens far oftener . . . virtually a union card of shamanism. So that in many cultures it still persists, the epileptic is revered. And for reasons presumably that other people in the culture sense and understand, respect. So, that's what I meant by that. I meant a lot more by that too, but that'll do for now.

QUESTION: I'm sure you're aware that alcoholic withdrawal symptoms can simulate an epileptic seizure. I've seen this firsthand, the fits, and just like in your film this can be resolved in favor of the protagonist.

FRAMPTON: If that's true I'm in a constant state. Because I'm constantly withdrawing from alcohol, and, at the same time, constantly reentering it, as promptly as possible.

Yvonne Rainer at the Cinematheque, April 6, 1978

(shows CHRISTINA TALKING PICTURES)
[Editor's note: The film, of course, is Kristina Talking Pictures.]

QUESTION: I was noticing how listless a lot of these narrative readings were, the actors and actresses, and I was wondering if this was something you directed them to do or if it was something they chose to do, and if you directed them I was interested in hearing something about that.

RAINER: In the longer passages we did pretty much as we were able to, especially the scenes in which I appear. They're basically recitational, flat, non-emotive somewhat, yeah, monotonal recitations. I was interested in the language, and not getting into character. I thought of us, or all the people, as vehicles for the language, and not of course as actors engaged in creating some kind of verisimilitude of reality.

QUESTION: I began to feel there was this kind of ambient indifference, an exhaustion, which interested me.

RAINER: There's a melancholy to it. It's a melancholy film.

BROUGHTON: Which brings me to my main question about the work. Such a lot of effort goes into the making of a film, especially a long film. I would appreciate very much hearing from you what, what was your strongest urgency behind the making of the film.

RAINER: To, go on.

BROUGHTON: To just go on?

RAINER: To make another film.

BROUGHTON: To keep, to keep going on . . . on and on. Is that what you mean?

RAINER: Well, to try out some things that were pressing on my imagination. There were a lot of hunches that were pursued. Tracked down. So much in the way I make films exists in the mind for so long before you film. And I guess that a kind of pressure that builds up and you have to do it. I don't know how else to explain it.

QUESTION: So much of what I got from the film was about language as a substitute for feelings. The one time when the image was touching, the image was absent and there would be a description of the image in its place. The conception being about not making contact?

RAINER: Some people take the particular stylized enactment very literally, as being about alienation. That wasn't on my mind at all . . .

QUESTION: But that there is a role of language . . .

RAINER: Language replacing intimacy? But that's sort of the same thing. I was interested in what they were saying and especially Raoul in the bed. At that point the story and his character and the reality of his person were all subsumed or subordinated to what he was saying . . . There were a few things, cutting for gesture, a certain kind of continuity of gesture, or discontinuity, like "the new ships are not built to last" and the camera comes upon his hand on her hand and removes it. There are little things like that that are almost, I know, invisible in the general density and clutter of the language.

QUESTION: Would you comment on how you come to film from your previous activity, dance?

RAINER: I got involved in writing stories, biography, autobiography, psychological subject matter and my movement investigations had never been concerned with these things either directly or pantomimically. So it seemed I should go into a form that had more latitude and flexibility in how I could combine images and language. For a while I did multimedia performances and gradually there was a period when I was both dancing and making films. I guess, mainly, I lost interest in performance and keeping, in investing the kind of energy and time in dancing that was necessary for me to make movement that interested me. It was a gradual and a natural kind of process.

QUESTION: I'd like to know about the references to the concentration camps. Whether you personally have a relation . . .

RAINER: It was a matter of being old enough in the Second World War to have a very strong sense of Evil for the first time. My first awareness that terrible things could take place in the world. I was only seven. It's a very clear memory of the war and this — shadow. When I was a dancer it was something on my mind that I couldn't deal with this in dancing. Even though there were modern dancers who attempted, uh, narrative metaphorical dancing about this thing. I never knew how I would do it in a way that would interest me . . . And maybe this is one of the compelling things that propelled me out of dance to another form where I could try to deal with this kind of content. The remoteness. I needed a more distant form, and film seemed to give me that permission . . . The choreographed body has been replaced by the choreographed camera and movement within the frame, both in terms of activity and in relation to the camera and between shots, from shot to shot . . . As a dancer I was interested in stillness in relation to motion. Motion could be contrasted to stillness, absence of motion. I was interested in people becoming, being used in ways objects could be used — carried. They could lose their mobility. And when I started making films, I would have people in tableau vivant, or posing before the camera as though they were posing for a still camera rather than a movie camera. So there were these references, now transposed to film. Here there's another dimension, the morality of images. How do you deal with atrocity? Do you have a famous person talk about it, or do you have unlikely people talking about it — Elvis Presley and Doris Day, or do you have a photograph of emaciated corpses tacked up on the wall. My own question and dilemma . . . Or do you have a documentary like NIGHT AND FOG? . . . I did not try to make anything so ambitious as that. And I'm doing something that may be somewhat suspect, making poetry, making art of this material . . . I'm not looking for a LOOKING FOR MR. GOOD-BAR audience.

(San Francisco Art Institute, April 4, 1978)

RAINER: This film I'm working on is being shot in bits and pieces. I have an idea of the subject matter, or subjects, one of which is German terrorists. It's got a lot of information, straight information in it in the form of rolling titles and voice over. And the visual stuff is to be quite unconnected, episodic. It's already shot in different parts of the world. I shot a little bit in Berlin where I was on a fellowship for a year and some will be shot in New York, and now I'm shooting this out here in a house that does not appear anywhere else in the film. This . . . This film is not, although it has story and it has a character, it's on the level of comic strip. They're kind of two-dimensional. They have names, they have characters, activities, histories that are told to you in voice-over. You never get a sense of characterization or psychological dimension by seeing or hearing them speak . . . In my second film there are no characters at all. It's he and she and it's all emotional situations, it's not enacted in any way at all. All the emotional melodrama is in the soundtrack, the voice-over. Then in this last film (KRISTINA TALKING PICTURES), there's more attempt at characterization. One person is a lion tamer and the other person is someone who worked on a super tanker . . . There's a whole discussion by actors and it's cut in a certain way that probably owes something in terms of precedence to Maya Deren's AT LAND or Buster Keaton in THE CAMERAMAN: where he walks into the screen, he starts to sit down in a field and then he falls down off a chair, and the scene keeps changing and his actions keep getting aborted by this change in scene and it's cut so he's exactly in the same place in the frame [actually, this sequence is in Keaton's *Sherlock, Jr.*]. And in this section I'm talking about in my own film, the same thing happens. One person has a monologue about acting, specifically about the acting in Godard's films and she keeps finishing the different parts of the phrase in a different part of the room so you get the continuity in speech but total disjunction in terms of what she is wearing and where she is in the frame and in the room and what she is doing . . . But the problem that comes up in the discussion itself. The conclusion by one of my people is that in Godard's early films, the people are either too young, too pretty, too middle class or too — there was something else, to be convincing as real people, because he made real films, he never fooled around with the image illusionistically . . . In that realistic format, the characters aren't believable. They disappear into the film.

Abigail Child

VIOLENCE

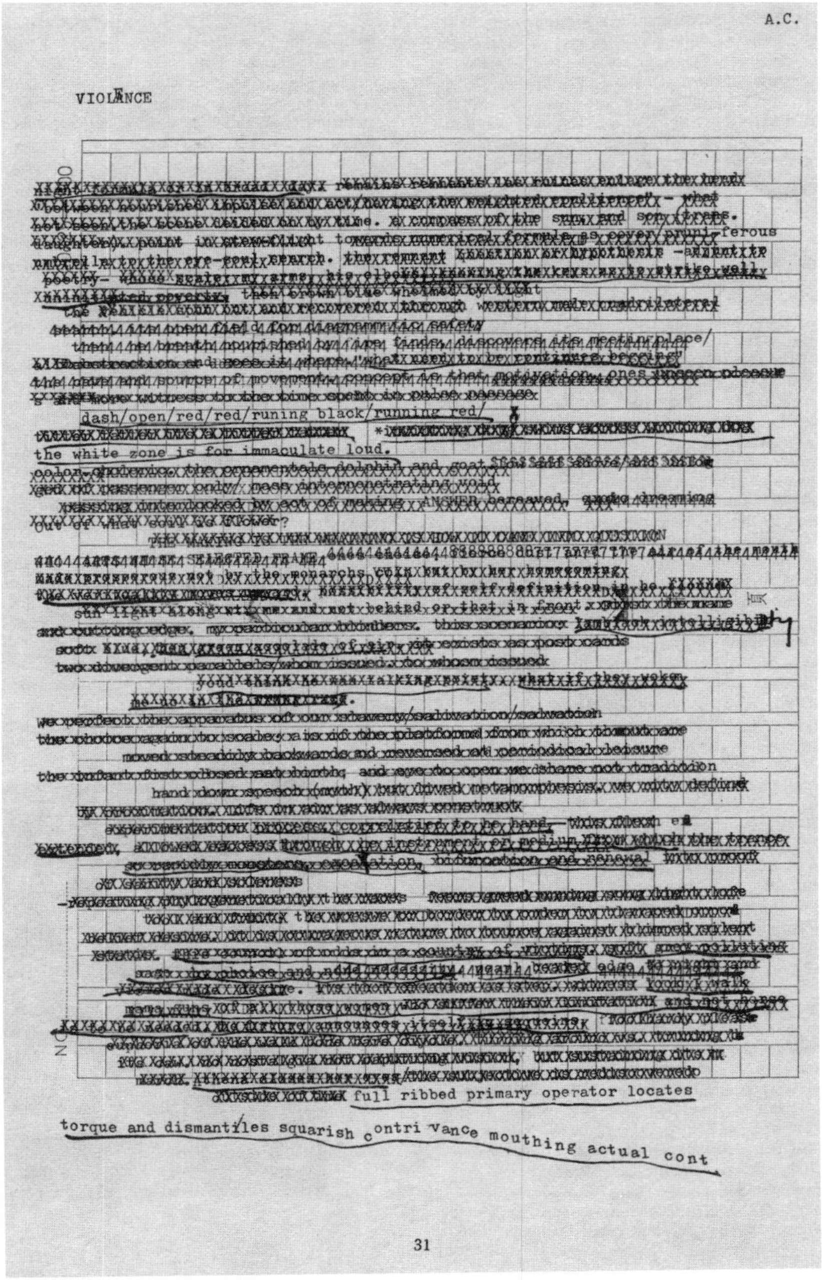
A.C.

VIOLENCE

dash/open/red/red/runing black/running red/

the white zone is for immaculate loud.

full ribbed primary operator locates

torque and dismantles squarish contri vance mouthing actual cont

31

—

FROM *CINEMANEWS*, 78.5

James Broughton
SOME UNSEEN LIGHTS

In the beginning there was no camera there. In the beginning Adam and Eve had only their eyes to see with. Did they see things as well-focused as we do? Do we see more accurately because we see everything through a lens? Or, is the matter the other way around? Does the seeing of everything through a mechanism make all of our world more unreal?

. . .

Now that everyone is engaged in picture-taking and picture making, is Maya, the universal web of illusion, more widespread than ever before? Do we actually see our world with less clarity? Is, therefore, self-deception more universal than it has ever been in human history?

. . .

Adam was given the task by Jehovah of naming all the creatures in Eden. Naming Day was a challenge to Adam's poetic invention. On the whole he didn't do too badly, although he was often unimaginatively monosyllabic, viz: cat, pig, ant, dog, ox. But certain of his namings have a lyrical aptness, such as hippopotamus, chimpanzee, porcupine, daddy longlegs, and cassowary.
Yet the questions remain: Did Adam take pictures of them?
And if he didn't, how could he remember what they looked like?

. . .

Another vital question: might Eve have escaped Temptation if she had been too busy focusing and had needed to back away from the Serpent in order to get more of the Tree into the frame?

. . .

Furthermore, are there more people taking pictures nowadays than there are people looking at them?

. . .

Einstein said: 'Everything should be as simple as it is, but not simpler.'

. . .

I am a poet who happened to make films (just as I happened to be born in California). My films have been generated by my desire to see what I feel, not merely read about it. Like that wonderful old question: How do I know what I mean till I see what I've said?
Hopefully, said Robert Creeley, I write what I don't know.

. . .

In order to perceive the Light, the eye must itself have some quality of that Light.
Light is not just lightness, or being light in the head.
Light is also the Great Reflector.
Gandhi said: 'Turn the spotlight inward. Bring forth what you find there.'

. . .

We strive for perfections. But all works are flawed, like life itself. Life is imperfect as we experience it, because we are each of us only a part of the wholeness of human consciousness. The fully realized work, like the fully realized human being, is a rare phenomenon.
Shakespeare didn't need to leave behind any apologetic autobiography. He fulfilled himself in the life of the imagination. And so he still exists.

. . .

Vertov said the eye of the camera is the great revealer.
Brakhage said the camera is the eye of the maker.
Broughton says the camera eye is the great deceiver.
Because the camera has its own fantasy of how the world appears.
This is not at all the same vision as any human being's. The despair of the filmmaker: trying to make the camera see his fantasy the way he sees it.

. . .

Fellini: 'I am congenitally incapable of dealing with reality impartially. My rapport with everything that surrounds me is always altogether private and individual. My response is solely that of my own fantasy, feeling, and emotions.'

. . .

It is easy to find fault with our betters as well as our peers. In fact, fault is the easiest thing to find. Fault-finding is the critic's specialty.
I prefer to be grateful rather than snooty. Be grateful for the artists we do have: for what they touch and reach and reveal. They are also you, they are extensions of your own knowing.

. . .

The world is divided between those who view humanity as hopeless and those who view humanity as hopeful. These could be called the Dark and the Light views of mankind. Let us choose to be on the side of the Light. Who wants to live in a dim view?

. . .

Where is Art going? I am asked by an interviewer, What is its future?

My reply: The future of art is the least of our worries in the modern world. The future, in art or anything else, will come to us as it will. It is already inevitable. In any event the New only comes into being through a rediscovery of the Old. There is nothing new except what has been forgotten.

Art is renewed by returning to ancient roots.

One can only predict the future in terms of a revival of so-called dead forms. What the subject will be, or the particular way in which an old form will be revitalized, rests with the unpredictable artist and what he is reacting to in his own time.

. . .

John Cage: 'You don't listen to what it ought to be. Listen to what is actually happening.' The truly contemporary artist always attends to what everyone else is ignoring. He doesn't choose what to do, it chooses him. Hence he often cannot explain what he is doing, or why.

Don't nag him: you will never understand art if you are too inquisitive.

Braque: 'In art what matters cannot be talked about.'

. . .

'Where do we go from here?' Thank goodness we don't know. Or, on the other hand, we don't have to go anywhere.

In any case there is nowhere to go.

If one must predict the future, we will probably go forward. Or backward. What is sure: what you expect won't happen.

. . .

Art is made in the now, not in the future.

If you can live long enough, everything ultimately comes back into fashion. So take heart: the art world is a lazy susan. If you find art too formal now, anticipate an imminent return to informality. If you think it too chaotic, look for a revival of the tidy.

. . .

Personally I believe in Delightments, Incitements, Enlightenments, and Liberation Machines.

—

FROM *CINEMANEWS*, 78.6/79.1

^{THE}CINEMANEWS

#78-6 & 79-1

THIS ISSUE:
HARRY SMITH
GEORGE KUCHAR
BRAKHAGE
SIDNEY PETERSON
LEN LYE
& more

Cover of the *Cinemanews*, 78.6/79.1, with photograph of Ernie Gehr by Meryl Glick.

Art Spiegelman

SKETCHBOOK (NOVEMBER–DECEMBER 1977)

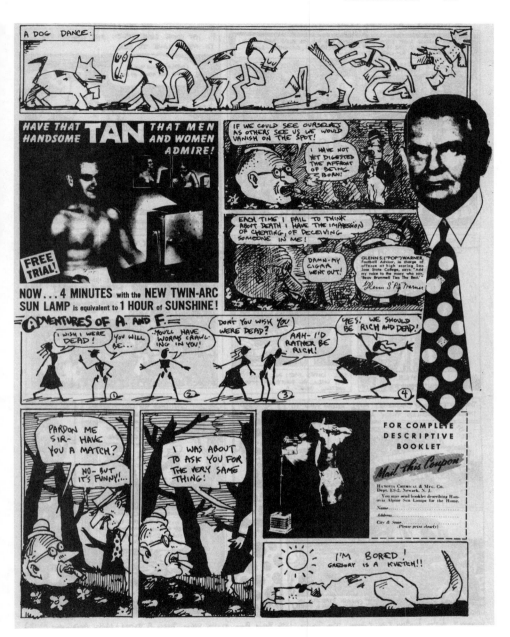

Diana Barrie

TO WHOM IT . . .

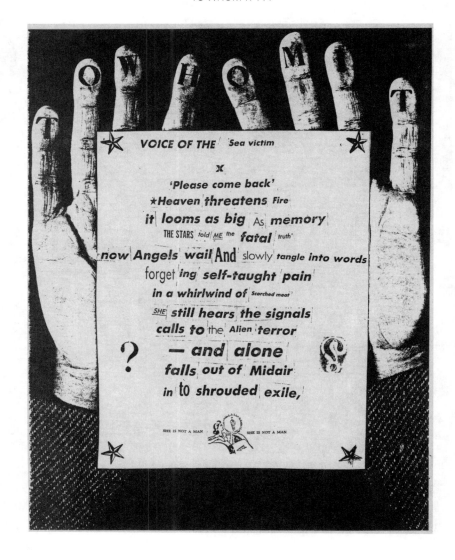

—

FROM *CINEMANEWS*, 79.2/3/4

Larry Jordan

SURVIVAL IN THE INDEPENDENT–NON-COMMERCIAL–AVANT-GARDE–
EXPERIMENTAL–PERSONAL–EXPRESSIONISTIC FILM MARKET OF 1979

Museums are just a lot of lies, and the people who make art their business
are mostly imposters. — Pablo Picasso, from *A Statement*, 1935

The bourgeois do not hesitate to affirm that their social order has permitted an extraordinary cultural development and that art, among other
things, has conquered unexplored regions until then apparently inaccessi-
ble to the mind . . . The very special value accorded to art by the bour-
geoisie brutally unmasks the vanity of its aesthetic concepts erected under
the pressure of class interests totally foreign to cultural preoccupations.

The ruse consists essentially of warping the normal relationship
between man and the world so that it is no longer possible to use the object
for itself but always for motives perfectly foreign to it: A diamond is desired
not for its intrinsic properties — its only authentic qualities — but because,
being expensive, it confers on its owner a kind of superiority over his fellow
man and constitutes a concrete expression of social inequality . . .

Things are no different in art. Capitalist hypocrisy, always refusing to
take a thing for what it is, lends to art the characteristics of a superior activity, although it lacks any resemblance to man's general activity. While usually man MAKES something, accomplishes some task within an ordinary
range, the middle-class artist claims to EXPRESS elevated sentiments relevant only to himself. Here bourgeois individualism is pushed to the
extreme, that individualism which isolates men and permits each one to
consider himself superior to his fellow men with whom he has no real
contact. — René Magritte, *L'Art Bourgeois*, London Bulletin, 1939

During the late 1950's and throughout the 60's American experimental film movements paralleled the general political and social movements of the country at large
with its counter-cultural, anti-establishment ties and its shock tactics aimed at
middle-class values. Along with this sociological alignment, the American avant-
garde film movement relinquished, by and large, any claim to aristocratic financial
support, choosing to attempt a people's art movement, which in most cases sought
support from its own audience. This does not imply that no college funds or private
donations ever reached filmmakers' pockets, or that no cinematheque had its private
patrons. But overall, individual ticket sales at cinema clubs, college organizations
and museums paid exhibitors' expenses and film rentals of "underground" 16mm
films.

This situation of "people-support" was an attempt, unknowingly, to institute a popular art support system more near to the "object-for-what-it-is" concept of the foregoing Magritte statement, and to by-pass the museums and art dealers condemned by Picasso in 1935.

This system, in the late 1970's, has all but failed.

Even though it has been buoyed up by public grants to filmmakers and film organizations, the American Avant-garde film movement is floundering for lack of an audience sufficient to support it; and though far from going under, it has certainly failed to fulfill the expectations of the 60's.

It is not mere coincidence that the sagging of the independent film movement parallels the 70's return of youth to the bosom of "The System." Students in these times want and demand to be trained not for idealistic purposes, but to take their places within a social order they have chosen not to fight, if not to condone. The transition period began with the concept of "changing the system from within." One rarely hears about changing the system in America at all anymore. Even the remnants of the non-commercial film movement, though ailing, have very little desire to change. And the "underground" aspect of the 16mm expressionist film movement has entirely disappeared along with the existence of any really significant counter-culture element.

The social tendencies of the 70's have effectively destroyed a people-supported film-art movement. In the present mood of conservatism the "people" wish more and more to identify with the establishment, the System, with *success*. This leaves any counter-culture element virtually defenceless, since the System (not the government, which has almost become a counter-culture element itself) is embraced by so many of the people. Today the Establishment is in a position to simply approve counter-culture and absorb or neutralize it. That is why the glamor of the Hollywood story-film has recaptured the imaginations (certainly the attentions) of the young people who once delighted in the irreverencies of the underground film. In the 60's the underground film spoke to and reflected the post-dadaist tendencies of youth.

On reflection it can be seen that it was not an American public who abandoned support for the avant-garde film. During the 60's the support was not for art; it was not even for avant-garde film. It was for a form of social change coincidentally advocated by the "underground" or counter-cultural film.

This social movement has had its effect and is over.

Times move on. In the late 1970's we are faced with an entirely different situation. Many experiments have been tried to establish new support systems for that part of the avant-garde film movement which remains intact. However, hundreds of new films and filmmakers join the ranks each year (from the film schools), and the attempts have been sporadic and decentralized. None of the more recognized film-makers who emerged from those movements of the 1960's now make a living from the rental or sale of their works, exclusively, whereas the top painters and sculptors do.

Today's filmmakers in the U.S. make films and pay their food, utility and mortgage bills by a complicated combination of:

Teaching
Grants (public and private)
Tours and appearances
Film rentals
Print sales
Commercial film jobs
Private patronage (rare)
Non-film-related employment

This is a very time- and energy-consuming system. With even the best-known film artists in the United States unable to make a living at what they do best, there is a lid on the top of this profession which is as firmly sealed down today as it was 20 years ago — a lid which does not exist for painters, sculptors, print-makers and others in the plastic arts. These artists, or those at the top of their profession, have achieved one very important result unavailable to personal filmmakers: the opportunity to work full-time in their studios, *and get paid for it.*

Of course the reason painters and sculptors get paid for their work is that they give up their paintings and sculptures. *They sell them,* with the knowledge they will make many others. I am told by painters that the sale of work not only frees them from time-consuming business dealings, but it makes a very healthy draw on their sources of creativity: new paintings are drawn forth by the sale of older canvases. Not so with filmmakers.

Film, by its very nature, seems to cry for duplication. And film exhibition seems to call forth a proliferation of prints from any given original. Avant-garde filmmakers have tried to buck the art system, become independent of it too. These and other highly emotional reasons have caused the American avant-garde filmmaker to shy away from any serious consideration of selling originals of films. Many who began as painters say they became filmmakers for the very reason that they did not want their works bought by one private collector and hidden away from sight. To suggest to most filmmakers that they sell an original film will bring on a reaction similar to suggesting they sell a child. It is a more or less *violent* reaction implying a certain degree of immorality on the part of the one making such a suggestion.

Yet filmmakers seem to accept this business of scattered film rentals, prints being eaten alive in deteriorating school projectors, teaching a few days a week, running here or there for an appearance (most of the money going to the airlines), trying to get a grant every three or four years — *and* work on their films — year after year. Perhaps it is just this disruptive, distractive and martyrly system which is responsible for so many disjointed and unsatisfactory avant-garde films. That element of primary concentration on the work at hand, which commercially financed films do at least have, is almost entirely lacking in the production of personal films. True artists will work under *any* circumstances, from Van Gogh to Picasso. But one imagines a society which pays its artists for honest labor, just as it does its other professionals.

The question is: *Who* will pay the film artists?

It is quite possible, even probable, that avant-garde filmmakers will *never* be paid properly for their work so long as they insist on remaining aloof from the support systems of the established arts — that is, from galleries, museums and private collectors.

When one looks closely (and honestly) at who has always supported "personal" art since its emergence in the Renaissance, one finds that it is private wealth. The fact that I do not *like* that statement does not make it less *true*. The church has supported church art. With some exceptions, the state has supported approved social art. Private patrons and collectors have supported "personal" art. Possibly wealthy persons imagine there is an affinity between their own individualism and that of an artist who is concerned principally with his or her inner world of images, allegories and metaphors.

And it is at this precise moment that one must face the general outcry against "elitism" in art. In 1939 Magritte condemns an individualism "which isolates men and permits each one to consider himself superior to his fellow men with whom he has no real contact." (One wonders if this view still remained in his later years.) Be that as it may, does Humanity benefit from the existence of "personal" art, or does it not? If it does, then it should be supported and the cry of "elitism" abandoned. If not, then "personal" art should be abandoned and all the Magrittes, Ernsts and de Chiricos junked.

One suspects that it is not so much a questioning of the *value* of personal statements by artists as the aura of *inaccessibility* of their work which brings on the cries of "elitism." (I am speaking of other than the suppression of personal statements by artists in a totalitarian society where "elitism" is but a thinly disguised tool for enforced conformity.) This apparent inaccessibility in the traditional media such as painting and sculpture consists both in the obscurity of the subject matter and in the castle-like enclosures of museums and private collections surrounding many of the works. All this tends to exclude the man and woman on the street from a kind of secret society of art hierophants, and to create a social division as described by Magritte.

But what if there is a natural, even evolutionary meaning to the process of "personal" art? What if it were a first rudimentary step toward the *abolition* of the very thing it seems to engender, namely class superiority and lack of contact between human beings? And what if it were so revolutionary as to be a step toward the complete abolition of all "government"?

If this were indeed the motivating drive behind all "personal" art then those producing it, the artists, would be justified in keeping it alive — not to enhance the false "superiorities" of the wealthy, but by *using* private wealth (as they have always done) for their own purposes so long as private wealth exists and is willing to patronize them.

If there really is a quality beneficial to all Humanity concealed in "personal" art, then it is as well for artists to receive a portion of that wealth as for it to go to the manufacturers of expensive automobiles, to criminal gambling interests, or to governmental tax structures which in turn pour it into the pockets of munitions makers. When private wealth no longer exists, we will speak of other means of support for artists. But so long as leftist factions regard "personal" art as "elitist" and refuse to support it, we must *use* the bourgeois system that exists. It is not the specific duty of artists to abolish private wealth. Nor does the sale of an artist's work to a wealthy collector in any way condone the principle of private wealth; it merely makes use of that person's wealth for the pursuit of cultural aims, which is as it should be.

In searching for this concealed quality of benefit to all Humanity, one imagines a world in which each man and woman could make available to every other man and woman pictures of their inner lives. In such circumstances it is hard to believe that fear, isolation and alienation could continue, but would drop away in the evolutionary process like obsolete organs of the human body. Fear having been abolished through individual openness, the dominance of one human being over another becomes unnecessary, ridiculous even. One imagines a world composed *entirely* of part-time personal artists, devoid of "geniuses" — those who have led the way — in which no power trips are necessary, and in which each human being looks into every other human being's inner, personal world without fear, admires it, cherishes it, but is never forced to obey or imitate it — a world in which *every* human being has developed the capacity to rely on its own inner strength, not in order to hide or escape into it, but in order to share it, to make it available to every other interested human being, but never to force it on another. One foresees a world composed of equal but individual strengths rather than a collective, single ideological strength.

And this, I believe, is essentially what "personal" artists are unconsciously trying to bring about, driven by powerful evolutionary forces toward a natural rather than an artificial equality. It is really only the system of "geniuses" that is "elitist," not the *process* of personal art. We are growing out of our primitive "ant-like" collectivism into a new individualized collectivism, one that will have neither a socialist nor a fascist orientation, and certainly not a capitalist one. This society, in which personal film will certainly play a great part, must exist on individual orientation. Masses will look even to fascism for external orientation, because human beings must have orientation in order to have meaning — real or artificial — to their lives. This is basic.

In order to move smoothly toward such a goal it is essential for artists to drop their paranoid defense of one school, style or form of art. To combat, for instance, "structural" film, or to defend it inordinately, only adds to the confusion and delays the process of wide-spread individual orientation, through personal art, as a means to social equality. "Isms" will fall away in time if we are willing to drop the truly self-indulgent part of personal art — insistence that only our own aesthetic ideas are valid — and concentrate on its strengths, which I take to be its infinite variety and its revelatory function.

Personal art by-passes the "how" of feeding the world and goes directly to the "why." It is vitally important to know that we can live equally without fear or external control before we are motivated to devise the exact systems necessary to provide for our physical needs. In my view it is exactly a hint of this knowledge that personal art provides.

Though the wealthy have a history of supporting personal art, personal art is not a concomitant result of aristocratic decadence. Personal art has always duped and played upon the vanities of the powerful because there was nowhere else to go. When a socialistic state will support personal art with a greater commitment than it will support a military, I will favor that system as a temporary measure, until the totally revolutionary consequences of personal art are fully understood, and those consequences in turn supersede the socialist state itself.

Meanwhile, I suggest that if avant-garde filmmakers want to be able to get back to their work full-time, they had better reconcile themselves to doing what every painter has to do: sell their work.

Admittedly, the system of art-selling depends on overvaluing a work of art, elevating it to the "genius" category, and proclaiming it a safe "investment." It is important for blood money, amassed by exploitation, to be transmuted into peaceful purposes through art. So long as artists themselves realize the long-term goal and do not fall for the "genius" business, no harm is really done in selling art at high prices. So long as wealth exists there is no reason why artists should not have enough of it to continue their work in peace and with dignity. This is exactly what any professional expects and deserves.

Purchase of film *prints* has never greatly interested art collectors for the very reason that a *print* is of no real value as an investment. Only one-of-a-kind originals (from which the collector can make prints or not) have saleable value — saleable, that is, at prices which will be of any sort of real help to the film artist. Progressive collectors *will* collect films (as they do Video) under the right conditions. Perhaps when the time is right the withdrawn Warhol originals will be for sale.

My first round of investigation among collectors elicits the following objections to buying films as "collectables":

1. "Why buy an original?" says one. I would inherit the filmmakers' headaches: making prints, renting the films, replacing damaged footage, etc."

I see this as a very superficial objection, and one easily overcome when collectors are made aware that it is exactly the old model of distributing films that they are looking at. Why should they try to *rent* their films any more than their paintings? They will eventually be asked to *loan* film prints for "film concerts" and festivals, as they do paintings for exhibitions. When they sell the film original is when their monetary gain will be realized. The model is exactly the same as for any other form of plastic art.

2. Another collector objects to sitting guests down in a dark room and "forcing" them to look at a new acquisition, in which they may or may not be interested. While with a painting or sculpture they can walk around it, talk about it, go to another room if it does not interest them.

At first glance, this may seem like a superficial objection; but it is not. It is a very real one, a human, social one. But this is a technical problem and can be overcome with daylight presentation rear projection. Film prints in Super-8 cartridges can almost eliminate a non-technical collector's loading headaches.

There would be other problems which analysis and technical application could also overcome.

The only *major* difficulty I find is on the side of the filmmakers themselves. As I have mentioned earlier, suggesting they sell an original is like suggesting they sell part of their soul, or at the very least one of their children. Emotional objections will be the hardest to overcome, because an emotional objection stops further thinking. Or else it will use other supposedly "practical" considerations to reinforce it.

A film seems very fragile and vulnerable to its maker. The fear of its mistreatment is great. 'Will a collector muddle it in some incompetent, non-caring lab after all the problems and headaches I've nursed it through?' Again, it is a technical problem. Why cannot filmmakers remain consultants to collectors and educate them in the protection of their investment, which I'm sure they'd be very appreciative of? Wealthy collectors can afford, possibly already have, humidity controlled bank vaults, in which to store originals. How many originals have we seen lost by fire, nomadic tendencies of filmmakers, lab casualties, etc., while in the possession of filmmakers themselves? Collectors who paid handsomely for a film might give it a better protection than the filmmaker. Filmmakers often lose interest in early films, for instance. Collectors would not. And who, by the way, is presently doing anything to preserve the American Avant-garde films of the 50's and 60's? A few black and white negatives have been put aside by Anthology Film Archives and that is about all. Placing value on film originals and their subsequent sale would go far in this direction alone.

As to exposure, it is true that those films sold to collectors would probably not be available for rental to (and destruction by) every film society and college group in the country. But people who own expensive art usually find very effective ways to show it off. Participation at film festivals would surely remain viable, perhaps under the filmmaker's supervision. And the distinct new possibility of "film concerts," handled by professionals, arranged by museums, etc. — film concerts similar in tone to classical music concerts — arises. I find this an exciting possibility.

Later I will discuss what I take to be the advantages gained by young filmmakers, cinematheques, and other showcases for experimental films.

In respect to the soul-wrenching act of parting with one's work: First of all, it is not necessary — or even possible — to sell everything. Nobody does, or hardly anybody. But painters, whose tradition goes back to the caves of pre-history, have grown up somewhat more than filmmakers in this respect. Filmmakers, whose entire history goes back only to Edison (or Lumière, whichever you prefer) have not yet come to realize that it is possible to be a *professional* artist and in no way become a "sell-out" to popular taste. (Even now, under the film *rental* system, filmmakers are constantly tempted to make more and more "rentable" films. On the other hand, collectors tend to acquire the more individualized and distinctive works — those works not usually recognized by the public at large. But it is amazing how soon the public appears when it comes to understand that a work of art is valuable.)

Another serious problem that has grown up with the avant-garde film movement is the identification the filmmakers now have with theaters, cameras, equipment, audiences and the whole mystique of the *film* world. But I suspect that most, once they overcame their fears about the security and availability of their work, would just as soon see their work in museums as in classrooms and college auditoriums.

Then we have the word, 'filmmaker' itself and that identification. To say that we are not artists (elitist connotations), but 'just filmmakers,' places us in that old and useless competition with theatrical filmmaking. It also relegates us to the constant frustration of dwindling audiences who don't know or understand or respect us. Occasionally curiosity brings out an audience for experimental films at a theater. When that audience discovers there is more "entertainment" at the commercial theater, they fall into the common misconception that experimental films aren't much good, and usually don't bother to return. At least at a classical concert one knows about what to expect.

It is sad that placing a money value on a work of art elevates it to respect. But this is true. (I have not given up on trying to *educate* a broader public to avant-garde film, but I do not expect them, as I once did, to support it.) At present audiences who do come to avant-garde film showings somehow cannot value the films very highly for the very reason that the *filmmaker* always owns the films. The subtle, but never-missed, implication is that if nobody else wants to own them, they're not worth much, not important, just a passing phenomenon. This is a poor position to be in when the films have cost so much and taken such a long time to make.

But film artists, in my view, have been too long intimidated by their own counter-cultural identifications on the one hand and fear of the art "establishment" on the other. While this mistrust is natural in a young artist, it becomes highly unnecessary in a mature one, and has put avant-garde filmmakers in a very isolated position today.

Maturity is one of the most difficult problems facing the avant-garde film artists today — or rather the lack of it. I am speaking of the infighting among filmmakers themselves. I have seen more alienation result from public speeches made by film-makers, condemning other filmmakers, than by the films themselves. Audiences who hear harangues directed at colleagues perceive filmmakers as immature, para-noid children — another reason not to take them seriously or value their works. (Incidentally, from my own experience I have found that one of the primary reasons governments cite in refusing to give more money to independent filmmaking is what they call a 'lack of seriousness' on the part of the filmmakers. They are refer-ring to the constant bickering and squabbling that goes on between rival film cliques. Of course the filmmakers are under the strong illusion that they *are* being serious and carrying the banner of the One True Art Form when they defend them-selves and their group.) In the United States this disease manifests itself primarily in individual filmmakers taking pot shots at each other, while in Europe, particularly in France, it is the immaturity of factionalism and political intrigue among groups of filmmakers.

But once filmmakers — film artists — adopt the broader view of the need and desirability for as many different forms of personal film as there are individuals mak-ing them, these problems will be relieved. I have seen this factionalism grow in America in direct proportion as the audiences dwindled and the showcase facilities dried up (in the last five years). I have observed that in France established filmmak-ers fight to keep new filmmakers from moving in on their already very small territory. It is like overpopulation and too little food. The rats begin to fight. And altruistic principles go for very little when one's very livelihood is threatened. It would be well, in my view, not to take the various "schools" of filmmaking too seriously. We must beware! There are all the signs that the fanatical conversion to, or hatred of "Structuralism" can have the devastating effects of religious warfare. No one wins. Everyone lies bloody and defiled.

Once film artists admit that they *are* just visual-sound artists who happen to work with the medium of film rather than paint and canvas or some other, and give up the illusion that they work harder, have more difficulties and expenses, and are a special "upper class" of the art world, martyrs all, they can once again have access to money for themselves, their films and their children that will just be spent elsewhere, and for possibly less cultural purposes. Access to *every* support system available — left-wing, right-wing, or center — goes hand in hand with the maturation of film and film artists.

I think that if several small groups of recognized filmmakers were to form "stables" of artists willing to sell originals of their shorter works, handled by professional art dealers willing to work with the collectors *and* the filmmakers to solve problems that the lid could be blown off the top of this pressure cooker where there are too many filmmakers, too many films and nowhere for young filmmakers to go.

It would certainly be a first step.

If film became valuable through purchase of originals, the intensity of interest centering on cinematheques and promising younger filmmakers could only increase. The entire field would once again open. I am convinced that the old models are worn out and no longer serve us, but also that our traditional showcases need not be abandoned. They would function much as they do now, but with renewed interest and appreciation and respect.

The second step would be to re-activate the traditional militancy of the avant-garde film movement to force an awareness among all museums of modern art that the situation as regards film art and artists has changed. No museum should be allowed to feel adequate unless they have an active film exhibition and acquisition program handled by a film curator who has more than superficial knowledge of personal film and filmmakers.

With the first sale of a five minute film original for $10,000 or more the face of the art world would be changed overnight. Film would be a valuable commodity, which at present it is not. And no one could ever shrug it off again.

—

FROM *CINEMANEWS*, 79.5/6

Peter Seaton

HOW TO READ II

Peter Seaton

HOW TO READ II

A and the the and and's to a the a is is or and the the sweet
and and to this sweet marrow of one and in and has the the at
is in in the complimentary in a the of ask of and marrow and
were the to is for to the the the walls and at is in in is of
the technically or in the or of were of and or spot flanked the
the the all and and as a with among for the the to the is for
of for for elements in the in by with of on the of purpose for
of the of an buzz faces in the the to devises elsewhere in half
undress the seated boy the of the at in left this each and of
as of of and in of as than of the undress than immediately to
for the and catalogue the in is three a the as the the the the
the in flesh a the the the the to the that's the of or in or the
the that anything's city and to of the that and of with seated
the of of it the to things the our she wings of into in and in
and present and as its as the's the boy and I'd the the of for
and period own or and a the and assign in the a of the and to
are on of like for at it it's brought country blue or of as in
the in the and that it as is at to the the to the the is is
available in a as in it the sketch of in of in of and is at
this in's to in it in available in a and and a the it in where
the in the the the as to into to in the's than or poetry the
the to in the date the naked in any that adapts to by a that
into the of for and the to in the of the to are a and the of
is of the and the of the a of on of the central representing
to the fine a and all in the almost its the for to be into at
of illustrating the of an the in all and it's and in the that
the of are more than to with of from of the as the for eras
the that the for the the of some that the and the anyway street
hunt with at with at at and the of the in the at is a of who
the of to a in the of the the's of the in is a of the a and a

3

for the a or it's scheme for as and that the and the and its of
on the to a with a on the the a in the of the the of ate like
to of the to at with the lines of and as as a with a to and like
an the for the to an and an of and in or the the on the and for
on the and the to the is the the it the a a to in the an for an
a to of the for and a for formed forms his message's stagger so
so so to as it its of in at with a a of that the and that it a
and as it it the of in to for the of the at the to the of the
of a is the of and the in the is to the of the to sites the an
and in the the in are of and the and that a and the and that a
and at a causal company body is a is that each and and of or a
generate a for the at the to on and of in and to it the that a
and is is of in its to is is in the it sits on of the of the a
and it in midair and the says that in that of the the flanking
the of of that are or and that and and and as to in all of of
metal the extension trim keystone women their or the the of on
the ultra its the used to a in the of the a the the and and
the of the for the the is the of the the and are of some of the
worlds the of a the worlds a some of a the the worlds of some
of the worlds for the the worlds the worlds the worlds the worlds
the worlds worlds the the worlds of a with of lining like this
one the the to as is to it in the and the of the the worlds to
it as the worlds is to it the the the like an that were in that
were that were and the is the and is of inside the the or from
the that in the experience the in the from the of the that something and at and the a to the of the of the and a to the of and
a to the of and its of to that is something it is is in a or
the as a of are with the its and and like a for the the than
the and it to the in of the it in the and a to the of the it in
the and a that to the of the in the is a the the to the relative
natural the of the to in the in of of and through the that or
and the the is a than the or the to the of the are and of and
of and the an a and a the in the and an is of the of it the on
the a and in the of the a.

4

—

FROM *CINEMANEWS*, 79.2/3/4

Jackson Mac Low

1ST MILAREPA GATHA

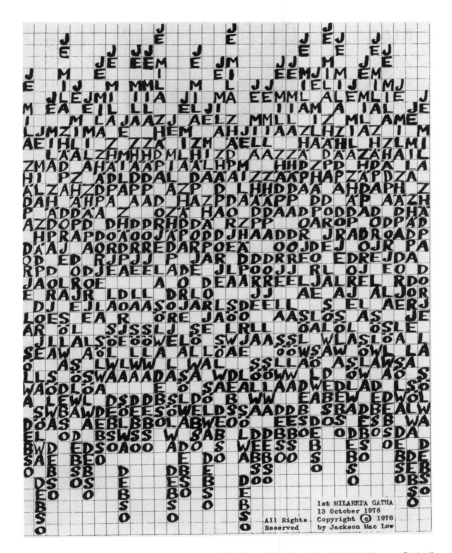

[Editor's note: The following is from Jackson Mac Low's explanation of "1st Milarepa Gatha," © *1976, 1980:* **The "1st Milarepa Gatha" is one of a series of performance pieces composed from time to time since 1961. The term "gatha" was adopted for them on analogy with its use to designate short poems by Zen masters and versified portions of Sanskrit sutras. In**

Gathas composed before 1973 and many made since then, transliterations of mantra — sayings or prayers repeated for meditative purposes — are lettered on quadrille graph paper, their placements being largely determined by chance operations. In this Gatha, the mantram associated with the Tibetan Buddhist Master and Boddhisattva Milarepa (A.D. 1052–1135) — "Je Mila Zhädpa Dorje La Sölwa Debso" — is lettered vertically down each column of squares. Each transliteration begins on one of the top ten rows of squares, as determined by chance operations involving random digits. . . .

Mac Low explains that this Gatha may be performed by one or more people, each functioning as a speaker or musician, and each starting at any square and moving to "any one of the eight squares adjacent to its sides and corners": "Vocalists may say names of letters; any sounds the letters may stand for in any language; syllables, words, or wordlike letter strings formed by letters adjacent in any direction(s) . . ."; instrumentalists may translate the letters into various "pitch classes (in any octaves). . . ."]

—

FROM *CINEMANEWS*, 79.5/6

Warren Sonbert

FILM SYNTAX

This is a potential shot sequence for a film that I'm working on now. I'll list 5 or 6 shots, and describe them. Shot A is a priest in a tent at an ethnic Filipino festival, held in Dolores Park (S.F.) a couple of weeks ago. It's very dark in the middle of the frame; he's sitting down towards the back and he's eating. In the midground, in front of him, are a pair of hands, exchanging money, paying for food. So the hands themselves have a dehumanized feeling because they're detached from any figure we might see. And I think the components of this shot put forward the idea of the greed of organized religion, the Church bloated, stuffing itself, in very conventional cliched terms.

Shot B is a sort of neutral shot: a band of gleaming light on water, moving in contrast to the preceding still shot. It's abstract: water, light. These neutral shots, of which you saw a lot in the last film (DIVIDED LOYALTIES) are like after-dinner sherbets, there to cleanse the palate before the next more highly charged image.

The next shot, C. On the left foreground, a little girl is dressed as an angel; it's Halloween in New York. She's got a full set of wings, halo, silk white tape, the works. And she's blond. Her mother is bending over her to tie a bow around her neck. Then on the right back middleground is an old man, gnarled, pushing himself along in a wheelchair. Perhaps an alcoholic, certainly at the end of his rope. The girl is oblivious to his presence; she's looking in the other direction. She's very smug and content; there's a scowl on the old man's face. We have a series of contrasts here, all within the same frame: old/young; she just beginning life, in perfect health, protected by her mother, angel tending angel/he's alone, isolated. At the same time, because they're in the same frame, instead of reinforcing shot A (the bogusness of organized religion), it raises the possibility, the potentiality, the spectre of miracle happening. The idea that she may cure him. He may find himself miraculously restored to his health and good graces.

The next shot, D. Another neutral shot. Let's reinforce the idea of serene objectivity. A burst of fireworks, let's say, a form of creation, a generative effect. Also continuing the idea of light, as opposed to the act of dissolution.

Finally in this series, let's reinforce the ambiguity, making shot E a clergyman shaking hands with some of his parishioners who are leaving church. This is again the clean image of organized religion, antiseptic, socialized, smug and efficient. Not the frenzied intention of a miracle motif. The image then can reinforce the negative qualities of shot A but at the same time strengthen the positive aspects of shot C. In other words, there's a place in religion for the mystic, impractical, unpredictable, direct, uncodified aspects. So again, the spectator takes away what he brings to it. Either complacency confirming what he feels about the drawbacks of organized religion, or an objectivity about what might be religion's hope-filled qualities. The neutral shots should reinforce this, since the figurative images have such built-in negative connotations.

Let's try another series. Shot A: a witty, urbane, solo person at an outdoor cafe sips some wine and smiles at the taste and fragrance, ambrosial, then notices something nearby, perhaps some behavior or activity at a nearby table: his expression changes to abhorrence, eventually culminating in a sneer.

Cut to B: a bridge, immense, expansive, far away. Both shots are still, but this one is very wide angle, and the other close. But all of a sudden, this bridge, several seconds in, after definitely establishing the serenity or rather placidity of the image — there's an intense explosion and the bridge wavers, crumples, disintegrates, blows up, crashes. Here we have two different images as far apart in content and construction as possible, and yet the psychological manifestation of A (displeasure, contempt) becomes the physical actuality of B (dissolution, disintegration). What can we do with C? Let's have a group activity of construction or planning. It could be some workmen building a house (definitely not tearing one down), or simply some people having a discussion, planning, exchanging ideas. So what are the qualifications at work here? One can look at it as if human activity is folly since all is dust eventually — this is the negative reaction; or that despite everything one continues rolling the rock up the hill — a more beneficent view. Or, again, both — which is ideal.

The job of editing, which distinguishes film from theatre or simple (minded) photography, is to balance a series of ambiguities in a tension-filled framework.

Neutral shots are usually non-figurative (4 seasons, 4 elements, implying country, landscapes, non-urban; animals can be contained within them). As soon as a human figure with its myriad of different interpretive gestures and expressions appears, the image takes on a complexity denser than any image without one.

I think the films I make are, hopefully, a series of arguments, with each image, shot, a statement to be read and digested in turn. Each work as well is about a specific topic: CARRIAGE TRADE, a film I made about 10 years ago, is about travel, transportation, anthropological investigation: 4 continents, 4 organized religions, customs; about time with its 6 years in the making and cast of thousands; about how the same people age and grow and even change apartments over 6 years. RUDE AWAKENING is about Western civilization and its work/activity ethic and the viability of performing functions and activities. DIVIDED LOYALTIES, the film you just saw, is more about art vs. industry and their various crossovers. And my new product, tentatively called NOBLESSE OBLIGE, is about journalism, reportage, news events that you might see on the 6 o'clock report, how the news is created, how it might affect our lives, and journalists' responsibilities.

The great hero in film history is Brakhage, who "liberated" film. He made the tactile qualities the major concern and showed that "mistakes," errors could have an expressive, demonic, psychological function. Images could be overexposed (too bright) and underexposed (too dark). That dirt, splice lines, flare-ins and flare-outs, the dots that end and begin a 3-minute roll of rushes, all could have a transforming purpose. He questioned the entire 19th century sensibility of the composed wide-angle art-gallery framework. He suggested that all budding filmmakers take an ice-pick to their lens to destroy Renaissance perspective. He also has this near-equivalent of Pollock — these thick overlays of impasto, almost including the paint-tube caps, with his drawing, painting, scratching on film, scraping away the emulsion, using oil, water, ink, magic marker; even, in a film called MOTHLIGHT, to go so far as to crush the wings and bodies of moths and other insects onto a strip of film.

He opened up the use of hand-held cameras so that the personal movement of the filmmaker would be underlined, as opposed to the commercial filmmaking industry that was superficially objective and always used tracks and grids for camera movement. He and others who followed (because, up to Brakhage, independent New American Cinema was almost exclusively obsessed with the clinical psychodrama, an offshoot of German Expressionism and its Freudian symbols that eventually became a tiresome deadend) not only exploited the turgid, muddy images potentially to be recorded filmically, but also opened up all sorts of patterns in the camera and editing (clipped shots, frenzied progressions in which the camera could toss, fly, spin, and whirl).

Brakhage's unique personal concern would also be involved in trying to discover the inner states of beings other than the adult human: children and babies, dogs, cats and insects, beings not yet born, or already dead. He proved that the images of the personal are of universal validity, and by their very nature superior to the studio-manufactured images that with rare subversive exceptions (Hitchcock and Sirk) just coddled, patted you on the back, and reconfirmed what you already knew or wanted to hear.

Hitchcock, like Renoir, Ozu, Rossellini, and to a limited extent Cukor and Ford presented worlds in which everyone had their reasons, that guilt was to be shared and experienced by all — films that threatened, that shook up, that called into question existence and roles — all in their individual styles and personal inflections. Sirk, besides slyly commenting on consumerism, respectability, bourgeoise cul-de-sacs, status and community acceptance, also was perhaps the most avant-garde of commercial Hollywood filmmakers (or even non-Hollywood; his films are much more "farout" than Buñuel, or Cocteau, or Godard, or any of the other non-commercial sacred monsters), since his primary technological obsession (through which his literary concerns would surface) was about the very two-dimensional qualities of the screen image with its interacting tensions trying to portray three-dimensional activities. Hence the purposeful flatness of his images and constant subject matter of glass, mirrors, reflective surfaces, emphasizing the formic qualities of film: his unique content considerations. Maybe it sounds simplistic, but his people and their concerns are so shallow because their medium of conveyance is so shallow: i.e. film. And he got away with it for 20 years in Hollywood, making lots of money for Universal, getting almost as much freedom as Hitchcock in his denunciations of capitalist mentality, and creating a very avant-garde body of work, with wit and humor, but foremost, being concerned with film vocabulary and form, unlike any other commercial filmmaker.

If Brakhage and Sirk are the great heroes and pioneers of the independent film and the commercial film respectively, then Eisenstein must be the great villain of both editing and even of the film image.

In Eisenstein you can spot the good guys and bad guys a mile away. Here is nothing but a knee-jerk reflex. And to think that Hollywood silent acting has been criticized for the snarling-villain-cringing-heroine school of acting — which is nothing if not Eisensteinian. One famous example: some known political figure (who is now on the outs in a party parlance) will be shown haughtily strutting about in gold lacquered palatial settings, arrogant and supercilious. Cut (and out of nowhere, mind you — not even to a continuing narrative strand) to a preening peacock. There are no shades, subtleties in Eisenstein, it's all black or white. No two ways to think about anything — it does all the work for you, no gradations, no surprises. Even his supposed elongation of (film) time was set in motion way before by Griffith. But really what is most damning, besides such mob pandering juxtapositions as Cossacks with pigs, is the total shirking of working with compositional spaces. It's all up front — the meaning is all contained in the foregrounds, with receding, weak, unplayed backgrounds. Now in the entire history of the cinema, from Griffith to Brakhage, it is this shifting tension, or, hopefully, tensions among the three fields of background, midground and foreground that constitute a genuine filmic sensibility. What is going on among these various planes and the spaces between provides commentary, reflection, qualification and placement. There is this lack of density in Eisenstein, that along with Cocteau (a totally pre-cinematic sensibility), and Buñuel (stuck in an anachronistic Dadaist groove), make them the most overrated trio in official cinema guidebook history.

Let's talk about the horizontal/vertical motion of film. Unlike poetry and art, in which it is up to the viewer, spectator, reader how much and in what way he responds to the art object (the reader can take his own time, skip ahead, dwell on words and phrases; the viewer can look at the whole painting first, or any detail), the auditor of a piece of music or the watcher of a movie is controlled by the artist. The difference is durational. In very much the same sense as one hears a series of notes, chords, or tone clusters, one sees a progression of a series of shots. The horizontal aspect in film can be looked upon as the subject matter itself (in the narrative literary context — what are these specific images: raccoons or policemen or flowers or whatever); in the same way the horizontal dimension of literature is what happens next: events, narrative; in music the melodic line, the theme. The vertical aspect is how all this is (literally) colored, how long the shot lasts, the exposure — is it light or dark, how is the image framed, what is contained within the frame, what is left out, is the image moving or is the subject matter within the frame moving — all this corresponds in literature to the actual words that tell the story or propel the reader: the languages, the grammar, the syntax; in music to the length and dynamics and coloration (instrumentation) of the notes. This is the old saw about form vs. content, which had been solved long ago: i.e., the two work together, can't have one without the other to provide the meaning(s), thrust of any work of art. Now, in music, with the 2nd Viennese School (Schoenberg, Berg, Webern) for the first time in history, with the exception of very worked-out controlled Bach fugues, both the horizontal and vertical aspects were controlled by a very systematic and totally exhaustive predefined grid or overlay or blueprint. Not only did so many notes, and of a specific kind and order, all have to be played before they were allowed to come round again (Schoenberg's contribution), but even the length of the notes or chords, their instrumentation or attack would be graphed ahead of time (Webern's contribution). Very rarely has this been attempted in film, with not only the flaw of the specific images, but their qualities as form taken into consideration to provide a specific framework in approach.

So really film is basically musical: any movie with a soundtrack is already a very mixed-up medium, a hybrid, a bastardization. Of course soundtracks help carry matters along, do all the work, as it were. It's hard to think of Connor or Anger with-

out their tracks — but that is exactly the acid test: Harry Smith's EARLY ABSTRAC-
TIONS and LATE SUPERIMPOSITIONS can survive without their early Beatles
goading, but INAUGURATION OF THE PLEASURE DOME cannot (as wit-
nessed by the recent pulling of the at least exotic and idiomatic Janacek Mass in
favor of a very undistinguished rock track [by the Electric Light Orchestra]).
Brakhage, Menken, Vertov, have all shown that to purely watch the images is a
much freerer, broader experience than any track would add. The film can truly
breathe this way — go many more places than it can anchored to sound. Somewhere
along the line the divergent rhythms of film and sound get in each other's way —
unless you're concerned with film theatre which is a whole other kettle of fish.
You'd have to cut an image on every note, chord, or sound-effect for the rhythm to
be accurate to the image and then you'd have a series of redundancies, reinforce-
ments. To object to silent film would be akin to having to have a Scriabin sonata on
in the background while one would read Bernadette Mayer, or being plugged into
earphones while looking at a Vermeer — being told what to look at or listening to
some of the early Franco-Flemish school, Joquin or Dufay. Just as ridiculous and
infantile. To have to have a soundtrack is not taking film seriously.

Knee-reflex reactions: I remember a show here at the Cinematheque not too
long ago in which a series of minimalist or structuralist films (not exactly arrivistes:
Snow, Brakhage, Frampton, Sharits, Gehr) had the audience so incensed and threatened by lack of any identity figures that they would throw beer bottles at the screen.
The viewing mentality was not quite ripe for these films and still has a long way
to go.

One of the joys of independent/personal movies is the fact that, given cultivated
eye and form, everyone's approach is unique. In a hand-held field everyone has a distinct way of moving; it can be clipped or gliding, tentative or aggressive; how tall or
short the person's stature; it can be a situation in which one is relaxed and knows the
subject matter intimately or one in which you have to catch the material on the sly
as it were, it can be reportage, home movie or documentary. You learn about your
way of seeing by viewing your rushes: given a wide-angle to close-up lens (let's say a
12 to 120mm zoom, though I'm not saying to use zooming in & out — one of the
banes of modern film technology), one can frame all the gradations between ultra-
objectivity (wide-angle) & selectivity (close-up). Of course, there is something inherently fascistic about the close-up — the doggedly insistent exclusion of various visual
fields — but like any other gesture, used sparingly, appropriate for a given effect. One
can show some hands performing a function in an early shot of a series, & then later
clarify the mystery by placing it in a long shot. What is excluded from the visual field
has just as much a voice as what is included. Very long takes with a minimum of
visual activity automatically invoke leisure, repose, or a meditative state. Short,

active, heavily spliced series of images conjure frenzy, generative, fiery forces. An overexposed image (too bright) tends to flatten the visual field, remove the apparent dimensionality of the image, a bleached effect. An underexposed shot (too dark) lends mystery & a forbidding quality; murky, literally understated, even a sinister quality. Then there are the myriad varieties of movement. Is the camera still or in motion? Is the object within the frame in motion? And the camera still? Are the camera & object(s) going in complementary or divergent directions? Again, each variation will produce a different effect on the viewer (but not to be understood divorced from the other film components). Because we are Westerners & have been trained to read from left to right any directional pull of this order will produce a pro-gressional effect/ reaction. And, oppositely, any right to left pull will register a sub-tle regressional attitude. Thus, one can reinforce positive or negative poles on the same level as over & under exposure. And what about the vast field of movement? Is the movement a hand-held pan in which the camera is stationary but moves on an axis in one direction or another, left to right, up to down, down to up, laterally, or in circles? Or is it tracking, by the filmmaker's own momentum, or by a moving object? This opens up more fields. Is the track conveyed by car, boat, plane, bus, train, bike, wheelchair, roller coaster, swing, being pushed out a window, & if the background medium registers this then it will cause a specific reaction/interaction in the viewer. Then there's the matter of lap dissolves (one shot fading out & another shot fading in towards the end) & superimpositions.

Film stocks: the texture of the image, the various tactile modes. Of course, color as opposed to black & white, but some stocks have a grainier look than others. And one can use indoor film outdoors (which gives a very blue tint to the image) or out-door film indoors (with non-natural, non-available window light) which gives an orange hue to the visuals. There is slow speed film — ASA 25 — Kodachrome II — which one would use in a very bright light normally: midday, on the Sahara, on water; then ASA 64 MS or tungsten, ASA 125, or Ektachrome ASA 160 (very fast film); there is even ASA 400 for color. Fuji film from Japan, Ferrania film from Italy; in B&W we have Plus X & Tri X & 4 X. ASA's from 40 to 400. One can use nega-tive B&W as opposed to reversal, or Ektachrome Commercial which has a very soft grainy almost viscous visual field; & especially fun are out-of-date stocks or film in which the emulsion (film coating) is starting to break up so the dot-like, fiery, exploding aspect of the celluloid image is constantly in motion. One can use light leaks & flares, & camera breakdowns (the film not being properly threaded & so not quite being in the gate to give the image a fluttery momentum). All these potentials are like different brush strokes to provide a change, an expressive reversal or chasm to be plunged across.

Where the camera is placed can provide punctuation to the images. If the camera is tilted up at the objects they can be invested with stature or foreboding, larger than life, looming over one. Ford used this approach invariably, giving his heroes an exuberance they might not have had with an eye-level approach. Also, by tilting up one includes more of the natural surroundings, particularly clouds & sky (& Ford had the most poetic clouds in film history — they are almost an instrumental voice), thus emphasizing man's benign interaction with the elements & stressing a positive attitude towards progress, civilization, a hopeful attitude. But this is not a strict rule. When Janet Leigh goes into the car dealer's bathroom to count her recently stolen money in Hitchcock's PSYCHO, the camera is tilted up & the background stalls evoke a sinister, something-could-swoop-down or burst-out nagging possibility.

Tilted down, the impression usually conveyed is one of Olympian detachment, eye-of-God attitude, it is all unfolding for us, this is just one cog of many, there are millions of other events like this happening all over all the time. The importance of such-&-such an activity is placed, dwarfed, commented on. This is the usual viewpoint for an establishing shot in a conventional narrative film. There is a danger in over-using a these-are-all-worms-underneath-the-rock attitude, & it is hard to think of a filmmaker who would consistently approach his subject matter this way.

Then there is straight eye-level which would be the standard — Hawks hardly ever strayed from this framing. There is the whole German Expressionism school, which, as has been increasingly pointed out, was not just limited to Prussia in the 20s, but overwhelmingly influenced all of Hollywood when, because of the war, & even before, many German directors (Lang, Murnau, Preminger, Siodmak, Wilder, Lubitsch, Ulmer, Zimmermann, etc.) came over here. It was the hallmark of Welles &, to a more limited extent, Cukor & Hitchcock, & even the early psychodramas of Maya Deren, Kenneth Anger, Brakhage.

A good film to check out would be Carol Reed's THE THIRD MAN, in which one is hard put to find a straight-on shot — every image seems askew, awry, tilted right to left, left to right, up to down, down to up, so as almost to induce nausea. Usually this is meant to invoke an all's-not-quite-right-with-the-world attitude, as well as states of psychological disarray, frenzy, upheaval — all underlined without having to move the camera. Or one can start out in a flipped position & move the camera either 180° or 360° to complete a circle.

2 classic examples spring to mind: 1). in Hitchcock's SUSPICION, when Grant brings Fontaine the last poisoned glass of milk (she thinks), with a lightbulb put in the glass to really give it a luminous, highlighted quality, we see him enter from her point of view as she's in bed, & then the camera comes half circle round as he strides across the room to place the milk at her bedside. 2). Then there's a very similar take

14 years later in Nick Ray's REBEL WITHOUT A CAUSE, again from a character's point of view, this time James Dean's, as he's stretched out, hung over, very confused about his relation to his parents, friends, the world; his father enters, dressed in a very frilly apron, to talk to him, again a 360° turnabout. Both instances show very subjectively a state of anxiety or confusion or helplessness, both unthinkable without German Expressionism, even though Ray was American & Hitchcock British.

Now point of view usually means that we are seeing images unfold distinctly through the eyes of a character (in narrative film context). Hitchcock is the arch exponent of this; he built a whole film around it, namely REAR WINDOW, though all his works partake of it. One goes back & forth between seeing images objectively (the theater's 4th wall, as it were), & subjectively (a character's reactions to what is going on in his or her situation). It is very seductive & allows for very quick identification on the viewer's part; it is one of the hallmarks of manipulative cinema & really why film is the true 20th Century extension of Greek cathartic theatre — we are made to experience very directly the upheavals that occur to the character. Of course independent, personal films, especially if they are of the lyrical, diaristic variety, can be looked on as totally point of view: what the filmmaker sees of the world & experience; or the opposite: totally nonpoint of view, with every image having a detached, observational quality: one is there to record without investment & not to put the audience through base paces.

(CONTINUED NEXT ISSUE)

Abigail Child

THE FILMS OF ALINE MAYER

At the source, an exposure.

Light upon the obscure origin of our own categorical imperatives.

Processes of quest under lie formal exploration.   The form a form of permission.

Shapes edge.   deliberate welter.   slipped returns wt trees of beginning Reversing
(a swan).   first material: *MATER.*

Felt density.   balls moon eggs.   vitreous fluid.

MINI NG POINT — the obsessional essence of its psychical mechanism.

The fear has not yet split up.

Water spots restless constancy marks overviews views shades abutts.   primitive
plane transfigures rectangle. *DB.*   celluloid self-developing (in & out of
transient sublets).

End always the BODY.   an anatomy sustained by history.   datum abstracted from a private life & enacted as a rite.

Of bugs wch we think first are bees but become trapped swarming maggots (ARE ladybugs).   *HONEY.*

From white to grey to black, next-to-nearly nothing: *DISPERSION.*   granular flow of film, THAT exposed to air.

In reaction to all this Aphrodite as a class-conscious goddess works herself up into a great rage.

Wch point the rejection — Aline leaves NY in 77, goes to Buffalo, abandons films, speaks of them as limited artworld OBJECTS.   Tho her work differs from related sculptural concerns of Vincent Grenier or Richard Serra in her persistent emphasis on ritual & the unconscious.   came to know myth in its personalized form.   THE FILMS STAND ON THEIR OWN.

Returns to NY this Fall to show S8 sound film @ Collective's CIRCA CINEMA this Jan

Obscurity vs. speaking out.   underside enraged, outside an addressing, outside entirely.

Shakes off the disguise imposed on her by time & emerges in *WORD OF MOUTH.*   of woman as sexual object & as well about art making.   process vs. construction.   both form.

STILL concerned with density & light potential of the film's surface, still transfiguring.

A fan behind hanging appears counting was who, in sync, stand-in for more complicated version, SNAKE, dense damage, SADISM, peeing turtle/bound hand/ sacrifice woman.   funky homage to Vertov's "Enthusiasm".   tackles manhandled image.   move to able down-turned claw.   pornographic —

The power of reminding a human of their own prohibitions & inducing them to transgress.   lures . . . fleeing.   read she for starts.

Turns to reality with risk   passion   energy   SURVIVAL

Discarding myth, Mayer describes her next as documentary.

MINING POINT: thru playing touch, cells form, need not stop, implementing growth.   and with that the necessary optimism encouraged to stand against all possible invitation to fall.

Gary Doberman

LETTER, DECEMBER 24, 1979

[Editor's note: All portions of Doberman's submission were printed in unusually small type-face, making the piece difficult to read (in Doberman's view this choice was an implication on the part of the Cinemanews *editors that his essay was unimportant). Later, the body of the piece was reprinted in the 80.3/4/5 issue by editors Diane Kitchen and Gunvor Nelson, in a typeface so small that the essay cannot be read without a magnifying glass—their satire of what they felt had become the overly contentious and pretentious intellectual tone of the* Cinemanews.*

I have eliminated a short, earlier letter of February 26, 1978, to Peterson in which Doberman expresses his excitement about Millennium Film Journal.

At some point, Peterson apparently suggested that revisions were warranted in "New York Cut the Crap," which Doberman believed was "an attempt to CENSOR my article." I have included the piece in precisely the form that the Cinemanews *printed it, and that Doberman seems to have submitted it, with all misspellings (and/or creative spellings) and misremembered titles intact.]*

Victoria Z. Peterson
Millennium Film Journal
66 East 4th Street
New York, New York 10003

Dear Miss Vickie,
You really should learn to quit while you're behind, instead of continuing to make an even bigger ASS of yourself. Do you really expect me to believe any of the SELF SERVING CRAP contained in your letter? Come on, Miss Vickie, just because I live in New Mexico and can see a landscape without going to a museum like you New York folks, doesn't make me naive.

The moment I heard your neurotic rantings start coming at me over the phone, I smelled a Set-Up. Almost two years after the fact, Miss Vickie has pangs of con-science about her treatment of the writer of an article entitled "New York Cut the Crap" (NYCC). Suddenly Miss Vickie is out to right all wrongs. What does the Z stand for these days — Zorro? Frankly, you're a terrible LIAR. You really are a disap-pointment. I expected much more style, a little dramatic flare, perhaps. I fully expected a letter from you after I hung up on you twice (my God, you people are easy to read), but I expected a YARN, Miss Vickie, not a YAWN. This really is a dis-appointment; you New York people must be slipping: even the behavioral psychol-ogists in these parts provide more entertainment.

Nowhere in your letter do you mention that, unbeknownst to me, my acceptance of your apology on December 16th was Brakhage's stipulation for permission to pub-lish in the Millennium Film Journal the Brakhage/Creeley Buffalo transcript you were so frantically soliciting.

I hung up on you twice December 16th because I find Set-Ups rather tasteless. I knew immediately you were setting me up, but I wasn't sure of the specific reason. Stan filled me in later that night. I realize it is not within your limited Behavioral Repertoire to understand friendship among filmmakers. You use people, especially those with a public presence, like Molloy used his sucking stones. You see, Miss Vickie, I find the Millennium Film Journal to be a Whore/or. You are so used to either committing usury with another person or entering into collusion with them that you forget there is a certain resistance left in this country. By giving me the pleasure of hanging up on an editor of the Millennium Film Journal (excuse me if I don't use your pet MFJ acronym), I symbolically HUNG UP on the entire SELF SERVING INSTITUTIONALIZED ACADEMIC FILM SCENE IN NEW YORK now symbolized by the Millennium Film Journal.

Not so ironically these are the very issues discussed in my article. That's quite a coincidence! "CUT THE CRAP"! You never had any intention of printing my article. Maybe, if I had allowed you to thoroughly CENSOR most of it, you might have published it but then there would not have been anything left anyway — so what would be the point. After reading the first issue, I smelled a lack of guts. For this reason, I enclosed a cover letter with the article giving permission to print the article only in its entirety. Two years later, you are still in such fright of my article that nowhere in your rather pathetic letter do you even mention the article by name. You are displaying the fear of naming generally associated with Black Magic.

I had never heard of you or your journal. You called me up and solicited the article. Remember, "Sweetheart"? You said you wanted input from the Midwest. We have such wonderful Midwest Indians in New Mexico. (Later Howie solicited my films.) Your letter makes my article sound like all the other academic dribble that goes to make up the primary content of your magazine and that I was too arrogant to allow revisions like the others. God, have we, considering the beginnings of independent film, come to this? Revision is really a euphemism for an attempt to CENSOR my article — one of the first — that attacks New York, "Structuralism," the Institutionalized Film Scene, and by inference Miss Vickie, the other editors, Howard Guttenplan and the Millennium Film Journal, while also discussing specific aesthetic issues. Wouldn't logic suggest that since the article was an attack on New York institutions and in need of "revisions" that publishing it would make New York look good and us provos out in the Midwest look even worse?

This is obviously a closed journal dedicated to the advancement of the careers of those people involved with it — witness the article on Miss Bradshaw and Howard Guttenplan's films in the first issue. The people doing the real work in film are catching on to what the Millennium Film Journal is all about. Only those looking for jobs in INSTITUTIONS will continue to be published.

AND I haven't forgotten, Miss Vickie, your logic for allowing the editors to censor my article. In order to get into a film show, you fulfilled the show's demand to put a sound track on a previously defined silent work. This is how you defined "revisions." I believe that is when I started screaming about integrity. Wasn't that the word you had to look up in your dictionary after our phone conversation.

You really blew it, Miss Vickie. Boy, are Howie and the rest of the "little rascals" going to be angry with you. You see, Miss Vickie, your LYING has so thoroughly PISSED ME OFF that I am going to make this letter public and offer to make the article public. The folks out there can make up their own minds. Did Millennium refuse to publish the article because it was in need of editorial help OR was the refusal to publish a self serving decision? The article would have presented another view and stimulated discussion, but the Millennium Film Journal, as I have said all along, does not have the guts to print it.

Remember, Miss Vickie, that the Senior Citizens Home for Aging Structuralists in Roswell, New Mexico mentioned in the article is still holding a room open for you. Your reservation is long overdue.

So long Miss Vickie — it's been a pleasure.

Gary Doberman [hw]

Cc Richard Myers, Robert Creeley, Ed Schwartz, Don Yannacito, Tom Heady, Jim Healy, Carmen Vigil, Robert Jacobi, Jim Baumohl, Mark Hartman, J. Michael Stewart, John Luther, Sarah Woodward, Stan and Jane Brakhage, Willie Varela, Bob Maestas, Barry Archer, Bob Haller, Howard Guttenplan, Jonas Mekas, Hollis Frampton, Gerald O'Grady, Diana Barrie, David Shapiro, Alister Sanderson, Fred Worden, Sidney Goldfarb, Bruce Jenkins, CinemaNews/OPEN LETTER, Sally Dixon-Block, SWAMP/Southwest Media/OPENLETTER, S. Suzanne Vitiello, Larry Jordan, Barbara Lena, Claude Chamberlan, Dave Lee, Sonja Rae, Edith Kramer, OPEN LETTER: Film Department/Chicago Art Institute, Film Section/Carnegie Institute, Pittsburgh Film-maker's, Rosalind Krauss, Bill Wees, P. Adams Sitney, Gary Adkins.

I've sat on the article long enough. Even though I would write a very different article today, this one still holds water. Copies are now available upon request. Seasons Greetings!

NEW YORK CUT THE CRAP

I

"Suddenly a cinema of structure has emerged" (Sitney, 1969). These seven deadly words written in New York launched the structural "ism" into the filmic atmosphere. Seven words triggered an aesthetic that for a decade would serve as a back brace for the spineless. The absurdity of Sitney attributing the prejudicial term "structure" to a body of new films by Gehr, Frampton, Snow, Landow, Sharits and others in critical opposition to Brakhage, Anger, Deren, Menken, etc., as if the latter lacked essential filmic structure, should have served warning of more absurdities to come. Unfortunately, a certain lazy critical mentality which thrives on confusion found structural film a welcome habitat for their parasitic minds to play the most deadening aesthetic game in the short history of independent film. Until very recently they appeared well on their way to squelching any other form of creative making by labelling it a quaint Romantic holdover undeserving of attention from the Post-Modern critical mind.

I realize full well that filmmakers such as Hollis Frampton and Ernie Gehr who were labelled structuralist by the critics denied the label. Although Hollis Frampton stated, "I always somehow hope that I would never myself get into one of those situations where I had to have a bur under my saddle of that kind," the denials were not made in a forceful enough manner. Unquestionably, great and singular films were thrown together into the structuralist box and left to collect dust in the critical closet: among others, Brakhage's *My Mountain, Song 27, Riddle of Lumen* and *Text of Light*; Ken Jacob's *Tom, Tom the Piper's Son*; Ernie Gehr's *Serene Velocity*; and Hollis Frampton's *Critical Mass, Maxwell's Demon* and *Surface Tension*. Barry Gerson, Bill Brand and J. J .Murphy, to name three, used structural gamemanship to make a name for themselves; in the end structuralism used them up. In the "art"? schools, sons and daughters of middle level bureaucrats had a brand new fad to imitate. A new breed of student films started rolling out seemingly scripted from and with all the excitement of daddy's efficiency studies on the movement of office workers to and from coffee machines.

New York breeds provincialism like its sewer system breeds alligators. However, it is not necessary to use an elephant gun on gnats. The poor structuralist like the aging bureaucrat needs a place to reap his rewards. I have applied for a grant from the National Endowment for the Arts to build a Senior Citizens Home for Aging Structuralists in Roswell, New Mexico. Roswell is a hot, dusty crap hole on the edge of the Great Plains. The Great Plains is the perfect physical expression of the structuralist mentality: flat, monotonous, seemingly never ending. Just think of the structured dialectic of flat against monotonous to be argued in Roswell forever. In addition,

Roswell offers the predictability of structured meals at a wide selection of fast-food restaurants and cowboys strutting on the streets. At the home, a well-trained staff would offer structured play and social activities. Prune juice supplements would be served with the wrinkles removed. To make the prune juice supplements even more appealing, they will be shaped in some unitary form like a box which gives the immediate impression of insisting on "the similarity of its overall shape." (Naturally, we cannot guarantee the resultant crap will be uniformly structured.) And, of course, the residents would be free to give each other lectures of a structured measure.

To prevent critical messes such as structuralism in the future, I make the modest proposal that critics, historians, exhibitors and film academics submit to a system of *marking* which identifies their common caste. A bolex should be tatooed on their foreheads in the color of Victorian Pea Pink so that everytime they look in the mirror, they will be reminded where films originate. Certainly, film art does not originate from them. This caste system would hopefully inspire a little humility and responsibility among these untouchables. Anyone refusing to submit to this *marking* would be prohibited from speaking or writing publicly on film. Since I readily acknowledge there are a few good people on the other side of film making, there would be exceptions. But, you, ask who would make such momentous decision? I have spoken to Ernie Gehr and he has submitted his resume for the job.

II

Last April at Mills College in Oakland, Hollis Frampton expressed the desire to be a woman and a musician in his next life. I appreciate that statement because my ideal filmmaker has always been androgynous. Paralleling emerging feminine consciousness in the sixties, the predominantly male New York art world reacted by retreating into the machismo or Machino of intellectual cowboyism. The barbed mental wires of *Over*-rationalism replaced more complex relationships with the Muse. With all lines of communication to the Muse disconnected, New York "artists" turned to the computer, the bureaucrat's best friend. David Antin defines the Machino's fundamental axiom:

> . . . it is necessary to define the medium of action, the elements that are acted upon and the operations that are performed upon them to make a work or a body of works. The defining act has become a mechanism for generating work or, to use the somewhat more appropriate computer technology, a program.

It all sounds fine until you imagine films projected in this museless light. Mel Bochner states the trap of Over-rationalism with great eloquence:

> When one is trained within our culture, and one has been indoctrinated to the separation of thought and feeling, when one has, in effect, inherited Cartesian dualism, one wants to believe that a Conceptual art *[substitute Structural Film]* is going to be

the answer. An art which achieves wholeness by elimination of the visual and emotional factors. But an art which terminates ambiguity is not an art at all. Pure concept is not a penultimate.

Film is the art of cutting shadows out of light and projecting them into form through time: Continuity Veils is a good name for this art. Over-rationalism, a basic withholding of emotive force lines within a film, builds into that film a predictability that will not allow for its continued existence in the light of time. Over-rationalism has led to a body of work that die stillborn at the first projection and can only be sustained by what Samuel Beckett referred to as "incessant critical salivation."

Among others, the following films have only been sustained by "incessant critical salivation": Barry Gerson's *Groups III, IV and V* and probably all the rest of his output; Bill Brand's *Touch Tone Phone Poem* and probably the rest of his structured output; J. J. Murphy's entire work; Michael Snow's *La Region Centrale, Rameau's Nephew According to Diderot with Thanks to Andrew Young [“Rameau's Nephew” by Diderot (Thanx to Dennis Young) by Wilma Schoen], Standard Time* and possibly *Wavelength*; Joyce Wieland's *La Raison Avant La Passion, Sailboat* and *Dripping Water*; Morgan Fischer's complete works with the possible exception of *Production Stills*; Gary Bedyler's *Hand-Held Day, Venice Pier Film*, the rest of his "sculptural films" excluding perhaps *L.A. Freeway [Pasadena Freeway Stills]* which just might have enough metaphorical wit and be enough of a conjuring act to survive. I dislike even mentioning Gehr's *Wait, Still* and *Transparency* because I find *Serene Velocity* to be one of the greatest masterpieces in the history of film. With respect for the assured greatness of Peter Kubelka's other films I will, with reluctance, include *Pause* and, possibly, *Arnulf Rainer*.

Sitney from the critical angle launched us into this mess but other factors sustained the confusion. Antin's fundamental axiom was the perfect seducer of filmmakers. The art being so young, and yet so much having been done, what easier way to make your name in lights than by making filmic tautologies. And why not. There was ample evidence that "artists" in other fields were falling over each other to develop the proper computer "program," that punch tape ticket into the pages of Artforum. New York "artists" of the seventies were not content that Jasper Johns should have the only Soho mansion. David Antin's fundamental axiom permeated the film world at the point defined by Stan Brakhage at Millenlium:

> There was a drive emerging in totally different ways and from different people, to put strongly, in the first place, primary place, as content the film's being, it's coming into existence and being existing as the major subject matter.

Set theory, chance operations and mathematical scripts are favorite construction tools of structuralist filmmakers. Using these tools to build a film is not inherently wrong: *Serene Velocity*! Making films that radiate out along the lines of Brakhage's definition is also not inherently wrong. The danger is always a too easy academicism, a film keyed on one idea alone. A film emerging from this definition, yet unable to spring metaphorical echoes beyond this definition dies from tautological narcissism; the failure to reach beyond its own existence. To give the label of structuralist to any fine film is to degrade it.

By Brakhage's definition of structural thrust and gamesmanship Ken Jacob's *Tom, Tom The Piper's Son* is the absolute structural film: a film made out of another film. To the academic mind, the content of the film is the artifice's "coming into existence" from the rephotography of the original material. The film is seen unmetaphorically as an autopsy of the cinematic experience. This film could so easily have reached the screen in a trite schematic package. In fact, rephotography has littered the screen in many slight variations by other filmmakers. *Tom, Tom The Piper's Son* is saved because Ken Jacobs acted like an artist for once. This film is not a conventional structuralist autopsy stinking of formaldehyde. *Tom, Tom The Piper's Son* under Jacob's cinematic knife opens to reveal a granular physiology which survives the autopsy transformed into a hypnagogic symphonic shadow play — "a seeing with one's own eyes" — with a dual temporal sense: the great rhythms of the rephotography and a referential temporality to the original material. Film creating its own internal time sense is a dominant clique both as "continuous present" and as tautological reference, usually on the sound track. (All Morgan Fischer's [Fisher's] work is an example of the latter.) The tautological references to the original material reach metaphor because they move within the pulsating imagery and rhythmic insistencies of the dancing rephotography. Jacob's diverse creative approaches to the rephotography make multiple memory skeins out of the same particulars of the original material which trigger, in addition, compositional and story superimpositions from the viewer's personal remembrance of that particular passage. Thus, the rephotography strikes memory chords of the original film which establishes a metaphor for the mind moving in memory thought or thinking analogous to musically composing. *Tom, Tom The Piper's Son* and the great Brakhage films are two moieties of the same tribe. Watching Jacob's film or Brakhage's, any film definitionally structuralist such as *Wavelength* comes back re-membered as an academic foreigner to great cinematic rituals. The only predictability in Jacob's film is the constant anticipation of more delights to come.

Structuralism is the perfect academic making, the perfectly tailored Academic Hollywood. The collusion is perfect and quite clear: the filmmaker just needs one self-evident idea to dissect the filmic body; nevermind if the patient dies from loss of blood after his life is cut out. This Three Stooges mentality for knocking out a film gives Herr Professor a film so easy even he can write about it, thereby ensuring his tenure and the filmmaker's name hallowed in print. Hollis Frampton said the European brand of intellectual structuralism ". . . rescued more failing and undistinguished careers in American universities than almost anything else since the theory of relativity." Among film professors structuralism in the American independent film has saved more careers than anything since the French New Wave. I have seen film professors who were unable to deal in any meaningful dialog with such films as *Meshes of the Afternoon* or *Anticipation of the Night* find their tongues reborn upon viewing the structural films of Snow, Wieland, Gerson, et al.

Most filmmakers have a tendency to think of lab technicians as mere appendages to laboratory machinery. It is true most lab people have their toes stuck in literal curves. There are, however, a few lab technicians who make brilliant theoretical comments or pose great filmic riddles shrouded in "lab lingo." Since these people work with film from the inside, who better should know about film "coming into existence." The lab people are the only meaningful structuralists and they will have none of it. I have discussed structuralism with lab people straight out and with the aesthetics veiled in "lab lingo" and their insights are more profound than the orthodox structuralist filmmakers and critics. They find structuralism so self-evident as to be silly nonsense. The film world is much too snobbish to listen to some blue-collar worker who learned his trade in the army and never went to college. Consequently, on the subject of the film's ontological existence, we take the word of academics, who avoid like the plague physical contact with film itself, over men and women who work with the physiology of film day after day for years.

III

The word fame is from the Greek, fama, which means rumor. Rumors of artistic greatness are often exaggerated but probably less so than the rumors of an acknowledged artist's demise. The general art public is much like a circus audience watching the tightrope walker: applauding his agility but secretly wishing for a false step. The vultures should know that the dry periods are, more often than not, preludes to the masterpieces. The creative process is an obsession with the bemusing; the mysteries of artistic conjuring cannot be read out like an athlete's statistics.

There is an unspoken taboo among "established" filmmakers which prohibits the public criticism of another "established" filmmaker's work. The slightest criticism of the work will sometimes end or temporarily suspend a long standing friendship. The contemporary critical tradition established for films will determine to limits beyond imagining the light in which posterity will envisage them. Conceptual art which started with the self-proclaimed "noble" commitment to by-pass the art commodities market quickly degenerated into Monumental Nick-Nacks for an Amarillo ranch and an Italian count. Structuralism has gone far beyond disagreement over a few films by makers otherwise respected. A desperate need existed to confront the one-sided structuralist polemic and make the situation, at the very least, a dialectic. For various reasons, such as the desire to deny the existence of their past laudatory pronouncements on structuralism, certain members of the private club of "established" film people apparently wanted to promote a general amnesia on the subject. The high priests of structuralism, at the same time, stood guard to protect their idol from any form of questioning.

Enter Stan Brakhage at Millenlium with the necessary verbal skill to debate the high priests and jog those with amnesia. Debating art in the heat of the public moment is a difficult task for anyone. I take this opportunity to go on record supporting Stan Brakhage's courage at Millenlium in bearing witness to the situation. Brakhage's confrontation with the structuralist beast in its New York lair unfortunately involved tangling with old friends. The guts to speak out on controversial issues has been seriously lacking in most quarters. With all the furious attack on Brakhage since his Millenlium appearance, I get this sickening smell that Brakhage broke the rules of a very exclusive club. Considering Stan and Jonas shared the struggle for the recognition of a film art, Jonas's attack in the Soho Weekly News on Brakhage's life is both silly and sad. It fell on Brakhage to speak-up because of the inaction or lack of debating skills on the part of others. Like so many times in the past, unpleasant historical obligations fall on Brakhage through the abdication of others.

IV

Again, although referring to painting, Mel Bochner pinpoints the problem with structural gamesmanship:

> There is a necessary skepticism lacking. The kind of thinking being done is too deductive. It's art problem solving. But where do "problems" come from? They don't come from art magazines. . . . Art is not illustrating ideas, particularly received ideas. Art has to do with the intent of the work — how it moves out, how it structures itself from a central preoccupation. A central preoccupation can't really be a formal problem, such as how you deal with the edge of the canvas.

Michael Snow's films (like certain painters) suffer from a too easy belief in analytical geometry; easily recognizable detachable structural parts with an overall geometrical composition: *Standard Time, Wavelength,* and *Rameau's Nephew According to Diderot with Thanks to Andrew Young.* The end product is an easily recognizable consistent style for the critics who desire each filmmaker to maintain a rigid style of making throughout his career. This packaging has caused critical visual senile dementia (Senile is defined as having advanced in reduction by erosion to a featureless plain that stands everywhere at base level.) and the subsequent refusal to seek out the imaginative workings of each individual film. Remember the hostile reaction from some quarters to Brakhage making *The Pittsburgh Trilogy*. The critical mind is a collection of a limited number of shoe boxes dependent on the stylistic vogue of the day. Great grief will befall any artist whose films resist the critical closet. Barry Gerson has the best stylistic shell game running. Gerson's predictability of simplistic camera movements is trite enough to be immediately recognized by the critics as style. Joyce Wieland's *Dripping Water* which Jonas Mekas equated with saintliness is only imaginable as a very shabby "reading" of Buddhism.

Brakhage, in what I consider the strongest passages of *Sincerity, Reel 1*, used the grid as a metaphor for restricting vision. This metaphorical seeing has more seeds germinating in it than the grid as the symbol of psychological enclosure. In *La Region Centrale*, Michael Snow employed a machine in an attempt to break beyond the compositional grid and basic geometric forms. At this point in his filmmaking the grid and the resultant geometric forms became equivalent to the internal boundary problem painters such as Pollock, Rothko, Kline, etc., tried to force their way out of by enlarging their canvases. Snow, I imagine, experienced correctly exposed film and geometric composition as an internal limitation equivalent to static matter. Snow sought out a machine which he felt would generate the necessary filmic critical mass to shatter the composition into luminosity. Again, I imagine Snow at this point was unconsciously involved with the luminosity of Brakhage's films. Snow desperately wanted to achieve the luminosity but still retain what he considered systematic objective generation of the film. His object would be created with the maker out of composition, quite literally hiding out of sight behind the inorganic (rocks).

It's a brilliant strategy on paper, a very seductive gambit. Snow's strategy leads to an early checkmate through the misunderstanding of a fundamental creative paradox. Ezra Pound acknowledged the paradox early on in *The Cantos* by beginning the third canto with "I sat on the Dogana's steps/For the gondolas cost too much that year." I believe Frampton understood the paradox when he wrote of the *Hapax Legomena* series: "Such 'double-vision' — that is, the superimposition of a personal myth of the history of one's art upon a factual account of one's own persona — certainly does not originate with me." Any maker's domicile with reference to his work is situated in the paradoxical coordinates of always remaining equally in and out of the work. The work arises through the unique particulars of person to a state of objecthood leaving the maker outside upon completion as visiance to his work. Every cell in the maker's body is replaced every seven years until his death. The film cells remain constant so that given proper preservation through others' attentiveness the film object survives the maker to once again unravel its veiled continuity.

All films are equally filmic objects. Regardless of their divergent working methods, Ernie Gehr is as much in evidence both in and out of *Serene Velocity* as Brakhage is domiciled with respect to this paradox in *Star Garden*, for example. The withdrawal of the maker to a position "lonely as god, parring his fingernails" (Hugh Kenner) to create an emotionless object for the apperception of the audience is impossible. There is an acronym of the computer specialists worth keeping in mind: GIGO (garbage in, garbage out). Thus, they acknowledge the computer as a mere extension, for purposes of quick calculation, of the intelligence of the man using it. Structuralists mistake the employment of a machine or modified set theory as a methodology for being a machinist, one who makes objects. In this way object is confused with being "free from personal feeling or prejudices" — a mistaken objective stance.

The withdrawal of emotive force is impossible. The machines that assemble television sets are not free from human "personal feelings or prejudices"; likewise the machinery used to prefabricate instant slum housing. Machinery constructs objects with no priority to the claim of objectivity. Scientific objectivity is, in fact, no more than a group of people with similar subjective world views, prejudicial stances, one uping everyone else by labeling their viewpoint "objective" and agreeing to temporarily play by common rules. The Jewish Golem legend nails downs generally and specifically the false steps of Snow's machino. A rabbi in the Prague ghetto is bored with the everyday menial chores around the temple so he uses somesuch as his Kabalistic knowledge and creates a figure constructed in the form of a human being and endows it with life to do "the chores." The Golem ends up running amuck much like Cesare, the somnambulist, in *The Cabinent of Dr. Caligari*. The Golem legend forewarns of the dangers of a too easy belief in machine technology.

Snow's Golem machine is programmed to make camera movements the human body is incapable of making. It's dandy on paper, but in actuality the imagery and the temporal intelligence generated by the machine are far inferior to Brakhage's luminosity of image and body generated camera movements and the small articulations shifting along the edges of the frame.

Perhaps because Sitney knows Brakhage personally and is also under Harold Bloom's prejudices, he would think to himself when watching Brakhage films, "Stan is moving the camera this way which means he's sad or happy or expressing himself or whatever." These projections led to the chapter in *Visionary Film* on the lyric film and this definition of it:

> The lyrical film postulates the film-maker behind the camera as the first-person protagonist of the film. The images of the film are what he sees, filmed in such as way that we never forget his presence and we know how he is reacting to his vision.

Watching a Brakhage film, I see into and through the film on the screen not into Brakhage's personality. There is no correlation between the film and the maker's personality. Films arise from person which is a much deeper and nebulous quality than the superficial sense of personality. Personality is never a sufficient center. The opposition of the lyric film against the structural film for reasons of critical definition is another dead end. Films do not express personality along the lines of the "this is self-expression" clique. Great film art realizes person through a filmic object without the maker necessarily having reached consciousness of his person in daily thought or in creating the film. Likewise great film will reveal only fleeting glimpses of the maker's person. Complexity of consciousness resides in the film on the screen. The maker vanishes; the film object remains not as a track of the maker's reactions but as a measure of its own nervous system reacting to being pierced with light.

The insistency of the solidity of the cinematic illusion in Gary Bedyler's *Venice Pier Film* or Snow's *Wavelength* does not make them ("incessant critical salivation" not withstanding) any more objectlike or objective filmic objects than the play of light at the window in, say, Brakhage's *Star Garden*. Brakhage's play of light at the window has the power of equal gravitational mass. Refractive light is as much cinematic "sculpture" as ex-sculpture Bedyler's emphasis on mass. Filmmakers are conjurors of illusions. The absolutely deadly mistake of confusing the illusion with reality is a straight line into the "Jaws" of Hollywood.

V

Even with a preplanned mathematic shooting script, Ernie Gehr said he waited two years to find the right place to realize the film. He thought he could complete the shooting in a few hours: he remained in the corridor from early evening until sunrise. Because Gehr is an artist even with a script, he was alert to the light at every moment of filming; the incredible blue sunrise pattern is a result of this attentiveness. The problem with a script of any form is the attempt to exactly match the environment with the script, thereby losing that which actually charges the environment. *Serene Velocity* which is the result of Gehr's person and his attentiveness is a masterpiece of a perfect emerald shattering. It vibrates conclave and convex alternating pulses of the mind/body dualism transcended. It is not a simple unitary object but rather exists in the paradox of both being unitary and a pixilated collage. It is not just a corridor insisting on its "similarity of overall shape" but a corridor that would have aroused Franz Kafka's interest.

At one point, Brakhage's masterpiece *Text of Light* got lassooed by the critical rope into the structural corral. Instead of seeing the great light metaphors, the critics "read" the form as unitary, developing along one axis with a seeming lack of representational content. They were oblivious to the prismatic rock carvings of totemic presence, an Easter Island sculptural garden of light, to name just one miracle of metaphor. *Text of Light* is, as Michael McClure felt upon his first viewing, "one animal" but this "one animal" radiates one of the most complex metaphorical skins and transformational physiology of any animal in the filmic wilds.

$\cdots$

Intermission: structuralism does lead to some amusing contradictions. A Hollywood movie becomes a structural film from its machinelike withdrawal of person and lack of photographic reaction to visual phenomena. The Hollywood production apparatus is a machine shop programmed to produce similar objects. Hollywood is a very successful celluloid experiment in manufacturing deadening visual constructs. Millenlium, S.F. Cinematheque and Anthology Film Archives do not screen experimental films; the local movie theatre serves that function.

· · ·

There is one further assertion from Sitney to discuss:

> He [Brakhage] has never addressed himself to a definition of the essence of his medium — although tautological references to the materials occur in most of his mature work.

I find this a shabby envisaging of Brakhage and of film art in general. Every great film by insistency on its own agency adds metaphorical knowledge of the medium among its other relevations. Tautological definition does not need to wear a sub-title. *The Riddle of Lumen* through exposing itself to light gave us new definitions for patterning light on the screen. The collision of images in *The Riddle of Lumen* gives that film the energy for continued existence through time. Achieving lasting value through the light of time defines the essential perimeters of the cinematic medium. In a back-handed way, Sitney in his article "Autobiography in Avant-Garde Film" confuses as much as he changes the statement above: " . . . and although he may sometimes deny it, considerations of the ontology of cinema consistently take precedence over the observation of phenomena in his work." The latter part of this statement is an absurdity. A critical theory of film unable to discuss the inseparable interwoven pattern of ontology, the bones of the matter, and the metaphorically radiating skin is not worth its name. *Riddle of Lumen* was also at one point roped into the structural corral because of the assumption there was only one answer to the Riddle. What worthwhile riddle ever had only one answer? *The Riddle of Lumen* we call cinema remains open.

Film art is not a question of technique, art problem solving, proficiency at manipulatory gamesmanship, or a question of lyrical expression teeming with emotion in critical opposition to the apperception of emotionless filmic objects. The film on the screen gains the urgency of its own agency as it goes about its necessary activity of either delighting, amusing or bemusing us or being an awefull experience of all three. Filmic agency is imparted by a person regardless of tools out of their unique set of particulars. Art is a healing experience of the mind/body schism through the integration of thought and emotion impregnated into matter. This integration is all that finally does matter.

Every great film is a new and singular beast with its own nervous system and our continued blessing.

Notes

Anyone wishing to further discuss the issue can reach me at:

1125 Lafayette, N.E.
Albuquerque, New Mexico 87106
505/266–0863

The David Antin quote: Occident, Spring 1974 p. 37.
The Mel Bochner quotes: Artforum, June 1974.
The Stan Brakhage quote: Soho Weekly News, November 24, 1977.
The P. Adams Sitney quotes:
  definition of lyrical film, *Visionary Film*, p. 180.
  "essence of medium," *Visionary Film*, p. 258–9.
  "Suddenly a cinema of structure has emerged," Film Culture, No. 47,
    Summer 1969.
The Hollis Frampton quotes: Cinemanews, November/December, 1977.
The Samuel Beckett quote is mentioned by Frampton in Cinemanews.

Photograph by Peter Hutton.

—

FROM *CINEMANEWS*, 80.1/2

Warren Sonbert

FILM SYNTAX (CONTINUED)

The following is the second part of a talk presented by Warren Sonbert at the San Francisco Art Institute in December 1979. It will be published along with 10 other lectures in the forthcoming issue of HILLS magazine (220pp/$5: 36 Clyde, San Francisco), and is published in the Cinemanews by their courtesy.

In any case there is no such thing as a correct shot — breaking rules has proved effective; the grammar exists to be undermined. So film has evolved its special language. On the lens the filmmaker has a series of f-stops which either let in or shut out light. These are like organ stops or pedals that provide tone and coloration. And there is no correct reading that one gets with a light meter — there is only the standard mean and it is up to the filmmaker to decide what will be appropriate. Of course, all this is dependent on development, what one's lab will do to it. You never know how it's going to look until it comes back from the lab. But there is a certain amount of insurance you can provide (albeit of the fairly expensive kind), which is to overshoot, or make a series of takes where each time you film the same object you vary the exposure, one or two stops up or down. And one can extend this even further by also varying still shots with moving shots, going left to right and right to left, tilting up or down and so on: then, while editing you decide what you'll need.

A few words about the length of images. One of the banes of TV is that people can superficially "read" the content of images fairly quickly; the information can fly by pretty rapidly so that the viewer is able to get the selling point on immediate contact. Slow films (Ozu) drive people up the wall. Now, given a certain standard mean of what is long and what is short, one can modulate series of shots of varying length that, as a group, might all be deemed fast. But there is a world of possibilities between shots that last as long as 20 seconds, those as short as 1/4 of a second, and all the gradations between. People are a lot more sophisticated than 50 years ago as far as what they can take in when an image goes by fairly rapidly (the figurative characters within the frame and their possible interactions both in and out of the frame; the taking into account of the off-screen space; their reactions, gestures, expressions, clothes, make-up, class, sensitivity; what are the byplays between characters and filmmaker: are they strangers, friends; are they aware they are being filmed or taken by surprise; is it day or night, city or country; what is the active focal length: close up, midshot, wide-angle; is the camera moving, which way; is the object in motion; what is the exposure like, or camera angle; which element takes precedence, both in reading a shot and making the leap to the next image; how do we both tie them together or be made aware of their differences). Is the point similarity or variety? And one can latch onto a key or grid, but that may dissolve, be upset.

Some people are disturbed by the brevity of some of my images — particularly those that one might label "beautiful" or "ecstatic." They are over before one has a chance to barely luxuriate in them, they are taken away before one can nestle and coo and cuddle in the velveteen sheen of it all, so that feelings of deprivation, expectations dissolved, even sado-masochism arise. Very often a cut occurs before an action that is in process when we first glimpse the image is completed. This becomes both metaphor of frustration, hopes dashed, and yet of serenity if you like — that perhaps all of this activity has been going on, is going on, will be going on, and even all at the same time. That we are privileged viewers of many sectors of humanity, none taking particular precedence over the other.

I believe that the nature of film lends itself to density: one can't pack in too much, albeit with rests, breathing spaces. It isn't necessary to have the totality of resonances immediately graspable, one should be able to return. The works I've made have met with two seemingly contradictory reactions: either people regard them as very enjoyable, light, airy, pleasurable, everything being very giddy and beautiful; while others regard them as dark, sinister, hopeless, claustrophobic, negative, minor key (And I indeed regard the works in a Mozartian key scheme: *Carriage Trade* being in E-flat Major, broad, epic, leisurely, maestoso; *Rude Awakening* in D minor, brooding, cynical, fatalistic, dancing on the precipice; *Divided Loyalties* in C Major, agile, dynamic, spry, with a hint of turbulence ((and even this scheme of keys can be seen as a classical instrumental concerto: first movement setting the scene and the longest in time and investigation; the second movement a dark melancholy adagio; the third a breezy rondo to clear if not quite dispel the heavy air, gracious, with a let's-get-on-with-life feeling, a caper and a capper to what has gone before.)))

So again, the ambition might be seen as an attempt to hold finely balanced series of tensions in which one can read images a variety of ways, sometimes in contradictory stances so that there are many possibilities of interaction. Not that any interpretation will do, or that it doesn't really matter what particular order presents itself — the works are definitely about specifics, each image a statement in series of axioms and postulates to produce an argument of a flexible non-didactic kind. A plus B will produce a feeling of C, whether it is anxiety, or pleasure, or commentary, or awareness, or whatever. Usually works are mirrors of what is contained already in the viewer, and it is the role of the creator to "place" or qualify these reactions. Lead the viewer down one road only to diverge onto another, upset inbred expectations at the same time as exploiting those very cliches.

Let's take a shot analysis of some images you've just seen — in *Divided Loyalties*: after a series of very short images, all bursting with motion and activity, the height of frenzy, so that the eye is both very involved, glued to the screen, and at the same time lingering to focus on something concrete and steady (these have almost all been nature materials and the camera or objects are in a variety of motions), the climax of which is a Coney Island Tilt-A-Whirl shot, a burst of revolving motion — metaphors of going in circles, going nowhere, aborted energy conflicting with spasms of life forces in play — the eye is highly geared now — This is followed by the first still image in some time, and the first figurative image as well, — the viewer is held now, forced and even anxious to have an anchor — so you show them something both appealing and shocking: specifically, a line-up of very handsome homosexual bodies all with shirts off, having a good time, gingerly moving even in the same right to left motion as the Tilt-A-Whirl shot; so that the shock is both on a narrative and visceral level.

This is followed by a moving shot (as opposed to the still shot of albeit moving bodies) of a cemetery with the gravestones carrying over the same horizontal blocks as those preening bodies. So we get an overly obvious cliched reaction of dust unto dust, all is vanity, almost of a biblical oppression, and lest anyone think this is rabidly anti-gay (which it is), this is followed by an affluent heterosexual couple at a luxurious breakfast table, very uncommunicative, obviously at loggerheads, fed up with each other and themselves, a *Citizen Kane* quote, the pettiness of their supposed just-completed argument qualified by the gravestones image (why squabble when death is just around the corner); this specific duo contrasts with the anonymous group of gay guys, as well as the fact that they are indoors in a domestic setting, as opposed to a public outdoor gathering-hole. So both the straights and gays come into criticism and are linked to death and dissolution; though one would never cut from one to the other, it is clear enough they are linked by the more neutral yet charged image of the cemetery.

The couple at table is followed by an image (movement left to right) of a series of train pans of rather bleak apartment building exteriors (though bathed in glorious late-afternoon sun), evoking the feeling of well-what-is-going-on-behind-these-windows — perhaps similar scenes of alienation and estrangement (and in contrary motion to the movement strand in between the previous figurative images).

This is capped by a very short figurative image of a bocci ball game in Paris, the only part that we see is the player hitting the target, brief enough only to communicate that fact, no intro or aftereffect. The camera angle, by the way, moves down continually throughout this series: the group of guys is shot from a second storey window; the couple at table, at eye level, intimately, staged (though the characters are told not to be aware of the camera); and, finally, the ball player is shot with the camera looking up. Also, the emphasis of figures moves from group to couple to individual. All of this keyed for both contrast and continuance. The brevity of the player has a playfulness and acts as punctuation almost like a period.

This is followed by an almost equally brief shot of two sailboats passing each other — upside down, which conveys the obvious tinge of all's-not-quite-right, an upsetting of the normal visual stance, yet echoing the couple at table because of the two-figure emphasis (yet a contrast as well, because this set is only objects), but emphasizing the visual pun of "two ships passing in the night," unaware perhaps of the needs, desires, frustrations of one another. One fairly narrative shot, one that is specifically staged like the couple at table, can carry endlessly a narrative guideline in which to judge many of the images around it. And there is a narrative element to these works, glimpses it is true, but on an equal footing with the documentary/diaristic images.

Another set: A young man is seen in close-up, though unaware of the camera's presence, sitting cross-legged in yoga position, very happy, dumb stoned smile, watching something.

Direct cut to his field of vision, which is a band of rock performers. We go from single to group, from male to female (since the act is predominantly made up of women). And, again, the man is shot straight on, whereas the women are shot from the right. They are out there to please, and apparently they are doing so, judging from the all-embracing approval given them by the onlooker. Now, as a visual icon, a viewer carries with it a proxy of the viewing audience — looking at itself as in a mirror, although how much this resonates depends on the actual self-reflective qualities of the cinema viewer.

From the group of women performers we cut back to the solitary young man, eyes now closed in what seems to be ecstatic reveries, underlining a particularly non-reflective state, perhaps an avoidance of reality as his stoned demeanor might indicate.

Then a cut to a very castles-in-Spain image, specifically, a sailboat on a very smooth, reflective lake, with a tower-castle on the right very much in balance with the sailboat on the left, though the figures are contrasted, one (illegible line) closed, to this castles-in-the-sky image, we underline the element of wish-fulfillment; this is the removed from reality image the young man would seemingly like to conjure up, which is, of course, the primary base emotion of the typical cinema audience trying to step outside reality, to have dreams bestowed on them.

So how can we provoke guilt, recrimination for this shirking of responsibility. The lake-castle-sailboat image is followed by a shot of another young man, standing as opposed to sitting, who is bleeding profusely from the head, dazed, not by drugs but from some dire car accident (as will be confirmed later on by a doctor running to attend him). So perhaps that removed from reality image is present in both their consciousnesses, but from very different circumstances. This not only qualifies the young man's fleeing from reality, stuffing himself on pleasure, but it also qualifies and upsets the cinema audience's demand for a good time from movies; there is somehow a link, a chain, by the very act of editing, of putting shots/images next to one another, that says our pleasure is somehow at the expense of another's suffering. Of course, the reaction on the audience's side is dependent on a lot of self-cognizance and the ability to digest and assimilate fairly rapid images, to contain and place them, standing on the outside as it were.

This is emphasized by the next image after the dazed, bleeding man, — which is a close-up of a Cezanne painting being cleaned. The image of art naturally refers back to the artist-filmmaker, saying that art is both objective and merciless, the film-maker being both callous and opportunistic, sharing in the guilt, taking advantage just as much as the audience of other people's misfortune to build his argument. There is a coolness, an objectivity that seems almost cruel and ruthless, to follow this image of human suffering by an image of, very specifically, art going about its own business as oblivious as the drugged young man and the audience wanting to be entertained. Engaged in an activity of casual everyday banality, though the response might be different if one recognized that this work is not being painted, only cleaned, the dirt being stripped away. The metaphor would then allude (without lessening the guilt shared among the drugged young man, the cinema audience, and the artsy filmmaker) to the young man's closed eyes, but would focus on the process of reopening, of lifting the veils of obscurance. Here again we can have our cake and eat it . . . Yes the artist is cool and detached, but the reason is to shake up and disturb. So the argument is not so much an original work of art being composed, but the fact that art is being revealed, in the causal link of images. This is followed by a shot of a photographer (again, a stand-in for the filmmaker) in a crowd, New York Easter Sunday, with about 40 different still cameras around his neck, desperately turning around and around looking for something to film, shoot, contain within the lying objectivity of still photography in which just an instant is recorded. This image is a criticism of a whole art form, the fact that nothing has a valid reality outside of the whole chain of images, which is what cinema is; so this image of non-artist (funny enough in itself) becomes just another underlining of the responsibility of the artist and viewer.

Question and Answer period following talk:

Sonbert: Criticisms, or questions?

Barrett Watten: One of the things you left out about Eisenstein, is the social context in which the artist operates. To really simplify matters: Eisenstein was addressing a largely non-discriminate and mainly illiterate mass of people, and so the obviousness of his use of film as an educational medium has to be taken into account. And so if he's using a fairly stock set of images to demonstrate a political point, that's operating across a much bigger gap than the kind of film you're proposing, which, in fact, works off an incredible sophistication and work of the film industry over the last 50 years. Your entire vocabulary presupposes a real intimacy with what American Hollywood film and personal film has been. And that leaves the question of what language is and the assignation of values within the film as exterior to the film, in a way.

One thing that just came up was the woman cleaning the Cezanne, okay? And then there's a great take on what art was, etcetera. Now it wasn't clear to me what she was doing, although I did get the sense of coldness, and the art industry, and what she looked like, and what this thing was, and how it was mounted and so forth. Now there's an articulation from your viewpoint that goes even farther than what I can see in the frame. It has to do with reading into the act of making this work of art that is correlated with a tremendous amount of other art. And that's exactly what Eisenstein didn't have available to him. What he did have, basically, was cubism, a kind of simultaneity which he was then extending into a medium which he was more or less creating as he went along.

Sonbert: In the same time that Eisenstein was making those propagandistic narrative films, Vertov was making a whole other body of work, also directing himself to the masses, also under the control of the Soviet party policy. And he opened up an incredible amount of poetry and ambiguity in his images. If you compare "Man with a Movie Camera" to any of Eisenstein's films of the 20s, it's much broader, looser, air is constantly being let in to his images. And they're not shoving you into thinking one way or another. I think Eisenstein suffered because he was dealing in narrative, with characters, how to present them as being good or bad. And Vertov was more in a documentary frame, so that automatically everyone was given a certain stature, which Eisenstein could not do, because he was anchored to narrative.

Watten: I don't think you can just throw out Eisenstein without considering whether he was completely in control of the irony that his reduction of the signification of film, — in other words, does he know what he is doing? Does he show us what there is to see? And the condition of history that Eisenstein was dealing with was one that was inescapable, while Vertov's position was one of ambiguity and distance, and may not be the way one might want to look at a period like that.

((Eisenstein's literalism is highly ironic. Like that figure of the little kid on the throne in the Winter Palace seems to me like the figure of or the ability of the film-maker to do whatever he wants, which is an incredibly libidinal image, you've got this sexuality which just cannot be gotten away from. (And the image of the 14 year old with the shaved head sitting on the Emperor's chair. That's like Eisenstein's ability to do something to you.) As an artist he was completely aware of what his activity was. It was working within a State structure. You're not talking about extrinsic and intrinsic ideas when you're talking about Eisenstein and Vertov.))

Sonbert: Eisenstein almost invariably had the camera down, tilted up, full face, full in the frame, with very diffuse backgrounds. They all seem to melt away. Whereas Vertov placed his people within specific contexts; you get an idea of environment, of spaciousness in his very images that you don't get in Eisenstein's, which are much more controlled, but more claustrophobic, to me. I'm not making Eisenstein out to be, like, a total non-talent.

Watten: Eisenstein identified with power, and so his irony is of a different order than that of somebody who's bucking power.

Sonbert: Okay, it's great that he identified with power, but I don't have to identify with him because of that.

Ron Silliman: I kept getting the impression from your talk about your work of an assumption of a standard of literacy. Like, this shot will create these responses. And I find that when I see your work I go through a process of needing to identify the image before I can read it. And that varies. If I recognize Anne Waldman in the back seat of a car, then I have to recognize her before I can then proceed to look at it. If it's just a woman in the backseat of a car I can begin to read that image a lot quicker. I'm not always sure at what level I'm immediately expected on your part, for example, to recognize Anne Waldman, recognize Nicky and Jerry [Nathaniel Dorsky and Jerome Hiler] (who I assume a larger number of people might not recognize), and there was one scene where people were hitting one another with sacks, where one of the people was somebody I knew from my *job*, who I assume *you* might not even recognize. So how does that impact with what the shot is going to be? You're assuming a fairly high and consistent standard of literacy, which is a little like defining your audience in advance.

Sonbert: No, I don't feel that. If you get the added embellishments, the overlays, that's fine, they can add to it, maybe change inflections. But usually it's pretty low base level standard of what information one can grasp. It's not necessary to recognize that's Anne Waldman, flanked by Douglas Dunn and Larry Fagin, as it turns out. It's enough that three people, grumpy, hung-over from the night before, not really talking to one another, are in the back seat.

Unidentified: Watching your film and hearing you talk about it, I think there are like two different processes maybe dealing with the two hemispheres of the brain. When you're watching the film you're only dealing with the sensual qualities of the film. You don't really have the time to think about the narrative in the way that you talked about it. It seems like the narrative is very important to you because you spent a lot of time talking about it, rather than color or form. But is it humanly possible for us to deal with the narrative and the sensual qualities at the same time?

Sonbert: There are certain things you feel, react to, register right off. Even here today, there was a huge amount of audience response, laughter, to an image which generally has not gotten that much reaction. Specifically, the man holding his trophy, which somehow falls out of his hands. This is contained within a very specific series of shots. Which is that a woman comes out of what looks like a theater, she's taking bows. So we get the feeling of applause, fame, acknowledgement, celebrity. This followed by a shot of this bridge being raised. A sort of physical manifestation of bestowing honor. Then we see a shot of a rainbow. Again, the visual pun: the pot of gold at the end of the silver lining of the rainbow, which we've just seen, which drops away.

Now, I don't know if people got all these lines, but I think they had a sort of intuition. I'm not forcing, I would never show, Kubelka has this policy when he makes films of always showing them twice. I'm not that didactic. If you want to come back to it again, that's fine. And I think that when you do, more things open up, more connections, lines, reactions. But hopefully, the works can function on many levels. And sometimes people just feel this thrill about going along, being shoved along every moment. That's basic one level. Then maybe later they can come back and have more happen for them.

Unidentified: The question that I have is: does what you call the intuitive response to the narrative come from the information within the frame or the relationship between frames?

Sonbert: It's both.

Unidentified: My feeling is that, in seeing it, it's more the information within the frame than the relationship, right now, on the first viewing.

Melissa Riley: Can you talk about how you compose, when you go out with your camera?

Sonbert: Right . . .

Lyn Hejinian: That leads back to the question of literacy, too. In other words, are you reading, in the editing room? Do you have an initial, naive possibility? Or do you go out and look for someone to drop a trophy?

Sonbert: There are a few images where I went out, almost after it was set, because I felt I needed more dark, turbulent, sinister images. Specifically the woman floating at night in the swimming pool. I almost wanted to have a death, murder, evoke that.

Usually I'll go out and shoot what interests me, attracts me. Usually it's public display, festivals, energy, activity, people concerned with precision and control.

When I get back rushes, I'll see a series of images and I think, that's the one that's really working for me. But I won't as yet — until I gather so many rolls of film over so many years. Like, this was three years. Then I'll think, okay, I've got enough. Then I'll start to build these art works.

Kathleen Frumkin: That opera sequence, that first woman dressed in black, bowing she stumbles, and there's a pun on the trophy dropping. But I began to recognize the costumes as from *Aida*. And then further on there's a shot of neon from the Aida Café. So what interested me in that was how much you carry around via memory. Or actually that the world speaks to you in its chronic images. I don't mean chronic in a bad way, but something that is consciously on your mind. So that seems to be a very literal thing, and not necessarily narrative.

Bob Perelman: What happens is, as you see the film more, your time sense dilates. You know what's going to happen, so you don't have this initial moment of worry and you can read the finer points. The film really seems to get longer. The first time it whooshes by.

Something like that happens in poetry. I was over at Intersection when Ron [Silliman] read part of *Tjanting*, which I find extremely easy to listen to. It seems like he's being very deliberate, and not demanding pyrotechnics from the audience to keep up. But then I heard somebody behind me say, Yeah, I didn't get much of that, I just closed my eyes and got some images.

So, the language that you have in common with the viewer is under dispute at every point. And, finally, the only thing you can do is to go on your own familiarity. You've seen this stuff for three years in making it. So you'll just have to take a stand: Yes, this guy is hung-over; Anne Waldman is in the backseat and not talking, and that's what it is. The question of resolving the language, the time scale and the fineness of the language, finally has to end up in the artist and then: here it is for people to see as many times as they want.

Caroline Savage Lee

"WHAT'S A PICNIC WITHOUT POTATO SALAD!"

It was a lovely day for a picnic and lovely it was at the Canyon Reunion Picnic on September 30th in Tilden Park. Although Bruce Baillie, renowned founder of Canyon, had suggested the gathering of filmophiles only days before, quite an array of Canyon talent enjoyed the feast, engaging in loose conversation and casual film activity. Bruce managed to post bright directional signs in conspicuous locations in

Hollis Frampton, Beverly O'Neill, and Pat O'Neill, photographed by Maddalena Rangel.

the Berkeley Hills and despite a decision to picnic elsewhere in Tilden, people found the sight. "We just remembered to meet near the tennis courts," remarked Diane Kitchen, "and so here we are."

A near disaster was averted by the problematical derring-do of Carmen Vigil who, with a bit of savoir-faire and boy scout ingenuity, gathered pine needles, paper and twigs to light the charcoal for the barbecue. The Canyon crew remembered all the barbecuing essentials except the lighter fluid. Once started, the fire blazed beautifully. First on the grill were the hot dogs, organic and turkey. They were an appetizer, a short of sorts, before the featured chicken, turkey tails and Italian sausage. A procedural question arose concerning the sequential application of the barbecue sauce but that was resolved effortlessly by the sauce's creator, Michael Wallin, declaring the proper approach.

As more picnickers arrived, they brought more goodies for the airy feast. Diane Kitchen made a delicious fruit salad. Janis Crystal Lipzin brought the famous potato salad, prompting James Broughton to declare, "What's a picnic without potato salad!" Larry Jordan brought French bread and Caroline Savage Lee baked an herb-onion bread. Carmen provided everyone with an abundance of his homemade Cabernet, vintage '78 and James and Joel complemented that with two thermos bottles filled with cold, crisp Chardonnay. Chick Callenbach joined the festive group with a simply ravishing salad of lettuce and sprouts. Tony Reveaux and friend Rebecca brought a scrumptious apricot pie. Gunvor Nelson brought a friend from

Sweden. Mark from Oakland attended with numerous questions of filmic import for the film luminaries. Michael Wallin and Richard Beveridge, the Co-op crew, provided the barbecue delectables. Bruce Baillie with German Shepherd Bill arrived late in the day with a wonderfully charming pot of brown rice. In all, everyone enjoyed the moist morsels.

The picnickers ate and talked. Joel and Caroline tossed a frisbee. Andalou, Richard Beveridge's dog and Carrie, Caroline's nearly year-old daughter battled over the same favorite toy. A Bolex appeared and all candidly performed. The camera was passed around for all to place their individual mark on the film event.

As the day faded away, so did the guests. Richard went to Marin to film the Dalai Lama. Others drifted homeward. Bruce's reunion was a pleasant chance to eat and reminisce about what was and conjecture about what will be. And to sum up, a quote from Gertrude Stein's word portrait, *Picasso* (1909):

> One whom some were certainly following was one who was completely charming. One whom some were certainly following was one who was charming. One whom some were following was one who was completely charming. One whom some were following was one who was certainly completely charming.

> Some were certainly following and were certain that the one they were then following was one working and was one bringing out of himself then something. Some were certainly following and were certain that the one they were then following was one bringing out of himself then something that was coming to be a heavy thing, a solid thing and a complete thing.

Freude Bartlett

LETTER, MAY 16, 1980

Dear Editor,

This unhappy impulse to write to you comes after reading the last issue of the CinemaNews. In the last few years there has been a noticeable and dismal decline in the spirit of communality which graced the founding and early years of Canyon Cinema and the CinemaNews.

The CinemaNews was once a lively source of information and exchange. There has always been critical writing in the news and that includes filmmakers being critical of other filmmakers work. This criticism was often satiric, humorous, and pointed. As reflected in the last issue, however, it has degenerated to the point of ugliness . . . even hysterical cruelty. The CinemaNews has become a mean-spirited, gossip mongering rag.

I am referring specifically to the Doberman and Hills' articles. In them I detect a strong element of envy and the vindictive desire to take vengeance on those with whom they disagree or perceive as more successful or more powerful . . . to wit, the Doberman/Peterson exchange and the backhanded swipe at George Griffin in the Hills' piece. These remarks are not directed toward film work, they are directed toward fellow filmmakers. They are not serious, critical comments, they are personal insults.

In terms of appreciation and financial success, the amount of pie available for film artists is too small for the independent film community to divide up into such camps as Doberman versus Peterson or Hills versus the world.

Best to save one's energy and talent for defeating the real enemy. How pathetic to pick on fellow passengers in the same small bus. It's called fouling your own nest and I do wish you'd clean it up.

Sincerely,

—

FROM *CINEMANEWS*, 80.3/4/5

Bruce Baillie

LETTER, LATE JUNE [1980]
Elizaville, N.Y.

Dear Everybody,

Was down in Alabamee recently. Will Hindle was burglarized, way out in the country, while doing show in N.Y. this winter. Lost original Bolex, among other irreplaceable tools.

I've been trying to get through to the film community to ask people showing films to please donate proceeds of one show this summer and send to: Steve Aronson, American Federation of the Arts, 41 E. 65th St., NYC, 10021. I have asked the Pittsburgh Filmmakers to dupe and mail such a request (for a comrade in need), using the Carnegie mailing list. Also to Canyon for a showing, also several NYC sources. *No response*. Are we engaged with communications or are we not!?

I miss everyone out there and the West herself, but here we are, and the days here are good, the birds sing and so on. We are shooting the last section to my last film, the *Romance*. It is called, *The Cardinal's Visit*. Elliot Caplan and I working together. If fall shows any basic life stability, the long process of putting the whole work together should be underway.

Best to all

Chick Strand at the Cinematheque, March 6, 1980

Question: The title SOFT FICTION seems to imply that there is a manifestation between documentary and narrative fiction . . .

Chick: Well, *that* could be it. I chose SOFT FICTION because the film is dealing with memory, and memory does change . . . becomes soft around the edges . . . The reality then is changed. And too, true, the line between fiction and reality is soft . . . the more media we get, the less we know where it is.

Q: The women that told the stories, did they ever tell you those same stories prior to being filmed, or was that the first time?

C: Not exactly. The whole film started out when I was at an art show, and the first woman, the woman that felt herself turning into this bannister . . . we were walking out, going down the stairs and there was a wooden bannister. And she said, "Oh, this really reminds me of the time I felt myself turning into a bannister." She's an English professor. (audience laughter) And I thought, this is a really bizarre story, I have simply got to film it. Then people would ask, "What are you working on?" and I would tell them. And they'd say, "Well I have a story." Then they would jump into their stories. For instance, the heroin woman said, "Oh, I was addicted to heroin in New York . . . " and then I would say, "Stop, don't tell me anymore. Wait til we get the camera," because I wanted it really fresh. So that's how it happened. Or I would hear rumors about someone. But these women are dear friends . . . We all have stories . . . (pause) . . . Any other questions? . . . Am I off the hook so easy?

Q: Was that a true story about the cowboys?

C: All those stories are true. (audience laughter) All those stories are true. And every one of them was filmed with the woman whose story it was except for the one about the cowboys, and that was another woman reading a letter from the woman who had the experience.

Q: Why didn't the woman whose story it was tell it?

C: I didn't ask her that, I just agreed that I wouldn't show her or get her name involved . . . she wanted to be anonymous. The others didn't care.

Q: Did the women have anything to do with choosing the setting that they would tell their stories in?

C: No. Except for the nude woman in the kitchen, the setting was usually my house. I wanted it dark and subdued and it was also chosen because I could borrow a sync-sound camera; I usually hand-hold everything but that camera was too heavy so I had to put it on a tripod. I also wanted to make it real easy for myself to relate to the woman I was shooting. And that was to me one of the most incredible parts of making the film, was my relationship to the women when they were talking and being on camera, and doing it knowing the result, knowing that they would be on this big screen and a lot of people, strangers, would see them. It was intense and amazing to film them. More than anything else . . . Unbelievable. Just unbelievable. And them telling it on camera acted as an exorcism, in a way, for the experiences that they had. They all felt better. And when I showed it in L.A. most of them came to the show, and the audience knew that they were there; and it was an incredible experience.

Q: There was no symbolic intention between the abstractness, the camera movement, and the rigidity of the monologue?

C: Not that I was aware of at the time. There might be . . . it might just be a part of me. But I think mainly and frankly it was because the camera was very heavy and I didn't want to hold it. I wanted to be able to move away from the camera and not concentrate too much on camera moves, to be able to relate to the women, to encourage them by my facial expressions so they could speak to me rather than just the camera. Usually it was the woman and me and the camera in the room and that was it.

Q: There was one woman that was not filmed in sync-sound . . .

C: Oh, the woman in the kitchen. Right. Well, I know why she isn't talking to the camera . . . I filmed her early on and I wasn't sure when I could get sync equipment . . . and I didn't really want every one to be straight on like that. So she told me her story on tape. She was a student of mine, she told it to me over the course of three evenings, several times. And so I had the tape, I had her voice, I had the story. And I always wanted to experiment a little with 'in time,' real time things, so that seemed like the opportune moment. I wanted to shoot her doing something in its entirety, without cuts.

Q: It is curious about her. She's nude and exposing herself so thoroughly while she goes about making herself breakfast; and then on the soundtrack over that she is telling the story about an incestuous relationship with her grandfather. There is a lot to see there . . .

C: I wanted her to appear vulnerable but strong . . . just in the way she moves through the world . . . not trying to look good . . . with no pretensions. So we both talked about how she would appear and we came up with the idea of her in the nude, making breakfast . . . a sort of ritual.

Q: And how about the woman who dropped the suitcase?

C: She also told me a story which I didn't use about an acid trip that she had that was quite devastating. I didn't use it, didn't film it, but I used her. I see Amy, the woman with the suitcase, the woman on the train, and she's the woman behind the waterfall at the end, as the traveller, the woman on a journey, the woman completing it all, the woman coming out the other end whole . . . and more than whole, with the addition of coping with the experience and making it constructive. It's hard for me to explain because I don't deal with my films that way . . . analyzing them beforehand . . . but it's sort of as if she and the other women take the responsibility for having had the experience. It's not that they take the responsibility for the experience happening, but for 'having had' it.

Q: The woman who is travelling, she comes to your house and she's knocking on the windows, and you're obviously there with the camera. I kept wondering why you wouldn't let her in. (audience laughter)

C: Why I wouldn't let her in? She talks too much. (audience laughter) No, I don't know. I just had this funny idea. I don't know what possessed me to do that. I thought it would be a good idea. She came and knocked and rattled the door. It might be because I had a pan that started upstairs and went down and ended up on that woman. It seems to me I was thinking I wanted somehow to connect the knocking with that. I like the idea of wandering through houses that seem empty and locked, secluded . . . with no way of entry.

Q: Yeah. After the wandering through the house I got a very clear idea of you with the camera so that it seemed like she's looking in but then on the other hand . . .

C: Right, see she's me . . . on the outside curious and trying to get in. But then I'm also the camera and on the inside too.

Q: That bothered me too. It seemed like you were protecting the chambered walls of your privacy . . .

C: That's part of it, yeah.

Q: . . . but then what about the woman in the chair?

C: In the chair. You mean why is she there?

Q: Yeah and oblivious to the camera.

C: Well, another silly thing happened. We were there filming her for the bannister story and gradually it dawned on me, oh I'd better get a pan of the house, because we'll be moving soon. So I went upstairs while she was sitting downstairs and I started panning the house, I just kept coming and coming and she was there in the chair and I just panned over her. I had every intention of cutting before her or maybe not using it, I didn't know . . . perhaps it's not as random as that. I have ideas and even write them down but in the course of working on the film it might change.

Q: It was good. I thought it enriched the whole . . .

C: Yeah, I'm just convinced that if it's . . . it's some sort of obsession to me to make films and I'm convinced that it works out. There's a lot of stuff I shoot that's dumb and stupid and I never use, and doesn't relate. But somehow, funny things happen, or appear. I just know not to put it off, but to follow the feeling I have about it at the moment. And I guess it's sort of a zen attitude. Not to push too much. It'll come.

Q: On the moving shot of the woman riding horseback, did you shoot that from a car going alongside?

C: There are two women in that scene. I love to shoot with the telephoto lens, six feet away. So I had them ride, as well as they could, six feet away from me and I just followed them . . . and got what I could. I got dizzy a lot.

Q: How did you shoot FEVER DREAM? That was beautiful.

C: I shot that one in the ivy in the front yard.

Q: Could you discuss the making of FEVER DREAM?

C: Yes. FEVER DREAM is very explicit. I think most women . . . I don't know, I do, I'm not gay but I do have sexual fantasies about other women. And that's what that's about. Did you get that? (audience laughter) But there is also an element of mystery and love between two people . . . a gentleness and tenderness. That's the image.

Q: Could you talk about KRISTALLNACHT?

C: KRISTALLNACHT, Yes. Um . . . I don't know why but I'm still obsessed by all of that . . . the holocaust. I suppose because it still goes on. And Anne Frank to me is symbolic of all innocent victims, male and female. And that to me . . . the film is just sort of a memorial to her and to all people who get caught up in things out of their control and done under . . . Two or three years ago I went to her house in Amsterdam. I'd never been to Europe before so the places I had imagined as a young girl during the war when the news came back from the camps had remained in my mind . . . stuck in past time. And of course Anne Frank's diary affected me a great deal. So when I went to Amsterdam I could just, I just, I took all away the present and I could just hear those hobnail boots down that street; and when I went to the place where she had been hidden in the attic, I was just chilled. So that experience is relatively recent to me. KRISTALLNACHT too, refers to a night in which there was a mass killing of Jews because someone in the Nazi party had been killed so they just went to the ghetto and started killing people. KRISTALLNACHT is the name of that night . . . I'm not Jewish either . . . (pause) . . . Any other questions?

Q: Could you explain a little bit about the film with the really old footage in it?

C: The really old old footage, LOOSE ENDS, is what it's called. I started out with almost nothing in my mind about what was going to happen. And I had an experience at Filmex last year. One night there was a very interesting film about death made by some French people [Strand is referring to *Of the Dead* (1981) by the Belgian Thierry Zeno]. Several scenes that went on for a long time about death in one way or another, and one of the first was, I think in Southeast Asia; a woman had died, and the camera stays with the woman all through the funeral ceremonies which took about five days. So during the course of the five days, very close up of the woman, we see her face begin to decay. At the end of the five days, five cattle are brought and slaughtered, speared through the neck. Everybody in the audience, oooohhh, ooooohhh . . . was very upset. OK, the film goes on . . . goes to Mexico City and we see a guy dying of a knife wound, we go to India and see really close up a funeral pyre and the corpse being blackened, consumed by fire. And it's very hard to sit through this. We go to the Philippine Islands and see a guerilla kill one of his comrades after talking to him about how they've been good comrades and he doesn't like to do it but after all, the first guy betrayed. After the film, going out into the lobby, the thing most people talked about was how awful it was to see those five cows killed. And that really threw me for a loop. That's the significance of the horse that gets it in my film. To set you up in a way; because everyone goes ooooooohh with the horse and the theater is perfectly quiet later on with starving people, bodies getting thrown into pits. It's sort of a strange thing, I think we don't like to think about human death . . . Besides, it's us, we do it to ourselves . . . but we don't really, kids don't do it, other people don't do it. So, as the film evolved I realized that I had something of a statement . . . my own feelings about starvation . . . 12 million people this year will die of starvation . . .

Q: I thought it was two movies in a way.

C: There are a lot of different sections. Sure it's all . . . it's me there. Ada Adams, the clumsy student is me and Miss Brown the teacher is me . . .

Q: The film reminded me a lot of LAND WITHOUT BREAD, that attitude of . . .

C: Yeah, I've had somewhat that attitude too. And I like Buñuel a lot. But it's a hard film to explain. You either get it or you don't.

Q: LOOSE ENDS to me had . . . a kind of an uncontemporary feel and I like this quality. Just the fact that it's in black and white. Have you got any comment on that, and also how do your audiences, say under 25, react to it?

C: Ah, being a teacher I find that the new bunch of freshmen that are coming in don't have the background, they don't even really know what happened in the sixties. So it's difficult . . . but they get it somehow. They get an impact but they don't get all the nuances, or all the tricks I play, or all the relationships; but that's OK, I don't care. I want a film that everybody or most people can relate to and they don't have to catch the inside jokes. Now what was the first part of the question?

Q: That kind of answers it . . . it was that the sense was very intentional. I was reminded of some of the early Bruce Conner stuff. Just because it was a film collage; it's a mood and a thing I don't see people doing anymore.

C: Bruce Conner's A MOVIE was one of the first experimental films I saw back in the early sixties; I really liked it and I like it to this day. It was very hard for me to say to myself, it's all right to use stock footage, that's Bruce Conner's scene. My feeling was, I've got all this stuff and it would really be dumb not to do it my way. I still like his work very much and 5:10 TO DREAMLAND sets up a mood and is very beautiful.

Q: Where did you get all the fantastic material in LOOSE ENDS and CARTOON LE MOUSSE?

C: I work at this school and they had a film library that nobody ever used; and a secretary's husband had 12 big reels of old stuff he used to show his family, old newsreels and cartoons and things. So I had thousands and thousands of feet of it. I thought it would be fun to make a movie with it, see if I could make something out of the puzzle. I understand there's another bunch of film hidden away on campus that I'm going to search for.

Q: Where do you get your music? Do you write some of it?

C: No, it's all stolen. I can't write but now I'm going to take a music class cause I think it's time. . . . I want to start doing my own music.

Q: Where do you find your music?

C: Oh, various places. I record a lot, in the field and from records . . . and also this school had a radio station at one time so it had a whole lot of tapes of very obscure things. I guess I work like a collagist in music as well as images, from found things. I get all of my material together and look at it over and over and over and then I pick out the things I think I might use. And then I just start. I usually edit . . . I almost do a fine cut right away and lay three tracks at the same time, and it just falls. I don't know why, it just works that way. Then I take things out, change them around later. If I knew what I was going to do beforehand I'd be bored. To me it's a new adventure every time. And every time I really plan on something, it looks blaaah.

Q: With all that material from other films, do you have the kind of access where you can cut it directly or do you contact print it?

C: I had a print, this old crappy print, it was real brittle and stretched, that had been in the library for years and years. And I had a student whose father owns an optical effects house in Hollywood, so he ran off a master from it with a wet-gate. I had to blow up some of it because the frame line showed, or slow it down, step it, things like that . . . (pause) . . . Any other questions? . . . Gee, I came, 500 miles . . . from Hollywood.

Q: Has Hollywood influenced what you do?

C: When I first went to L.A., I had decided to go to film school because I wanted to learn how to use the equipment, that's the usual reason why a lot of people go . . . and I lived in Berkeley at the time. I actually threw the *I Ching* to ask it if it would be cool for me to go to L.A. . . . Yeah, sure, I've lived there fifteen years now and I'm really a Southern Californian. It is a different life down there, so sure it has influenced me.

Q: You said you're working on new films and you went back to Mexico. Are they more like your other Mexican films?

C: Well, sort of. I got hooked into making another film about Anselmo, the guy that was in COSAS DE ME VIDA; and this is a continuation of that, more or less, deeper inside of him, his wife and family, and the woman that he has two other children by. We're real close. And two or three other films, abstract kinds of things . . . I think. I haven't seen most of the footage, I've been too poor to have it developed. I had some of it developed but it's been sitting in an icebox for a long time and it was real hot for about two or three months so the color's real strange. I don't know if I like it or hate it but I'll live with it.

Q: What's your attraction to Mexico?

C: My attraction to Mexico? Well it's right down the freeway from L.A., number one, so it's easy to run off down there. I went there about fifteen years ago and I just got into it. To me, Mexico is surrealism . . . just being there. It's a different culture, it's beautiful, it's just incredible to be there.

Q: I'm curious to know what you were doing in SOFT FICTION with the scene where the woman was reading the letter about the cowboy. There was a strange tension set up because this woman was a victim, yet she enjoyed it or she was trying to make light of it, there was an element of humor interjected and I wondered about that.

C: Are you sure she was a victim?

Q: Um . . . yeah.

C: Why?

Q: Because she wasn't in control of what she was doing. She didn't want to, she felt questionable.

C: Well why did she go up there in the first place?

Q: Well, that's what I'm asking you.

C: I'm not her. (audience laughter)

Q: Could you say how you feel about that scene?

C: Sure, not only do I have sexual fantasies about other women but I also have sexual fantasies about several men at once. Don't you?

Q: Uh huh.

C: To me, that story is a sexual fantasy lived out . . . and ah, sort of a freeing kind of thing. I know for a fact that it was a freeing thing for her.

Q: That was a true story?

C: That is a true story. But it's not just the experience, it's how she came out of the experience, what she did with the experience, made it a constructive part of her life rather than destructive part of her life. It's that tenacity, that kind of spirit that I'm really enamored of. Like Anne Frank. To turn it around and not to have been victimized. I mean it doesn't erase the thing but if you come out whole, if you come out no longer the victim in your own mind, then that's great. You've gotta survive the best way you can.

Q: So did you get a lot of footage and edit it out?

C: Only Cameron and Amy.

Q: Could you tell us about Cameron?

C: Cameron is a very interesting woman. She's a painter. She's the woman in SOFT FICTION who talked about the young girl with the flush face and who had a man who wanted to marry her, who gave her his memory. Well that's a true story of Cameron's, more or less. Cameron first appeared in Kenneth Anger's INAUGURATION OF THE PLEASURE DOME as a young woman. So that's another reason Hollywood influences me, because I know people like that, years later. And Amy is the one that told me the story about the LSD trip. It was just too incoherent. (audience laughter) She came over. She phoned me up the next morning and said, "I'm just out of the hospital. I had a terrible acid trip. I'm going to come right over and tell you." But she was still up and the tape isn't good. Well, those were the women I found and those were the women I used. Just those. I didn't go out looking. I just waited and they came to me; so in that way the rodeo thing also belonged.

Q: Was that the first time the woman had read that cowboy letter?

C: Yes. She'd never seen it and she doesn't know the woman who wrote it.

Q: I'm wondering if maybe the tension that was set up was a voyeur quality.

C: Of course it is! I mean sitting here is a voyeur kind of thing. Yeah, in fact afterward she and I talked about it, the woman who read the letter and I. And I asked her if she ever felt like that and that's why she smiled at the end, that knowing smile.

(audience laughter) I don't know, I don't know whether this stuff's supposed to come out about women.

Q: How was it set up that she was the one to read it?

C: She's a handwriting expert that I know and I had this idea that she would analyze the writing. I gave her a part of the letter that had nothing to do with the story and filmed her analyzing this woman's handwriting. Well, it was interesting but . . . enh . . . what she did was to automatically read the letter and comment on the writing as she read . . . Does that scene bother anybody?

Q: It bothers me because it hits really close to home . . . those kind of fantasies that are semi-masochistic . . . and I don't know how I feel about that . . .

C: You mean your own thoughts about it?

Q: Um hmmm.

C: Well, here, just call me Abby, but . . . (audience laughter) You've got them and everybody does, not everybody but a lot of us do, so it's all right. (audience laughter) I don't see it as masochistic as much as an exploration . . . It's just that some people don't see the difference between wanting to explore and wanting to be hurt in some way . . . It's what society says we can't do, have sex in a dark dormitory room with a bunch of cowboys who seem to have the upper hand, that turns us on the most . . . And I suspect that in your fantasies . . . putting yourself in a situation where you aren't actually forced, but more or less have an excuse not to be able to get out of it, so as to be able to carry it through in your mind with a clear conscience. What I think the problem is, is that if we admit to these things, we seem to be laying ourselves wide open to the myth that women want to be raped.

But it's not the same thing as rape. Rape is a violent power trip . . . But be smart about it, don't say, well I like this so here I am, kind of thing. It's all right . . . and it isn't. I mean it's just part of, I can't say human nature because it's maybe our culture, western culture particularly, but . . . it's OK.

Q: Why did you use the song "Death of a Maiden" at the end?

C: Why did I use it? Well I have this other friend who is the wife of one of my colleagues at school, who sings, and I saw her sing one night and I said, "Cathy, would you sing for my film?" And she said, "OK." I told her to pick out a song, and that's the song she picked knowing nothing about the film. (audience laughter)

Q: Would you choose to have that kind of ruthless lighting regardless of what she might have sung?

C: Yes. I shot it on the stage at school. It had dark curtains, I wanted her to come from the dark, a pale face. She was the one that chose to wear the black dress. I'm not very good with lighting, I just sort of put it at 45 degree angles to the side.

Q: The lighting turned out to be very appropriate to the song.

C: I think so, yeah. I used my eye, and it looked right. I don't like to carry around a lot of stuff, like lights. So it was all a set-up job on the tripod.

Q: What were the subtitles from?

C: In LOOSE ENDS they come from LAST YEAR AT MARIENBAD. In the Anne Frank film it's haiku. In SOFT FICTION the only subtitles were the words to the song.

Q: You said you weren't gay and you weren't Jewish, what else is there . . . ah, what's your cultural background?

C: I'm really WASP. Both sides of my family came to the United States in the 1600's, came through New York and the midwest and into California. I'm a fourth generation Californian; and none of them ever made it. None of them ever got rich. My great-grandfather was here in 1849 and then decided to go to Calusa, California and be a farmer, dirtfarming. That is my cultural background. I was brought up an atheist but my parents were very conservative politically. I was raised in Berkeley.

Q: Very conservative atheists . . . (audience laughter)

C: Well, see we never ever used the word atheist. My grandmother went to a Methodist Church but my parents never did. They believed in nature I suppose . . . my mother was a very sweet woman and she would say that God was nature. Yes, they were Goldwater people. We don't talk about politics anymore. My father has never seen any of my films . . . my mother is no longer alive.

Q: Do you want your father to see your films?

C: No, not particularly. I was going to show him and my mother some of my early films. I brought the projector but my mother was dying. She just didn't have the strength to see them. Now my father relates the rigamarole of setting up the projector with my mother dying and he just cannot bear to do it. I don't blame him.

Q: So he does know that you're a filmmaker?

C: Oh yeah. Just today I flew in and I went to see my father and my stepmother. And today for the first time he asked me definite questions about my films.

Q: This was the first time?

C: This was the first time. When I moved down to L.A. to start studying film I was 34 and I had to ask him for some money, and you know how parents give you money sometimes, with all those strings attached? I remember him telling me, "You'll never be an artist. Don't kid yourself. You should be a teacher." A grammar school teacher. Well, I am a teacher. A college professor and now he's sort of proud. It's probably because I don't bug him anymore. You know when you're young and you're much different from your parents, it gives you great thrills to just really give them a bad time . . . our righteousness in our twenties. Well I've learned. They don't have to know everything about the way you feel . . . My father is old now. I want to give him as much comfort about my life and the wonderful things he did that contributed, in ways he doesn't even know, to the happiness I have . . .

Gunvor Nelson

CONVERSATION WITH CHICK STRAND

Gunvor: How do you feel about your show last night?

Chick: When you are in that situation people fling questions at you and you answer the best you can . . . and sort of stumble through it hardly remembering what you did . . . hoping that you said what you really meant.

G: You are good at answering calmly . . .

C: I certainly did not used to be! I would get real defensive . . .

G: . . . with an edge of irony and humor in your answers where you get both your philosophy and stories across.

C: Well whatever . . . I don't know about philosophy.

G: . . . or your personality.

C: That's it! It all comes out eventually but I don't know what I want to amplify.
   I get this feeling that we have another role to play that is put upon us by other women . . . sometimes . . . by what is expected of women artists . . . and that is to make films about women and make them a certain way. Make certain statements. Those statements have been made already over and over and over.

G: Not knowing the filmmaker I would not have been able to tell if these films were made by a woman or a man.

C: Sure. I just happen to be a woman making those films.

G: It's your particular world that you're representing and your choices. That's what is interesting about them rather than some kind of expected common denominator. They wanted you to solve their problems.

C: That was really interesting! . . . and to make up for it I spilled some beans about myself in front of everybody to make them feel easier. I guess that comes from teaching, where you get students that come in with all these crazy problems or need some help or support or sympathy or . . . I find that I get impatient when I deal with younger students.

We have such a conglomeration of memories and it is involved . . . We are evaluating a lot of things now . . . our feelings . . . How much creative energy do we have? Is it a fountain that comes or is there just a certain amount?

G: I think the well is deep and unfathomable . . . but how much oxygen have we left . . . or heart?

C: I am working two jobs so I can do my films. It is driving me crazy! To think there is no time for reflection . . . I just sort of do it. All that energy that goes into caring about the students . . . that goes into teaching . . . we do somehow care about these damn students. That's the crazy part of it. It's not crazy, it is part of what makes us artists. But, ah, to chuck it, ah, my God!

G: If I had the money I would maybe teach now and then, but not like this grind.

C: It is a grind, but it is my choice and I will keep on doing it. It is nurturing in a way.

G: We have to trust the beauty that is here.

C: Of course. Marty and I talk about all this and we are very pleased with ourselves and we feel we are really doing what we want, playing a lot. We are very happy. Anxious, anxious too.

G: Two jobs like you have would drown me.

C: Totally crazy. It's all week long except for Fridays, but on Fridays you usually write that report, figure out that budget, read that script that you know you are going to hate, or go to that faculty meeting. .

G: It's getting to be too hard to scrape together the money for film . . .

C: I can't even conceive of calling it a business. We will never make our money back . . . much less make money. God. I have given up thinking. It is the same kind of mess I get myself into when I do think about those NY people who set up the "holier than thou" hierarchy of "who is who" in filmmaking. Maybe I am wrong thinking this, but the concerns back there seem artistic and intellectual and maybe our concerns here are more cinematic. They might disagree and see it the other way around.

G: Artistic and cinematic? What do you mean?

C: This seems to be a question that is constantly discussed, the "difference" between East Coast films and West Coast films . . . perhaps East Coast films can be discussed more intellectually. They seem to be interested in art movements and philosophies that can be stated verbally . . . using film as an extension of these philosophies as seen in painting etc. And West Coast films can be discussed more on an emotional level . . . maybe it is the difference between being a left side of the brain person and a right side of the brain person . . . Also the ocean is on the wrong side of the road there. And you can't tell me that does not have anything to do with it. We live differently. A lot of us live in the country. We live quite isolated from each other because the distances are so great. We are just different animals I guess.

G: We refuse to be put into niches . . .

C: We hate it!

G: . . . and resist dividing the world into neat compartments . . . cleanly placed.

C: I know it! On the one hand it is the joy of making films, or it is placing yourself in history . . . and then why bother. Those films are often boring . . . and I can't read about it. Maybe we here are more concerned about human issues.

By God I love making films! Getting into it! I just love shooting. I love looking at the rushes and figuring out the sound! It's incredible!

G: I'm envious of those who have films that are on the verge of being edited.

C: Ohhhhh . . . !

G: . . . to cut into.

C: That's what's driving me. I've had this film shot now for almost a year, and two-thirds of it still has to be processed. Six films in there. And it's crazy. There is something like 20,000 feet shot. Finished and ready to go to the editing.

G: What a fantastic place to be.

C: It is.

G: You are going at it like a fiend.

C: I am . . . I am obsessed. I can't stop . . . I love it so much . . .

G: That obsession, is that connected to age? There is no time?

C: That is part of it. The realization that time is leaving. It's harder to move around physically.

G: Could you be without film? Could you paint instead?

C: Yes I could . . . there always has to be something, even gardening although film is the most remarkable because it entails all. Time . . . music . . . painting in a sense . . . writing . . . photography. I would not be lost, totally lost without it. My life . . . the quality of my life is the main thing. It's the drudgery, busywork that makes us crazy.

G: You used footage from the slaughterhouse film, LE SANG DES BETES. It comes from such a beautiful film and is made by such an artist that I have a hard time seeing it in any other film.

C: Yeah, I can understand that. I am a believer that art can always be tampered with.

G: I would not want people to use my footage in another film.

C: Yeah, yeah . . . that is valid certainly. I don't know how I feel.

G: I confess I have used bits and pieces of other people's music.

C: Yeah, I know it is hard to draw the line . . . real hard. I'm going to try to do some of my own sound. I'm looking forward to it.

G: For your films last night I would probably have used more abstract sounds. Your music many times distracts from seeing the film. Like in KRISTALLNACHT which for me was a fantastically visual film, even though the soundtrack was more abstract, the drumbeat at the end was very disturbing and prevented me from experiencing the picture. I wanted to float away.

C: That is also one of the problems in filmmaking, in having to do it all. Now I want to have my own sound-vision come through. I want to get into sounds myself instead of having to adapt stuff which I don't really like. I just have not had enough access to equipment. But now I do.

G: It's mostly the ready music that disturbs me. Also many times in your films I don't have the reference. I wonder where this jazz piece comes from or what it stands for. I don't have the knowledge of the symbolism.

C: I really love to play with sound, to work through and develop my own style. You know we really are still beginners . . . that's the urgency, realizing that we have twenty pieces, twenty films together, all together. Big deal! We are still just beginning . . . just learning.

G: But think how many frames!

C: That does help.

G: That does help.

C: It is a total thing. I feel I'm still in a sketchbook stage.

G: But I see how skillful you are.

C: It's also plodding through and being able to see, being able to edit out, being ruthless enough and understanding about holding onto it. And steady and powerful and not letting loose of it until the right time. It is a process in learning how to see.

G: It is learning how to select, how to trust in your own choices. It is dangerous to become too skillful, too slick.

C: That's the other end of it, yeah. Because as we learn patience and learn not to compromise, then we tend toward, lean over to the slick area.

G: Your latest films have surface dirt.

C: That's these prints . . . I cannot believe (laughs) I have such awful first prints. I took it to a lab because I needed it quick. The guy there said that he would print it on 7260 and I had no idea about it. He said that it would look just beautiful and I think that was because he didn't have any experience in timing the right stuff. But it is very contrasty, it prints so light that I had to have an optical print made instead of an electroprint, which cost $600. He did not clean the film before it printed. He did not tuffcoat the print and it has just crap all over . . . but I had to use them. In the meantime I've taken it all to another lab but they are slower than the seven year itch and they did not get them to me in time for this show. So the soundtrack was awful because even then he printed it too light, so all that hiss, and it drops out . . . Oye! The usual thing. But I did not want to say that at the show because it becomes in the realm of excuses and hell, I just . . .

G: Well, I was going to say it was nice to see, because it was perfect and not perfect at the same time.

C: You cannot be perfect! I like that aspect of it and I think in terms of getting too slick and losing substance, a different kind of substance for the surface quality of it. I don't know. And what is hard too, is realizing as we go that it is more than in our hearts. It is not more than making films. But more enters into it with showings like this, what they write about it, and what they say in N.Y., "blah, blah, blah." And all this goes in the head somehow and sort of clatters around in there and it is hard to dispense with it.

G: I don't have that sort of feedback that often so when I make a film . . . it's all new territory.

C: Yeah, scary.

G: And when you work for two years on something you have to zero in on the film itself rather than all the other things that are out there, so . . .

C: So when it is finished is when the other things come into play.

G: Yeah. But then it is already done so you can't do much about it.

C: Yeah, I know, but it is all there, lingering somehow. It is really crazy. It is hard for me to thrust out and tell people I have a new film . . . another western kind of thing, but I am really thinking of getting up a little brochure and sending it around to all those places in *Filmmakers Newsletter*. But I really don't know my motivation behind it. I have been trying to sort it out.

I don't like to have that a part of my filmmaking or read about whether other people are going to like it or worrying about if I am going to be recognized or anything like that . . . because that can be real deadly. On the other hand I like to travel and show my films. I have a good time. I like the performance aspect of it, the theatrical aspect of it. But also I have tried ever since the beginning of Canyon Cinema to support the movement in general.

G: I am very pragmatic. Travelling with the films I can usually get more money than for a regular rental . . . Money for film . . . Also part of it is getting a different perspective. It's like a jump into another world and then a jump back to your own place.

C: . . . and see what is going on . . . see what people are doing . . . what people are thinking. How else are we going to travel? Have adventure?

G: . . . but it gets rather tiresome to do often.

What somewhat confuses me about your films is that they have an inherent connection, a similarity in the way certain things were filmed, and then cut into different films.

C: I see all these films as one or parts of one, all that at the same time, even in the found-footage.

G: I have a hard time distinguishing one film from another even though they have different titles. For me, it would be easier with one title and then movement I, II, III, IV and so on, and maybe also have subtitles.

C: After I finished them I realized that there were some connections. I should have known because they were done at the same time. I don't see them as quite that connected.

G: Oh, I see.

C: I see elements between them, but for instance, the one for Anne Frank I like to separate because it deals with some different aspect of me. It is almost facetious to say that I see them as one piece but they can be seen that way. I wonder if these new films are all going to be the same.

G: Are they all shot in Mexico with color?

C: They're all color. One, two, three, four . . . are shot in Mexico. One is shot in Vermont, Sante Fe, and Mexico. Another one is shot in L.A. . . . and another is L.A.

G: I make one film at a time and they don't become many films.

C: This last bunch . . . I was mainly going toward one film. It was SOFT FICTION and I shot and shot and shot and I realized too many other things. And for the new ones I had money and went to Mexico with no idea of what I was going to do. I took a whole week and thought of nothing but what I could do down there . . . and that's fast, I mean . . . imagine allowing ourselves one week to figure it out. I took 15,000 feet with me, and what are you going to do with that . . . you are here smart-mouth and now what? So I thought . . . luxury . . . and I started shooting after a week knowing pretty much what I was after, separating the films. We were there for six weeks and of course they evolved as I was shooting. But they were all films all along. Whether they will stay that way I don't know.

G: How could you keep track of all that?

C: It is hard. I have done it mainly because of limitations of my time and the way my job sets me free or does not set me free. And then in the springtime I'm only obligated to teach one course at Occidental College, and at CalArts we get out about a month earlier, it's a little lighter then.

G: You have only one course?

C: And then teach summer school. I teach four classes.

G: You're crazy.

C: So that my really free time is only from July to August, just more or less a month. I have worked two jobs for so many years I can't believe it. Up to two years ago it was only parttime at each place but now it's been fulltime at one place and parttime at the other. If they ask me back to CalArts I will do it for one more year to pay those lab bills.

G: Without any grant support it is really hard to make films these days.

C: It's impossible.

G: What a nice thing it would be to be a writer.

C: Ahhhhh! Just a typewriter and some paper. I think often of that. You can take it anyplace.

G: Right. Or a little tape recorder.

C: Yeah I but I can't write. I might though, because I didn't think I could make films so I could probably do anything . . . but I don't want to write, I want to make films.

Ben Van Meter

Bloomfield School
Organic Nursery & Garden Supply
6691 Moro Street (707) 795-0977
Petaluma, California 94952

LETTER, C. 1980

[Editor's note: The following letter was sent to Canyon Cinema but was not published in the Cinemanews.]

To Canyon Cinema Members, and Readers of the Cinemanews,

(Bruce, Bob, Bruce, are you still out there?)

Enough is enough, already. I quit. For awhile, I found the incomprehensible, elitist ramblings of the Cinemanews slightly amusing. The issue before last, however, came with a bit of prose attached that even I could understand. It said, in effect, that Canyon thinks that I owe it money for my subscription to this tree-wasting collection of anti-life irrelevancies. PSHAW!

The new issue, #80, needs only one thing to make it a perfect comment on the Olfactory Essense of Current Elitist Cinema. It could even be a monthly feature. A scratch-n-sniff fold-out of Brakhage's or Snow's or Kubelka's ass-hole.

Please tell me exactly how much you think I owe you, remove my name from your membership, subscription and mailing list and send my films back a.s.a.p. Good luck in the ever expanding world of Olfactory Art, suckers.

(Bruce, Bob, Bruce are you still out there?)

Humbly,

—

FROM *CINEMANEWS*, 80.6/81.1

Henry Hills

New York City

LETTER, SEPTEMBER 10, 1980

I wish to apologize to George Griffin for my irresponsible and irrational reference to his name in my article, "Catholic Filmmaking in America," in *Cinemanews*, No. 79.5&6. I do not know the man and am only cursorily acquainted with his work. I felt the gravity of my error only a few days after publication when, on visiting L.A., my friend David Wilson expressed to me puzzlement at my pronouncement, explaining that seeing one film in a group show say might give one impression, while viewing an entire program of Griffin's films showed clearly a maker struggling with a specific set of problems, a particular sensibility. My original motivating impulse was a feeling that the Brakhage/Doberman attack on "Structuralism" was misdirected and that the more apt target would be the so called "soft core." The real enemy is television. The real enemy is the ever increasing homogeneity encouraged and enforced by monopoly Capitalism. I used a name as a symbol (probably not a very apt and certainly not a very clear one) without regard for the person that that name referred to. For this I feel ashamed. It was not only "mean-spirited" but also politically abominable. I had been mulling for some weeks over how to somehow at least partially make amends when Freude's apt and carefully worded letter appeared in *Cinemanews*, No. 80.1&2 and afforded me the opportunity to respond. The irony of being linked in someone's mind with Gary Doberman was overwhelming. I am not at all bitter or rigid; I was, however, at the time of assemblage of the issue in question, suffering the effects of a particularly raw N.Y. winter and, rereading that issue at this time, that tone seems to have infected much of what was included, a tone particularly foreign to what one might expect to find in a publication coming out of San Francisco. I do, however, find some of the points Freude makes to be erroneous. I'm sure that old Canyon was glorious, but when I arrived in San Francisco in 1974 it no longer existed. James Broughton and George Kuchar (and later for a period before he left town, Robert Nelson) were the only older filmmakers who ever came to Cinematheque. There were younger filmmakers, however, working out their own aesthetic concerns, many of which were perhaps quite different from those which motivated the original Canyon group, and they were encouraged by a lively flow of films and visiting filmmakers from all over. Additionally, Malcolm LeGrice's presence at the Art Institute encouraged an increased concern with intellectual and political issues. There was (and is) still a sense of community, but as the number of showcases and hence possibilities for travel had greatly increased in the 70s, this community was more national than local. It was this community that the *Cinemanews* began to address. I hardly find the *Cinemanews* of the last few years to be a "rag" (having included words and/or visual works of the like of Brakhage, Broughton, Conrad, Frampton, Gottheim, Hutton, Jacobs, G. Kuchar, Landow, LeGrice, Lye, Mekas, R. Nelson, O'Neill, S. Peterson, Rainer, H. Smith, Sonbert, Wieland, etc.): it is, in fact, my favorite magazine, and I don't think I'm alone — we have received many words and letters of encouragement, as well as increasing subscriptions and sales at bookstores and showcases around the country. I hope to see it continue to grow. Anyway, it's no longer "Hills versus the world." Please accept my apologies for whatever hard feelings I have caused. I hope to be more careful and caring in the future.

Chick Strand

Tujunga, California

LETTER, SEPTEMBER 18, 1980

Has it been twenty years since those first exciting days . . . such vivid memories of those times. After those first showings in Bruce's backyard in Canyon . . . films some-times shown on a sheet . . . always good popcorn . . . some wine and fine friends . . . the excitement of experiencing the films which to us were so new, such a wonder-ful art . . . becoming a weekly thing . . . finding places to show in Berkeley . . . the authorities always at our backs . . . showing in my front room, Chick Callenbach's backyard in the summer with Strawberry Creek rushing down to the bay in back of the screen adding another soundtrack . . . showing in the Bistro Café run by the Wobblies, rushing to SF to pick out the paper for the programs which we printed up on the Wobblie "press" . . . meeting Brakhage for the first time at James Brough-ton's . . . Jane coming to talk about the filming of *Window Water Baby Moving*, Albert Johnson coming to play music for a silent film . . . Pauline Kael coming to talk about film . . . Will Hindle . . . so many people helped . . . writing the *News*, no grants, no officiality, really by the skin of our teeth, holding on . . . money for rentals coming from our food money . . . hand-painted posters . . . how I know the feel of all the buildings along Telegraph Avenue and Grant Street . . . when late at night we would staple up our posters on every empty space. We thought we would run out of films to show in six months . . . after four years we were still going . . . three times a week . . . ending up with a more or less permanent place to show at Stiles Hall, California College of Arts and Crafts and the Coffee Gallery. Bruce and I worked almost everyday . . . but it wasn't work really . . . sitting out in the sun deciding on what films, writing program notes, sending out the programs . . . Sometimes Bruce's mother would print them up on her church mimeograph machine . . . We were constantly looking for places that would let us show the films . . . dressing up in our city clothes . . . but there was always some reason it couldn't be done . . . some law . . . or the films suspect. Once, driving across the bridge to set up our show at the Coffee Gallery (we had to take along with Bruce's projector and screen, my bureau to raise the projector up high enough), the screen must have bounced out of the back of the truck . . . I went back to Berkeley and got a sheet . . . the show went on on time . . . the next day one of Canyon's unsung heroes bought us a new screen. On the surface Canyon appeared to be made up of a tight organization of many peo-ple . . . but we were very loose . . . Bruce and I made the decisions . . . I guess as pardners . . . I know he had the clearest vision . . . but we had so very many helpers I guess with some sort of good faith in what we were doing . . . it certainly wasn't done by committee . . . it was street theater . . . The Tripps Festival I think was the end of the beginning of Canyon . . . it was our last great feast . . . other people were willing to take over . . . and Bruce and I wanted to go on with our lives . . . the avant-garde film scene was changing . . . becoming recognized, getting organized . . . it was time to leave it and get on with making films . . . But for those four years Canyon was a lifestyle for us, a great part of our lives . . . a time of great learning, expectation and fulfillment . . . it was wonderful . . . and we were right, it didn't end, Canyon kept going, more unsung heroes . . . keeping the hope, commitment and joy alive all these years . . . for all of us, for all of the filmmakers.

5 : Maintenance

Between 1980 and 1990, Canyon's income from its distribution efforts roughly doubled. In 1980–1981, Canyon's total income was $28,841; in 1990–1991, it was $76,255; and this expansion of the business continued for another decade: in 2002–2003, income reached its all-time high of $179,184. A number of factors seem to have contributed to this gradual but consistent rise in fortunes (see the year-by-year listing in appendix 2). Most obviously, the interest in American independent cinema, particularly within educational institutions, was growing. Of course, experimental and avant-garde forms of cinema have never received the level of attention that commercial cinema, or even documentary cinema, has, but more and more teachers were incorporating avant-garde work into film history courses, and some were developing courses that focused on avant-garde film (Michael Zryd discusses academic support of avant-garde cinema in "The Academy and the Avant-Garde: A Relationship of Dependence and Resistance," *Cinema Journal* 45, no. 2 [Winter 2006]: 17–42). Further, Canyon itself was working to maximize its attractiveness to those interested in teaching avant-garde film, specifically by regularly producing new, expanded catalogs.

Canyon's two competitors for academic film-rental dollars were, and I expect remain, the New York Film-Makers' Cooperative and the Museum of Modern Art's Circulating Film Collection. *The Film-Makers' Cooperative Catalogue, no. 6,* published in 1975, was not revised and expanded until 1990; and the Museum of Modern Art's *Circulating Film Library Catalog,* which appeared in 1984, was followed by a single supplement, in 1990. Canyon, on the other hand, published its *Catalog 5* in 1982 (Dominic Angerame, Andrew Moore, and Michael Wallin compiled and edited it). An update index appeared in 1985 and was followed in 1986 by *Catalog 6* (compiled and edited by Nina Fonoroff and Melanie Curry). "Film/Video" supplements to *Catalog 6* appeared in 1988 (compiled and edited by Angerame and Curry) and in 1990 (compiled and edited by Curry and Amy Stewart); and *Film/Video Catalog 7* (the "25th Anniversary Issue," compiled and edited by Curry and Heather Mackey) appeared in 1992; it was followed by supplements in 1993 (compiled by Curry, Alfonzo Alvarez, and Heather Mackey) and in 1994 (this one compiled by Alvarez, Curry, and Angerame). The final printed catalog—the Canyon catalog is now online—was *Film/Video Catalog 2000* (edited by Christine Metropoulos, assisted by Susan Vogel, Kevin Barnard, Alfonso Alvarez, and Andrée Johnson). It seems likely that the rise in Canyon

Covers of *Canyon Cinema Catalog 6* (1988), with cover image, "Homage to Marey" (1986) by Joel Singer; *Canyon Cinema Catalog 7* (1992), with cover image, "Deus ex Machina" (1987) by Bruce Conner; and *Canyon Cinema 2000* (catalog no. 8), the final book-form Canyon catalog, with cover art by Pat O'Neill.

CANYON CINEMA

CANYON CINEMA
FILM/VIDEO CATALOG 2000

revenues during the late 1980s and early 1990s was a function of Canyon's regularity in issuing these catalogs. I remember receiving the regular supplements and finding them distinctive and often impressive as publications.

The Canyon catalogs not only kept potential renters up-to-date on exactly what was available but also were engaging (this was also true of the catalog and supplement for the Museum of Modern Art Circulating Film Program). The covers of the catalogs and supplements were elegantly designed and included artwork by noted artists and Canyon filmmakers: William T. Wiley (*Catalog 5;* Wiley's drawing was entitled "Eye Can't Yawn Cinema," referring back to Diane Kitchen's Canyon malaprop contest of 1975); Bruce Conner (the update index of 1985, *Film/Video Catalog 7,* and the 1994 supplement); Joel Singer (*Catalog 6*); Rock Ross (the 1988 *Film/Video Supplement*); Robert Nelson (the 1990 *Film/Video Supplement*); and Pat O'Neill (*Film/Video Catalog 2000*). The listings themselves were often illustrated by stills and frame enlargements, and sometimes by collages, drawings, and photographs supplied by the filmmakers.

The Canyon catalogs sometimes included surprises. *Catalog 5* is prefaced by a brief essay by William S. Burroughs, "Take Nirvana," in which Burroughs theorizes about film history, arguing that Hollywood has crippled cinema by refusing to appreciate the camera's ability to achieve "a nirvana of uncritical acceptance." From the "zero point," he explains,

> the filmmaker can build in many directions. He can travel where no one has ever traveled before. He has a section of film time: he can speed it up, slow it down, run it backwards or do all three at once. He can randomize, scramble, overlay, flash forward or backward, cut in other material, substitute other sound tracks. He can negate or disintegrate image and meaning. He can speed up a command to slow down, and slow down an urgent "Hurry up!" His lynch mob can sing "Do the same to others as you would have them do." His saints can spit curses. . . . He can grow corn while you wait, or stop the sun in the sky. He has become God for that section of film time. From a point of zero preconception, he can break down all preconceptions.

According to Burroughs, the film industry, afraid of what might happen if people made their own movies—movies that were expressions of their real dream lives—has worked to retard film's expressive capacity and has supplied, instead, *meanings* ("You begin to see what meaning means? It means someone else is doing it. . . . You still need that? Then perhaps the camera is too much guru for you"). How much Burroughs understood Canyon or knew particular avant-garde films I don't know, but he seems to have imagined many of the kinds of cinema that Canyon distributes.

A different kind of surprise appeared in *Film/Video Catalog 2000:* a twelve-

I want to assure film programmers funded by the National Endowment for the Arts that my movies will never contain obscene or indecent material. You will not see the denigration of the objects or beliefs of the adherents of a particular religion or non-religion. Neither will you see the reviling or debasement of any person, group or class of citizens on the basis of race, creed, sex, handicap, age or national origin.

This is my pledge to the citizens of this great nation. I will maintain these high standards at all times

BRUCE CONNER

Bruce Conner page from *Canyon Cinema 2000* (catalog no. 8).

page photo spread by Bruce Conner with eleven pages of stills from films, introduced by a photograph of Conner in military dress and his "pledge to the citizens of this great nation." This seems to have been, simultaneously, a kind of tongue-in-cheek camouflage directed at moral conservatives on the look out for "pornography" and a way of distancing himself from the tendency of some Canyon filmmakers to foreground the outrageousness of their films in their catalog listings—a tendency that in the 1990s had had some unfortunate consequences for Canyon's relationship with the National Endowment for the Arts.

The marked increase in rentals during the late 1980s and early 1990s may have emboldened some to feel that Canyon could handle rentals of video as well as film. The minutes of the April 22, 1993, board meeting (by Dominic Angerame) describe "an intensive two hour meeting" between Bruce Conner, who had requested the meeting, and the board of directors (the board at this point included Clair Bain, Daniel Barnett, Linda Tadic, Jeffrey Skoller, and Michael Wallin, though Bain and Barnett were not present on April 22). Conner had asked for the meeting in order to address his concerns with how the current board was running Canyon Cinema, concerns instigated by the fact that "recently a policy was created to allow any video maker to join Canyon Cinema as a voting member." In Conner's view the specter of dozens of videomakers becoming voting members of Canyon seemed, at worst, likely to transform Canyon from an organization devoted to the distribution of 16mm prints—what he would later call "the only distribution center that truly respects the handling and presentation [of] film and also pays the film makers on demand with full accounting" (Conner interview)—into a video distribution center run in the interests of those committed to new technologies. Even at best, such a change would seriously overburden Canyon's staff (Angerame was the lone full-time staff member; David Sherman was half-time), placing Canyon's film distribution in jeopardy. Further, Conner contended, the decision to admit videomaker members was being taken in clear defiance of Canyon's articles of incorporation and bylaws, which clearly indicated, "The number of directors of this corporation will be four" (article V) and "All members shall have equal voting and other rights. Each member shall be entitled to one vote which may be cast in person or by proxy" (bylaw VII) at an annual meeting in April.

During the following year the board's way of doing business and the specific issue of admitting videomakers as voting members were the focus of the organization. With the assistance of legal advice (supplied by Peter Buchanan, hired by Conner; and Felicity Hammer, retained by the board), it became clear that the organization was legally required to rely on the articles of incorporation and bylaws rather than on what had become over time the usual way in which the board functioned (the five-member board had sometimes made decisions without consulting the members, and when it did contact them, it did so by distributing ballots and tallying those that were returned). During 1993–1994 the bylaws were revised, input from the membership was sought and received, and on April 19, 1994, the issue of video came to a head at the annual membership meeting where new bylaws were discussed. The proposed bylaws indicated that Canyon would distribute not just "film," but "work"—opening Canyon's doors to all moving-image technologies. For some members the apparent resistance to video was a defiance of Canyon's original mission (the original announcement of Canyon Cooperative, after all, had indicated that the organization would be "a federation of willing devotees of the magic lantern muse, consisting of artists engaged in the creation of 16mm film, 8mm film and other related light and image production media"). For others, the resistance to video had simply become pointless and old-fashioned (as Stephanie Beroes said in her April 14, 1994, letter to the membership, "Look to the future!! C'mon guys! WAKE UP! Video 'works' are vital to the survival of Canyon Cinema").

It was true that opinions on the issue generally depended on the person's age. As Jeffrey Skoller indicated in his May 25, 1994, letter to the membership after the meeting, "What seemed clear from the meeting and letters sent regarding this issue is that positions are somewhat generationally bound. The older generation who began working in the 50's and 60's are most preoccupied with the safety, preservation and continued accessibility of the existing work already in Canyon. And while supporting this work, the younger generation is trying [to] see how Canyon can be a viable place from which to distribute new moving image media." Ultimately, as Skoller suggests, the debate was less about whether video could be art, or deserved to be distributed and preserved, than about *where* this vital activity could best be done. At the time there seemed little clear evidence that Canyon's going into video distribution would add enough to its revenues to justify burdening the organization's small, efficient staff with further work or to allow for hiring additional staff. In the end new bylaws were approved without opening Canyon's membership to videomakers; and what had become the informal policy regarding video was confirmed and remains in place to this day: Canyon is a *film* distributor, though it does sell videos/DVDs.

The other major issue for Canyon during the 1990s was the organization's relationship with the National Endowment for the Arts. Beginning with *Catalog 4* in 1976, the production of Canyon catalogs had been supported by the NEA, along with the California Arts Council and various other donors (Lucasfilm in the case of *Catalog 5*); and from 1992, by a few ads included in the back of the catalogs. NEA support continued through *Film/Video Catalog 7* (the NEA money was not used to produce supplements, except in 1993 and 1994), but in 1997 Canyon received word that congressional representative Peter Hoekstra (R-Mich.) had instigated an investigation into NEA funding by the Subcommittee on Oversight and Investigations. Derrick Max, a professional economist on the subcommittee, contacted Canyon, asking for a copy of the most recent catalogue. David Sherman put *Catalog 7,* along with the 1993 and 1994 supplements, in the mail and soon learned via the *New York Times* that Hoekstra had found "many parts of Canyon's catalogue" objectionable: "First you look at the photographs—one was of several young boys that were naked. . . . There are several descriptions that are sexually graphic or offensive descriptions. Things that describe graphic sex or other kinds of things that caused us to say 'We'd like more information about those things'" (Jon Brandt, Hoekstra's press secretary, quoted in the April 16, 1977, *San Francisco Bay Guardian* in a story by Nina Siegal; I assume the image of the young boys Brandt refers to is on page 99 of *Catalog 7,* an image from Phillip B. Roth's *Boys/Life* [1989]).

Angerame learned that offended committee members had also been upset by an image of elderly lesbians kissing that had been used in *Film/Video Supplement 1994* (the image was a still from Barbara Hammer's *Nitrate Kisses* [1992]). According to Deborah Zimmerman of Women Make Movies, another distributor investigated, Cheryl Dunye's *Watermelon Woman* (1996) had drawn the first attention, and other filmmakers focused on in the investigation were Su Friedrich, for *Hide and Seek* (1996), and Yvonne Rainer, for *MURDER and murder* (1996): the Committee "hijacked our 25th Anniversary year; it was depressing and debilitating, and in the end we lost close to $200,000 in funding over the following years (until 1996 we had received NEA support regularly for a decade)" (Zimmerman, in an unpublished interview, June 5, 2006).

The NEA promised it would stand by Canyon. Indeed, Canyon was awarded a $15,000 grant in January 1997. But in the end, the grant was rescinded: Angerame believes "Jane Alexander sacrificed our organization to save the NEA" (unpublished interview with Angerame, January 23, 2006). *Film/Video Catalog 2000* was funded by grants from the San Francisco Arts Commission's Cultural Equity Grants Program and from the Tamarack Foundation, and by individual donations. Since the brouhaha, Canyon has received NEA money only once, a $10,000 grant in 1999 to support an effort to help potential users find their way to the Canyon collection; that money has helped to produce this volume.

At the end of 1994, Timoleon Wilkins, with help from Dominic Angerame and David Sherman, began publishing what he called the *New Canyon Cinemanews* ("the official member publication of Canyon Cinema, Inc."), a quarterly that lasted into 1996. Wilkins's *New Canyon Cinemanews* was, quite consciously, a flashback to the *Cinemanews* of the Diane Kitchen era and before. It included the sorts of items that had characterized the first decade of the *Cinemanews:* letters (including letters from Bruce Baillie, Chick Strand, and Tom DeWitt [now Tom Ditto]), minutes of Canyon board meetings, listings of new films available from Canyon, poems, reminiscences, photographs of filmmakers . . . And the *New Canyon Cinemanews* looked like the original journal: Wilkins chose similar type-faces, recalled the Exothematic Man to duty, and used layouts evocative of the early years (at 8½ x 5½, the *New Canyon Cinemanews* resembled the *Cinemanews* of 1969–1972). One bittersweet difference between the *New Canyon Cinemanews* and the earlier publication was the inclusion of obituaries of Canyon notables, including Earl Bodien (1943–1994) and Warren Sonbert (1947–1995). That, despite Wilkins's efforts, the *New Canyon Cinemanews* did not have a long run is primarily a testament to the arrival of digital technology; indeed, in some ways, Pip Chodorov's FRAMEWORKS listserv provides many of the kinds of opportunities offered by the *Cinemanews* during its early years and by the *New Canyon Cinemanews* (in fact, FRAMEWORKS sometimes hosts filmmakers and scholars who were familiar to the *Cinemanews* readership: Fred Camper, Bruce Baillie, and Jon Jost, for instance).

In recent years Canyon has functioned as an effective and efficient small dis-tribution business, and only that. It is no longer a nexus of a range of film activ-ities. Of course, it continues to be identified with the Bay Area, but for those in contact with Canyon, whatever informal interchange exists is a result of renter and rentee both being glad to have each other as a resource. The Canyon board continues to function and to be made up primarily of people from the Bay Area or with a close connection to the region who believe in the value of independent cinema and in artist-run, not-for-profit distribution. Dominic Angerame's long tenure as director of Canyon has at times caused some controversy. At one point, Robert Nelson conjectured that periodically having new, younger directors might re-create something of the energy of the early Canyon distribution. But there seems little question that Angerame has run the organization with com-mitment, skill, and integrity. Angerame has been practical and diplomatic, and especially in recent years has become a vocal defender of the independent dis-tribution of 16mm and of Canyon in particular (contributing, for example, to the FRAMEWORKS listserv).

As of 2007 Canyon remains a precarious but solvent distributor, though the arrival of DVD, and in particular the production of DVDs by film artists whose 16mm prints are distributed by Canyon, has been affecting rentals and causing serious concern. Angerame has said on the FRAMEWORKS listserv that the release of the *by Brakhage* DVD (*by Brakhage,* produced by Peter Becker and Kate Elmore for Criterion, and released in 2003, made available twenty-six Brakhage films, including *Window Water Baby Moving* [1959] and *Mothlight* [1963], two of his most frequently rented films) has clearly hurt 16mm rentals. Because it is precisely the most frequently rented filmmakers who are likely to have the opportunity to transfer their work onto DVD, the proliferation of DVDs by these filmmakers could have a substantial impact on Canyon. On the other hand, some believe that as the films get more widely known as a result of the DVDs, interest in screenings of the "real thing" will grow.

The beginning of 2006 looked problematic enough for Canyon Cinema that Angerame and the Canyon board decided to send out a letter asking for donations. "Canyon," the letter explained, "is now, for the first time, experiencing the possibility that it may not be able to continue to operate in the same way that it has taken for granted for so many years." Two specific problems are cited: "the proliferation of DVD and soon HD media projection in museums, classrooms, film festivals," and the real estate markets of San Francisco. In 2002, after it had become clear that its long-term tenure at 2325 Third Street was endangered by real estate activity in that area of San Francisco, Canyon moved to its current address at 145 Ninth Street. The move resulted in a substantial increase in rent and utilities, though the new space had the advantage of locating Canyon Cinema in the same building as several other noteworthy arts institutions: the Film Arts Foundation (publisher of *releaseprint*), Frameline (sponsor of the San Francisco International LGBT [Lesbian, Gay, Bisexual, Transgender] Film Festival), the San Francisco Jewish Film Festival, and the National Asian American Telecommunications Association—perhaps enhancing the distributor's profile in the Bay Area. By the end of the 2006–2007 fiscal year, however, Angerame and Nathaniel Dorsky, president of the board of directors, were surprised to be able to announce in the annual "Report to Our Filmmakers" that "this year Canyon Cinema is economically solvent," as a result of increased rentals and several substantial donations, including a $25,000 donation from LucasFilm.

I continue to hope that an increasing number of college professors teaching film history will recommit to 16mm as one of the valuable instruments on which cinema can be played (I am paraphrasing Gene Youngblood: "Cinema is the art of organizing a stream of audio-visual events in time. . . . There are . . . at least four media through which we can practice cinema—film, video, computer, holography—just as there are many instruments through which we practice music" [Metaphysical Structuralism: The Videotapes of Bill Viola," *Millennium Film Journal* 20, no. 1 (fall/winter 1988–89): 83]). And further, I continue to hope that increasing numbers of those who see themselves helping their students to understand cinema will make use of the remarkable collection Canyon has accumulated and has worked so hard to make available. It is conceivable, of course, that, in time, the bulk of the 16mm prints currently maintained and rented by Canyon will disappear or be archived, vestiges of a long-obsolete technology. But, as of 2006, the Canyon collection remains very much alive; it's not ready for the archive yet!

Conversation with Dominic Angerame, August 2002

MacDonald: You've been the director of Canyon longer than anyone.

Angerame: I've been here since 1980—since I was thirty! I'll be fifty-three in October.

MacDonald: How did you become involved with Canyon?

Angerame: I guess my route to Canyon Cinema started when I was making movies in Chicago. I remember coming across an old Canyon Cinema catalog— it had to be the 1974 catalog—and I told my (now ex-) wife, "I really want these people to distribute my movies." I didn't feel confident enough to send a film to Canyon until around 1978, when I deposited a film called *Neptunian Space Angel* [1977]. Little did I know that within the next year or so my wife would visit San Francisco and fall in love with it and would talk me into moving out here.

I had just graduated from the Art Institute of Chicago, and I was planning to take a job with the CTA [Chicago Transit Authority], collecting tickets; and I told her, "Well, I'll apply to the San Francisco Art Institute and if I get accepted, we'll move to California." And that's what happened. I was at the school about a year, and struggling to get by. One of my grad-student colleagues, Margaret White, was working part-time at Canyon Cinema and so the name came up again, and I said, "Oh, I have movies there."

Margaret said she was going to leave the Canyon job—she had married an Iranian filmmaker and they wanted to go back and film the Iranian revolution— and there would be a position open; if I was interested, I should go to Canyon and set up an interview with the board of directors.

That's what I did: in May of 1980 Margaret and Michael Wallin showed me the office. I had worked in film distribution in Chicago, distributing medical movies, so I wasn't totally unfamiliar with the process. And they told me that the next week there'd be a board meeting, and I'd be interviewed. The board liked me (one member happened to be a former colleague from the Art Institute of Chicago) and hired me.

MacDonald: Who was on the board?

Angerame: I remember Tony Reveaux, David Gerstein, Karen Holmes—there were others. The important thing was that Michael Wallin, the director at that time, and I had a decent conversation and we knew we could work together.

The intimacy of the place was obvious, but at that time Canyon was very chaotic. All the people working there were part-time students, like myself, working about twenty hours a week for about three dollars an hour. When I first came in, I sat down with Michael and we decided to eliminate a position, so we'd only have two positions and could increase our hours to half-time. I would do the film shipping and inspection and the bookkeeping, and Michael would handle all the film orders and deal with the clients.

And then, we talked about how to go about publishing a major new catalog. I applied for an NEA grant—the first time we had applied in five or six years—and they gave it to us. So we went into production. We were the production managers, and the editors and proofreaders, of *Catalog 5*—the black catalog with the drawing of the eyeball, by William Wiley, and the minute that catalog was released, in 1982 (it took us two years to get it out), business boomed. We saw such a tremendous interest in the work, that we established a policy of publishing a supplement every summer, when business was slow. We'd pay ourselves money from the grant to work on the catalogs, so we had work in the summer *and* new catalogs regularly. I've kept that tradition going up until relatively recently: now, the supplements are online, and we save the money of publishing hard copies of supplements.

MacDonald: That was an important way in which Canyon distinguished itself, not only from the New York Coop, which didn't have a new catalog for many years, but even from MoMA: you never quite know what MoMA has.

Angerame: Right now, we have a decent amount of money to use as seed money for the next major catalog. Of course, the trend of the future is that we probably won't print as many hard copies. We try to keep our Web site up-to-date on a month-to-month basis.

MacDonald: At what point did you become director of Canyon?

Angerame: Michael Wallin and I shared the directorship until around 1984–85, when he began to have major back problems and couldn't do the work anymore. Michael resigned after five or six years of hard labor and generosity with his time—because we were so underpaid. I had to hire someone else to come in, and it seemed unfair to me to still be a *co*-director, because I'd already been there for five or six years and had a good handle on what was going on with the business. I talked to the board about this and we decided to hire a person to come in and do the books. That way the bookkeeping responsibilities would be off of me; the other person would share the shipping and inspection duties. I would handle all the bookings and would become the director. That started around 1985. The first new person, Wendy Blair, only lasted a couple of years: Wendy had a child and left to deal with the family; and then in 1987 David Sherman took over her job.

I had been able to get an Andy Warhol grant to help photo-guard most of the collection, and we hired David for that project. He had worked for six or seven months on that grant, and when Wendy left, David was a natural fit. So I asked the board to hire David, and David worked here for twelve years. He was in charge of the shipping and inspection, though I still did some of that. Neither of us worked full-time, and Mark [Toscano] and I still don't, so we need to share responsibilities.

MacDonald: During the long period when you've worked at Canyon, I know there have been a number of fairly substantial brouhahas.

Angerame: Well, soon after I got to Canyon, there was a time when the board couldn't function because they were so busy arguing and screaming at each other. Around 1983–84, Dean Snider was a board member. Dean wanted all the films at Canyon Cinema distribution to be available at the theater he and others had started, called the No Nothing Cinema; and he was getting tremendous grief from the other members of the board, who just didn't agree with his philosophy or his aesthetics. These would turn into incredible shouting matches.

I think Dean wanted Canyon Cinema to be more integrated into the San Francisco film community. The No Nothing was an attempt at a revival of the original Canyon Cinema in Bruce Baillie's backyard. Dean had great admiration for Bruce Baillie, for Robert Nelson, for Chick Strand.

The No Nothing Cinema was started as a result of an earlier controversy—and I was part of this—where several filmmakers took over the Cinematheque. This was in 1981, when Carmen Vigil was director. Carmen was refusing to show any of my films, any of Dean Snider's films, any of Mark Stern's films, any of Marion Wallace's movies, any of Michael Rudnick's movies. So Dean and Tony Merritt had a meeting with Carmen, and said, "Carmen, look, we've been making movies for years, and you've not shown any of them. What's going on?" And Carmen says, "Your movies stink!" That pissed us all off, so we decided we would take over one of the Cinematheque screenings.

We barricaded the projection booth. Dean ran the projector; Lynne Kirby read a manifesto. Bruce Conner was there with us. We showed half an hour of our own movies. Carmen tried to turn off the electricity, and called the police. Before we left, we put the originally scheduled film—by Owen Land—back on the projector. We also published a newspaper called *Cinemattack*. It has interviews with Dean, and me, and others. I changed my name, called myself "Pete."

Carmen's board of directors freaked out after we took over the projection booth; they established a screening committee that would be deciding on shows, and Carmen didn't like that. He quit, and that's when Steve Anker came in.

So Dean and Rock Ross rented a warehouse south of Market, where the baseball stadium is now, and created the No Nothing Cinema. Dean's philosophy, and mine too, was to have an exhibition center that was totally open. Dean realized that, working at Canyon Cinema, I had a great access to a huge film library and to filmmakers. And that's where things between me and Dean got a little weird, because he wanted to show everything from Canyon Cinema at the No Nothing *for free,* and wanted me to oversee these screenings. I wasn't sure I wanted to take on the responsibility of the projection, cleaning, and inspection — plus these screenings wouldn't generate any revenue for Canyon. The controversy over this ended by alienating a number of filmmakers, including Snider and Michael Rudnick.

MacDonald: There were other controversies too, including the one about video.

Angerame: Yes. Nobody seemed to know how to handle the distribution of videotapes. Do we just rent them for two dollars a pop, like Blockbuster? How do we inspect them? How do we catalog them? What kind of material do we accept? There were people on the board who wanted to accept anything: How to Play Golf, How to Maintain Your Motorcycle, whatever. We were getting overwhelmed by people sending in grade B sexploitation movies. And there was a real fear by a couple of members that Canyon Cinema would cease to be controlled by filmmakers.

MacDonald: I can imagine all sorts of logistical problems. If you suddenly were a major video distributor, your catalog would have to be twice as large.

Angerame: And who pays for that, and maintains that? How do you hire staff? The membership fees we've charged over the years don't cover that cost. Basically, we did a compromise. We decided to allow people to distribute videotape, but for sale only. And people had to buy the tapes sight unseen; we wouldn't get involved in previewing.

MacDonald: You only allow people who have films in the collection to distribute their videos, right?

Angerame: No, we decided that people who are not film members could join for a higher, onetime membership fee, and could deposit videotapes for sale only.

They could not vote for the board of directors and therefore, they could not take over. One of our board members felt it was illegal that we would not allow video members to vote, illegal and also not right; and that's when major controversy broke out. We ought to accept video members, and we ought to open the doors, and we should become a nonprofit organization and set the wheels in motion to become a distribution center not just for motion picture film but for video and digital technologies.

MacDonald: I've looked at documents from that controversy and have talked to some of those involved, and it seems to be one of those situations where something is theoretically correct—why make a separation between film and video?—but practically devastating. Sure, everyone wants to be open to video, as well as film, but video has its own distributors, and *they* don't distribute 16mm film.

Angerame: That was my point of view as director. I kept saying at our board meetings, "Look, *this* is what I know how to do. There are other distributors for video. If someone wants to distribute video in the way Canyon distributes movies, why don't they start their own company. Why are we required to do this?"

During the video controversy, the board gave me a gag order; I could not speak to Bruce Conner! They ordered me not to give him any information about what was going on, and they went out and hired a lawyer who would seek an avenue to nonprofit status. The lawyer had some ideas; she wasn't sure they would fly. Bruce became indignant that the filmmaker members of Canyon Cinema were not notified as to the process that was going on. This is what Bruce's constant battle is. He feels the filmmakers need to be informed about major processes—that Canyon is not the property of the board.

MacDonald: So was this when he got all those proxies and held forth in that famous meeting?

Angerame: That's correct. The organization almost dissolved. Luckily David Gerstein had the wherewithal to adjourn the meeting at the very beginning, so discussion could happen, because it would have been devastating.

MacDonald: How do you mean?

Angerame: I think there might have been a call to dissolve the corporation. Or at least many people there would have decided not to be a part of it. I think the right action was taken, because what came from that meeting was a sensibility that we needed to form a democratic committee to research, once and for all, the pros and cons of being a for-profit or a nonprofit corporation.

We asked for volunteers from that open meeting to be on a committee that included myself, Larry Kless, David, Bruce, Ala Alvarez, and Irina Leimbacher—and through months of process we decided that the for-profit corporation was the *only* way we could go without getting into an enormous complexity and making the organization no longer a democratic organization controlled by the filmmakers. We decided we would be a shareholder corporation. The shares are fictitious; they don't really exist, but we treat Canyon as a shareholder corporation.

MacDonald: The idea of democracy at Canyon is complex, because Conner, Brakhage, and Anger and a very few others make the money that supports the organization and all these other members.

Angerame: I've realized over the years that if you removed the twenty-five most popular of our filmmakers from the organization, we'd lose maybe 50 percent or 60 percent of our income. Now the thing is, Canyon can *also* not exist without that other 40 percent or 50 percent, which comes from lesser-known filmmakers. We cannot afford to lose *any* of them. We *can* afford to lose people whose films don't rent for fifteen or twenty years, but the other 40 percent of our income is from people who rent modestly. We just can't afford to run a business on the top twenty-five people. Freude Bartlett tried to do that in the seventies—a major failure. Drift tried to do it—another major failure. I've seen it again and again with people who try to market just the cream of the crop. They end up ripping off the film artists and not paying the kinds of royalties they're supposed to be paying, and they fall apart.

I think our strength is our diversity. Running Canyon is a double-edged responsibility: there's our responsibility to the filmmakers to uphold our agreement with them, and it's up to them to uphold their agreement with us, by paying annual dues.

MacDonald: In addition to the film/video controversy, what other moments strike you as pivotal during the time you've been director?

Angerame: Well, about three years ago there was a major conflict between the staff and the board. David and I almost walked out and shut the doors behind us.

MacDonald: What was the controversy?

Angerame: There was a lack of confidence in us on the part of a couple of people on the board. The staff was asking for a raise, so that we could continue to live in San Francisco with escalating living costs, and the board was refusing to give us the raise. They wanted accounting figures; they wanted economic statistics—and they weren't believing the information I was giving them, which *was* totally accurate. We got into a two-year fight where we couldn't do anything;

it stalled our Web site. In the end, I think that's what pushed David to quit—at least indirectly.

We all have big egos, and even on the board there's a lot of professional jealousy. During that time period, Bruce Baillie was invited to Bangkok and couldn't go. He wanted me to go and represent him. And the board was telling me not to go; I think some members of the board were just jealous. I don't know how else to understand it.

It's a hard thing to put your own issues on the back burner for the greater cause, but I continue to be involved with Canyon because I realize that Canyon *is* the greater cause. It's part of the greater cause of experimental filmmaking, and when it succeeds, we all succeed.

MacDonald: And if it were to fail . . .

Angerame: Then there's nothing. And that becomes very clear very quickly once you think about it.

MacDonald: I'm curious about this moment when you and David were under fire. Can I know what you two earned at that point?

Angerame: I think I was making $28,000; David was taking three months off and going to Bisbee, so he was making $14,000 or $15,000. We hadn't had a cost-of-living increase for a long time. Canyon had a surplus in the budget, and we asked for the surplus. We said, "Look, we've been saving the company a lot of money, but we can't live like this."

At first, the board agreed to give us something like a 4 percent increase retroactive over a year, which was nothing. It was disgusting. And so when David left, I came up with a business plan and made some demands. I now make about $40,000, which is barely livable in San Francisco, and Mark makes $24,000 or $25,000—much more than David did. But business has been really good, and my philosophy has always been if the business succeeds, you put that back into your staff, or you do *something* for them. Otherwise we lose people, and I can't hire good people for $10 an hour. When I first got here, all of us were on food stamps. It was a dismal employer-employee situation. Right now Mark and I have medical benefits. We don't have retirement, which is a problem—I should have dealt with that a long time ago.

MacDonald: Why do you think business has improved?

Angerame: I think there are several factors. San Francisco is definitely one of the world's capitals of experimental filmmaking, so there's a lot of interest here, and there are a lot more people now with a genuine interest in seeing projected experimental motion pictures.

MacDonald: So a substantial portion of your business comes from the Bay Area?

Angerame: We used to get an enormous amount of business from California, but now that has dropped somewhat. Now it's the East Coast, and since Brakhage has been in Colorado, rentals have been coming in from that area. And Chicago. And a lot from Europe. I think the inefficiencies of the other distribution organizations have sometimes sent people to us. Over the years, we've built up a lot of confidence that we'll get the films to them at a fair price.

I learned when I worked in distribution in Chicago, that you have to do what you say you're going to do. You have to build up confidence with people. If you don't do that, the whole place is doomed to failure. It took me years to earn Bruce Conner's confidence: he only had one movie with us when I started working here. It was years before he would give us other prints.

Another Canyon controversy was that David and I had a gag order about movies. If somebody called me up and wanted suggestions, we couldn't give them suggestions. But together, David and I have seen probably half the collection! Why can't I tell somebody that I believe this movie is a good optical printing film? It was ridiculous.

So we had major discussions, and finally the board passed a policy that we did have the right to promote the movies, which has led me to go into other areas, such as curating for the San Francisco Film Festival; and I think we're going to do a series at the Museum of Modern Art next year. We want to promote the organization.

MacDonald: What's your sense of the job now? Do you feel in it for the long term?

Angerame: That's a good question. I never expected to work at Canyon for more than a year or so. I figured that once I graduated from the Art Institute, that would be it, but I've found it so challenging and rewarding that I'm hooked.

Addendum, May 2006

MacDonald: I understand that recently you've begun to notice a falling off of film rentals.

Angerame: It began about a year and a half ago; our last quarter of last year (2004–2005) showed a large slowdown.

MacDonald: How do you account for this?

Angerame: It's largely about DVDs. I noticed in the specific case of Brakhage, our most rented filmmaker, that his rentals dropped off once the Brakhage DVD was released [see p. 409].

MacDonald: I'm surprised because there's been a lot of talk, especially on the avant-garde film listserv, FRAMEWORKS, about Brakhage's insistence that that DVD not be used in lieu of rentals of 16mm prints. Marilyn Brakhage has made this point, as has Fred Camper, who supplied the written information about the Brakhage films included in *by Brakhage.* Of course, most academics who rent the Brakhage films or buy the DVD are probably not on FRAMEWORKS.

Angerame: Unfortunately, the DVD doesn't *say* that it is not intended for classroom use or public exhibition. If I had been consulted when the DVD was in production, I definitely would have suggested that they make that explicit on the packaging.

The way it is now, a college library will buy a copy of the DVD, and that will take care of all classroom use of Brakhage's films for the foreseeable future. They do buy the DVD at an institutional rate, but still, I don't think the filmmaker gets much return on a DVD purchase—and it's a real problem for us.

MacDonald: Have DVDs other than *by Brakhage* cut into rentals?

Angerame: When Kenneth Anger releases his films on DVD, I'm sure the same thing will happen. I would hope that he'll put something on his DVD indicating that it is not for classroom use or public presentation, but I've not been able to reach Ken recently, so I don't know whether he's thinking about this at all. [*The Films of Kenneth Anger, Volume One* was released in 2007 by Fantoma; the DVD box, in extremely small print, does say: "WARNING: For private home use only. Any unauthorized public performance, broadcasting or copying is a violation of applicable laws. Violators will be prosecuted"; and the DVD brochure indicates that "16mm film rentals for classroom and public screenings" are available through Canyon Cinema, and provides the relevant Web addresses.]

MacDonald: Exactly what is the size of the recent drop-off in rentals? How serious is your financial crunch?

Angerame: Our expenses are still high. Our rent is higher than it was two years ago, and in general the cost of living in San Francisco continues to go up. Rentals, our main source of income, are down. And our videotape sales are *way* down; there's enormous competition from Re:Voir [Re:Voir, which is run by Pip Chodorov, was founded in 1994 in France to produce quality VHS tapes of noteworthy avant-garde films]. It costs anywhere from $8,000 to $12,000 a month to keep our office running; that's with salaries and benefits, and postage and rent and everything else. We need to do about $24,000 in film rentals per month, which we don't do. We're losing something like $2,000 a month.

The first quarter of this year (2006–2007) ends in May, and right now we're doing a bit better than we did last year (we've grossed $34,000), but still it's not enough to make me think that it's going to bounce back up to where it should be. Ideally, it should be $45,000. Last year, the same quarter was $26,000; but the year before that, $43,000; and the two years before that, $40,000 and $40,000.

MacDonald: In some recent years, from 2000 until 2003 especially, there was a considerable jump in revenues, as big a jump upward as the recent jump downward.

Angerame: Right after Stan passed away, we had a huge rental from Japan for the Brakhage films, about $20,000.

MacDonald: Probably everyone was renting Brakhage in the months after his death.

Angerame: Everyone *was* renting Brakhage. Actually, I had been expecting a deficit that year, but the Brakhage retrospectives saved us. The interest in his work will continue, but the demand for the films seems likely to taper off from those first years after his death. And now there's the DVD.

MacDonald: I understand that Bruce Conner has withdrawn his films from Canyon.

Angerame: Yes, we'll take another hit—about $20,000 this year. Bruce was about 15 percent of our business.

MacDonald: What does the board plan to do about this problem?

Angerame: It's very unclear. We have drafted a letter asking for donations—and some donations have been coming in—but as yet, we don't know what *can* be done.

PORTFOLIO

Tom DeWitt

Dear Board:

Regression. Article II regression.

The original *Articles of Incorporation* refer to "cinematic art." The *Revised Articles* refer to "motion picture film." The former is inclusive. The latter is exclusive. The word "cinematic" has a very broad connotation. It includes all motion media. It was presciently written and has far more validity today than the revised version which will only narrow Canyon's scope.

I appreciate that you wanted to update Canyon's mission. Unfortunately, this critical part of the *Revised Articles* are the proverbial shot in the foot. It will handicap the corporation far more than the original statement of purpose.

Film, with its punched holes, mechanical pull down, incandescent lamps, scratch-prone, color-unstable, and extremely expensive emulsions may not survive far into the next century. How long will raw stock even be available to make prints? If there are no film labs left, should Canyon end distribution? Suppose the film prints are deemed too valuable to rent, but video copies are available. Will this create a situation by which some other medium will jeopardize Canyon's mission to distribute the work on film thereby violating the very purpose of the corporation?

Why lock Canyon so explicitly into commerce in the film medium? It's suicide. We are motion picture artists, not motion picture film artists. It is not the physical medium that defines us. It is our vision and creative talent.

Moreover, the use of the English language in Article II is ungrammatical. One does not say, "media is," rather, "media are." Medium is the singular. The last sentence should read either, "Should any other medium be incorporated into Canyon Cinema, Inc., it will in no way jeopardize Canyon's mission to distribute work on film." Otherwise write, "Should any other media be incorporated into Canyon Cinema, they will in no way jeopardize Canyon's mission to distribute work on film."

I have not heard anything about my proposal to restrict video to optical disk distribution and sale. Please give me some feedback.

Best test cement

George Kuchar

San Francisco Art Institute
800 Chesnut Street
San Francisco, CA
94133 415/771-7020

[Editor's note: This letter is handwritten and undated.]

Dear Jeffrey [Skoller]:

Best of luck on your far-sighted plans for the future. Having seen the hard work you put into your films I know that you love that medium and are not out to destroy it. It has destroyed you.

As a previous victim of celluloid abuse, I salute your march into the digital decades ahead. The founding fathers of thy filmic tradition are either dead or dead and still walking. The stench of vinegar dessicates their edge-numbered droppings. Their temples to cinematic exposition reek of funeral fumes. The young in our houses of learning are taught to cannibalize the Canyon classics. They now come to eat us . . . the so-called master chefs. I go gladly to the banquet table and hope that you rosy-cheeked, young people carve us up with the most technically advanced utensils. I go in peace by piece. Farewell for I must get back to editing my latest video so that I may have leisure time in the days ahead to manipulate the CD-i, interactive player.

Best wishes,

P.S. and B.S.: The true motivating powers of madness and perversion have been replaced by correctness and croissants. God have mercy on us all!

Robert Nelson

March 31, 1994

To Canyon Cinema Directors and Members:

I am pleased to hear that a long overdue membership meeting is about to take place. It is my hope that enough of the membership attend so that a quorum may legally transact some of the urgent business at hand. In order to assist that possibility, I have assigned my proxy vote to Bruce Conner. I urge any other members who cannot attend to assign their proxy vote (in writing) to someone who will attend.

I label the following notes and suggestions "miscellaneous" because they are supplementary to the main issues of creating legal and appropriate Articles of Incorporation and legal, appropriate and functional bylaws.

Film vs. Video

The I.D.D.I. (Independent Drum Drummers International) last year voted 165 to 9 to *not* allow bongo-drum makers into their organization. The steel drum makers of the I.D.D.I. knew that the far more numerous and growing ranks of bongo-drummers would divert the focus and dilute the energy away from the specific needs that had originally inspired the charter group to form (grants from oil company suppliers and welding, cutting-torch and acetylene access).

Often it is not just an arbitrary or exclusionary impulse that causes individuals to form a group. The collective pursuit of shared interests and benefits sometimes is reason enough to collectivize and form criteria for memberships.

The technological and economic basis of filmmaking and film distribution is distinct and differs significantly from the techno-economic base of any and all other media and any and all other media distribution. Film also has the distinction of being a medium that is (perhaps) dying in front of our eyes as services and support systems wither and shrink while costs escalate.

We don't invite artists from other media to be members of Canyon Cinema because to do so would blur our collective focus and create factions of divergent interests. Once we lose our collective purpose we create a minority in our own ranks that is in competition with the majority interest.

Of course video is a worthy medium. Of course video artists are as good as filmmakers. Of course video artists are worthy of support. Of course they should have their own organization in order to collectively pursue their goals and interests. If someone wants to form a sister organization called *Video Canyons* I would even vote to loan them our mailing list at a reduced fee. Let's support our desolate brothers and sisters of the independent art world whatever their tools or production.

Films may not be in the world for very much longer, but for now please, let's keep Canyon Cinema for filmmakers only. No video distribution or sales . . . only films. If we limit ourselves to films and filmmakers we will be able to continue to define and agree on our collective interests.

At some point in the near future at the upcoming meeting or as soon as is appropriate I hope that some form of the following motions will be presented and voted on:

MOTION: THAT the new Articles of Incorporation and bylaws specifically limit membership to filmmakers.

(and further) that Canyon Cinema does not distribute or in any way become financially involved in the distribution sale or promotion of any art produced in any medium other than film.

(and further) that only filmmakers with prints on deposit and who are otherwise in good standing be considered members.

(and further) that only members be eligible to become DIRECTORS. . . .

Sincerely

Stan Brakhage

April 11, 1994

To: CANYON CINEMA COOPERATIVE MEMBERSHIP
(appropo issues relevant to April 19th, 1994, Annual Membership Meeting)

1) I would not personally be in favor of any rule which (for example) could exclude Bruce Baillie's "P 38 Pilot" or the videos of George Kuchar; but it seems to me quite obvious that Canyon Cinema cannot afford (financially, that is) to accept the deluge of videos now pouring into it: it would seem reasonable to me to accept ONLY those videos by members who have films in the Co-Op.

2) I object strongly to the use of the word "work" in the currently suggested new by-laws, inasmuch as it is quite clearly a loop-hole which runs counter to the stated objectives of Canyon Cinema in its original by-laws *and* in those proposed by the newly suggested by-laws — i.e. that Canyon Cinema was created for and is dedicated to Film.

3) I object strongly to any rules which would preclude members from, or make it difficult for members, attending meetings of the board of directors — thus am very opposed to the rule suggested in the newly proposed by-laws that 12 days notice must be given previous to a meeting one wants to attend.

4) I wish to make it quite clear that I am not opposed to the current board of directors, that I have nothing but sympathy for them in consideration of the legal complexities which have befallen them (the need to re-write the by-laws . . . not to mention the current confusions as to the future state of the medium of Film vis-à-vis other media of moving imagery); but I (who DO very much believe in the future of Film) would plead, with the members of this organization dedicated to Film to have a little faith in that future — especially in the light of the enormous number of young film-makers absolutely dedicated to that medium at present . . . young people far greater in number more purely so dedicated (i.e. UNdistracted by video or by specious hopes for careers in Hollywood somesuch) than at any

previous time in history — far more, for example, more clearly dedicated, than in the 1960s.

5) I have given my proxy for this evening's meeting to Bruce Conner; and I wish that, and all other proxies, to be honored in this meeting: but I do fully understand that the decisions made by vote in this meeting cannot be absolutely binding on the board's final decisions re-writing the by-laws inasmuch as they must factor (briefly because of the expense) thru a lawyer and with The State of California. I think the votes of this meeting, however, must be recorded and sent to the full membership, along with the finally proposed new by-laws, so that the membership-at-large have a way to gauge just exactly how responsive the board has been to the votes of this meeting in its final proposal when that membership-at-large votes on the new by-laws being proposed

Blessings, [hw]

—

FROM THE *NEW CANYON CINEMANEWS*, JANUARY 1995

Bruce Baillie
LETTER FROM CAMANO ISLAND, OCTOBER 10, 1994

[Editor's note: Baillie included several footnotes at the end of his letter; I have placed the information in those notes within brackets at the point in the text where the notes are called out. I've put Baillie's notes in quotation marks to distinguish them from my interpolations.]

[. . .] And so it went. *Many* adventures and tales to recount.

We discovered James Broughton was living in San Francisco. There was a section in the pre-Brandon catalogue devoted to James' work as well as to the films of Maya Deren, Willard Maas, Sidney Peterson and others. I met James one dark night at his home where I found a wonderful empathy and sense of camaraderie toward the impossible tasks ahead. The (later) Brandon distribution center whose earlier name eludes me at the moment, (Audio-Brandon?) was out on Clement Street, managed by Willard Morrison. Willard also became a friend through many years, and eventually took it upon himself to include some of our films in the "experimental" section of his catalogue. In 1963, he also advanced me the sum necessary for 6 or 7 rolls of EK film, my first color [*"To Parsifal"*].

Will Hindle lived on Vallejo Street, off Van Ness, across from a Chinese laundry. He would cross the street to pick up two or three laundered shirts, artfully wrapped in transparent bags, and perhaps buy a few things at the corner store which is still there. His closet, shared with roommate, George ——, whose last name will likely remain forgotten ["A biography is currently in the works by Ms. Diana Whatley, Tampa, FL., with cooperation of an attorney in Huntsville, Ala. Funds for same are very much needed: Any assistance gratefully received c/o Canyon Cinema"], was a memorably long and scrupulously exact recess with trousers and slacks on the one side, separated according to their owners; shirts and jackets being on the opposite. Shoes — polished — beneath hanging clothes on both sides. It always reminded me of a page from an uptown clothiers' catalogue!

As well as the works of Paul Hindemith (*Pastorale d'Eté*), there were albums of musicals — *Oklahoma*, and so on, one or the other usually playing. I also recall pieces of San Francisco architecture arranged around the apartment: the base of a column, part of a church window, a Victorian door frame, etc. In the rear was Bill's studio area, for editing, shooting interiors and titles, recording and commercial still photography. He used only simple equipment; e.g., measuring by hand the quarter-inch non-sync sound master for his first several films. Sometimes Kikuko, the dogs and I would bring over food while he was working. I would help out at times by running through reels of sound while Will was editing film. We later worked together for CBS I think it was, doing a segment for the *PM West Show*, annual Fiesta in a studio car, accompanied by a fellow (whose jacket I still wear after he left town without his clothes in 1963), an escapee from the Presidio Army Hospital. We had a good time together, I wonder where he might be now.

All this for another occasion, mentioned here because Will Hindle was a special friend and artist with whom I worked closely for some time, and for whom there was vital interest in the shaping of our Canyon Cinema. I will always remember the "silvery" images he was able to get out of his Bolex, especially through his 3" Kodak lens, which I was privileged to use one or two times. His mother still lives, at the age of more than one-hundred years, in the state of Alabama.

Pauline Kael began occasionally to write of our "precious" films. She was always a good friend and a severe, literate critic. Jordan Belson lived in SF and made his abstract masterpieces there in an austere, lovely, monastic apartment. He photographed through holes in small pieces of board. He had a tiny, precise and quiet 16MM theater in his small apartment, the best for its scale I have seen. Kenneth Anger lived for a time, I remember, in rooms he occupied above a nice little theater somewhat east of North Beach, near the old open market, with its lovely and mysterious, usually Gay apartments looking out on the carts and stalls of fresh produce below. I can still see his big Kodak single-lens 16MM in its velvet-lined case — was it blue? He did A-roll only, using a frame splicer and mylar tape on one side. I also recall his buck Rogers collection — large theater posters, the Buck Rogers ray-gun (which I also remember actually on sale in the 30's at the toy counter of Woolworth's) and the small cast iron rocket ship. I traveled extensively one year, '64 or '65, with his famous *Scorpio Rising*, Vanderbeek's *Breath Death* and my own *Mass*.

Larry & Patty Jordan lived in SF, later north of the Golden Gate — he was the first "independent filmmaker" I'd heard of. Speaking to Patty across the Bay by phone in Early '61 or so, I was making my first naïve inquiries . . . how, where to begin, etc.?! Later, we often showed Larry's work at Canyon and crossed paths through the Midwest, New York, etc., along with other film artist-friends such as Stan Brakhage, Ken & Flo Jacobs, Stan Vanderbeek and Ed Emshwiller & his family.

Jonas Mekas and crew were moving into the new Anthology Film Archives: I recall an early showing with Gregory Markopoulos making an appearance, wearing a long beige cashmere coat off the shoulders, Fellini style, followed by his entourage.

As the custom of touring with films matured, between '64 and the beginning of the 70's, approximately, one found various places on the map where he/she could feel at home: In NYC I always stayed with filmmaker Charles Levine and his mother. Mrs. Levine kept us alive with her cooking, especially the chicken soup! I enjoyed as well my few stays at the old Chelsea Hotel, where Brendan Behan and Dylan Thomas had stayed — gold plaques outside on the front, also Harry Smith, I believe (no plaque). I used to give roses to all the ladies in the bar next door, and a case of champagne with bread and cheese to my audience when I showed in NY. And there was Leslie Trumbull to come along and run Filmmakers' Cooperative for such a long time, on Lexington Avenue, where it is managed now by M. M. Serra.

We had Ann Arbor and the yearly film festival, founded by George Manupelli, an old friend in whose house I used to stay, premiering new work year after year. For exercise in winter blizzards, along with composer, Gordon Mumma, we would shovel cars out of the snow or shovel older people's walks, no charge. For a short while there was Pocatello and the hot spring, until poet Ed Dorn and a circle of other brilliant professors were asked to leave by the city's fundamentalist fathers!

I was traveling in '65 through both places, shooting *Quixote*, with a quick run down to Selma, Alabama, from Ann Arbor, Michigan. David Spellman of Aberdeen, SD, had loaned me $25 to get off the ground — I gave a show at the college in Bozeman for $50 attended by three students and one teacher (It was a football night). The first leg of *Quixote* was more or less sponsored by my dear friend, Tseng Ching, a music fellow at Mills College — we traveled together, with my dog (Mamma) through the Southwest before I struck out in the winter for the north. I will always be grateful to Ms. Tseng and numerous other friends — and the free, outdated film we picked up in an Hollywood alley — for helping me to make that film. It was not until a year later that I was able financially to develop the closet full of negatives.

And for a time there was Sally Dixon's in Pittsburgh. A very lovely lady who gave her three-story home over to our importunities, arranging our shows, etc. A local film group formed there, where our friend, Robert Haller first appeared to us — now with Anthology Film Archives in NY. There is some unfinished material I shot at Sally's for the *Roslyn Romance*, from the "later Pittsburgh period," in my own archivery. It was/is of an hilarious supper with Sally, Ken Anger, Robert Haller, myself, Ondine, and Roger Jacoby — we were creating an impromptu Western script that wouldn't stop. At Sally's, I took to sleeping on the floor in the cellar next to the washing machine, while — I recall — greeting the newly arrived Kenneth Anger (he gave his entire Magic Lantern cycle at Carnegie Mellon University in Pittsburgh to an audience of 6 or 7, entirely indifferent to the size of the turnout, answering questions professionally, then retiring again to Sally's, where he took the upstairs suite). In the cellar, I was occasionally blessed with a lovely companion for the night, or an afternoon, it was always a joy to visit there. With my dog, I would sometimes carry out overdue maintenance on a faithful black VW (a Beetle with seats removed, bed installed; carrying food, water, film, clothes, tripod, recorder and tools).

I recall the kindness of Sally Dixon and her honest concern for us filmmakers; she and James Blue together at the Pittsburgh house toiling over a plan to create free health insurance for all of us!

Gerald O'Grady in Buffalo, many visits, many shows, good times. He lived like an ascetic — 3 shirts, 3 pairs of black/navy blue socks, 3 trousers, one jacket, 2 or 3 ties, one worn pair of black shoes. Bed and briefcase. I slept in his apartment once, but Buffalo had become too noisy for me. Stan B. and I visited there, speaking of . . . our comings and goings. He had his small 8MM at the time. I presented Jerry with a general's star, from my boyhood collection. This was the last time I saw him.

To more or less confine this monograph, as Sherlock Holmes might have remarked — or this extended NEWS, to the earlier, California days, perhaps to conclude with a few more notes: We held our first official festival by returning to Canyon, it was about 1964. On the program were films by Stan Brakhage, Larry Jordan, myself, Ken Jacobs, Allen Downs (my University of MN teacher, later moved to Mexico), George Manupelli, Stan Vanderbeek, Ed Emshwiller, Jonas Mekas, Lloyd Williams, Gregory Markopoulos, Paul Beattie (who was another of the very early Bay Area filmmakers), Bruce Conner, Christopher MacLaine, Dave Myers, Marvin Becker, Will Hindle, Carl Linder, Jack Smith, Chick Strand, Michael Putnam, Ben Van Meter and others.

Ron Rice came through town with two ladies. It was to be his last run. They needed a room and some editing equipment, enroute to Mexico. Chicky and I visited them one evening, Ron editing in a corner, hanging his film on lines of women's undies strung across the room. He shot 50' rolls of surplus machine-gun film. He never returned from Old Mexico. His film, *The Flower Thief* was shown from the early 60's to the present.

In '64, Rockefeller saved me from a debtor's life, in the final nick of time, as I was going into my best few years. I had moved north to live at Morning Star, 40 acres owned by Lou Gottlieb ["A doctor of musicology and member of the Limelighters, then retired near Sebastopol, CA, to pursue self-knowledge and open his property to others."]. In the beginning there were only four of us, Lou, Ramon Sender (SF Tape Music Center), artist Wilder Bentley, and myself. We took turns cooking while Uncle Lou told us stories evenings by the great medieval fireplace. I rented a small cabin for my film work and set up a place to sleep with Mamma-dog under the trees with tarp, buffalo robe and lantern. We found our way at night by identifying the trees against the sky, to where the trail led off to the left, walking the next leg by memorizing the distance. Later, Morning Star was a famous commune. Lou willed the property "to God," arguing brilliantly in the local courts his right to allow free access to his land. Every word of the daily proceedings then was printed in the Santa Rosa paper.

Sometime in this period, or a bit later, Canyon Cinema moved to a sail loft in Sausalito and was run by a very nice woman, whose name was possibly Jan [Jan Lash], God forgive me for not recalling her name. At this time too, we had our Cinematheque at the SF Art Institute. Edith Kramer, who is now at UC Film Archives, took over Canyon Cinema next and stayed for quite some time. Nearly everyone had a go at it through the years.

Brakhages came to San Francisco for a year or so — early 60's — and were fondly embraced as a part of our lives and works at that time. I remember both Stan and Jane asking me directly, "Why are you doing all this?!" or some such. I replied, "Because it needs doing —," which seemed to be a doubtful response, though it was the simple truth. I also recall asking Stan if I could borrow his B&H. "Yes," he said, "I would loan it to you if you asked, but I would never be able to use it again." I have since had to give a similar response to the same inquiry. A camera, like a horse, never works right again once loaned ["At Bard College, Peter Kubelka was asked by an innocent student about the fun and the 'wonder' of being able to carry a camera everywhere through one's life, to which he replied (roughly translated), 'There is no *fun* in such commitment, only toil and perhaps terror!' Also refer to the introduction to Stan Brakhage's published lectures, Chicago Art Institute." I assume Baillie is referring to Stan Brakhage, *Film Biographies* (Berkeley: Turtle Island Press, 1977), and/or Stan Brakhage, *Film at Wit's End* (Kingston, NY: Documentext, 1989)].

Charles Levine came to SF for a time. Bruce and Jean Conner showed up somewhere in our lives, I can't recall exactly when, though I believe they have lived at Sussex Street forever. Bruce Conner, a great all-round artist and athlete, also managed Canyon Cinema for a time. Charles was in San Francisco, as "Ambassador from New York" (Jonas Mekas' title) in 1966, where he made three films during his stay. In June of that year there occurred the founding of Canyon Cinema Cooperative, with meetings at the Haight Street Theatre and the SF Museum of Art. Among those involved in its formation at that time were filmmakers Ben Van Meter and Tom DeWitt, as well as Charles Levine, Larry Jordan, myself (at times), John Schofill (later director of the film dept., the Chicago Art Institute), Earl Bodien, Lenny Lipton ["Lenny Lipton had a column in the *Berkeley Barb*, the only regular review & criticism of and for 'independent cinema' at that time"], and others. Earl and Charles were to author the first charter and settle the Co-op in an Haight Street rental: We had scheduled two rather large showings — according to Charles' information — one in San Francisco, the other at UC, Berkeley. Jonas Mekas generously contributed $1,000; along with another thousand, Canyon Cinema Cooperative, managed by Earl Bodien became a reality in the summer of 1966.

Robert Nelson came around before '66, when we were neighbors with the Tape Music Center. I recall Canyon premiering his first works. Then Gunvor Nelson's films: with daughter, Oona, at their house by the sea north of the City . . . where I stayed one night — the house guest in an Ingmar Bergman movie, visiting the lady guests in those various nooks and crannies of that marvelous manor of my memory. (Perhaps this was why for so many years I remained an uninvited guest at the SF Art Institute, in spite of their honorary MFA and my infamous seminar, "Alternatives to Success.")

On and on —

Remembering things past — the mid-50's, after the University at Minnesota — Sally Stanford's, amongst the house boat community of Sausalito. Saturday nights riding across the Bay and Golden Gate Bridges on my Matchless twin, either to Sally's or North Beach's Old Spaghetti Factory — my friend and chef, Don __, who was as well a former P-39 pilot. Perhaps sampling too many of the lovely wines, I would stand on my head against the back of Sally Stanford's place or elsewhere in the darkness and do vertical push-ups in order to clear my head. This period, when I lived in the old Lydiksen house in Canyon which now haunts my dream life as archetypal home of the spirit.

Late 50's. Phyllis Diller was appearing at the Purple Onion in SF, while the former radio voice . . . of the invisible *Shadow* was being murdered aboard his Sausalito houseboat.

In our early filmmaking years, the labs were especially helpful and often friendly: The elder Mac McKinney, of Multichrome on Gough Street helped get me underway, along with other original mentors already mentioned. At the time I had a 400' capacity Kodak projector that scratched film, and my (new) Bolex. My first halting tests with the camera and exposure meter were on B&W Plus-X reversal, with my two dogs out on the beach, near the amusement center (I recall that lovely, classic merry-go-round). Mr. McKinney made beautiful EK prints (later of *Castro Street*, '66). Mac had a WC Fields nose, like a glass hen's egg in color — from long exposure to toxic photo chemistry. His son, Mac II took over for some years before Multichrome disappeared. He was also a good man. Somehow in the end there was great difficulty in recovering our various film originals.

Scott Bartlett and I met one sunny afternoon outside Multichrome — I had just delivered the A-B rolls for *Mass*. We went to his place and looked over his set-up, where he did re-shooting and high contrast color developing — I can't remember exactly how he was achieving his interesting effects. Scott lived with Freude at the time — she too became a filmmaker and film distributor. Scott and Tom DeWitt worked together on *Off-On*. When I was ill in Ft. Bragg ('70), his dear sister came up north to stay awhile; she appears in *Quick Billy* ["*Quick Billy*, the title was given me by my old friend, Paul Tulley. Charlotte Todd (also appearing in the film), Paul & myself created Reel IV together"]. She and her brother are among many friends in my life whom I shall never forget.

Other SF labs were, and are, WA Palmers and Monoco, both still doing good work. I have several quite decent S-VHS video masters made recently at Monoco. Palmers have done most of my printing: Ms. Kay Kibby was a wonderful help there for twenty years.

We filmed the protests against atomic testing in the Pacific — the infamous SF Courthouse scenes: Shoulder to shoulder with the men in big suits (FBI or CIA), "We know who you are!" etc. The napalm trucks came in and out of Martine, north of Berkeley. Day and night vigiling along the road. Footage somewhere in my archivery.

Ah yes, one more note. There still exists somewhere in Berkeley, an entire set of lovely blue mohair theater seats which belong to Canyon Cinema. Alas.

Another big thanks to Chicky Strand and to Dominic Angerame, Steve Anker, David and crew for carrying on after thirty-four years of Canyon Cinema, the subsequent and contemporary SF Cinematheque, and now and again an occasional NEWS! Apologies, finally, for what I may somehow have forgotten. I hope to atone in the current writing I am doing, now in a sixth year: *Memoires of an Angel*, a combination of narrative and autobiography.

Hellos to all from Lorie and daughter, Wind in Camano Island.

Appendix 1: Canyon Cinema Employees, 1969 to the Present (name and dates of tenure)

Edith Kramer	1969–1970
Don S. Lloyd	1969–1972
Ken DeRoux	1969–1973
Peter Hutton	1970–1971
Jan Lash	1970–1971
David B. Boatwright	1971
Paul Lawrence	1971
Dagny McClosky	1971
Eugene J. Kenney	1972
Paul Marioni	1972–1973
Susan O'Neill	1972–1973
Adolfo A. Cabral	1973–1974
Rene Fuentes-Chao	1973–1974
Diane Kitchen	1973–1977
Roslyn Schwartz	1974
Larry J. Huston	1974–1975
Wolfram B. Zimmermann	1974–1975
Diane M. Levine	1974–1978
Vincent Jean Grenier	1975
Carmen Vigil	1975–1976
Charles Wright	1975–1976
Shelley Diekman	1975–1977
C. Rock Ross	1975–1977
Douglas Wendt	1975–1977
John H. Joy	1977
Joseph Van Witsen	1977
Janet Perlberg	1977–1979
Richard H. Beveridge	1977–1980

Abigail Child	1978
Michael Wallin	1978–1986
Ann Cole	1979
Margaret J. White	1979–1980
Dominic Angerame	1980–present
Andrew Moore	1981–1982
Toney Prussia Merritt	1983
Mary Marsh	1985
Wendy Blair	1985–1989
Amy Stewart	1988
David G. Sherman	1988–2000
Charlotte Hill	1991–1994
Suzann Rucigno	1993
Timoleon Wilkins	1995–1996
Vertna Bradley	1998
Lisa Sousa	1998
Michael Rosas Walsh	1998
Steve Polta	1998–2000
Klara Grunning	2000–2002
Pamela Harris	2000–2003
Mark Toscano	2000–2003
Michele Silva	2003–2007
Jan Doyle	2007
Lauren Sorensen	2007

Appendix 2: Canyon Cinema's Gross Rentals and Sales, from 1966 until 2006–2007

Year	Sale Films	Sale Video	Sale Rentals	Total
1966–1967	0	0	$9,000	$9,000
1967–1968	0	0	$15,000	$15,000
1968–1969	0	0	$40,000	$40,000
1969–1970	0	0	$54,000	$54,000
1970–1971	0	0	$38,000	$38,000
1971–1972	0	0	$41,000	$41,000
1972–1973	0	0	$28,000	$28,000
1973–1974	0	0	$37,000	$37,000
1974–1975	0	0	$32,000	$32,000
1975–1976	0	0	$30,000	$30,000
1976–1977	0	0	$26,000	$26,000
1977–1978	0	0	$32,000	$32,000
1978–1979	0	0	$30,000	$30,000
1979–1980	0	0	$38,000	$38,000
1980–1981	0	0	$28,841	$28,841
1981–1982	0	0	$31,093	$31,093
1982–1983	0	0	$38,541	$38,541
1983–1984	0	0	$42,567	$42,567
1984–1985	0	$1,575	$51,205	$52,780
1985–1986	0	0	$51,307	$51,307
1986–1987	0	0	$52,055	$52,055
1987–1988	$2,734	0	$56,587	$59,321
1988–1989	$1,140	$1,684	$69,639	$72,734
1989–1990	$895	$5,768	$65,823	$72,486
1990–1991	$8,495	$2,545	$65,215	$76,255
1991–1992	$1,559	$2,837	$63,671	$68,067

Year	Sale Films	Sale Video	Sale Rentals	Total
1992–1993	$2,195	$2,589	$75,475	$80,260
1993–1994	$4,543	$3,026	$63,777	$71,348
1994–1995	$15,102	$4,209	$60,792	$80,103
1995–1996	$13,407	$4,858	$67,847	$85,753
1996–1997	$28,182	$6,351	$74,284	$108,818
1997–1998	$7,206	$10,622	$78,568	$96,395
1998–1999	$7,857	$18,308	$90,896	$117,063
1999–2000	$4,997	$7,265	$103,780	$116,042
2000–2001	$8,024	$9,065	$107,146	$122,765
2001–2002	$8,027	$14,878	$131,171	$154,076
2002–2003	$38,517	$12,833	$127,834	$179,184
2003–2004	$6,921	$14,291	$133,203	$154,415
2004–2005	$9,530	$10,673	$120,429	$140,632
2005–2006	$7,334	$20,275	$102,342	$129,951
2006–2007	$11,225	$6,860	$112,395	$130,479

Acknowledgments of Permissions

I am grateful to the following individuals and organizations for permission to use the documents and images reproduced in this volume. The listing is alphabetical by the last name of the permission grantor; when a single grantor has given multiple permissions, they are arranged in the order in which the relevant documents appear in *Canyon Cinema* (in dating the documents in this listing, I have used the title *Cinemanews* consistently, regardless of what the particular variation of the name was at the time of the publication).

Bruce Baillie: Program announcement for fall 1963 Canyon Cinema series; "Report from on the Road, Filming" (*Cinemanews*: May 1965); "Letter from Chapala, Mexico, Jan. 24 or so" (*Cinemanews*: Feb. 1967); letter to *Cinemanews* (July 1967); "Bruce Baillie's Prejudiced Guide to Film Festivals" (*Cinemanews*: Sept./Oct. 1967); letter to *Cinemanews*, "August, Beginning of September [1968]" (*Cinemanews*: 68.7); letter to *Cinemanews*: 70.3; letter, Mar. 1975 (*Cinemanews*: 75.3); letter, late June [1980] (*Cinemanews*: 80.3/4/5); "Letter from Camano Island, October 10, 1974" (*Cinemanews*: Jan. 1995).

Diana Barrie: "To Whom It . . ." (*Cinemanews*: 78.6/79.1).

Freude Bartlett: Poem by Scott Bartlett (*Cinemanews*: 70.4); letter, May 16, 1980 (*Cinemanews*: 80.1/2).

Robert Beavers: Essay on [1965] Ann Arbor Film Festival by Gregory Markopoulos (*Cinemanews*: June/July 1965).

Evan and Diedre Beckett: Drawing for *Canyon Cinema Catalog 4* by Adam Beckett.

Herman Berlandt: "What Is a Poetry Film?" (*Cinemanews*: 77.1).

Marilyn Brakhage: Letter to *Cinemanews*: 70.1 by Stan Brakhage; "Remarks Following a Screening of *The Text of Light* at the San Francisco Art Institute on November 18, 1974," by Stan Brakhage (*Cinemanews*: 75.2); letter to Henry Hills, January 13, 1978, by Stan Brakhage (*Cinemanews*: 77.7); letter to Canyon Cinema Cooperative membership, April 11, 1994, by Stan Brakhage.

Arthur Cantrill: "Right Back to the Billabong" (*Cinemanews*: 70.4).

Abigail Child: "Matinee" (*Cinemanews*: 77.7); "Violence" (*Cinemanews*: 78.3/4); "The Films of Aline Mayer" (*Cinemanews*: 79.5/6).

Bruce Conner: "Letter from San Francisco, February 18, 1967" (*Cinemanews*: Mar./Apr. 1967); "Letter, August 6, 1968" (*Cinemanews*: Aug./Sept. 1968); "Letter to the Board of Directors of the New York Film Makers Cooperative, dated May 16, 1969" (*Cinemanews*: 69.4); letter to *Cinemanews*, May 27, 1969 (*Cinemanews*: 69.4); letter to *Cinemanews*: 72.1; eight drawings (*Cinemanews*: 72.2); cover of *Canyon*

Update 1985/Index; letter to *Cinemanews,* September 22, 1968 (*Cinemanews:* 78.2); Bruce Conner page from *Canyon Cinema 2000, Catalog 8.*

Ken DeRoux: Posters advertising screenings at the Canyon Cinematheque at Intersection; "Canyon Cinema, What Next?" (*Cinemanews:* 73.1).

Tom DeWitt (Tom Ditto): Letter to Canyon board of directors, 1994.

Gary Doberman: Letter, December 24, 1979, and "New York Cut the Crap" (*Cinemanews:* 79.5/6).

Carol Emshwiller: Letter to *Cinemanews:* 69.5 by Ed Emshwiller.

Joe Gibbons: "An Art Liberation Front Dis'course on Avant-Garde Film" (*Cinemanews:* 77.6); "ALF Communique" (*Cinemanews:* 77.7).

Barbara Hammer: "Body-Centered Film" (*Cinemanews:* 77.6).

Henry Hills: "Hyper Kinetic Stan/dards" (*Cinemanews:* 77.6); "George Kuchar in Europe" (*Cinemanews:* 78.2); "Child Labor" (*Cinemanews:* 78.2); "Robert Nelson Interview" (*Cinemanews:* 78.3/4); letter to *Cinemanews,* September 10, 1980 (*Cinemanews:* 80.6/81.1).

Peter Hutton: Letter from Bangkok (*Cinemanews:* 72.5/6); photograph (*Cinemanews:* 79.5/6).

Larry Jordan: "Survival in the Independent–Non-commercial–Avant-Garde–Experimental–Personal–Expressionistic Film Market of 1979" (*Cinemanews:* 79.2/3/4).

Jon Jost: "I Lost It at the Movies or Electro-Videograph Interface Meets Mr. Natural" (*Cinemanews:* 70.2); "Underground Myths and Cinema Cooperative Realities (Some Concrete Policy Suggestions)" (*Cinemanews:* 72.1).

Diane Kitchen: Photograph of Peter Kubelka (from cover of *Cinemanews:* 74.5); "Chick Strand's Recollections of Canyon Cinema's Early Beginnings with Added Commentary from Chick Callenbach" (*Cinemanews:* 76.2).

George Kuchar: Drawing for *Canyon Cinema Catalog 3;* photograph of George Kuchar on set for Larry Jordan's *The Apparition;* "Thundercrack" cartoon (*Cinemanews:* 77.6); "The Dietrich Dossier" (*Cinemanews:* 77.7); letter to Canyon Cinema board of directors, 1994.

Saul Landau: "An Essay on Censorship" (*Cinemanews:* Oct./Nov. 1964).

Don Lloyd: "Whatever Became of Canyon Cinema Cooperative?" (*Cinemanews:* 72.2).

George Manupelli: Letter from the Ann Arbor Film Festival, April 1, 1965 (*Cinemanews:* June/July 1965); "On His Blindness" (*Cinemanews:* Oct. 1965).

Jonas Mekas: Letter, May 20, 1969 (*Cinemanews:* 69.4); "Aunt Kastune" (*Cinemanews:* 78.2).

Emory Menefee: Review of Sheldon Renan's *An Introduction to the American Underground Film* (*Cinemanews:* Nov. 1967); response to Bruce Conner's letter, August 6, 1968 (*Cinemanews:* Aug./Sept. 1968).

Gunvor Nelson: "Chick Strand's Recollections of Canyon Cinema's Early Beginnings with Added Commentary from Chick Callenbach" (*Cinemanews*: 76.2); "Conversation with Chick Strand" (*Cinemanews*: 80.3/4/5).

Robert Nelson: Drawing celebrating the completion of *The Great Blondino*; "Open Letter to Film-Makers" (*Cinemanews*: July 1967); "The Brussels Festival" (*Cinemanews*: Jan./Feb. 1968); "The Swedish Proposal for New American Cinema, and Some Miscellaneous Notes" (*Cinemanews*: Jan./Feb. 1968); "Some Thoughts about the Bellevue Film Festival Two Weeks after Judging It" (*Cinemanews*: 68.7); letter to *Cinemanews*: 70.4; letter to Canyon Cinema board of directors, March 31, 1994.

Yoko Ono: Fan letter from John Lennon to Bruce Conner (*Cinemanews*: 69.1).

Lyle Pearson: "Waiting for Godard at the Front: The Palestinian Cinema Institution" (*Cinemanews*: 75.3); "Prayag in 35mm: The Film and Television Institute of India" and "Correction to 'The Palestinian Cinema Situation' Issue #75-3" (*Cinemanews*: 75.6).

Joe L. Phillips: Letter from Will Hindle to *Cinemanews*, Dec. 1967/Jan. 1968; "Letter from San Francisco, April 1968" (*Cinemanews*: Apr./May 1968); letter from Will Hindle to *Cinemanews*, September 10, 1968 (*Cinemanews*: 68.7); letter from Will Hindle to *Cinemanews*: 69.1; letter from Will Hindle to *Cinemanews*, Jan. 1970 (*Cinemanews*: 70.2); "Recuperating at His Forest Place in the Mountains of North Alabama," by Will Hindle (*Cinemanews*: 74.6); "Letter, Lower Appalachians, Late June, '76," by Will Hindle (*Cinemanews*: 76.4).

Angeline Pike: "Rebuttal to Robt. Nelson's 'Open Letter to Film-Makers,'" by Bob Pike (*Cinemanews*: Aug. 1967); "Notes from the Creative Film Society: Pros and Cons of Theatrical Bookings" and "More Notes about Theatrical Bookings," by Bob Pike (*Cinemanews*: Apr./May 1968); "Notes from the Creative Film Society," by Bob Pike (*Cinemanews*: May/June/July 1968); "The Story of a Closet Cine-Drama . . . or . . . from Isolation to Immortality," by Bob Pike (*Cinemanews*: Aug./Sept. 1968).

San Francisco Cinematheque: Instructions for building an optical printer; announcement of the publication of the Canyon Cinema *News* (1962); first page of the first issue of the Canyon Cinema *News*; photograph of Ben Van Meter (*Cinemanews*: 70.4); photograph of Edith Kramer and cow (*Cinemanews*: 80.3/5); inside cover of *Cinemanews*: 70.3; minutes of the Canyon Cinema board of directors' meeting, May 20, 1970, by Loren Sears (*Cinemanews*: 70.3); photographic portrait of James Broughton (*Cinemanews*: 70.4); two photographs of the Canyon Cinema board of directors meeting (*Cinemanews*: 72.3); photograph of Canyon Cinema T-shirt; pages designed for *Catalog 3* by George Kuchar and Ben Van Meter and for *Catalog 4* by Adam Beckett; cover of *Catalog 4*; discussion with Peter Kubelka at the Cinematheque, October 3, 1974 (*Cinemanews*: 74.5); cover of *Cinemanews*: 76.3; discussion with George Landow at the Cinematheque (*Cinemanews*: 77.2); cover of *Cinemanews*: 77.4; cover of *Canyon Update 1985/Index*; cover of *Cinemanews*: 77.6; "Hollis Frampton in San Francisco" (*Cinemanews*: 77.6); discussion with Tony

Conrad at the Cinematheque, February 28, 1978 (*Cinemanews:* 78.2); discussion with George Landow at the Cinematheque, May 18, 1978 (*Cinemanews:* 78.3/4); discussion with Hollis Frampton at the Cinematheque ["St. Hollis (Part 2)"] (*Cinemanews:* 78.3/4); discussion with Yvonne Rainer at the Cinematheque, April 6, 1978 (*Cinemanews:* 78.3/4); cover of *Cinemanews:* 78.6/79.1; photograph of Hollis Frampton and Beverly and Pat O'Neill (*Cinemanews:* 80.1/2); discussion with Chick Strand at the Cinematheque, March 6, 1980 (*Cinemanews:* 80.3/4/5); cover of *Canyon Cinema Catalog 6*; cover of *Canyon Cinema Catalog 7*; cover of *Canyon Cinema 2000*; Bruce Conner page from *Canyon Cinema 2000*.

Caroline Savage: "What's a Picnic without Potato Salad!" by Caroline Savage Lee (*Cinemanews:* 80.1/2).

Peter Seaton: "How to Read II" (*Cinemanews:* 79.5/6).

Joel Singer: "How to Cope with the Question Period" by James Broughton (*Cinemanews:* 75.4); "A Rune for Jerome Hill," by James Broughton, "Tomfool for President," by James Broughton, and "A Prelude for Brakhage," by James Broughton (*Cinemanews:* 77.2); "Windowmobile," by James Broughton (*Cinemanews:* 77.3); "Some Unseen Lights," by James Broughton (*Cinemanews:* 78.5).

Warren Sonbert: "Film Syntax" (*Cinemanews:* 79.5/6; © The Estate of Warren Sonbert); "Film Syntax (Continued)" (*Cinemanews:* 80.1/2; © The Estate of Warren Sonbert).

Art Spiegelman: "Sketchbook" (*Cinemanews:* 78.6/79.1).

Barry Spinello: "Letter to John Schofill" (*Cinemanews:* May/June/July 1968); letter from Oakland, California (*Cinemanews:* 69.3).

Chick Strand: Photograph of Chick Strand in the 1970s; letter to *Cinemanews:* 72.1; letter to *Cinemanews,* September 18, 1980 (*Cinemanews:* 80.6/81.1).

Anne Tardos: "The 1st Milarepa Gatha," by Jackson Mac Low (*Cinemanews:* 79.2/3/4).

Albie Thoms: "Australian Coop News" (*Cinemanews:* 75.5).

Ben Van Meter: Letter to Canyon Cinema, c. 1980.

Willie Varela: Letter to *Cinemanews:* 77.1 and "Excerpts from a Conversation with Stan Brakhage."

David White: Letter to *Cinemanews:* 77.7.

Index

359; German Expressionism, 344, 349, 350; independent media distribution, 31n17; George Kuchar, 281–88, 282*illus.* *See also* Brussels Festival; London

exhibition, 2–4, 216–21; advertisements of, 14*illus.*, 15*illus.*, 105; commercial, 102, 105, 108, 127–28; damaging films, 103–4, 132, 137; duping, 105, 108; Esquire Theatre, 105; finances, 88–89; hand-crafted films, 106; low quality, 132, 137; No Nothing Cinema, 412, 413; Provincetown Playhouse, 87–88; Rivoli Theatre, 105, 108; Sydney Filmmakers' Cinema, 210, 211; theatrical bookings pros and cons, 102–5, 108; Total Mobile Home, 8–9; Uptown Theatre, 102, 105, 108. *See also* Berkeley exhibition places; Canyon Cinema exhibition; Cinematheque; film festivals

Exothematic Man logo, 10, 11*illus.*, 408

Experimental Cinema Group, University of Colorado, 129

experimental film, 1, 29n1, 30n5; Australia, 140, 210–12; Baillie exhibition, 8; Brandon on, 31n12; distribution, 4, 87–88; Kramer teaching, 73–74; Landow, 309; San Francisco as capital of, 416–17; understanding, 56; video, 19–20, 255–56. *See also* avant-garde film; New American Cinema

experimental writing: "Child Labor" (Hills), 293–95; fan letter to Bruce Conner (Lennon), 122*illus.*; "The Films of Aline Mayer" (Child), 350–51; "1st Milarepa Gatha" (Mac Low), 341–42, 341*illus.*; "How to Read" (Seaton), 339–40*illus.*; "Hyper kinetic Stan/dards" (Hills), 263–66; letter from Bruce Conner, 297*illus.*; "Matinee" (Child), 273*illus.*; "The Swedish Proposal for New American Cinema, and Some Miscellaneous Notes" (Nelson), 99–101; "Violence" (Child), 319*illus. See also* poetry

Expressionism, German, 344, 349, 350

F

FACETS, 254

Fagin, Larry, 372

Faisal, King, 206, 208

Fall of the Romanoff Dynasty (Shub), 263

al-Fateh, 205, 206, 207

Fat Feet (Grooms), 108

Faws, Manfred, 206

FBI, 81

Feetfear (Baillie), 119, 136

Feinstein, Peter, 26, 296

Feldman, Marty, 311–12

Feldman, Robert, 13

Felheim, Marvin, 61

Fellini, Federico, 321, 426

Une Femme Douce (Bresson), 213

festivals. *See* film festivals

Fever Dream (Strand), 381

FFFTCM (Hindle), 95, 102, 103

Fiddle-De-Dee (McLaren), 4

Film and Television Institute of India, 212–15

Film Arts Foundation, 257

Film at Wit's End (Brakhage), 428

Film Biographies (Brakhage), 428

Film Culture, 34n41, 221

film festivals: Ann Arbor (AAFF), 42, 54–62, 93, 95, 96, 426; Baillie's "Prejudiced Guide to Film Festivals," 65, 92–93; Bellevue, 70–71, 72, 93, 115–17, 223; Berkeley, 107; Brussels, 65, 93, 96–98, 116; Canyon, 217, 218, 299–300, 427; Carthage, 205–7; *Cinemanews* on, 37–39, 42, 43, 54–62, 65, 92–93; Cracow, 93; Film-maker's/Festival Contract, 70–71; Foothill College, 37, 94, 113; Japan, 68–69, 93; London, 113; Midwest, 37; New York, 113; poetry-film, 230, 231–32; San Francisco, 37, 88, 94, 121, 232, 417; Tripps Festival, 397–98

Film Form (Eisenstein), 264

Film Forum, India, 65

Film Guild, Gould's, 30n6

Film Images, New York, 88

Film in Which There Occur Edge-Lettering, Dirt Particles, Sprocket Holes, Etc. (Landow), 305, 308

Film-Makers' Cooperative: Japan, 65, 69. *See also* New York Film-Makers' Cooperative

Filmmakers Distribution Center, New York, 187

Filmnews, Sydney Coop, 211

film-painting, 123–25

Filmpiece for Sunshine (Schofill), 120

Designer: Nola Burger
Text: 8.25/13.25 Electra
Display: Univers
Compositor: BookMatters, Berkeley
Indexer: Barbara Roos
Printer and binder: Sheridan Books, Inc.